CRITIQUE OF
BORED REASON

CRITIQUE OF BORED REASON

On the Confinement of the Modern Condition

DMITRI NIKULIN

Columbia University Press

New York

Columbia University Press
Publishers Since 1893
New York   Chichester, West Sussex
cup.columbia.edu
Copyright © 2022 Columbia University Press
All rights reserved

Library of Congress Cataloging-in-Publication Data
Names: Nikulin, Dmitri, author.
Title: Critique of bored reason: on the confinement of the modern condition / Dmitri Nikulin.
Description: New York : Columbia University Press, 2021. | Includes bibliographical references and index.
Identifiers: LCCN 2021011178 (print) | LCCN 2021011179 (ebook) | ISBN 9780231189064 (hardback) | ISBN 9780231189071 (trade paperback) | ISBN 9780231548151 (ebook)
Subjects: LCSH: Philosophy, Modern. | Boredom. | Philosophy, Ancient.
Classification: LCC B791 .N55 2021 (print) | LCC B791 (ebook) | DDC 128/.37—dc23
LC record available at https://lccn.loc.gov/2021011178
LC ebook record available at https://lccn.loc.gov/2021011179

Columbia University Press books are printed on permanent and durable acid-free paper.

Printed in the United States of America
Cover design: Julia Kushnirsky
Cover image: Paul Klee, *The Time*. Copyright © 2021 Artists Rights Society (ARS), New York.

Contents

Foreword   vii

Abbreviations   xv

Acknowledgments   xxiii

1. A Conceptual History of Boredom   1
2. Boredom and the Flâneur   53
3. Critique of Bored Reason   85
4. Being and Boredom   119
5. The Nonboring Well-Being   148
6. Scandal   175

    In Place of a Conclusion: On Method   233

Notes   241

Bibliography   279

Index   295

Foreword

This book is a critique of bored reason. Obviously, if reason is pure thinking—either thinking itself as its other in logical categories or thinking the relationships with others, or the other of the world, in its properties—then it should not be bored. Reason can be bored only if it has nothing other than itself, which it establishes, and has a history of being only with itself, which it reflectively studies. While almost all philosophical concepts originate in classical antiquity and live on through various, sometimes unexpected, historical transformations, boredom is unique in that there is not even a word for it in classical Greek. The discussion of boredom is conspicuously absent from ancient thought. My claim, therefore, is that boredom and reflection on it arise properly only in modernity—in the wake of the emergence of the modern subject. Everyone gets bored once in a while, not only people of all ages and cultures but also animals, yet boredom becomes the pervasive mood of existence and the proprium of the subject only in modernity.

Modernity is a complex set of interacting and interwoven social, cultural, political, and historical processes and phenomena that establish, define, and describe theoretical cognition, practical action, and productive activity. Among the concepts that determine it, perhaps the central and most significant is that of the modern subject, which is internalized by us and through which we perceive and construct our social, natural, political, and psychological reality. The modern subject establishes itself as universal, rational, and necessary, and understands itself as self-defined by (excessive) reflexivity and self-awareness. Being a historical (self-)construction, it considers itself as its own transhistorical achievement in history, which is ultimately produced by itself. Most importantly, the modern subject realizes itself as autonomous, as self-legislating and self-sufficient, uniquely asserting a normatively binding moral law, which is meant to be universalized and appropriated by each. And yet, such a subject makes the otherness of others only a task to be achieved, and in this way renders interlocutors redundant in theoretical investigation and practical action.

In this way, the modern subject releases itself from the bond of and with others. It is always a singular collective without and outside of plurality. Exclusive of others, the modern subject is the only actor in and of the theoretical, practical, and productive drama of modernity, being its protagonist, playwright, director, and spectator at the same time. In the absence of others, the modern subject is utterly lonely, solitary, and monological in its being and thought. Hence, it is inevitably bored.

The philosophical study of boredom, therefore, is also a critique of the concept of the modern subject as the realization of universal reason in its transformations and vicissitudes. Being very familiar, boredom is utterly unfamiliar. Boredom is an evasive concept and is thus difficult to grasp and inquire into. Indeed, it is difficult to understand the proper question to be asked about it, which is why it comes under a different name even in closely related languages (*tédio*, *noia*, *aburrimiento*). One might make a distinction between passion as a natural physiological phenomenon experienced by all humans at all times—and emotion as a culturally processed and trained passion. While the basic or universal passions might be relatively few,[1] a number of emotions, such as saudade or тоска, are culturally specific and are difficult to translate and render precisely into a different cultural context.[2] Yet, as I argue throughout the book, boredom is not a mental state or a psychological emotion but rather the inalienable proprium of the modern subject, which does not define the subject in its essence, since the modern subject does not have an essence beyond what it freely and autonomously assigns to itself; rather, boredom is that without which the subject cannot be thought and with which it is mutually substitutable. Paraphrasing Aristotle, one can say: if modern subject, bored; if bored, modern subject. In this sense, boredom constitutes the very *conditio moderna*.

In its historical rendering, boredom is the response to the improper or inauthentic existence of the contemporary bourgeois city dweller, who is thus caught in the net of boredom, which signifies the utter inadequacy of their existence. Boredom is thus a very modern phenomenon that lies deep in the constitution of modern life and cannot easily be uprooted. Rather, boredom needs to be carefully analyzed as a profound symptom of the crisis of our time and a sign of our situation of being with—or without—others, and in—or outside—the world.

For this reason, there is much interest in boredom, which is perceived in the nineteenth century as "le mal du siècle," and which becomes a prominent theme in its literature, defining the characters and alter egos of Goncharov, Dostoevsky, Flaubert, and Baudelaire.[3] These inspired singers of the bleakness of boredom are all born in the first quarter of the nineteenth century, so that their flourishing coincides with the tightening bourgeois grasp on the world.[4] Establishing a keen interest in boredom thus coincides with the development of the novel, where boredom accompanies the ordinary, rather than exceptional, perceptions and emotions of bourgeois life, which yearns for greatness amidst the banality of the everydayness that is, as Lefebvre puts it, "forever unchangeable, unchangeable in its boredom, its greyness, its repetition of the same actions."[5] Despite the attempts of the modernist novel to get rid of the boring familiar in its experiments with estrangement, boredom does not loosen its grasp but persists in the flux of self-directed and self-recording over-reflexive thought. As such, boredom becomes the main hero in Sartre and Moravia and transpires virtually in the majority of literary and cinematographic works, even when they intentionally try to achieve distance from boredom through the spectacle and narrative of tragedy and horror.[6]

The reflection on boredom in philosophy is already important in Pascal and Kant, and becomes central to Simmel, Kracauer, Heidegger, and Benjamin, who all critically explore and attempt to overcome the construction of the modern subject, bored with itself in its regal solitude. In discussing their works, I intend to show that, despite their differences, they all share an understanding of boredom as symptomatic of our situation in the social, political, and natural world as it has been historically defined by the construction of the modern subject. If philosophy is indeed a heteroreflection in that it reflects on something that is not its own, on a radically different other than thought, one could say that philosophy always thinks the improper—that which should not, and perhaps even cannot, be thought. This improper, then, is the proprium of modern thought, which is boredom. As such, it can only be considered by unthinking the (usual) thought, or even by not thinking. Therefore, as both Kracauer and Heidegger agree, since we cannot overcome the deep rootedness of boredom in our own being, we should embrace it. This might then lead to a profound and nonboring experience that would become (re)defining of our being, perhaps even beyond description and thought. However, each one does this in his own way: Heidegger by heroically committing himself to the expectation of a novel possibility that would reveal itself from within the depth of our Dasein in the resolute moment of vision, and Kracauer by lying determinedly on a sofa.

In what follows, I attempt to alternate a systematic interpretation with a conceptual historical approach, so that they can support, partly clarify and simplify, and partly question and complicate each other. For if systematic interpretation simplifies the understanding of a phenomenon, allowing us to see general trends and regularities, conceptual historical interpretation complicates it, allowing us to see many bypasses and roads not taken. The systematic chapters are shorter, because long-winded and overly detailed theory is boring. And the conceptual historical chapters are longer, because close and careful reading of an engaging text is never boring (at least, not boring for the reader, but not necessarily for the reader of the reader, who can easily get bored and, as a result, irritated with long stacks of subordinate clauses and the minutiae of the not yet established meaning...). Throughout the book, I use a method that is explicitly clarified only at the end—as the pendant to the "elements" of the critique of bored reason—and that I call *demontage*. It is meant to restore—to their original and unedited form—the multiple narratives that have eventually been presented as one single argument through their demolition and montage, cut and glued into a single story by the sole producer and addressee of the modern subject. Demontage, then, intends to provide original, if always partial and incomplete, depictions of an event by multiple and independent, yet dialogically engaged, voices.

Boredom has recently become an intensely discussed topic in psychology, where it is being investigated by specifically scientific means—by research based on hypotheses that are tested through observation and staged experiment, the results of which are quantitatively (statistically) processed and analyzed. Contemporary studies in psychology, which for the most part neglect the historical and cultural situation that refers to the modern environment in which boredom transpires, take boredom as a long and slowly developing, inconspicuous yet powerful emotion, or sometimes as an affective state, which most people experience daily. Yet, once persistent, chronic, and acute, boredom strongly correlates with perceived negative states and aversive effects, such as apathy, anhedonia (inability to experience pleasure), depression, stress, anxiety, anger, aggression, loneliness, hostility, somatic disorders, drug and alcohol abuse, truancy, risk-taking behavior, and inattention. This prevents one from participating in a satisfying and preferred activity and often leads to making errors in everyday situations and work environments.[7] At the same time, many researchers stress the positive role of everyday boredom, which can stimulate creativity and make us explore, learn, discover, and invent new things, and to better navigate and change our social, cognitive, and emotional environment, especially when it is perceived as dull and aversive. As such, boredom can help us find a new purpose and set new goals for a fulfilling life, or at least organize our life in such a way as to minimize boredom and monotony.

The problem of boredom has once again come to the forefront of philosophical debate, where it has been discussed in a number of illuminating works, to which I will be referring throughout the text.[8] This renewed interest seems to suggest that we live in an age profoundly marked by boredom, despite troubling social and political conflicts, and exciting scientific and technological advancements.

In my own analysis, I argue that, in modernity, boredom appears under two guises: as vexing *ennui* and as unending duration. I subsequently distinguish and discuss three forms of boredom by using the concepts of same and other, which are not taken as opposites in a dichotomy, but rather as two categories that can be bound into a mediated dialogical unity without identity. In these three forms, boredom appears as indeterminate duration (boredom as same without other), as inevitable repetition and privation (boredom as other without same), and as inescapable self-abdication and self-incapacitation through odium and self-hatred (boredom as the rupture of same and other). These forms belong to the modern subject that unsuccessfully attempts to overcome boredom by various philosophical, scientific, and artistic means.

The modern subject tries to get rid of the inevitability of boredom by turning to the pervasive yet equally repetitively boring entertainment. In the absence of the real other, that remains always a task to be achieved, and thus in a situation where dialogical communication is impossible, entertainment as diversion from and substitution for well-being becomes a pointless and endless flight from boredom, which we can never escape. At best we can only embrace it, as both Kracauer and Heidegger claim, in order to make sense of the nonsensical. The modern subject takes entertainment very seriously—perhaps too seriously—which undermines itself as an engaging and playful activity. The modern subject is a playful subject. And yet, being lonely and tragic in its seclusion and the exclusion of the other, the modern subject always plays against itself, entertaining itself by a narcissistic (dis)play, boringly enacting the same game, even if it is trying to turn it into entertainingly innumerable different games offering seemingly uncountable possibilities of being other, which, however, is still the same but under a different guise.

The most radical attempt at a breakaway from boredom, predictable yet failing, is scandal. As I argue, scandal is always public, dialogically communicative, yet at the same time it constitutes a rupture in such communication. Besides, scandal is intrinsically comic, conceptually oral, loud, swift, and spontaneous. The modern scandal is the unsuccessful yet constantly repeated attempt of the modern subject to flee away from and get rid of itself. Scandal tests the existing explicit and implicit norms of thinking and behavior. Autonomous and moralistic, the modern subject constantly judges itself against itself. In the absence of the norms that would be established by the other rather than by the lonely, autonomous self, the modern subject comes repeatedly to challenge, question, and punish itself through scandal. This inevitably remains unsuccessful, since scandal is public and dialogical and as such is impossible in the absence of others. The modern scandal is thus a response provoked by the modern subject's painful realization that well-being as a dialogical being with others is unattainable.

The expression of the modern scandal is revolution, as an attempt at a radical break with the boredom of the lonely subject. As such, modern revolution takes three forms: the revolution in science (in theoretical philosophy, in the understanding of nature), art (in aesthetics, in the understanding of beauty), and politics (in practical philosophy, in the understanding of human relations). Hence, I trace the presuppositions and implications of the scientific, artistic, and political scandals of modernity.

And yet, the modern, all-pervasive boredom is only inescapable if we remain within the historical construction of the modern subject. But another, nonboring social and political world is possible, if we realize our well-being as being in dialogue, as being in comedy, and as being with others. Such an understanding of well-being presupposes an entirely different concept of the universal subject, which is the one in which we all participate, and which we enact in our lives. Such a subject allows for a distributed and shared common good, is not an inevitable being toward death, and is fundamentally plural in its being. Rather than being autonomous in its establishment of the moral law by a universalizable act of rational will, it is autarchic, or capable of establishing moral norms in a heteronomous exchange, through participation and deliberation by many independent yet dialogically bound and communicating participants.

One of the main insights behind this discussion is that dialogue is never boring. By "dialogue" I understand an always renewable, nonrepetitive, and communicative exchange between a multiplicity of mutually independent interlocutors, who, however, need each other to live in and off the dialogue. In dialogical communication, which is practical but not productive, everyone is included freely as equal in a shared, unfinalizable communication, which can always be meaningfully continued without a repetition of contents. For this reason, being as well-being is being in dialogue.

Against the self-perception and self-cultivation of the modern subject as tragic (inevitable being toward death, which makes well-being eventually impossible), the comic subject is always integrated with others and strives to achieve well-being on the chaotic public stage as the end of democratic political action with real and equal others. In comedy, there is no place for solitary being, action, or thinking, which are always shared with and distributed among others. Comic being is always being toward life, its renewal and assertion with others. The comic moral and political subject always comes in the plural and is already oriented toward others. Comedy allows for solving a problem or an initial complication by concerted acting, thinking, and working toward the resolution of the current conflict. The strived-for good ending of well-being is possible but never guaranteed, and can only be achieved by the common effort of everyone involved in action across customary divides. Social justice in comedy is accomplished by allowing the dispossessed, the poor, and the deprived to be the main actors who act together with others, which directs them toward the autarchic, rather than autonomous, freedom and equality that makes well-being possible. Such a well-being, then, is nonboring and can only be realized as being with others.

Abbreviations

The standard abbreviated forms for texts that I use extensively in the book are given below. Citations of classical Greek and Latin sources are shortened according to the *Oxford Classical Dictionary* (4th rev. ed., 2012). Classical citations are given according to their canonical form (Stephanus pagination for Plato, Bekker numbering for Aristotle, and book, chapter, and line numbers for other works).

GENERAL

DK   Diels and Kranz, *Die Fragmente der Vorsokratiker*
LSJ Liddel and Scott, *Greek-English Lexicon*
LXX Rahlfs and Hanhart, *Septuaginta*
SVF von Arnim, *Stoicorum Veterum Fragmenta*

AELIAN

Var. hist.   *Varia Historia*

ALCINOUS

Didask.   *The Handbook of Platonism*

ALEXANDER OF APHRODISIAS

In an. prior.	*In Aristotelis analyticorum priorum librum 1 commentarium*
In Met.	*In Aristotelis metaphysica commentaria*
In Top.	*In Aristotelis topicorum libros octo commentaria*
Anon proleg.	Westerink, *Anonymous Prolegomena to Platonic Philosophy*

APOLLODORUS

Lib.	*The Library*

AQUINAS

Summa theol.	*Summa Theologiae*

ARISTOTLE

An. post.	*Analytica posterior*
An. priora	*Analytica priora*
Cat.	*Categories*
De an.	*De anima*
De bono	*De bono*
De gener. anim.	*De generatione animalium*
De gen. et corr.	*De generatione et corruptione*
De mem.	*De memoria*
EE	*Eudemian Ethics*
Met.	*Metaphysics*
MM	*Magna Moralia*
NE	*Nichomachean Ethics*
Phys.	*Physics*
Poet.	*Poetics*
Polit.	*Politics*
Rhet.	*Rhetoric*

AUGUSTINE

De civ. Dei	*De civitate dei*
De duab. an.	*De duabus animabus*
Lib. arb.	*De libero arbitrio*
Trin.	*De Trinitate*

BENJAMIN

AP *The Arcades Project*

BOETHIUS

De consol. phil. *De consolatione philosophiae*

CASSIAN

Inst. *De Institutis Coenobiorum*

CATULLUS

Carm. *Carmina*

CICERO

ad Att.	*Epistulae ad Atticum*
De fin.	*De finibus*
De leg.	*De legibus*
De nat. deor.	*De natura deorum*
De or.	*De oratore*
Fam.	*Epistulae ad Familiares*

xviii *Abbreviations*

DESCARTES

AT	Adam and Tannery, *Oeuvres de Descartes*
Disc.	*Discourse on the Method*
Med.	*Meditations on the First Philosophy*
Med.	*Synopsis*
Princ.	*Principia Philosophiae*

DIO CHRYSOSTOM

Disc. *Discourses*

DIOGENES LAERTIUS

Vitae phil. *Vitae philosophorum*

EPICTETUS

Disc. *Discourses*

HEGEL

Enc. *Encyclopedia Logic*

HELLER

CB *The Concept of the Beautiful*

HESIOD

Theog.   *Theogony*

HOMER

Hom. hymn.   *Homeric Hymns*
Il.   *Iliad*
Od.   *Odyssey*

HORACE

Ars poët.   *Ars poëtica*

[IAMBLICHUS]

Theol. arithm.   *The Theology of Arithmetic*

ISIDORE

Etym.   *Etymologies*

KANT

APH   *Anthropologie in pragmatischer Hinsicht*

KRACAUER

L   "Langeweile"

LIVY

Ab urbe cond.   *Ab urbe condita*

LUCIAN

Vit. auctio   *Vitarum auctio*

LUCRETIUS

De rer. nat.   *De rerum natura*

MENANDER

Epitr.   *Epitrepontes*

PAUSANIAS

Perieg.   *Periēgēsis*

PHILOPONUS

In de gen. et corr.   *In de generatione et corruptione*

PLATO

Charm.   *Charmides*
Gorg.   *Gorgias*

Legg.	*Laws*
Lys.	*Lysias*
Phaedo	*Phaedo*
Phaedr.	*Phaedrus*
Polit.	*Politicus*
Prot.	*Protagoras*
Rep.	*Republic*
Theaet.	*Theaetetus*
Tim.	*Timaeus*

PLINY

Nat. hist.   *Naturalis Historia*

PLOTINUS

Enn.   *Enneads*

PLUTARCH

Eum.   *Life of Eumenes*

PORPHYRY

Isag.   *Isagoge*

PROCLUS

In Eucl.   *In primum Euclidis Elementorum librum commentarii*

QUINTILIAN

Inst.   *De institutione oratoria*

SENECA

Ep.   *Epistulae*

SEXTUS EMPIRICUS

Adv. Math.   *Adversus Mathematicos*

SIMPLICIUS

In Phys.   *In Aristotelis physicorum libros commentaria*

TERENCE

Ad.   *Adelphoe*

THEMISTIUS

In de an.   *In libros de anima paraphrasis*

THEOPHRASTUS

Met.   *Metaphysics*

Acknowledgments

I want to thank Richard Bernstein, Krishna Boddapati, Caryl Emerson, Rainer Forst, Simona Forti, Jeremy Gauger, Christoph Horn, Andreas Kalyvas, Elena Nikulina, Lev Nikulin, McWelling Todman, Massimiliano Tomba, Alejandro Vigo, and Samuel Yelton for their most helpful suggestions and discussions of various portions of the book. I am also grateful to Forschungskolleg Humanwissenschaften, and Alexander von Humboldt Stiftung, whose grants allowed me to work on the project in Bad Homburg and the University of Bonn. Parts of chapters 1, 2, and 6 were published as "The Burdens and Blessings of Boredom: Heidegger and Kracauer," *Kronos* 6 (2017): 120-32; "The Eternal Return of the Other: Benjamin on the Social and Political Effects of Boredom in Modernity," *Social Imaginaries* 4, no. 2 (2018): 135-57; "Laziness and the Cunning of Nature: Kant on Boredom," *Stasis* 7, no. 2 (2019): 122-36; "Hans Jonas, the Thinker of Ontological and Scientific Revolutions," *Giornale Critico di Storia delle Idee*, no. 14 (2015): 83-99; "The Promise of the Beautiful," *Revue internationale de philosophie* 69, no. 3 (2015): 289-301. They are reproduced here with the permission of the publishers.

CRITIQUE OF BORED REASON

CHAPTER 1

A Conceptual History of Boredom

Paraphrasing Kant, one can say that in philosophy mere theory without a history is empty, whereas history without a theory is blind. Combined with systematic interpretation, the history of thought is engaging and never boring. So I will begin with a conceptual reconstruction of boredom.

Under the influence of the humanists and the Romantics, ancient Greece came to be considered as the exemplary cultural, philosophical, and literary other against which modernity could understand itself. In order to see and enact a picture of oneself, one needs the mirror of the other. So the conceptual history of a term usually starts with classical Greek antiquity, moves on to its appearance in Roman sources, and then to its medieval, Renaissance, and modern uses. Within such a limited and fairly linear account, which appears necessary only post factum and that genealogy tried to rectify and challenge by pointing to alternative, now suppressed, side-lines of a meaning, the historical and philosophical passage of thought is invariably confined to the Western tradition. With the Romantics, such a historical restoration normally emphasizes the Greek and downplays the Latin heritage, and includes some non-Western sources (such as the Vedas and the Avesta), though from a specifically European perspective.

Most of the philosophical concepts that we use today originate in antiquity, so it might indeed be helpful to trace the changes in their use and meaning at different times and in different contexts, in the hope that we might reappropriate and rethink the concept in our current situation. Sometimes it is easier to detect an important phenomenon by finding out what is missing, rather than by discussing what is there. It is most remarkable that in Greek antiquity there is *no term* for "boredom." No doubt, in ancient Greece, as in any culture, people got irritated, vexed, distressed, depressed, and bored. However, boredom as an unavoidable and all-encompassing phenomenon is a specifically modern phenomenon and concept, the proper expression of the modern solitary subject. The contemporary cultural, social, and political world cannot be thought and lived without boredom. This also means that a conceptual reconstruction of boredom is thereby also the (not always boring) work of boredom.

Boredom makes its stage entrance only after the beginning of the common era, when subjectivity is already very much established in its self-understanding, both in the practical philosophy of the Roman Stoics and in the theoretical philosophy of the Neoplatonists and Augustine.[1] There have been attempts to show that a closer look at ancient texts should be able to detect several terms whose meanings are somewhat similar to that of modern boredom, although they are not quite the same.[2] As I argue in what follows, it is only in modernity that we have a persistent and acerbic philosophical and literary reflection on boredom as the predicament of the existential condition of the universal subject that thinks and acts in the absence of the other, and thus has to be forever familiar to itself and remain lonely in its sameness. Through boredom, we become aware of ourselves. Modern boredom appears under the guise of ennui (in Pascal), the pain of the soul in suffering from dullness, in which same and other remain separate and thus cannot communicate dialogically—and as *Langeweile* (which I will analyze in Kant), the emptiness of long and everlastingly repetitive duration, in which the recurrent same misses the other and thus inevitably lacks in novelty. To repeat, as a specifically modern phenomenon, boredom becomes a dominant theme in the nineteenth century.[3]

In antiquity, however, even if people get bored, they do not have a proper word or a concept for it. We find a set of related terms in ἀκήδεια, which communicates the meaning of carelessness or indifference in Empedocles;[4] ἀκηδία, which stands for indifference, apathy, weariness, exhaustion, neglect, and disregard;[5] κῆδος, for care or grief; as well as the verbs ἀκηδέω, to take no care for or heed of, and ἀκηδιάω, to be careless, exhausted, weary.[6] *Acedia* is then used in late ancient monastic tradition by John Cassian, defined by him as "weariness or anxiety of the heart" (*taedium sive anxietatem cordis*), which becomes the major sin of sloth and finds its explication in the works of Albert the Great and Aquinas.[7] In Euripides, ἄση signifies distress, vexation, or satiety.[8] In Plato, ἀνία means distress, sorrow, or annoyance.⁹ From Homer's depiction of Polyphemus to Aelian's description of the Persian king, we encounter ἀλύω, to be deeply stirred, agitated, or excited.¹⁰ In Plutarch, the related ἄλυς stands for languor, when describing the state of Eumenes's troops besieged in the confined space of the city of Nora with little place to walk and move.¹¹ In the Latin tradition, Lucretius uses *pertaesum* to communicate the sense of weariness and disgust which come out of standing in the same familiar place, and *odi*, for the aversion and loathing of the ailing mind.¹² In Seneca, we find *nausia*, literally "seasickness"; *taedium*, for communicating the sense of weariness and disgust; and *odium*, for hate and revulsion. Says Seneca:

> Others also are moved by a satiety [*satietas*] of doing and seeing the same things, and not so much by a hatred [*fastidium*] of life as because they are cloyed [*odium*] with it. We slip into this condition, while philosophy itself pushes us on, and we say: "How long must I endure the same things? Shall I continue to wake and sleep, be hungry and be cloyed, shiver and perspire? There is an end to nothing; all things are connected in a sort of circle; they flee and they are pursued. Night is close at the heels of day, day at the heels of night; summer ends in autumn, winter rushes after autumn, and winter softens into spring; all nature in this way passes, only to return. I do nothing new; I see nothing new; sooner or later one sickens [*nausea*] of this, also." There are many who think that living is not painful, but superfluous [*Multi sunt, qui non acerbum iudicent vivere, sed supervacuum*].¹³

A number of other terms (such as ὄχλος) express uneasiness, distress, disquietude, and annoyance in ancient literature,¹⁴ yet none of them conveys the exact contemporary sense of boredom as the expression of the loneliness and the proprium of the specifically modern subject.

Laziness and the cunning of nature: Kant on boredom. Kant is not only one of modernity's most remarkable systematic thinkers but also the one who, despite being deeply rooted in the tradition of scholastic thinking, epitomizes the main historical features of modern philosophy. Simplifying somewhat, one could say that modern subjectivity finds its theoretical expression in Descartes, and its practical one in Kant. Hence, I continue with the modern conceptual history of boredom in Kant, proceeding next to its discussion in the modernistic writings of Kracauer and Benjamin, and only then will I return to Pascal, so that the imputed "beginning" of my account can be reassessed and understood from within the middle and the end of the narrative.

Discussing the feeling of pleasure and displeasure, Kant dedicates an entire section in his *Anthropology* (1798) to the consideration of boredom and its role in human life. The section is called "On Boredom and Entertainment," which is a linguistic opposition between "long while" (*Langeweile*, or "boredom") and "short while" (*Kurzweil*, or "amusement").[15] Boredom for Kant is aversion or repugnance to one's own existence (*die Anekelung seiner eigenen Existenz* [APH 7:151]). This existence is not being as such, but rather being that is devoid of any content, insofar as it faces no change. It is empty being, or pure negativity. To be sure, being is that which does not or should not change, as opposed to becoming. Yet human being is the being that lives, is *alive*, and as such seeks a change that comes from the world in the form of perception, providing for a possibility of life, knowledge, and experience. We thus constantly strive toward, and need, new impressions or perceptions; otherwise, we feel the dull pain of boredom, which thus arises from the horror of the vacuous, from the emptiness of the soul, destitute of perceptions (*aus der Leerheit des Gemüts an Empfindungen* [APH 7:151]).[16] Stiff regularity bores us aesthetically.[17] Monotony, the complete uniformity in perceptions, leads to us disregarding our current state (APH 7:164). Boredom is therefore a response to the lack of impressions, to the absence of any signs or greeting from the world, of its frightening silence that leaves us in panic and the anticipation of death.

Even before Kant, Johann Georg Sulzer suggested that boredom is a painful mood of the soul that awakens a "mortal annoyance" (*ein tödlicher Verdruß*), which we cannot get rid of and that which arises from the impeding inactivity (*Unthätigkeit*) of our soul that constantly searches for new thoughts and impressions. And yet, boredom contributes to our happiness, to the extent that happiness has to be earned and cannot be enjoyed without first going through suffering and negative states.[18]

One might thus say that boredom is akin to *sensory deprivation*. When people are exposed to sensory deprivation, they often start to hallucinate, thus attempting to compensate for the loss of external (sensory) and internal (thinking as self-perception) impressions. Philosophically, this response is explored by Avicenna (Ibn Sina) in the "flying man" and by Descartes in the "cogito" arguments, which intend to show that the suspension or ultimate lack of sensory input leads to the realization of thinking as a reflective act of thought that has nothing else to think except itself. Perhaps our *dreams* are just similar responses to temporary sensory deprivation, in which we start producing images in order to cope with the temporarily nonresponsive world.

The fright (*Grauen*) of the everlasting sameness without any difference or novelty or the possibility of transformation is similar to the horror of emptiness (*horror vacui* [APH 7:233]), of the emptiness that has no distinctions or divisions, and is the triumph of the coincidence of the identical with the nonidentical. For the lack (of perception) or privation (στέρησις) has no qualifications and is distinct from anything definite, and yet at the same time cannot be distinguished from anything, because it is a pure negativity or nothing, a not-this and never-yet. Nothing cannot even cause anxiety, because anxiety is the fear of something whose cause we cannot understand. But "nothing" as privation is not a cause—or it is one only accidentally. The horror of nonbeing is the dread of death, and boredom is its sign.

Life, on the contrary, is a constant renewal—of perception and thought, an incessant leaving of a given state (APH 7:233). Life is the continuous abandonment of sameness that intends to preserve itself as sameness. Life is the assertion of oneness through a multiplicity of otherness that can never stop self-reproducing. The stop is a break that becomes the condition of the impossibility of the continuation of thought and the motion of perception. Boredom, then, is the unmediated, prereflective pain that is the indication of the possibility of such a rupture.

Double move at self-preservation. Yet the constant change and motion of renewal and the flux of new perceptions and impressions can be unsettling, annoying, and destructive. Here, Kant shares, probably without realizing it, the fundamental Stoic thought that nature has equipped us with means for self-preservation—*caritas sui* or ἐπιμέλεια ἑαυτοῦ—of each other and of the polis as the commonality that reserves our being together with others.[19] Cicero tells us that from the very moment a living being is born, it "feels an attachment for itself, and a tendency to preserve itself and to feel affection for its [current] state and for those things which tend to preserve that state; while it moves away from destruction and from those things which appear to contribute to destruction."[20] Boethius, influenced by the Stoics in his moral philosophy, maintains in *The Consolation of Philosophy* that all living—and thus mortal—things exemplify a "care for themselves" (*sui caritas*), which comes from an "exertion of nature" (*ex naturali intentione*); therefore, all things "seek naturally the continuance of their own survival, and avoid destruction [*quae sunt appetere naturaliter constantiam permanendi, devitare perniciem*]."[21]

Yet this striving at preserving ourselves is double and ambiguous, in that it balances two opposite moves. On the one hand, we have a propensity toward laziness and indolence, to the avoidance of tiresome and difficult activity and thus toward rest (APH 7:151). Yet, absolute rest is death, which causes aversion (*Ekel*) and fear. Nature thus has put an opposite tendency in us that echoes the fear of nothingness, of sameness without otherness, through a kind of suffering and pain, which is the incentive to life-saving activity (APH 7:235). Nature arranged for pain always to creep into pleasant sensations, which makes life *interesting* (APH 7:164). Boredom calls us to make explicit something that bothers us without realizing what it is that bothers us. Similarly, for Descartes, nature *teaches* us to preserve our being in unity with our body through a dull pain of negative affections, such as hunger and thirst.[22] Boredom is thus a *painful gift of nature*, a kind of negatively erotic striving that allows us both to live on and eventually to live well.

For Kant, we are by nature inclined to be lazy and keep at rest—and to suffer for it. The careful, constant balancing between the sameness of rest and the otherness of motion is what constitutes life in its suffering and enjoyment, in all its misery and glory. The cunning of nature is then meant to preserve us through the negativity of suffering, which is not accidental or meaningless but has the purpose of the renewal of our mental, physical, and even social life. Discussing the idea of history in which we all participate and that we cannot escape, Kant introduces the famous notion of "social unsociability" (*die ungesellige Geselligkeit*).[23] This idea, as developed by Kant, is similar to that of Mandeville, who argued that the negativity of private striving and egoistic interest does inevitably contribute to the public good.[24] Kant claims that the highest purpose of nature, which is the development of all our natural capacities to the highest degree, can be achieved by means of what nature has supplied us with care yet without our choice or consent—namely, by social antagonism or "social unsociability." Similar to boredom, social antagonism is based on opposing tendencies—the tendency to live in a society with others, yet also to live as an individual in isolation. The tendency toward isolation and living an individual, secluded life causes resistance from everyone around, which in turn awakens all of our powers and induces us to overcome the natural "tendency for laziness" (*Hang zur Faulheit*).[25] Nature's nurturing slyness thus comes with a propensity that we find in ourselves that embraces opposites, perpetuates conflict, enhances antagonism with others, and by nudging and forcing us through struggle and fear, brings us out of the natural state of slumber and rest toward the activity of life. Life is thus sustained and preserved as individual solitary activity through the pain of boredom, and as commonly shared social activity through unsocial sociability.

Work and boredom. Boredom is thus an indication of the inertia and dullness (*Trägheit*) of existence, of the satiation of any activity (*Überdruss an aller Beschäftigung* [APH 7:151; see also *Critique of Pure Reason* A x]). But the most important *intentional* activity proper to humans, for Kant, is *work*. Modernity understands the human being primarily as a *homo faber*. Work is difficult and painful, yet necessary and unavoidable, life-preserving activity. Everything important in life in the Kantian autonomous and production-oriented social world comes through work: human dignity, worth, and political standing are defined by the *how* and *what* of work as one's own work: produced, alienated, and appropriated once again. Idleness amounts to laziness and as such is morally reprehensible, and enjoyment and rest can only be justified as a deserved prize.[26] In order to have the right to moral satisfaction and pleasure in life, one has to toil and suffer first. Boredom, then, prompts us to act: it is a great motivational force. The entire edifice of modern morality is based on the idea of the morality of work and the inevitability of suffering that we need to go through in order to fulfill our duty. According to this approach, I do something even (and mostly) if I do not want to do it, but I still do it out of the unqualified sense of duty. The opposite teleological moral position suggests that I do something because I want to achieve a particular end, and I do so often because I enjoy the action as interaction with others.

Kant's moralistic pedagogical appeal to the youth urges them to love and embrace work and renounce pleasure, not to abdicate from pleasure altogether but to postpone it and have it ahead of you, in the hope of achieving enjoyment as a goal of work:

> Young man! (I repeat) get fond of work; deny yourself enjoyments, not to *renounce* them, but rather to keep them always in perspective as far as possible! Do not dull your receptivity to enjoyments by savoring them prematurely! The maturity of age, which never lets us regret having done without a single physical enjoyment, will guarantee, even in this sacrifice, a capital of contentment which is independent of either chance or the laws of nature. (APH 7:237)

This is already the maxim of a teleological action, which, however, is not autonomous, because it is not defined by an imperative of our practical reason, and because it posits means to an end that is contained neither in the activity nor in the lack of it. But most importantly, pleasure now becomes a *capital* that one needs to accumulate and grow with interest, in order to savor when one retires! And those who did not work or accumulate this capital apparently will not be entitled to pleasure.

Boredom is thus a force or impulse put into us by nature, an inevitable yet potentially beneficial force of suffering, which is not rational but sensible, and whose purpose is to avoid the immobility of stagnation and the lack of new perceptions. Boredom motivates us to work more. And if people try to overcome the dullness of work by trying to find pleasure in their work, they still, as Nietzsche puts it, "do not fear boredom as much as work without pleasure; they actually require a lot of boredom if *their* work is to succeed."[27]

While it is painful, boredom allows for postponing fantasies and anticipated pleasure that will come with the enjoyment of new impressions and perceptions. In this sense, boredom and work are similar but also distinct. They are similar in that both are a form of negativity that impels us to act and thus enjoy life as the result of necessary suffering (APH 7:232).[28] Yet they are also different in that work is a positive form of suffering that comes with a plan and projection of the anticipated result to be enjoyed. Boredom, on the contrary, is a negative form of suffering, indicative of the lack of perceptions of an empty soul that does not yet know what to enjoy.

But is thinking, then, a toil or an enjoyment? If it is work and is a means to achieve an end, it should be difficult and unpleasant and only be needed when we have to produce something—a conclusion of an argument, a solution to a problem, or a new item of knowledge. Such thinking is inevitably painful and boring. Kant clearly opts for thinking as hard, productive work, from which we have a chance to obtain rest (APH 7:234), and which produces not only theoretical novelty but also rejuvenates our will and generates morally upright, reasoned action—the source of our dignity. But thinking is pleasure and can testify to the joy of being. Such thinking is engaging, enjoyable, and, as Whitehead suggests, is interesting before it is true (Whitehead's proposition is itself interesting, although it might not be true!).[29] But in order for thinking to be enjoyable and not boring, it should be practiced and shared with others as a nonproductive activity in which the capital of joy is never accumulated but is always spent with others at the very moment it appears.

Opposing inclinations. Thus, in order to live the good life, we need to legitimately *earn* the enjoyment of it. For Kant, life and enjoyment are closely related, since in order to enjoy life, one must perceive it in its constant change and abandonment of the current state (APH 7:233). However, to be legitimate and acceptable, enjoyment, which always depends on accidental circumstances that are beyond our control, must follow the (moral) purposes that we establish and pursue (APH 7:237–38). At this point, Kant is a Stoic thinker who carefully distinguishes between what is up to us and what is not, between what we can properly choose and what we can't.[30]

Kant is even more Stoic when he claims—as a postulate that makes the good, enjoyable life possible—that *nature* has put certain impulses into us. The purpose of these impulses or inclinations minimally is to preserve life, and maximally to maintain a good, enjoyable, and socially shared life. To this end, nature has equipped us with opposite impulses: one toward rest, which preserves sameness through not-acting (laziness), and the other toward change, which keeps otherness and change through negation, suffering, and contentious action (boredom and unsocial sociability). We should surmise a (or even the) purpose of the impulse: it is an indication that something is going wrong in our life, and thus we should move elsewhere, toward a better life envisaged for us by nature. The good life, then, is a carefully maintained balance of sameness and otherness, which is never a given or guaranteed but must be sought and kept each time anew and in a concrete situation of human interaction.

The life-preserving impulse cannot be chosen by us, because it is an inclination or propensity (*Hang*), which shows that the very foundation of our life is uneven, skewed, and slanted, unless it is leveled and rectified by morally upright reason.[31] Moreover, such an impulse is not rational and is thus hardly controllable, yet it is clearly detectable in its working through (negative) action. Only then can the natural impulse in us become the subject of philosophical reflection. The beginning of philosophy, on such interpretation, is not the wonder of being but the realization of one's weakness and limitation.[32] The working of impulse is negative (the inertia of rest or the dull pain of boredom) but the result of its interaction with its opposite is, or should be, positive, producing the enjoyable and continuing life as the synthesis of sameness and otherness.

The art of deception. Yet there is another inclination or impulse that we need to recognize when we analyze our life stung by boredom: it is the inclination to be *willingly deceived* (APH 7:151–52). Kant is very strict and upright about mendacity, which for him is the condition of the impossibility of human interaction. The maxim "You should not lie" is the main prescription and the cornerstone of philosophy for him, so that eventually it will secure the eternal peace and flourishing of humankind.[33] The presupposition of a simple and straightforward correspondence between (physical and moral) reality and the truth about it as reflected in cognition and moral action is a fundamental basis of the modern attitude toward the world and oneself as an embodiment of a universal subject who establishes the truth by, through, and from within itself (the "through truth" or "thruth"). In order to be identical with, and thus truthful to, oneself, one needs to produce and recognize the truth that would be exactly as one produces and recognizes it. In its identity and sameness, the subject cannot and should not lie or deceive itself. One can be mistaken or deceived, yet intentional mendacity has to be ruled out because it upsets the order of moral communication by undermining, and morally and cognitively eliminating, the subject who sets the moral and social relations in the first place.

Mendacity, then, is lying with the intention to deceive the other without the other knowing it. For Kant, one may be mistaken (*irren*), but one should never lie (*lügen, täuschen*).[34] However, as said, nature has endowed us with the inclination to be willingly deceived. Therefore, it is acceptable to deceive (*betrügen*) when the deception is morally permissible and stays within the accepted moral limits (APH 7:152). Since the natural sensible inclination or impulse (toward rest and not-acting) is an obstacle to life and thus to the good life (for there can be no good life without life), one needs to act against this inclination. One way to do it is, as said, by work. Yet work is difficult and is a positive suffering toward an end. The other way to confront the inclination is by *deceiving* it. For nothing can be gained against sensible and sensual inclinations by force or sheer decision. Therefore, it is permissible to fight the enemy of our well-being by its own means: *to deceive the deceiver* (*den Betrüger . . . zu betrügen* [APH 7:152]). Here, the natural inclination to be deceived counters the inclination toward idling. In this way, boredom too can be deceived.

Kant apparently takes the deception of the deceiver *not* to be itself a natural inclination in us. Therefore, it should come as an artificial and artful device that needs to be and can be cultivated, organized, and properly presented. In particular, we are amused when we know (1) that we are deceived; (2) that the deceiver knows that we are deceived; and (3) that the deceiver knows that we know that we are deceived. If these three conditions are met, we enjoy the deception and call it fine art. Art *is* deception. However, it is the deception that does not lie but tells the truth about the world and ourselves by deceiving—that is, by presenting the fiction of things and actions, not the way they are or have been, but the way they *might or should have been*.[35] One should thus overcome the cunning of nature by the cunning of art, not by replicating or imitating nature—but by deceiving it. The art of modern subjectivity is, therefore, not the art *according* to nature but *contrary* to nature and its impulses.

The most socially acceptable and morally significant form of art is the one that, although played in the "as if" mode and often in imagination, is closer to the real life of suffering, enjoyment, and communication. This is theater. Hence, for Kant, the more cultivated people are, the more they are actors (APH 7:151). Contemporary psychological observations suggest that people tend to deceive more often and more willingly if they cooperate with others, which might be construed as cooperation in a theatrically shared setting.[36] Dramatic art is the art of showing people's interactions not the way they happened but the way they might have been. Therefore, an actor is a professional pretender, deceiver, and hypocrite: ὑποκριτής means "actor." As we know from La Rochefoucauld, hypocrisy is the homage that vice pays to virtue.[37] Yet the hypocrisy in theater is an intended pretense and deception that is understood and valued as such by both actors and spectators.

However, on the stage of public life we need to perform and impersonate socially acceptable roles, which is why we should wear good manners, decorum, and politeness. The appearance of the good might seem pretentious and insignificant, a kind of small coin (APH 7:152), can buy much and has been in circulation for so long that its devices have been obliterated almost to the point of being unreadable. But even a habitual appearance of the good in other people should be valuable. Such a theatrical, hypocritical acting is only a semblance of proper morality, yet it is permissible and in fact necessary because it leads to the seemingly deceptive and hypocritical but eventually habitual establishment and promotion of good morals. We fend off the pain of boredom by an aimless play (*zweckloses Spiel*) that nevertheless has a purpose, that of entertaining the immobile and immobilized bored mind of work and moral action. The purposeless game comes with the joy of play and thus contributes to the culture of the soul and the cultivation of morals (*Kultur des Gemüts* [APH 7:152]). As Kant claims in the *Metaphysics of Morals*, our duty both to ourselves and others is to contribute to the appearance of virtue in public through manners, politeness, and culture, by affecting each other through our moral qualities and sociability (*officium commercii, sociabilitas*), by acting with others and not separating from them, by cultivating tolerance and friendliness, and by the display of humanness and propriety (*humanitas aesthetica et decorum*).[38] The paradigm of such socially entertaining art is theater, because drama allows us to witness lifelike experiences and new perceptions, which drive away the "long while" of boredom through the "short while" of amusement and thus contribute to the renewal of life. The enjoyment of theater comes from the possibility of empathizing with the actors yet feeling lucky not to be in the same predicament (APH 7:238-39). This is tragedy. But when one rejoices with others and learns from them how to solve seemingly unsolvable social puzzles and to untangle apparently irresolvable situations through a common effort, this is comedy. Boredom, then, is a negative *mediator* between work as positive suffering, difficult and painful striving toward the best, which is tragedy—and culture as pleasurable entertainment and purposeless play that still has the purpose of the rejuvenation of life, which is comedy. If this is the case, and if culture can be taken as the means of increasing our capacity for even greater enjoyment (APH 7:236) through the deception of art, then culture can be defined as the socially and morally acceptable way of *regulating boredom*.

Boredom unto death. In the theater of moral and social life, wearing the mask of good morals becomes a *form of action*, and the appearance becomes indistinguishable from the essence of a good life. But the modern moralistic subject can, and should, entirely erase the difference between the appearance of the good and the morally good as such only *in itself*. The acting should stop in front of the lonely, stern gaze of oneself as one's own spectator, judge, and inquisitor, because the appearance and play here can only veil one's egotism, cover for moral trespassing—and even make one believe that one can redeem one's guilt, the source of an irredeemable anxiety (APH 7:153).[39]

This means that the ultimate coincidence of the good and the appearance of the good is *death*, in which no further action of the subject toward itself is possible or required. Boredom, then, is the death of the subject who is still alive but does not want to live on. This is why in his anthropology lectures Kant exclaims in desperation: "Boredom is the disgust that one has for a condition in which one finds oneself. It is the great ill and the cause of much evil."[40] Yet, since death is the ceasing of any activity of life (APH 7:235), one strives toward life, which, as said, is a constant renewal, the life of action, change, novelty in perception and thought, and interaction with others. Since the solitary and lonely monological subject strives toward life, it wants to avoid the death of ultimate solitude and self-reliance, and thus to get rid of itself, or commit suicide. Since the life of the solitary modern subject is boredom, the lack of life implies its own abandonment.

Extreme boredom can thus cause suicide.[41] The modern philosophical subject is fascinated with death and seeks to get rid of itself to make way for life as renewal and novelty. The lonely subject attempts to commit a philosophical suicide out of the sense of inescapable boredom, trying to achieve its death by various philosophical devices—by the "death of the author," intersubjectivity, fragmentation, "automatic writing," playing with various literary genres, intertextuality, transindividuality, or the introduction of unusual, provocative topics, etc.[42] And yet, the modern subject *cannot succeed* in killing itself, wiping itself out as morally corrupt and guilty. It forever remains its own predicament and unintended destiny, only protracting the inevitable and unredeemable lonely suffering, the boredom of the same inevitably encountering the same.[43] The severe and ruthless judge that is one's own conscience cannot allow for this: the monological, moralistic modern subject is not redeemable in its solitude. It is utterly serious and thus does not, should not, and cannot enjoy the engaging play in the theater of public life.

Boredom as a modern malaise. In contemporary debates, Georg Simmel's short paper "The Metropolis and Mental Life" sets the tone for the discussion of the importance of boredom for the constitution and perception of modern city life. The congestion of the city in medieval times leads Max Weber to stress the frequency of personal and political contacts. But a modern city grows, enlarges, and straightens its streets and alleys into avenues and boulevards, its own old self slain at the hands of Baron Haussmann. This urban self-straightening and replanning promotes the comfort and protection of the inhabitants but instills separateness and disconnection between them. For Simmel, the modern bourgeois as a city inhabitant is emotionally protected by the city, which imposes a rationally planned sheltering and safeguarding of its inhabitants. Such a protection results in a "blasé attitude," which is "an indifference towards the distinctions between things" caused by a precisely calculated and predictable life.[44] The collective change in emotional perception leads to the equally collectively shared attitude to life. The city as the place of modern dwelling, then, is the locus of social exchange and political interaction in which its residents share the same set of emotional and rational attitudes that are established and conditioned by the frame of the modern *polis*.

This position has been supported by a number of prominent sociologists who pay attention to functional connections between people in the complex mesh of urban social interactions, rather than to individual perceptions or thoughts. Émile Durkheim and then Maurice Halbwachs follow this line of reasoning when they argue that our thought and memory is collective in its nature, so that we always participate in socially shared collective representations and remember only within a collectivity or group.[45]

More recently, Elizabeth Goodstein, mostly following Simmel but also relying on Benjamin, Heidegger, and Musil, has argued that boredom is the effect of modernization, which results in the loss of "the meaning and purpose of existence in a world increasingly bereft of both religious and worldly certainties."[46] Boredom, then, is the expression of and reaction to the disorientation in the world, in which one cannot find meaning in terms of traditional religious and social structures. The meaninglessness of the world signifies for Goodstein the loss of traditional values, which transpires in the form of modern "democratized" skepticism.[47] Much of the contemporary discussion of boredom in psychology, in the works of Fahlman, Igou, van Tilburg, and others, also stresses the close association of boredom with meaninglessness. For Fromm, boredom is *the* problem of modern life, much more than cruelty or self-destructiveness, precisely because contemporary life is meaningless.[48] The thesis that boredom is a specifically modern phenomenon is certainly a tenable one, yet why the spread of skepticism inevitably leads to boredom remains unclear. For skepticism was already widespread and quite "democratized" in antiquity, which, however, did not know boredom as a collective social phenomenon and thus did not even have a word for it. For us, the uncertainty about our place in the world and its ultimate meaning should create anxiety; that is, the fear of the unpredictability of the consequences of our actions whose origin and logic we moderns no longer understand.

Kracauer's paradoxes of boredom. It is thus modern city life, with its inextinguishable dynamism, unlimited offer of entertainment, and the inability to pause for a while in order to make some sense of one's ever-unstable position in the middle of the well-regulated bourgeois flux of production, exchange, suffering, and amusement, with its seasonal ebbs and tides, that is the primary locus of boredom.

Perhaps one of the most significant modern, reflective, and critical accounts of boredom comes in a short piece by Siegfried Kracauer published in the *Frankfurter Zeitung* in 1924.[49] Kracauer's writing is stylistically elegant, philosophically condensed, and literarily engaging. In just four pages, he mentions and briefly engages with the themes (anonymity, alienation, inauthenticity) that preoccupied thinkers of the age and that would be developed at much more length and with scholarly ponderosity three years later by the author of *Being and Time*. Kracauer begins his discussion with a rather paradoxical claim: those who today have time for boredom but are not bored (*nicht langeweilen*) are as boring as those who do not come to be bored. This happens because their self (*Selbst*) is lost, remains unaccounted for, and has been long forgotten, since people live in an ever-busy, hasty world, without an aim or purpose, not lingering anywhere for long (*nirgendwo lang zu verweilen* [L 161]). Similar to Kant, Kracauer takes boredom to be *inevitable*, although in a very different sense. The experience of the inevitability of boredom inescapably leads us to encounter a number of paradoxes. Kracauer himself seems not to notice them, and yet they transpire and are implied in his discussion. For him, boredom is both a burden and a blessing. People—by whom Kracauer means modern city dwellers, wage office laborers who routinely do boring, tedious work, petit bourgeois who follow strict Kantian *Arbeitsethik*, the working ethics of duty, which they proudly uphold—reward themselves with their justly deserved contentment and satisfaction (*Genugtuung*) of fulfilled obligations, after which they customarily return to their city apartments to enjoy their deserved and earned leisure.

However, for Kracauer there is no nature—only urban civilization. Therefore, unlike in Kant, boredom is not a voice of nature in us but is intimately connected with culture with its emphasis on production that gets eventually rewarded with entertainment and leisure. The distraction, fascination, fantasy, and enchantment of city life are endless. They drive oneself from oneself, hanging and hazing about in the evening streets, from one night into another, lit with lights and advertisements. The fantastic world of cinema and the illusion of the presence of other places through radio (and later television and the internet), substituting for communication in cafés, are the expressions of the city life that becomes a perpetual self-contained run and activity of amusement (L 161-63). Kracauer is condescending toward the people of the (big) city, and yet, since he himself is one of them, he is not disdainful of the city inhabitants, unlike Heidegger, who cannot find a better way of describing the "contemporary city man" than as "the ape of the civilization."[50] Because city life is the life of culture, superfluous yet vivid and engaging, the sympathetic figure of a city dweller is that of a flâneur, gadder, wanderer, the observer of city life in its endless, fascinating minutiae, a frequenter of films and cafés who knows and loves the city. For the flâneur, the city is a theater in which every minor event may become meaningful and insightful, connected with the lived history of the city, and it was this aspect of experience that would be studied with love and care by Benjamin. Another figure representing the ever-curious city inhabitant is a *Lumpensammler*, ragpicker and tatter, which is what Benjamin calls Kracauer in his review of Kracauer's book.[51] Interested in the splinters and rags of what the city has to offer, a ragman or chiffonnier is a connoisseur and antiquarian, a collector and appreciator of the concatenated poetic and political activity of the city. The first such figure in the history of the city is probably Socrates, followed by Diogenes the Cynic.[52] In modernity, this is the flâneur, ever distracted and never bored.

Yet the leisure offered by city life (*die Muße*, ironically close to necessity, *der Muß*) is both a burden and a blessing. Here we encounter the first paradox (1): contemporary life provides people with much leisure, yet in fact they have no leisure at all, because they are as bored at their leisure as they are at their work, which means that most people lack leisure. Rather than being time off, time for freedom, leisure becomes an institution that pays for boring work. At one's leisure, one is allowed not to do anything, does not want to do anything, and is made not to do anything.[53] But this is boring.

Here, Kracauer introduces an important distinction between two kinds of boredom: the "right," "exemplary," "radical," "legitimate"—and a "vulgar" (*vulgäre*), ordinary, and mediocre boredom. The latter is the insatiable satiety of the improperly lived leisure that suspends leisure and cancels its blessing. The vulgar boredom is neither hot nor cold, but rather tepid: it neither kills (Kant's English gentleman) nor calls for a new life. It only causes dissatisfaction, which can be driven away by morally allowable distraction, and this ultimately testifies to moral uprightness. What Kant takes to be the purpose of boredom—the pursuit of duty, the establishing of moral character—for Kracauer is only the means to dispel the bother of inauthentic boredom. People are too busy to be bored, which is why they are bored, but not in the right way. Boredom, then, is the condition of modern human existence in its two different forms, which in fact are two sides of the same coin, with which the modern self both pays and charges itself.

This entails the second paradox (2): the flight away from boredom through distraction in the abundance of modern entertainment does not save us from boredom. Driving away from boredom makes us only more bored in a "vulgar" way. Rather, embracing boredom in its inevitability makes us realize that boredom itself is *not boring* at all, once we come to recognize its right, radical form.[54] Accepting boredom gives us back our leisure, which is not the leisure of fleeing away from boredom but the leisure for being bored, or rather for not being afraid of being bored. What we cannot avoid, we should accept, and boredom becomes our blessing.

The third paradox (3) is that boredom is a state of powerlessness and supineness, in which one cannot and does not produce anything, yet boredom is most creative. Kracauer's prescription for well-being is to turn away from vulgar boredom to the genuine one by a radical suspension of all commonly accepted distraction. On a sunny afternoon, when everyone is outside, one goes back to one's room, closes the curtains, lays on the sofa, and does the "spiritual exercise" of fully committing oneself to the radical boredom—by embracing not acting, by not doing anything, drifting away in thoughts and reveries.[55] In this way, Kracauer performs a radical *epoché*, yet not of thought or judgment—but of *action* that overcomes action. Rather than preventing boredom, one embraces it in the nondoing that surpasses and goes beyond *theōria*, *praxis*, and *poiēsis*. This radical boredom is the suspension of all action. In order to be properly bored, one needs leisure, which one should be able to know how to use. One should dare to be lazy, not to produce, make, or do anything. Paraphrasing Erasmus, one could call Kracauer's way *Pigritiae laus*, "Apology of laziness." This is exactly what Malevich advocates in his short piece "Laziness as the real truth of humankind" of 1921.[56]

Outlined ironically and in a sketch, Kracauer's way to the "legitimate" boredom goes through a number of stages (L 163–64). At first, one entertains certain ideas and even thinks of some projects, which, however, as Chichikov's grand projects in Gogol's *Dead Souls*, do not, and cannot, lead anywhere and are thus totally useless. Once one recognizes their ephemeral character, one comes to reject any thought and activity, marveling at the presence of the surrounding "not serious" little ludicrous beings, such as a glass grasshopper or a cactus. Their just-being-there testifies to the purposelessness of the activity of the constant production of new things, distractions, meanings, which makes one utterly and inescapably bored. Such a being finds *nothing* (*Nichts*) in its existence worth noting or of importance to the greater whole of the existent. Such a being is that which *is without being* (*was ist, ohne zu sein* [L 164]), a being that is present in its absence to the world of reality and purpose. But existence without (serious and purposeful) being is irritating, causes an inner unrest without any aim, and one can only be content with "not doing anything further than being by oneself and not knowing what one actually should do."[57] And finally, if one can wait long enough, one arrives at legitimate boredom, which opens the flux of passing images through a shimmering landscape that looks strangely like a paradise.[58] And here one encounters what one was always looking for but was always missing, the end of the journey, which itself is a journey. For the lack of a better word, Kracauer calls it "great passion" (*große Passion*). But it can probably be called anything, because everything is just a play of boredom in imagination against itself.

Hence, along the "way of boredom" one first needs to know how to be distracted; then one does not know at all what to do, other than just being with oneself by being bored; and finally, one does not even know how to be, what to know, and how to ask the right question, committing oneself to the oblivion of anything having a purpose, useful knowledge, and dutiful judgment.

Yet, one cannot force oneself to be rightly bored: radical boredom cannot be produced or be had on purpose. Rather, one needs *patience* in order to be bored. Boredom thus comes to those who are capable of being bored in waiting for it.

And so boredom, which does not produce anything, generates *nothing*, *Nichts*. The one who can be embraced and taken away by boredom is a kind of bored creator who produces nothing—the nothing of the daydream, of not knowing, and oblivion. Yet the nothing of boredom is *almost* nothing, which makes the bored creator an *as-if* creator who flows along with the fleeing appearances of the world of rattletraps, fantasies, and forgettings that the as-if creator makes up out of *prope nihil*.

This leads us, finally, to the fourth paradox (4): boredom alienates ourselves from ourselves (our self), yet it is the only way to go back or have access to our proper—"authentic"—existence (*Dasein* [L 163]), which is being bored without giving an account (λόγον διδόναι) of that which is and should be, of the *Sein* and *Soll* of the world and our action in it with and against each other. Here, Kracauer diagnoses what other thinkers of the age discus at much length: that we can get back to ourselves as living, nonproductive beings by facing the negativity of finitude, mortality, and anxiety. Kracauer is more benevolent: it is boredom, rather than death, that opens the way to our self and existence. Unlike in Kant, boredom in not opposed to pleasure but, if it is the right kind, brings its pleasurable blessings (*Beglückungen* [L 164]). Boredom is useless, yet it is most helpful. By itself, boredom is meaningless, yet it allows our actions to become meaningful. We live to the full only when we are really bored. Paradoxically, we are liberated from (vulgar) boredom by (radical) boredom. Happiness, life, and freedom—such are the blessings of the right, radical boredom for Kracauer.

Radical boredom is thus the way to its own truth, which is *freedom*. It is the freedom for our proper existence and the freedom from the fake life of purposeful production. Kracauer establishes the diagnosis of modernity. Modernity is born out of the spirit of boredom. But he also suggests a treatment by the remedy of philosophical homeopathy: treat the same by the same, *similia similibus*, evil by evil, poison by poison, *pharmakon* by *pharmakon*, boredom by boredom. In fact, philosophical thinking itself gets suspended by literary writing, the boredom of long treatises by a short newspaper article, attentive thinking by the *far niente* of doing nothing, which becomes the realization of freedom. To be is to be free, and hence, to be is to be bored.

Kracauer's discussion is notable in its being both a reflection on boredom and an exemplification of the way of boredom, of the working of boredom by being bored. As he hints at the end of his piece, the double reflection on boredom by thinking about boredom and acting out of it, might itself be boring, and it might even be written out of boredom. If the modern subject is forever stuck in the ongoing reflection about itself, there might indeed be no way out of such a reflection. Besides being boring, the boring reflection on boredom in boredom is a kind of self-praise, and although narcissism is alleviated and even suspended by self-irony, this is the way the praise of stupidity overwhelms and cancels stupidity.[59]

Yet Kracauer envisages the radical liberation and freedom from boredom by boredom, which might bring not only new experience but a new type of experience. The freedom achieved in boredom by being bored might even make radical boredom extinguish and transcend itself, so that, as Kracauer says (L 164), everything that is would be . . . , simply . . . The end of thinking at the end of writing as the end of being useful, not allowing for existence with oneself, at one's self . . . Just the ellipsis, which marks the inevitable elision in the existence without being, without knowing, and without acting, in total forgetfulness of these three. Only suspension points, which suspend any point of productive being, purposeful knowledge, and dutiful action . . .

Kracauer thus has to inevitably complete his discussion of boredom with an ironic self-suspension of what he said about boredom in order to elude the boringly serious and productive conclusion about boredom. The "great passion" is just passing on the horizon, and true boredom, which does not mitigate itself, keeps being productive—but only of trifles and bagatelles, as this boring one that Kracauer has just quickly written for a newspaper that we have picked up and read in haste...

Heidegger's poetics of boredom. There is no evidence that Heidegger ever read Kracauer's piece. Yet, much of what Kracauer said about boredom elegantly and often aphoristically, Heidegger thoroughly, painstakingly, and systematically elaborates in his 1929-30 Freiburg lecture course, "The Fundamental Concepts of Metaphysics," which marks the end of the flourishing of the Weimar era.[60] Strangely enough, boredom is in the air at a time that is marked by the highest and most original achievements in philosophy, art, literature, poetry, film, and literary critique, which are all expressions of the modern subject's attitude to life, thought, and nature. And yet, this subject is deeply bored, and the thinkers of the time cannot miss it in their thought.

In his year-long lecture course, Heidegger apparently intended to discuss the fundamental questions of metaphysics, which were announced as those of the world, finitude, and solitude. Boredom initially was not one of them. And yet, after the beginning of the discussion, Heidegger realized that boredom *is* a fundamental for modern philosophy and our attitude toward the world that cannot be missed, and thus the entire first semester turned into perhaps the most philosophically sophisticated discussion of boredom, conceptually intense, often laborious, but never boring.

The subject of boredom does not come up in Heidegger's earlier work and is referred to only rarely thereafter. This lecture course, which was published only much later and posthumously in 1983 in the *Gesamtausgabe*, stands out in Heidegger's work. On the one hand, it continues the development of the analytic of Dasein from *Being and Time* (with explicit references to it), and on the other hand, establishes the style of philosophical questioning of the self-investigating, uncensored thought that intends to overcome itself by using and then slowly evaporating established concepts and apparent distinctions—by an ever-deepening questioning of the ground of our being as being-there. By acting out his thinking in this way, Heidegger intends to provide a *critique* of contemporary philosophy, for which boredom is the main theme of a polyphonic variation in the form of a fugue, which, at the very end, will resolve into a single high-pitched sound culminating in complete stillness.

The concept of critique may mean a destruction and refutation of the opponent's thesis as false and untenable—or it may also mean an engaged discussion in which, even if the interlocutors disagree, they can still continue the dialogue in order to develop the original claim further. The critique of modernity, then, may mean its complete rejection in favor of retrieving a "premodern" or "original" understanding that has now been lost but still can be recovered through a nonmodern way of thinking that might help us understand who, what, and how we are in the world. But we could also question modernity in the hopes of articulating and strengthening some of its insights such that they might assist with establishing and reinforcing practices of thought and action that might then lead to liberation from the current oppressive practices that we need to investigate.

Heidegger, however, stays away from this latter kind of critique, which for him objectivizes the thought and thus misses the very ground of our being. Critique, for Heidegger, means providing the diagnosis of modernity and of our current condition (FC 75; GM 112), and, at the same time, if the inquiry testifies to our being sick, also suggesting the remedy. Similar to Kracauer, Heidegger takes the modern condition of both public life and philosophy to be debilitating and banal. We—the anonymous—"find no meaning for ourselves, i.e., no essential possibility of being any more" (FC 77; GM 115). The contemporary bourgeois—city—life is based on the self-reproducing planning ahead that is meant to satisfy *needs*, which tend to proliferate and can never be ultimately satisfied.

> For the renewed attempts and efforts which are constantly made to control these needs, to put an end to them, to convert them directly into order and satisfaction are just as hasty and boisterous. In keeping with this, it is not only individuals that are at work everywhere, but groups, unions, companies, classes, parties—everyone and everything is organized to face these needs and every organization has its program. (FC 163; GM 243)

Yet despite his apparent rejection of group-planning activity in favor of lonely, uninterrupted meditation in front of his silent listeners and during long walks outside the city, Heidegger will join one such party soon. Detecting that something is almost irreparably wrong with our contemporary situation, Heidegger fails to notice that he himself falls into its trap. Apparently, he does not want to become one of the many, but be one of a kind, showing others the way out of the impasse of "floundering self-defense against the needs" (FC 163; GM 243), into the sublime stillness of the proper vision of the goal beyond the banality of the modern condition.

For Heidegger, the satisfaction of needs is not a political or social question but a philosophical one: the incessantly busy and superficial activities of modern needs-oriented city life find their expression in ever-increasing disorientation, lostness, and illusion, which eventually comes out of abandoning or missing the very ground of our existence. Like Kracauer, Heidegger takes the modern ethics of duty not as countering the planning and ordering rationality that achieves particular ends through a coordinate effort, but rather as its very expression. The duty of being responsible means the duty of being then and there for a particular task, precisely at a place in the city grid and on a time of the city clock, which is not the time of being but the measured duration of the improper, "inauthentic" existence.

Since modern philosophy is a reflection of and deliberation about the contemporary situation, it is equally flawed for Heidegger. It is nothing but a "fashion philosophy" (*Modephilosophie*), and "a higher form of journalism" (FC 77; GM 115); which hastily tends to fill thick volumes with classifications of modern forms of life; which has lost itself in the city, in the form of "philosophy of life" (in the apparent misinterpretations of Oswald Spengler, Ludwig Klages, Max Scheler, and Theobald Ziegler [FC 69-74; GM 103-11]), and "philosophy of culture" (by which Heidegger clearly means Cassirer, the three volumes of whose *Philosophy of Symbolic Forms* had just been published in 1923-29). No doubt, both Kracauer and Benjamin will fit Heidegger's bill as "philosophizing journalists."

The central problem of Heidegger's lectures on boredom follows up, and explicitly refers to, *Being and Time*'s concern with Dasein, which, in us, has been summoned by being to question being beyond the existent or beings.[61] Dasein is always *ours*, not *mine*, and as such it makes us attuned with itself, puts us in the mood of looking for its being-there, which is always presently absent and transpires from its concealment. Dasein is not something that can be made into an object, the properties of which we could study and describe, because Dasein is neither objectifiable nor finalizable in any representation. Dasein is that which *is* there, is *there* (FC 77; GM 116). It makes it possible for us to be in tune or in the mood of listening and attending to what it discloses to us.

Dasein speaks to us from its unconcealed ground through the voice of its *Stimmung*. The term, which Heidegger uses throughout his published oeuvre, is usually translated as "mood" or "attunement."⁶² This is one of the key terms in *Being and Time*, central for the understanding of the critique of modernity, which also often appears in Heidegger's interpretation of Hölderlin and Nietzsche, but it is used in the lectures on the fundamental concepts of metaphysics more than anywhere else.⁶³

Mood, according to Heidegger, can be first seen as reflected in our everyday interactions: when someone is struck by grief, they seem to appear the same, yet altogether different in their presence with others. Here, the "how" becomes different. Mood involves others, yet it is not a thing, not a particular being, not something that is present at hand, not a mode of being; is nether inside nor outside, but even if it is not noticed, it is always there and present in our dealings with others. In fact, such an unnoticed, concealed mood is the most powerful. This allows us to first define it as the *how* of our being with others, which ultimately depends on our Dasein.⁶⁴ Although Heidegger constantly repeats the formula "our Dasein," his stress is on "Dasein" rather than on "our." Being with others, which potentially could lead to a radical critique of modernity, is derivative of the fundamental way of our being-there (or being-here) or Da-sein. In this sense, Dasein is also the deep ground for the normative, although not ethical, demand *to be there* (*da zu sein* [FC 165; GM 246]). In the end, despite its being social, Dasein for Heidegger characterizes us as being in attunement to the deep tune of our Dasein, hidden in its very ground and in need of being disclosed through a different kind of philosophical analysis, or rather, a philosophico-poetic description.

The mood, then, is the *how* that characterizes Dasein, and thus does not come and go according to a situation: it is always there because Dasein is always and already attuned, or is in a mood, from its very ground (FC 67-68; GM 101-3). Hence, we are already and always in a mood and are attuned to Dasein, so that the mood becomes a precondition of thinking and acting in a particular way. Because being in the mood (*Gestimmtsein*) is the fundamental way or mode (*Grundart*) of our Dasein (FC 89; GM 134), it needs to be understood. Understanding the *how* of Dasein thus becomes fundamental for the whole of Heidegger's project of the critical rethinking and redescription of the human being, which also means to redefine, retool, and rearm modern philosophy in its entirety.

Since we are already in a mood for something but do not yet know what this mood is, we need to become related to others, and this discovered relatedness

(*Bezogenheit* [FC 89; GM 134]) will then make transpire that which is in the ground of our being-there but not yet evident to us. In everyday life we cannot put ourselves into a mood just by an act of will: we cannot be joyous simply because we want to be, but something needs to happen in our life or we need to generate the mood through a collectively shared action, such as celebration. Heidegger's example of mood, however, is grief rather than joy, which is induced—he intends to avoid any language of cause and causation (FC 83; GM 125)—by an event, situation, or other people's interacting in the already established mood, which happens to us yet is not produced by us.

The fundamental mood, then, is not something that comes and goes but is already there. The "always already" (ἤδη) is the ancient way of characterizing being as being-here, distinct from becoming as never-yet. Dasein is always already somehow in a mood, is tuned and attuned (*gestimmt*). *Stimmung* makes clear, reveals how it *is* to one, "wie einem ist," and thus the being-tuned, *Gestimmtsein*, brings being to its there, *Sein* to *Da* (SZ 134 [§29]). The fundamental mood "must permeate [*durchstimmen*] our Dasein in the ground [*im Grunde*] of its essence" (FC 132; GM 199). But the mood is *not* dialogical: it tells us something quietly and indistinctly but does not respond or talk back—at least, not always. Fundamental mood is there as latent or sleeping, hence it can only be *awakened*. One needs to awaken the mood, a kind of a sleeping beauty, which will then allow us to grasp Dasein as such, as it is or can be in its possibilities (FC 68). The awakening is an acting (*Handeln* [GM 103]). There can be different moods in us, but apparently there is *the* mood of and in Dasein, because it is fundamental to it and to our essence. But who should and can awaken Dasein in its mood, and how?[65]

Philosophy and philosophizing. This brings us to the very fundamental mood of Heidegger himself, to the attunement of his philosophy to discovering and describing Dasein in its very ground. Heidegger takes it that he and his listeners (but not interlocutors) are engaged in an activity of utter importance when doing philosophy, because the truth of philosophy is that of human Dasein. For this reason, philosophy is something primordial and originary. Philosophy is the way in which we are summoned or even "attacked" by Dasein in its demand to discover or disclose itself in its deepest ground that makes philosophy, which thus "permeates the whole of human life (Dasein)," a risky and turbulent yet inevitable and most important activity. As such, "philosophy has meaning only as human activity [*Tun*]. Its truth is essentially that of human Dasein" (FC 19; GM 28).

But what exactly this kind of activity is depends on our understanding of philosophy. For Heidegger, the essence of philosophy is the knowledge, or cognition, of essence (*Wesenserkenntnis* [FC 154; GM 231]). This is a traditional understanding of philosophy since the time of Socrates, whose philosophizing was asking questions about the essence of a thing, action, or concept in the hope of arriving at its definition, to which he almost never got. The Socratic philosophy was thus the *questioning* of and about *what* a thing is, through questions and answers directed to the other. For Heidegger, however, philosophy is not a dialectical enterprise meant to establish a logically justified definition that would hold against any attempts at its further dismantling. It is instead the "comprehensive questioning" (*begreifendes Fragen*) of the very Dasein itself that comes from its essence (FC 132; GM 199), where others may be present but do not play a role. In this way, Heidegger avoids providing definitions or logically supported distinctions and conclusions, and when he happens to arrive at them in his lectures, he quickly erases or suspends them in order to continue the questioning even "deeper," to the very limit of philosophy. Philosophy as the proper metaphysical comprehension, then, consists in the unfolding of the right questioning, which, however, always remains without an answer, since philosophical answers do not consist in communicating established facts or logically achieved definitions (FC 185; GM 273). Hence, "philosophy is only there to be overcome" (FC 155; GM 232). As fundamental questioning and the invocation of Dasein, philosophy can only be meaningfully practiced as the act and activity of philosophizing: "Philosophy is philosophizing" (*Philosophie ist Philosophieren* [FC 4; GM 6]; see also FC 174; GM 258). And philosophizing means learning how to move in the depth (*Tiefe*) of Dasein (FC 131), and thus "grasp[ing] ourselves in the ground of our essence via the interpretation of the mood" (FC 118; GM 178), which, in the end, should lead to the "proper" (the "authentic," *Eigentliche*) understanding of Dasein (FC 136; GM 205).

Only through philosophizing as comprehensive questioning can the truth of Dasein become revealed in its unconcealment.[66]

Once we are concerned with the existent as a whole, we encounter φύσις, or the self-building ruling (*Walten*) that eventually prevails through us (FC 26; GM 39), or simply that which proceeds out of itself and needs only itself to transform. Heidegger evokes Heraclitus's fragments, which apparently contain the splinters of the originary understanding of being, since Heraclitus for him is the thinker and singer of the existent as a whole. Speaking and saying, λέγειν, is the opposite of hiding, κρύπτειν, which is established not by a speculative act of thinking but by the oracle (22B93 DK). What is expressed in speaking is the *logos*, λόγος, which is to be understood as taking that which rules in the existent as a whole (nature as φύσις) into the openness of the unconcealment, ἀλήθεια, or truth about the existent. That which has been hidden, concealed in things as a whole, is taken into the light by its opposite, the λόγος. But what is that which hides? For Heraclitus, it is nature or φύσις, which *loves to hide* (22B123 DK), always being playfully engaged in a hide-and-seek with serious (re)searchers and thinkers. In this way, the truth of things, of the existent as a whole, is revealed or opened through the originary saying as making evident or unconcealed (FC 26-29; GM 39-41). Unconcealment is also the way in which nature produces life: a living being is gestating in the concealment from both our eyes and reason until it comes into the unconcealment of the light of the world.

Unconcealment brings into the open the evidence of the existent in its entirety, and indeed of Dasein itself (FC 145; GM 218). Something that is present there at hand, that which can be objectivized and described through a finite number of properties and attributes, does not need to become manifest. Dasein, on the contrary, is *both* here and there (*da*), opening itself up and making itself available in its manifestness (*Offenbarkeit*) or "resolutely disclosing itself" (FC 149; GM 223). What is important for our discussion here is that the fundamental mood or attunement should become manifest through the philosophico-poetic analysis of the truth of our being there (FC 90; GM 136).

Heidegger's project of philosophizing by attentively listening to the words of his language and the ancient Greek philosophico-poetic lore aims at the revealing of the concealed into the openness of truth, which for him is at the very root of human Dasein (FC 29; GM 44) and is driven by homesickness to being as a whole (*zum Sein im Ganzen* [FC 5; GM 8]). Heidegger suspends the philosophy that objectivizes thought by straightening it through logical rules of engagement, doing so by philosophizing as questioning the existent by attending to what it says. Yet the openness to the saying that comes from the existent in its hiding might still conceal the same narcissistic reflective attitude of the modern self that one tries to overcome. And although it is *our* Dasein, as being there with each other, *Miteinander-Dasein*, Heidegger takes on the role of the speaker on its behalf, considering himself to have been appointed by Dasein itself, thus embodying the odd figure of an academic oracle who not only listens to what the Dasein tells him—but also interprets what is said. Hence, Heidegger is the Pythia who listens to the divine word and is inebriated and intoxicated by the superabundant fullness of the depth of being, uttering the oracle in a language incomprehensible to the listeners. Yet the oracle gets untangled and interpreted in accessible language by the priest. And Heidegger thus conveniently turns into the priest—or the "guardian," "director," or (academic) "supervisor" (*Verwalter* [FC 163; GM 244]) of Dasein—who can interpret and communicate the meaning of the heard through the said.

Waiting and boredom. But how does one get to the truth of the unconcealed? Because proper philosophical knowledge should be revealed in its ground and then interpreted, rather than, as we do now, progressively accumulated by ordered thinking that moves on to a logical conclusion, we are inevitably making less and less progress and eventually come to a standstill (FC 160; GM 237). What is left for us, then? Only Dasein's holding to itself in composure (*Ansichhalten*) against the hastiness of living and thinking, which cannot be overcome in an act of resistance by refutational argumentative thinking. The only alternative is *waiting* (*Warten* [FC 161; GM 240]), which leads to a suspension of unnecessary and superfluous idle talk and should provide a stop, a *hold* (*Halt* [FC 161; GM 240]). The philosophical maxim—theoretical, practical, and productive—then is *sta, viator*. Only by making a stop and waiting for the concealed to become manifest can the true originality (*Ursprünglichkeit*) of questioning provide and open up the possibility of the essential knowledge (*Wesenserkenntnis*), which is the task of philosophy (FC 162; GM 242).

Philosophizing as questioning that leads to a suspension of philosophical constructive thinking is neither passivity nor activity: it is something different. It is waiting in countenance, which allows for being there, fully awake and attentive to the possibility and necessity of our Dasein. Waiting *wakes*: it wakes oneself in and to the fundamental mood, the attunement that allows the very ground of Dasein, concealed up until the moment of questioning, to become manifest. The one who does not philosophize is asleep. Only the philosopher who has the courage to pause in purposeful thinking through unrushed "comprehensive questioning" can come to awake the fundamental mood of Dasein: "Only philosophizing is wakeful [*wache*] Dasein" (FC 23; GM 34).

While questioning in front of others, Heidegger himself always eventually hints at or finds the right answers, which he apparently has already found while being awake. Yet, contra Heidegger, one might assume that the real questioning might be the one without an answer, or even, in a more radical way, the questioning that has forgotten the question itself and for this reason ultimately has abandoned the questioning.

But what is this fundamental mood that we are meant to awake by philosophical questioning that comes to a stop in *waiting* for the truth of things and of Dasein to become unconcealed? Waiting means putting oneself in the state of *receptivity* for a more manifest and transparent understanding of the fundamental mood or attunement of the Dasein (FC 132; GM 199).

Without noticing that she still remains a somewhat shabbily dressed modern bourgeois, in her fantasy the philosopher rejects the ordinary and her own self, and fights for the sublime and the reestablishing of the concealed essence of the truth of our existence that is tarred by everyday haste. Yet apparently it belongs to the nature of the philosopher to be better understood than she understands herself (FC 155; GM 232), and so one needs to explain what her task is, which is only incidentally entrusted to a philosopher. So the suggestion is to stop and wait for the truth to come out of its unconcealment. And waiting may allow us to listen to the closest other of philosophy, which is poetry, insofar as the two share and recur in *logos*, although they do it differently, since now *logos* is primarily understood not as syllogistic and proving but as the word of the poet and the language itself.

Poetry thus becomes the paradigm for philosophy: "for philosophy is true what is true for the poet: 'create, poet, do not talk'" (*Bilde Dichter, rede nicht* [FC 154; GM 232]). Heidegger paraphrases here Goethe's famous dictum, substituting "poet" (*Dichter*) for the original "artist" (*Künstler*) and omitting the second line, which runs "nur ein Hauch sei dein Gedicht" ("let only a hint be your poem"). By making the citation into an enthymeme, Heidegger hints at the hint of the poetic image as clarifying the meaning of the fundamental mood of Dasein and indeed the necessity of Dasein itself, not through a logical analysis or a dialectical exchange but by a poetic intimation, in which creation amounts to waiting, and where the *logos* speaks through the philosopher-poet.

The poet is thus the model for the philosopher. Or, rather, the philosopher is a reflecting poet, the poet who first *creates* and then *talks*, interpreting her own creation. But the poet does not need to reflect on what she says and thus can allow it to be interpreted by others. In this sense, the philosopher is the aspiring poet who failed to become a poet. Perhaps one could even say that philosophy is born out of the spirit of resentment. One becomes a philosopher once one realizes that one has failed to become somebody else and thus can only reflect on the one whom one wanted to be but could not become. Plato aspired to be a great tragedian, Descartes a mathematician, and Nietzsche a composer, and when they failed, they turned to thinking about what they might but could not do. And Heidegger probably aspired to be a Romantic poet singing of the concealed beauty of nature—of the surrounding native fields, woods, and hills.[67]

If the blueprint for philosophical activity is poetry and the philosopher is essentially a poet, does this mean that what the philosopher does is made up and is a fiction of the productive imagination? The poet, taken by the Bacchic mania, as Plato describes him in the *Ion*, is an ecstatic and inspired transmitter of what is, of being; an empty reed that turns into a flute expressing the divine harmony, which then is passed on to the rhapsode and then to the listeners, thus connecting us listeners to being through one interlinked chain by way of transmitting the message through poet and performer. Yet the poet of the epic tradition, Homer, is not an ecstatic singer but a temperate historian, the one who knows what he is talking about and transmits the heard (before) into the said (now) with an utter precision and responsibility for each and every word that needs to be said, thus preserving them from the futility of oblivion. The ecstatic Platonic poet is also presented in the figure of the prophet who utters a divine commandment by first submitting to the divinity, and in the figure of the Pythia, who literally gets out of her mind in order to free space for the divine oracle that needs to speak through her. But the Homeric poet, who is in full self-control, to such an extent that she allows herself improvisation, is the one who creates or recreates what he has heard, knows, and what needs to be remembered and understood. This kind of poet needs an interpreter, as the Pythia needs a priest who will turn her gibberish into everyday language. Yet, in order to interpret, describe, and analyze the message, one needs to invoke that which will give it in the first place.

The task of philosophy, against the phenomenological description of the data of consciousness, becomes then the invocation of Dasein: "Not to describe the human consciousness but to invoke the Dasein in human being. This invocation cannot come about as a bewitchment or mystical contemplation but only through sober conceptual questioning" (FC 174; GM 258). Heidegger thus denies to the philosopher (to himself) the role of an ecstatic poet, an inspired prophet, or an inebriated Pythia—but claims for himself the role of the sober priest of being, a hierophant who listens to the poetic message of Dasein, interprets and translates it into vernacular philosophical language, reshaping and recreating it along the way. This should mean that as a philosopher one has to be a careful and meticulous interpreter, a hermeneuticist, of that which is said originally, in an original manner. But the original itself, the cryptic message, comes from an ecstatic poet or Pythia. Thus, there is always a temptation to turn into a Pythia, especially in front of so many listeners.

As a human activity of acting and doing (*Tun*), philosophy should be the creation of a word that would uncover that which is *there*, *is* there (Da-sein) but as yet is concealed, thus not really created but revealed by the philosophico-poetic diction. And this word Heidegger finds in Romantic poetry, in Hölderlin, and, for now, in Novalis. It is a prophetic or oracular word that cannot be contested, only listened to and interpreted. Novalis's word is that "philosophy is properly a homesickness (*Heimweh*), the striving to be everywhere at home" (FC 5; GM 7; see also FC 8-9; GM 11-12).[68] This is what philosophy is in its profound concealed ground: homesickness, nostalgia for being-there everywhere, wherever we happen to be, the desire to return to where we have always belonged, at home in our proper Dasein, despite having drifted to the vain and busy city, where the proliferated distractions keep us from hearing the simple and exercising the moment of the concentrated, simple gaze.

Moreover, the *logos* of language is not straightened by the correct normative literary use but the local idiom of the surrounding villages, fields, and mountains, the "dialect," that reveals the concealed, profound truth about our Dasein and about the existent as a whole, the things around us in which we are immersed, but which refuse our proper understanding of them. And the language of the surroundings, Heidegger's native Alemannic, tells him that "to be homesick" (*Heimweh haben*) means "to have long time" (*lange Zeit haben* [FC 80; GM 120]). But long time literally means boredom as "long while" or Langeweile.[69] Listening and attending in waiting is thus ultimately the attention to language, which will be the theme that Heidegger develops by wandering through his postwar philosophical woods.

It needs to be noted that in *The Fundamental Concepts of Metaphysics*, boredom takes the place of anxiety, or *Angst*, which is the fundamental mood in *Being and Time*, where, under the influence of Kierkegaard, Heidegger claims that it is anxiety that transpires in Dasein's flight from itself and from its authenticity, when facing being in the world (SZ 184-91 [§40]; see the discussion of anxiety below).[70] This means that there can be many different fundamental moods: "Every genuine fundamental mood liberates and deepens, binds and releases the others" (FC 182; GM 269). Why this is the case, we still do not know, because the different fundamental moods can be only experienced "through Dasein itself, and then only to the extent that we actually summon up the effort to be *there* (*da* zu sein). Hence it is just as mistaken to absolutize one single fundamental mood as it is to relativize all the possible fundamental moods with respect to one another" (FC 182; GM 270). It is thus only through the direct experience of the occurrence of Dasein that we can testify to different fundamental moods, which otherwise cannot be speculatively deduced from a concept or reduced to each other.

We only need to wait for a different fundamental mood to occur, as, for example, melancholy (*Schwermut* [FC 182–83; GM 270; see also FC 79; GM 119]). In order to awaken a fundamental mood, Heidegger again turns to listening to the word of the said, which in this case is a philosophical fragment that becomes poetic by being taken out of its context. The new fundamental mood is revealed through the hermeneutic interpretation of Aristotle's saying that everyone who achieved prominence in philosophy, politics, poetry, and the arts are melancholics (μελαγχολικοί).[71] So the fundamental mood is now changed from boredom to melancholy, without further notice or explanation. Having brilliantly discussed boredom in the fall part of his lectures, Heidegger abruptly abandons it for melancholy in the spring. Perhaps a seasonal mood change.

Three forms and two moments of boredom. Thus, despite the attempt to go beyond the rules of logic, Heidegger posits a syllogism, one premise of which comes from the *logos* of the poet (Novalis) and the other premise from the *logos* of the language (Alemannic): as philosophizing, philosophy is homesickness; and homesickness is boredom. Therefore, philosophy is rooted in boredom. Boredom is the fundamental mood of our Dasein that needs to be awakened and attended to in philosophico-poetic questioning in waiting.[72] As a practice, awakening boredom as the fundamental mood of our Dasein is achieved by listening to Heidegger's narrative, which is consistent and logically coherent, introducing a number of highly original and unexpected distinctions, yet can only be accepted (or rejected) in its very fundamental premises.

The modern subject, which is the lonely center of produced and acquired meanings, is primarily delimited by *negative* states: by ennui, anxiety, angst, fear, and dread. Everything that appears to be out there and have an independent existence, is the not-subject, non-ego (in Descartes), not-I (in Fichte), nonindividual (hence universal, in Romanticism), and only thus acquires its objective status, which precisely means nonsubjective. In line with this modern attitude, the fundamental mood has to be negative, something troubling, disturbing, unsettling, which, once awakened by Heidegger's philosophical acuity, appears as boredom.

How do we approach it? The immediate natural (or, rather, unnatural city-dwelling) attitude is to drive boredom away, to escape it, which seems easy, given the enormous amount of entertainment provided by contemporary life. Yet, in doing so, we inevitably act in bad conscience. Why? Because in boredom time becomes long, *Langeweile*, "long while," and yet we are constantly trying to make it short and eventually fall asleep. Hence, the major task is to awaken the fundamental mood, to let it be awake as boredom (FC 78-79; GM 117-18). By making time short through increasing entertainment, which becomes more and more overwhelming in the contemporary world, going beyond any visible scope of amusement-seeking activity, we shorten the time of our life instead of making it longer. We give up on our life. The time of our life becomes filled with nonsensical, distractive activity that is ultimately directed at the same bored and boring self, instead of becoming fulfilled with a few meaningful acts that reach out for the other.

The right attitude for Heidegger, then, is exactly the same as Kracauer has described before him: not to resist boredom but to "let it resonate" (FC 82; GM 122). Only in this way can we find something important about boredom as our fundamental mood, and thus about our very Dasein. If philosophy has to seek again the assertion of life against the mechanical encrustation of the artificial,[73] then boredom is the assertion of life (FC 188; GM 277).

Heidegger sketches three different forms of boredom, each one present in its two moments. The distinction between these three forms of boredom is again suggested by the genius of language, which distinguishes between the property of a thing (which may also stand for its concept), the state induced in me by a thing, and the thing or concept itself. The three forms, then, are (I) that which is boring; (II) becoming bored by something; and (III) boredom itself, or profound boredom.[74]

Heidegger thus starts by a philosophical questioning in which the three forms of boredom come from a (re)description of the situation of being bored. One might take the three forms of boredom as a version of the three Aristotelian fundamental categories of privation, matter, and form, where the boring in things corresponds to privation, being bored to matter, and boredom as such to form. Yet every concept needs to be fundamentally rethought and redescribed, so the traditional distinctions need to be avoided and may only serve as hints or signposts in the maze of Heidegger's thought. The two moments of boredom correspond to the situation itself, in which things produce and resonate with a particular form of boredom. One might take these two moments as a version of the subject-object distinction. Yet again, Heidegger intends to avoid by all means such substantivizing of that which needs to be kept open and made unconcealed, not through a rigid oppositional pinpointing but rather as released within the ongoing questioning of philosophizing.

(I) *Becoming bored by something (das Gelangweiltwerden von etwas)*. Heidegger begins by observing that boredom is something with which we are intimately familiar; yet, as a fundamental mood, it is not graspable by the usual methods of reasoning. We cannot observe boredom, but we need to let it emerge, since, without our consent, we have been already involved with it by trying to get rid of it (FC 91; GM 136). When we try to approach boredom through reasoning, it *disappears*, so we do not know where to begin (FC 94; GM 142). This might mean either that we need to find a different way to boredom, or that thinking about boredom is itself *not boring*.

If we do not know where to begin, we should still begin somewhere. Heidegger's way is an inventive poeticolinguistic and subtle, sophisticated philosophical redescription of the familiar and everyday, which, due to its frequent use, became obliterated, unfamiliar, and practically unknown. He starts by analyzing an everyday situation of boredom, which is strangely familiar yet becomes the familiarly strange. We are at a tasteless train station several hours before the train leaves (FC 93; GM 140). This is the situation when we try to get rid of boredom, because we are tired of waiting, which oppresses us. Yet boredom is neither waiting nor impatience, since waiting and impatience can be not at all boring (FC 94; GM 141). What we cannot miss noticing is that boredom is somehow connected with time in the activity of passing time (*Zeitvertreib*) (or the passivity of acting time out). Passing the time, then, is the "driving away of boredom that drives time on" (*zeitantreibendes Wegtreiben der Langeweile* [FC 95; GM 145]). It is a confrontation with time that whiles, drags on, lingers, and vacillates. By passing the time, we find ourselves being oppressed by being held or delayed by lingering time (*Hingehaltenheit*, Heidegger's neologism [FC 99-100; GM 149-52]). This is the first important moment in the encounter with boredom: being delayed by time as it lingers. We are not late: we were there on time before the right time, but we still have to wait. The situation of being held or delayed by dragging time is that of being in a prison. Although we are free to leave the station, we don't. This being bored by something that results in the oppressive hold of lingering time is also the situation of our life, when we have to pass the time, often not willing or wanting it, without reaching the desired end when we finally can move on and not be oppressed by the delay. In becoming bored, we are bored by something, but not looking for anything in particular, which means that we do not really know what we are looking for—for something that will save us from being oppressed by the delay, which can be the delay of our entire life, and thus can even lead to death.

We thus get engaged in a rather meaningless activity: we try to flee away from boredom as being held by lingering time, whose specifically modern form is an attempt to escape the vacuity and devastation of being held empty by engagement, into the endless activity—without stop or purpose—of being entertained, in order to become immersed in the fullness of things and life (see FC 101; GM 153).

This leads us to the recognition of the second constitutive moment of boredom, that of being left empty (*Leergelassenheit* [FC 101; GM 152], another neologism, in which Heidegger cannot miss *Gelassenheit*, composure, as the constituent of this second moment of boredom).[75] We become thrashed, emptied by things at hand that do not disturb us, but in doing so, we abandon ourselves to ourselves, and thus offer nothing (FC 103; GM 155). Things (the train station) refuse us in themselves by still being there yet not meeting us, by not allowing us to meet them in a precise moment. This is, then, a provisional definition (even if Heidegger tries to avoid definitions as finalizing the unfinalizable) of the first form of boredom that ties together the two constitutive moments of boredom. (I) Becoming bored is the essential being delayed in letting become empty (*Hingehaltensein im Leergelassenwerden* [FC 105; GM 158]), that is, by the things that did not let us meet them at the right time, and thus left us empty.

(II) *Being bored with something (das Sichlangweilen bei etwas)*. In the first form of boredom, something is boring. In the second form, we are bored with something. Here, we find the same two structural moments of boredom that we saw in the first form, those of *delay* and *emptiness*. Transformed within each form of boredom, the two structural moments of boredom are mutually independent, yet form an intrinsic unity (FC 106-7; GM 160-61).

The important difference between the two forms of boredom is that the first is linked with something determinate: a particular thing at a particular moment.

We can always say that we are bored with something at the moment when we are bored. In contrast, in the second form of boredom, we are not bored with anything specific and not at a given moment: here, "the border cannot be drawn" (FC 109; GM 165). The example of this kind of boredom is an evening one spends quite comfortably at dinner and conversation, and then only later realizes that it was utterly boring (FC 109-11; GM 164-67). Thus, in the first form of boredom (I) one is *immediately reflective* of being bored by something "outside," by a thing that refused in its meeting at the proper time. In the second form of boredom (II), reflection comes only *belatedly*, after the event took place, and thus comes *from us* (FC 118; GM 178). While in (I) we *do not want to lose time*, in (II) we *have time*, we give and leave it to ourselves (FC 115, 129; GM 174, 195).

There is thus a certain *carelessness* in our spending time: we do not care much about time and about ourselves spending our time, and thus let ourselves slip away from ourselves. We both abandon ourselves to the event that goes its own way—and, in doing so, leave ourselves behind, withdraw from our proper self (*das eigentliche Selbst* [FC 120; GM 180]). We are left empty again, but in a different way. Emptiness in (II) is not an absence of fullness and fulfillment of our actions in time when time stalls and the things refuse to meet us at the right time. Emptiness now is in a sense "formed" by our being careless with our time, by chatting it away in an imperceptible manner (FC 117; GM 177). The entire time we have spent seemed full and engaging at that time, but looking back we see that we managed to kill it and do not have any meaningful experience left of the entire evening. We meant to make it full but instead made it empty. All modern entertainment has this character of being seemingly full in its intense diverting activity yet being always empty in retrospect. By giving time, it takes time away and does not even permit one to pause to be with oneself. This is the structural moment of being left empty in (II), being bored with something.

Because time is spent during the evening so imperceptibly, and subsequently is perceived to have been empty and boring, we face something that we do not recognize and hence do not know, encountering it in the seemingly very familiar spending of time. That which is boring in the second form, then, is utterly unfamiliar, is an "I don't know what," which Heidegger poetically expresses though the alliteration of "un": *Unbestimmte und Unbekannte*, an "'undeterminate' and unknown" (FC 116-17, 126; GM 176, 190).

But what is our reaction to the utterly indefinite, where there are no limits? It causes *fear*, appearing in Shaftesbury's and Kant's works as the sublime that causes awe, as the infinite that startles Pascal, and as nothing as an indefinite possibility in Kierkegaard. The Romantic attitude to the unknown, however, is different: the unknown is the not yet discovered, and as such provokes curiosity and the desire to know, to find out, in order to transform our entire life. The modern hero of "discovery" is Columbus, who discovers the apparently unknown by subjugating and colonizing it, altogether ignoring that the unknown in fact has been intimately known and inhabited by people before him.[76] In uncovering the indeterminate, we need to be determinate and resolute (FC 119; GM 179).

So the task of understanding the unknown as its discovery and bringing out into the light of belated reflection is the oracular philosophico-poetic questioning that makes the concealed disclose itself to us. Through the serious, tragic, and solemn thinker, singer, and the hierophant of the indefinite unknown, that is.

But what do we discover? The oracular command is "Know thyself" (Pausanias, *Perieg.* X.24). In Heidegger's interpretation, when we depart from *boredom in us*, which we recognize only later, after having been bored, we do not really come to know something *in us*, something inner that needs to be reflectively recognized through introspection. Rather, the task of and for self-knowledge is to "grasp ourselves in the ground of our essence via the interpretation of the mood" (FC 118; GM 178). In other words, by interpreting and understanding boredom as the fundamental mood of Dasein or attunement to its base tune, we come to understand the ground of essence as it is in our Dasein that makes us what we are and have to be.

How does the other structural moment of boredom, that of being delayed or put on hold, appear in the second form of boredom? During the entire evening, being busy with chatting and thus creating an emptiness that appeared in the fullness of time as one time at the time, the very "during" (*Während*) did not even occur to us (FC 121; GM 182). While we do not notice the passage of time by not paying attention to it, time in the mean*while* does not release us but spreads stillness and calm (*Stille*) into us (FC 122; GM 183). Unlike in (I), in (II) time does not hold us but leaves us to ourselves, allows to be near here (*Dabeisein*), as part of the existent. But we are held still nevertheless. Hence, we stop time, make it stand still, although we do not make it disappear: we leave time to ourselves, but time does not leave us (FC 121; GM 182). Therefore, time *stands*, "whiles and endures" (*weilt und währt* [FC 122; GM 184]), and because this is not how we usually perceive time in its timing, it cannot be recognized and thus is indeterminate and unfamiliar. In (II), time brings us to a standstill, to the point. To a full stop. To . Or, rather, it suspends us in stillness and brings us to suspension points and (Kracauer's) elision marks (FC 108-9; GM 163-64, et al.). The ... stand(s)—in singular plural—indicating motion without moving. It stand(s) for being bored with something that then contracts to a point of "standing now," which, nevertheless, being the point of utter indeterminacy, still has the traces of these three dots, as three apophatic privative "un-/in-" for the indeterminate-and-unknown, or for the indefinite-indeterminate-unknown.

By spending the evening in careless entertainment and chatting, rather than conversing, we blow time away by making it *stand* (FC 124; GM 187). The three points of suspension turn it into a "now." This "standing now" is now what holds us still by making us pass away time as almost an atemporal activity, when the flow of time becomes imperceptible and thus makes time unfamiliar. The ... stand for the having been and the future as cut off, disconnected from the present in which we are present to what is happening by being disconnected with what has just happened and what will be. The past and the future here are not lost but are dissolved, interrupted, yet still tied to the *mere present* as disconnecting the have-been and the will-be (FC 124-25; GM 187-88). In the elision points, the middle point of the "standing now" is not connected to the other two that stand (still) for the past and future—but rather marks them as elided by suspending but not eliminating them in its current standing presence.

Therefore, in (I), the first form of boredom, time lasts and endures, while things and the existent as a whole refuse to meet us at the proper time. In (II), the second form of boredom, time stands still, does not move. By not moving, it holds us still, brings a delay. The second structural moment of boredom, that of delay and hold, comes in (II) as standing now, as time that *does not move*. However, the two structural moments, those of emptiness and delay, are not isolated, since by being immersed in the entertaining, by spending time in chatting it away, we make present whatever is going on. And by making it present, we bring time to a stand, to standing (*zum Stehen*). By passing the time without noticing it, or without paying attention to it, we make it stand. The time that has come to a stand forms emptiness, which stands (*stellt*) us, and thus holds and delays us. The structural unity of the two structural moments of (II), of becoming bored by something, is thus grounded in a "making present that brings the taken time to a stand(still)" of time (*in dem gegenwärtigenden Zum-Stehen-bringen der genommenen Zeit*, FC 126-27; GM 190-91).

In comparison, one can say thus that the two forms of boredom have two similar yet different structural moments. In (I), the first moment, being left empty (*Leergelassenheit*) appears as a lack (*Ausbleiben*) of fullness; in (II) it comes as emptiness building itself. And while the second moment, of being held or put on hold (*Hingehaltenheit*), shows itself in (I) as being delayed by things, in (II) it transpires as not being released and being halted by standing time (FC 130; GM 197).

Forgetfulness and standing time. When we bring time to standing, we become fully present in the situation, in which we only retrospectively will find ourselves utterly bored. But this being "entirely present" or "merely present" (*ganz Gegenwart, bloße Gegenwart*), or making the situation present to us, means being cut off from the *what, how,* and *where* of our have-been, and from what we have planned for tomorrow. This means being cut off in the passing now of the evening both from the past and from the future (FC 124; GM 187). In other words, we *forget* the past, being unable and even unwilling to remember it. The "earlier," "before," or "has been" is forgotten, although it is not forever lost. It will be retrieved later, after the standing now of the boring evening no longer has hold of us and is not making us empty by chaining us to the "entirely present."

Because we are locked in the "expanded present," time has come to a stand, and hence the "now" (*Jetzt*) "cannot show itself as the earlier," which means that the "now" can only remain "now" (FC 125; GM 188). There is thus no memory in the "now" because there is no past as holding to what has been, nor the anticipation of the future. It is a peculiar kind of stop that almost means death or at least the exposure of our finitude, which later—not *now*—becomes Heidegger's preoccupation. The "now" is the source of the aporias of the relationship of the discrete (now, νῦν) and the continuous (time, χρόνος) for Aristotle (*Phys.* 219b10–220a24, 222a10–b7). The "now" is the prototype of the mysterious *Jetztzeit* that for Benjamin might be the origin of history.[77] The "now" is the image of eternity for the medieval commentators of Aristotle, a now that encompasses past and future in one atemporal moment.

The "standing now," *nunc stans*, represents—stands for—eternity in which there is no passage of time and thus no change, no distinction between past and future but only one enduring moment of "now." Because nothing happens during the "during" of the evening, even if the entire entertaining event seems to be full of action, we are profoundly bored and make time stand, stop it, and thus assimilate ourselves to a creator who is utterly bored in the very ground of its existence, in its Dasein. We make the present be "entirely present" by stopping time, while allowing time to "stand" us.

The concept of "standing now" appears in Themistius's paraphrase of Aristotle's *De anima* (*In de an.* 110.5-111.20), where he argues that, unlike time, "now" is indivisible and hence is not related to change.[78] Moreover, since, unlike the soul, the intellect (*nous*) is nondiscursive, its thinking happens not in time (as does perception) but in the "now" (*In de an.* 110.22-24). The "standing now" as representing the atemporal unchangeability of eternity explicitly appears in Augustine, as the "all at once" (*simul*) in Boethius (*De consol. phil.* V. pros. 6), and later in Aquinas, who distinguishes between the divine "*nunc stans*," in which there is no passage of time and no distinction between past and future, and the "flowing now," "*nunc fluens*," of the created (*Summa theol.* I, Q 10, A 2, ad. 1; I, Q 10, A 4, ad. 2).[79]

For Heidegger, however, the standing "now" is a clear hint toward the nunc stans that is *not* eternity, which has no place in and for Dasein, whose essence is time. The "standing now" is that which bores, holds, and stands us. The standing "now" stands for standing time (*stehende Zeit* [FC 126; GM 189]), which is that unfamiliar, indeterminate, unknown—which stops and startles us—that bores us in our boredom. The essence of boredom thus transpires in the familiar, which is the time, in an utterly estranged and unfamiliar way, of the standing time. Hence, boredom itself springs out of the temporality of Dasein and is made possible by time itself, which is thus the source of profound boredom (FC 81, 99, 127, 133, 152, 157-58; GM 121, 149, 191, 201, 228, 236-37). This is Heidegger's unfolding of boredom as the profound mood in the "long while" of temporality. As the fundamental mood, boredom *now* becomes strictly set apart from anxiety, the other fundamental mood of Dasein, which thus precludes the possible understanding of boredom as either loneliness or the repetition of the same.

(III) *The profound boredom.* But we have to dig even deeper in order to achieve the very height of the situation of boredom. Paradoxically, "where there is height, there is depth [*wo Höhe ist, da ist Tiefe*]" (FC 129; GM 194). From now on, Heidegger will be using *spatial* and *contrasting* metaphors, which can be understood as implicitly erotic, describing the unknown and unfamiliar, yet most intimate: the very temporality of Dasein, which transpires through boredom. In the end, we are not looking for a dialectical definition of boredom—rather, we need to learn how to *move* in the "depth of Dasein" (FC 131; GM 198).[80]

The three forms of boredom differ in their depth (FC 156; GM 233). The third form of boredom (III) is the most profound: it is boredom itself. Whereas for the other two forms there are paradigmatic examples (the train station and the party), for the third form there is no such example. This means that the profound boredom, boredom itself, is ubiquitous and all-pervasive: it is always there with us, whether we miss boredom or try to drive it away in a particular situation. Again, the genius of language comes to the rescue in the initial hint of how to approach this ultimate form of boredom: "it is boring for one [*Es ist einem langweilig*]" (FC 134-35; GM 202-3). Here, two elements of what language reveals to us are important: *it* and *one*.

It is boring for *one*: someone—anyone, but not anybody in particular, and hence for everyone. It is given to one. Grammatically, it is given in the dative, *einem*. And etymologically—as a gift.[81]

One cannot escape boredom, because it is the most profound and proper mood indicative of what we are deep down, in the essence of our Dasein. Boredom is thus our human condition, which we should not try to escape but embrace and learn from. Here Heidegger and Kracauer are in full agreement.

It is boring for one: *Es*, the author and the namer (in the nominative) of profound boredom. *It* makes its famous appearance in "there is," literally as "it gives" (*es gibt*) in *Zeit und Sein*.[82] That which is, is *it*, and is grammatically neutral, as being itself. In the "es gibt," *it gives itself* to us as our Dasein, wants to tell us something through the constant painful disturbance of boredom. *It* bores us—but we do not know what it is (FC 115; GM 174). *It* appears troubling, because it is utterly impersonal, as in "it rains." Therefore, *it* is the familiarly unfamiliar, indefinite, unknown (*Unbestimmte, Unbekannte* [FC 134; GM 203]), which already made its appearance before, in the second form of boredom (FC 116-17; GM 175-76). *It* can be perhaps approached apophatically: it is not this and not that (FC 142; GM 214). Yet it is not nothing, because it speaks to us all the time, even if we do not want to listen, do not have time, are killing time, and entertaining ourselves to death.[83] *It* is rather *no one* (*Niemand* [FC 135; GM 203]), the Odyssey's Οὖτις (*Od.* 9.367-408), who speaks to one from the depth, and reveals itself in simple things and ordinary situations around us: during a walk through the city streets on a Sunday afternoon (FC 135; GM 204, which is also Kracauer's example!), the horizon of a plain, the snow when it snows. *It* speaks not to me but to the very self of the itself of Dasein. Thus, if in the (I) form of boredom we do not need to listen to boredom, in the (II) form we do not want to listen to it, in the (III) form we are compelled to listen to boredom as the oracle that we cannot escape, because it calls us de profundis, speaking the *proper* (*das Eigentliche*) of Dasein from its profound freedom (FC 136; GM 205).

The two structural moments of the profound boredom: emptiness and delay. With the two structural moments of the third and deepest form of boredom, Heidegger proceeds in reverse, first introducing being left empty and then being delayed, which is explained and deduced from emptiness.

(III.a) *Emptiness as indifference.* The first (formerly the second) moment, being left empty, comes now in a different form. Again, continuing with the philosophico-poetic description, Heidegger does not provide much of an argument as to why this should be the case, drawing on the resources of the language and building a coherent picture of the various forms of boredom. The emptiness now is neither a lack of fullness nor of fulfillment, nor privation, nor the nothing as a self-building emptiness where one's proper self can be left standing. Rather, emptiness now comes with *not wanting* any thing in any contingent situation (FC 137, 140; GM 206-7, 210). Emptiness is now *not wanting anything*. We do not want anything, because in profound boredom we are suspended and raised above any particular situation. For this reason, everything becomes *of equally great and equally little worth* (FC 137; GM 207). Everything is depressing. Everything is equally far removed and equally near. Nothing can be clearly seen, because everything that is too far and too close cannot be seen distinctly. Nothing matters, because everything is of equal worth (*gleichgültig*), or *indifferent*. We stand—are put—into the middle of the circle, the periphery of which is the existent as a whole, where all things are equally unimportant and thus are the same in their worth. Everything is at an equal distance from the horizon, and nothing can come in our vicinity.

The equal distance or worth, the indifference to every thing in every situation, means that in profound boredom the *existent as a whole* (*das Seiende im Ganzen*) becomes indifferent. But if the existent, all things, beings, are indifferent, this means that everything is *impossible*. Nothing can be done. Rien à faire. Nothing can be named and hence is anonymous, a no one, an Οὖτις. Doing is impossible. Not doing, not letting do and be done is possible. But it is profoundly boring—for one, from the depth of Dasein. The equal worth or the indifference of the existent as a whole now reveals itself to Dasein as such. The existent as a whole becomes indifferent, not to me as "I-ness" (*Ichlichkeit*), but to the self of Dasein itself as that which is here/there (*da ist*) in Dasein in us (FC 141, 143; GM

212, 215). This is Heidegger's substitution for reflection, when profound boredom brings itself to its self not through a systematic argument or an introspection but through listening—being *compelled* to listen to the unknown that is already there. To what end? To be *it*.

The modern subject, who always and inevitably reflects, is thus turned by Heidegger into someone—one, anyone—who is made, compelled to reflect—by its own, *proper* other, which is its self, the self of its Dasein. But the indifference of the existent as a whole to Dasein means that Dasein is now put (*gestellt*), located, delivered to the existent, in front of things and situations in such a way that they do not offer any possibility for Dasein to act, to do anything anymore. The existent as a whole refuses, denies itself in its entirety to Dasein. This is emptiness in profound boredom.

Kairos. The existent as a whole, all things, and every thing in particular can be considered to have its own *proper time* (καιρός), which is the time when we meet a thing that allows us to meet it and do that which is appropriate *now* and act within a range of possibilities in a particular way in this particular situation. Yet if we do not meet a thing in its proper time, we are refused, rejected, and denied by it, and become bored. The very essence of boredom, then, is *in time* and arises from the temporality of our Dasein. Hence, boredom prevails in *the very ground of Dasein* (FC 96; GM 144-45), which is why, from the essence of boredom, we can get a glimpse into the concealed essence of time (FC 99; GM 149). Boredom is possible and in fact necessary because everything has *its time*. Moreover, every Dasein has its time (FC 127; GM 191), which can be thought of as its *kairos*.[84] The essential in Dasein that we are looking for cannot be extracted by force or in haste (FC 130; GM 195). We need to wait for that to come out into the open through a not-rushed quiet and concentrated effort of questioning the awakened mood of boredom. The essential of Dasein, the realization of its possibilities, then, comes as a *meeting* of the proper time of things with the proper time of Dasein. But for now—for long time—the existent refuses and denies itself to Dasein, which becomes our predicament of being surrounded, put into, and stood in front of those things that do not matter, because they are all equally *the same*, all are far and close at *the same time*, none is here properly, and none is of any worth.

In the first form of boredom, a particular thing (the train station) refuses us its kairos, does not meet us in due time, so that we have to wait and are bored. In the second form of boredom, the entire situation (the whole evening) refuses us its kairos, which we notice only afterwards. And in the third form of boredom, *everything*, the whole of the existent, all things, refuse to ever meet us in their due time of the kairos.

(III.b) *Delay*. But why are we delayed when we encounter profound boredom? Again, Heidegger deduces the most profound characteristics of our being from language—from *German* language, primarily from semantics rather than syntax, which might in fact be more definitive of the structure of thinking. If the existent as a whole refuses itself to the generous offer of and from Dasein, this refusal (*Versagen*) is itself saying or telling (*Sagen*), which comes as an announcement (*Ansagen* [FC 140-42; GM 211-14]). The announcement, then, intensifies to the appeal, or calling (*Anrufen* [FC 143; GM 216]). The refusal needs to be told, and thus announced, which comes as an *announcing hint at . . .* (*ansagendes Hinweisen auf . . .* [FC 142; GM 214]). At what? At the suspension points and elision marks: . . . We encounter the suspension and elision once again, which now announce the refusal. The kenōsis of Dasein is left without response and recognition from the things, from the existent as a whole. The call of being in Dasein is left without response from the existent in its entirety, from things that remain mute. There is no dialogue that being could have established in and through Dasein in and for us. We only need to wait in profound boredom that is not caused by anything in particular . . . What does the announcement announce in refusal? It tells us through a hint about all the *possibilities* in and of Dasein, which the existent as a whole has missed by refusing it. These are the possibilities of *doing* and *letting do* (*Tun und Lassen* [FC 141; GM 212]). But they are being left uncultivated, unused, unexplored—because they are being refused.

And yet—. . .—the refusal of and to Dasein by the existent as a whole, in the midst of which we are, announces and points toward *that which* allows (*das Ermöglichende* [FC 143; GM 216]) for all essential possibilities of Dasein, which are now being refused, *in us*. *That which* makes Dasein possible, however, is *without content*, because that at which we are placed has refused Dasein and is thus being held empty. *That which* constitutes the possibility of acting and letting be, since it is contentless for us now, is *it*, *das* or *es*. *It* is present in . . . It is *possible* that *it* is being itself. But it is not named, cannot be defined, and rather can only be asked about. *It* is announced, hinted at. We drive away from the way it is announced, which is boredom. But if we wake boredom, embrace and turn toward it, we cannot miss the hint, announcement, or appeal. Yet we do not know what calls us from the depth. It cannot only *disturb* us. And this disturbance *compels* us. To what? To the edge, peak (*Spitze*), which is another way of saying that we concentrate on that which makes Dasein possible in acting and being-there, where we realize these possibilities in ourselves. This is what being held, Hingehaltenheit, means in the (III) form of boredom: being compelled to the original realization (*Ermöglichung*) of Dasein as such (FC 144; GM 216).

Temporal horizon. Since profound boredom is always there for one, it is not situation-specific, which is why there is no paradigmatic example of it. It happens to everyone, at *all times*, and everywhere. Semantically and perspicuously, it can be described as happening anywhere, in the whole expanse and in any *respect, prospect*, and *retrospect* (*Hinsicht, Absicht, Rücksicht* [FC 143; GM 215]). In this sense, temporality is now reduced to, and established by, the spatial determinations of *sight* (*Sicht*), *seeing*, and *looking* back, around, and forward, which are located on the plane characterized by *breadth*. Perhaps the three determinations of sight can even be taken to describe spatiality in its three dimensions, but Heidegger does not go that way, probably because he intends to avoid spatial descriptions of time, since space is characteristic of the existent as a whole and not of being, whose secret essence is time.

Yet the existent as a whole refuses itself to Dasein in *every* respect, retrospect, and prospect, which are perspective-sights (*Sicht*) of the current seeing, seen back, and seeing forward (FC 145; GM 218). These three perspectives encompass every doing and letting do of Dasein, all those possibilities that are announced through boredom yet are refused by the existent as a whole in its *what* and *how*, that is, in its *entirety*. And these three perspectives, although expressed spatially, define how Dasein allocates itself in and for the present, past (having-been), and future. These are temporal determinations, which, however, do not follow each other as one-after-another but are originally *unified* and *simple* in the *horizon* of time as such (FC 146; GM 219).

But why should there be such a horizon? Because the existent refuses Dasein *in every respect*. The existent remains—for the time being—impenetrable in its sight to us. It cannot be seen in its entirety or even in any of the three aspects. It refuses itself altogether. Yet the very possibility of such a refusal lies not in the existent, *das Seiende*, but in the temporal horizon where the three aspects are originally fused and unified. It is the temporal horizon that embraces all things, the existent as a whole, and makes it inaccessible to Dasein—in that moment—in the unified temporality.

The temporal horizon is again a spatial metaphor for the as yet unknown abysses (*Abgründe*) of the essence of time. Being a horizon, it suggests being one, unified, and only and always seen in *every* respect, yet as an unreachable *limit* that delimits (ὁρίζειν) time itself. Yet how time comes to have a horizon and whether past, present, and future are present all at once in its scenery—these kinds of questions are left unanswered, at least for now (FC 146; GM 219-20). What is important is that it is time itself that stands beyond the horizon and allows for the binding of the two structural moments of the (III), the most profound form of boredom.

Bann. Being left empty does not mean that the existent as a whole disappears. It is still there in sight, but it withdraws precisely *as a whole*, to the limit of visibility. It is now on the horizon, only and always seen, but not reachable. It always recedes—has receded—to the horizon, so that Dasein is not abandoned alone in isolation but is put precisely in the center, surrounded by beings, being as a whole, unable to touch or grasp it. The existent is now always seen but is never graspable. Dasein is nowhere and everywhere *at the same time*. The existent—the world—is all around but is never here or there (*da*). Dasein is thus put and placed in a strange position, becoming the master of a circle, *cuius centrum ubique, circumferentia nusquam*.[85]

But by what is Dasein carefully placed or intentionally thrown there? Apparently, by time itself, although why this is the case is not entirely clear. We can only keep questioning, at least for now. In order to describe Dasein's ultimate *situation* as being *in situ* embraced by the time horizon, Heidegger uses, as he often does, an archaic word that has a bearing on farmers' practices from the region that forever remained his own horizon of seeing, interpretation, and reference.

It is *Bann.* Among its various meanings, Bann primarily refers to (1) enchantment and entrancement, and (2) ban and exclusion. So it can be translated as spell-ban, or perhaps even transliterated as bann, once one keeps in mind its double meaning. The profound, inexorable boredom permeates our situation vis-à-vis the world, which recedes to the horizon, points at our Dasein, being everywhere and nowhere at the same time, exiled not to the periphery but to the very center of things. By being there, Dasein is under the *spell* and *ban* of time, not of time as flowing (in the [I] form of boredom) or standing (in the [II] form), but beyond them. Dasein is now *banned* in boredom, spell-banned by time in its temporal horizon. The bann, the enchantment and exclusion of Dasein by time, makes it impossible for Dasein to find its way to things, to the existent as a whole, which refuses itself and moves beyond the reach and grasp of Dasein, being in sight everywhere and at once, and yet unattainable. This is the ultimate sense of emptiness, of being left empty in the middle of the existent, enchanted and banned from the existent by time's horizon (FC 147–48; GM 221–22).

In the middle ages, the term "Bann," (coming from Latin *bannum*, which is also the origin of the English "ban") stands for the right to exercise power by submitting to a decree, edict, or proclamation. In canon law, it means excommunication (*excommunicatio*), the ban from ecclesiastic community and communication, which can be imposed on someone for past wrongdoings for a time.[86] It is this last meaning that Heidegger seems to have in mind when claiming that in modernity Dasein has been denied, rejected, and excommunicated from the existent as a whole.

Excommunication also implies the prohibition of the *communicatio forensis*, the inability to testify or file an accusation in court. For us moderns it means an inability to be a witness to Dasein's realization of its possibilities. Dasein is now refused, banned, and excommunicated from the existent—by *time itself*, by its horizon. In profound boredom, Dasein is banned into immobility, catatonia, lack of motion, into being imprisoned by being excluded from the things that refuse Dasein, into the enchainment that results in disenchantment with the existent as a whole.

This refusal comes as the "forgetfulness of being" (*Seinsvergessenheit*), which plays a central role in *Being and Time*, appearing in its opening line.[87] But the excommunication of Dasein from the things by which it is surrounded, by the existent as a whole, also means its exclusion from the community of others, banned by being itself.

The bann, the exclusion and abandonment, the spell-ban put on Dasein by time comes at the very limit of thinking, which is why Heidegger has to turn again to mythopoetic language. From its very abyss, from the unfathomable, ungrounded depth that cannot be reached by any sight from any perspective, being itself as time takes hold of us, takes us over in a flash-like moment of profound boredom. At this very moment, we are facing the undivided and undifferentiated unity, the one outside of many, the simplicity of the time horizon. Yet simplicity is very difficult, perhaps even impossible, to achieve in thought. Being utterly simple, in the absence and ban of the many, simplicity cannot be grasped, since grasping is an act of understanding that is reached by thinking, which binds multiplicity into unity by moving on discursively through a number of steps that occur in time and reproduce the structure of temporal succession.

The simplicity of vision. It is thus in and through profound boredom that time itself puts a spell-ban on Dasein and bans it to a proper distance from things: they are all here and yet move to the horizon. The expanse of the horizon is now seen as simple, unified, and one, where the three perspectives are fused into one, which places Dasein right in the center and yet does not allow it to distinguish clearly and see any thing, or anything by which it is surrounded. Nothing is one and simple, because time *strikes* (*schlägt*) Dasein into bann (FC 148; GM 223). Being spell-banned, Dasein is being refused by all things, by beings, by the existent as a whole. Yet, the temporal horizon is not simply there but participates in this refusal, because as the time of Dasein it banns Dasein, puts a spell on it and bans it from the existent as a whole, by attuning it through the most profound boredom (FC 150; GM 225-26). In boredom, Dasein stands amid the things of the world, surrounded by them yet disconnected from its very ground of possibility, from its proper being there. Being refused and rejected by the world, by the existent as a whole, Dasein is ousted to everyday boredom, which is just a hint at and the anticipation of profound boredom. In the commonplace, banal, and trivial, in everyday life, we lose the sharpness of sight and can only see things myopically in their blundered outlines.

But at this decisive moment of being spelled and bound by the spell, of being banned from the existent, Dasein has a possibility of freedom, of freeing itself. This is the moment of resoluteness, of resolute disclosedness, *Entschlossenheit* (FC 149; GM 223). Dasein now has to resolutely disclose, open up (*entschließen*) itself to itself as Da-sein, as being-there. Heidegger again goes along with what language suggests to him, which, however, is only *a* language, his language. He plays here with the meaning of the prefix "ent-" of removal, "schließen" (close), and "entschließen" (resolutely decide). Through profound boredom, Dasein needs to dare to claim or rather reclaim its being there, its proper place in being with the existent, where it has always been, and yet has been banned from, by the charm and spell of time in its horizon. The resolute disclosedness constitutes the very "fundamental character of existence, of human existence" (FC 295; GM 427), which in the end is the expression of the *loneliness* and *tragedy* of our being as the inescapable being toward death (*Sein zum Tode* [FC 295; GM 425-26; see also SZ §§46-53, 235-67]).

Dasein resolutely and decisively discloses itself, establishes and affirms its being "here," dares to be there at all against the spell-ban and exclusion from the existent that refuses the rapprochement with Dasein. Luther's "here I stand," "*hier ich stehe*," is the expression of the foundational act of self-establishing, modern autonomous will.[88] The act of the resolute self-affirmation has to be *there* for us to be at all.

But how and when does this self-disclosedness of freeing oneself occur? As an *act*, it cannot be premeditated, planned, or thought through, but is an act of resolve and determination that faces death and finitude; it can only come in an unexplainable *moment*. The language again comes to the rescue: this moment is literally the *moment of vision, Augenblick, Øjeblikket*.[89] It is the *look* of the disclosedness (*Blick der Entschlossenheit*), in which a glimpse into the full range of the possibilities of our existence becomes possible (FC 149; GM 224). The resolute disclosedness is thus released only at the moment that properly makes Dasein possible, opens up the fundamental possibility of its proper or "authentic" existence and action in the situation, in which it *now* finds itself (FC 169, 296; GM 251, 428; see also SZ §§61-64, 301-23). It is the blink of an eye when we are properly there–here, in this moment. In a very brief moment and for a very short while that becomes possible by waking the long while of fundamental boredom, we break away from the everydayness with its ordinary boredom and begin to exist properly (FC 295; GM 428).

(i) Augenblick is thus the moment of vision.[90] First, it is the *moment* of vision, which comes all of a *sudden*, a piercing and sharp moment, a point-like suspension of the indistinct continuum of the temporal horizon.[91] This moment does not come as a result of a number of intentional and calculated steps that secure the achievement of a goal. There is no secure method, like that of Descartes's *Regulae*, which would allow one to achieve the moment of vision. Rather, this sudden moment is a gift—of time itself, of being. But one has to stay vigilant in the mood of the awakened boredom, attuned to the tune of being, waiting for the proper moment (FC 132, 161; GM 199, 240), that of the kairos, which is now not that of things or of the existent as a whole but of being itself. This is not a passive waiting but rather resolute preparedness for the disclosure of Dasein, summoned by the bann of time. The moment of vision is *the* moment of "now," in which the essence of time becomes disclosed, always waited for yet always unexpected, and is a kind of revelation of the essence of our Dasein de profundis, from the mystical depth of time, which itself is not in time and thus can appear only in this moment. This is why the simple moment of vision is unpredictable and rare (FC 295; GM 428).

When the moment comes, it resolves, dissolves, dispels, and disrupts the spell-ban, the bann of time itself, which refuses Dasein the possibilities of its existence. Augenblick comes as a *rupture* of the bann of the profound boredom, of our being enchanted, spelled, and banned from the possibilities of the proper existence (FC 149, 151).

(ii) Secondly, Augenblick is the moment of *vision*: that which has been banned and has thus become not visible—receding to the temporal horizon, thus becoming indistinguishable—which, suddenly, *now*, in this moment, becomes distinctly visible as the very ground of Dasein itself within all its possibilities of acting and being. The moment of vision stands in similar relation to "look" as does an eye blink, which allows for sight or insight, *Einblick*. This is the response to Aristotle's understanding of theoretical vision as θεωρία, which Heidegger interprets as an attentive human relationship to being, in which being itself establishes the essence of human being.[92] Augenblick is the moment of the insight into the ground of Dasein, as being there, Da-sein, which is always *mine* (FC 296; GM 428). At this moment, the look, the glare of Dasein reaches into being as time that suspends its temporality into the sharpness of the moment of vision of itself through our Dasein.[93] This momentary act of glimpsing is an unmediated self-reflection, in which Dasein brings and wrests itself before itself—not in an act of thinking but in the binding, establishing, and realization of its own possibility of being-there (FC 165; GM 247).

In the moment of the proper regard, time is suspended: it does not procrastinate or stand any more, and the entire horizon gets contracted into one single point that stands out of time and yet *at the same time* is the whole temporality gathered into one blink of the eye. The moment of concentration of time brings us out of the extended and inevitably boring discursive thinking, which in its orderly manner follows the flux of time, to the nondiscursive moment of thought beyond thought, of the thought that suspends itself in its restlessness and can only be expressed later metaphorically and poetically. In his "comprehensive questioning" of boredom, Heidegger moves within a mesh of complex linguistic and categorical distinctions, which, however, is incomprehensibly canceled and suspended in the simplicity of vision. Now, at the end of his discussion of boredom, Heidegger can only claim that the distinction between the three forms of boredom is only provisional and fluid and that they differ in depth only (FC 157; GM 235; see also FC 129; GM 194).

Peak and breadth. Now, when we have a glimpse into the depth of Dasein, everything is very close to us and yet is unfamiliar, the unseen can only be described metaphorically and not in terms of familiar philosophical concepts. Despite stressing the temporal character of our existence, the wanderer through the woods and mountains chooses *spatial* metaphors to describe the unfathomable depth of time, which stands still and in front of which we suspend the flux of time in the moment of sharp vision. This should mean that boredom, even if being ultimately profoundly temporal in its constitution and essence, is still understood from reference to places that arrange temporal events: travel and railway stations, the house full of guests, the entertainment of the city, or the leisurely walk along its streets. *Loci temporis* are now substituted for the places of memory that locate temporal events in their succession. In particular, profound boredom is described metaphorically by breadth (*Weite*) and peak (*Spitze*), which, in their unity of the two structural moments, characterize the most profound form of boredom.

The refusal of the existent as a whole compels Dasein to the extremity, peak (*Spitze*), which is the moment of vision of the fundamental possibility of Dasein's proper existence. Yet this constraint eventually comes from the refusal of time itself in its horizon, which means that Dasein is compelled by the banning time itself in its proper essence, impelling Dasein to the fundamental possibility of its proper existence (FC 149; GM 224). Going even deeper through the layers of boredom compels us to the height of the look into the unfathomable depth, out of which every form of boredom comes. Moved by profound boredom, which thus becomes a productive force, the bann, spell-ban of the temporal horizon, makes the moment of vision disappear. In boredom as "long while," Langeweile, time becomes long. The lengthening of time is the expanding of the temporal horizon into the entire temporality of Dasein. But Dasein as properly existing has its own time, which is a short while (FC 152–53; GM 229): in the moment of vision our Dasein becomes "short whiled."

The proper existence of Dasein with all its possibilities can be thus regained *in a moment*, in this very moment of sharp vision, to which Dasein is compelled by boredom, by this bann. *The* moment, Augenblick, is thus the peak of time itself, the moment of its extremity and sharpness, which comes all of a sudden, in the blink of an eye, rupturing the spell-ban and disrupting the exclusion from things as a whole.

This moment of vision is the look of Dasein in three perspectival directions (FC 151; GM 226), that is, at the time horizon, where the present, future, and past are present in their fusion and entirety. Yet at the moment of vision, the continuum of the horizon is contracted into a point-like instant, a "now" that is standing and stood. Profound boredom makes us move again, tremble, *oscillate*, swing between the *breadth* of the continuity of the temporal horizon and the *point* of the discreteness of the moment of vision, between the breadth of emptiness and the peak of the sharpness of the moment of vision (FC 166; GM 247). But there is *no mediation* between the breadth and the peak, between the horizon and the moment of its interruption. One could say that the breadth locked into the undistinguished horizon is the Dionysian, and the summit of vision is the Apollonian moment brought to Dasein by time itself. The Apollonian and the Dionysian are not, and cannot be, mediated either. The breadth of the temporal horizon, the entire circumference of things that has receded into the unreachable, which banns Dasein, is interrupted and pierced by the moment of the simplicity of vision (*la simplicité du regard*, to use Pierre Hadot's phrase) that reinstalls Dasein in the center, where it properly is—everywhere.

In the end, through boredom it is time itself that banns, puts a spell on and bans, Dasein from the existent and refuses it a meeting at the proper time. And yet, at the same time it is the same *time* that summons Dasein by compelling it to the possibility of its proper existence in the moment of the acute vision in all its possibilities as grounded in the depth of time and being (FC 153; GM 230). Such is the mystical poetic picture of the breadth and peak, of the continuous and the discrete, that we as our individual Dasein have to relive, once we have awakened the monstrous sleeping beauty of boredom.

Liberation and freedom. Heidegger seeks to abandon the banality of the superficially boring petit bourgeois perception of the world by opening up the possibility of the moment of vision, of a sharp look into the depth of Dasein. In order to get to the truth of philosophizing, one needs to get engaged in unconventional and potentially dangerous philosophical acts, activity, doing (*Tun*), rather than in the boring production of true justified statements. Philosophizing as "comprehensive questioning" that seeks to wake the fundamental mood of boredom and elucidate it, is meant to *liberate the Dasein in us* (FC 172; GM 255), which up to now "stands before the possibilities it does not foresee" (FC 19; GM 28).

Because philosophizing is bound by the mysterious and dangerous fate of Dasein, this history is tragic, for tragedy is driven by fate, which determines our existence as being toward death (see SZ §§46-53, 235-67). Currently, in our superficially boring world, there is no mystery in Dasein, no fear and oppression, but liberation might, and should, lead us to encountering the mystery of Dasein again.

Freedom transpires in liberation from the superficial boredom by embracing the profound boredom as necessary for opening the possibility of Dasein's innermost freedom, which is originally made possible by the bann of time in its horizon that compels us to the sharpness of the moment of vision (FC 136, 149; GM 205, 223). Only then can one suspend the flux of temporal events, approach things, beings, the existent as a whole, and look into the abyssal and frightening freedom of our Dasein, seen as the absence of any oppression (FC 163-64; GM 244-45).

Questioning boredom is thus meant "to liberate the humanity in human, to liberate the humanity of human, i.e., the *essence* of human, *to let Dasein in him become essential.*"[94] Heidegger can only turn prophetic in delivering not a moral but still a normative oracular message to his followers and listeners: the liberation of Dasein in us means not establishing an arbitrariness of one's volition (*Willkür*) but loading and carrying the *burden* (*Bürde*) of Dasein. The fate of Dasein becomes our fate. Once awakened by the philosophical questioning of profound boredom, we are destined to wait for the moment of staring into the opening abyss of being.

So Kracauer and Heidegger agree in that, since we cannot overcome boredom, we need to embrace it. But while Heidegger embraces the profound boredom that might disclose radically new possibilities for us in the resolute moment of vision, Kracauer prefers an ironic yet perhaps no less resolute encounter with boredom, shielding himself off from the endless entertainment of the city life by exercising nonaction as doing-nothing, cherishing an Oblomov-style lazy and unrushed contemplation from a sofa, letting everything go, thus catching a brief glimpse of the unutterably unboring glimmering on the horizon . . .

CHAPTER 2

Boredom and the Flâneur

Though boredom is an acute symptom of modernity, its discussion need not be boring if modernity finds new ways to reflect upon and express boredom. Heidegger still uses the traditional genre of metaphysics with its careful subdivisions, which he means to undermine in the end by evaporating the very necessity of distinctions. Yet, other insightful critics of modernity turn to new genres: Kracauer to a paper feuilleton meant for a blasé reader, and Benjamin to painstaking yet unsystematic reflections that disclose boredom much more as a social and political phenomenon, rooted in the ideological boredom of the ruling class.

Benjamin: The power of rain. Benjamin turns to boredom in his posthumously published the *Arcades Project*, which was started in 1927—that is, right between Kracauer's and Heidegger's discussions—and which thus belongs to the same brief and intensely lived epoch when the acute sense of life was perceived in and as boredom.[1] The Convolute D of Benjamin's work, which encompasses the fragments and extracts from literary works on boredom and eternal return, contains some twenty pages on *Langeweile*. Since this is a mélange of fortuitous thoughts that Benjamin came across in his and others' real and written walks through Paris, nothing is central, and thus every fragment is equally important.

Speaking about boredom thus follows several different genres: short essay (Kracauer), a treatise based on lectures (Kant), lectures in the form of scholastic *disputationes* (Heidegger), and fragments (Benjamin). The semester-long lecture course is perhaps the most boring.

Before the Annales school, which makes nonhuman entities the protagonists of history (the Mediterranean Sea in Braudel), Benjamin makes Paris the main hero of his writing.[2] Paris is the capital of the nineteenth century. Therefore, it should be properly dressed. Paris chooses to garb its busy trade streets, which attract the most visitors, both those on business and idle passersby, with glass. For the city needs to set off its consumption districts not just as places of ordinary trade and exchange of goods but as those that dictate the style of consumption, thus defining the whole way of life that would rule the rest of the world through style and fashion. Gray from the soot in all its picturesque gradations (AP D1a,7), which is tattooed into the body of the city by the coal brought down the Canal St. Martin and burnt at every house, Paris brightens itself up with fashionable colors under the covers of its passages. Yet the immediate, perhaps unintended, purpose is the protection of these emphasized public spaces from *rain*.

(1) *The boredom of the weather.* Unlike Heidegger, Benjamin does not provide any systematic insights into boredom, its types or causes. And although his thinking is fragmented on principle, one can still distinguish three main interconnected forms of boredom in Benjamin: weather, waiting, and repetition.

In the old "cosmopolitical" opposition of the world to the city, the cosmos is the other of the polis, both defying and complementing the life of its citizens. The cosmic mathematical law counters the economic and moral bourgeois law. But for Benjamin, the modern opposition between the two is not that of a forceful collision or drama—rather it has a narcotizing effect, which is that of *boredom*: "Nothing bores common man more than the cosmos" (AP D1,3). Yet how does the cosmos appear to the hollow and stale contemporary city dweller? Not as the ancient cosmos, which was a beautiful and living being that showed itself in its splendor and fury to the political beings who protected themselves from it with thick city walls. Stripped of any apparent or hidden purpose, demystified and disenchanted, the modern cosmos appears in the tedious natural monotony of *weather* to the bourgeois, who protect themselves not by walls but by the glassed roofs of the arcades, and more recently, of enormous malls, exhibition centers, and stadiums. Therefore, the primary manifestation of cosmic power for the city inhabitant is annoying *rain*. "Rain makes everything more lurking, makes days not only gray but uniform" (AP D1a,9).

Similar to Kracauer and Heidegger, Benjamin takes boredom to be "the threshold to great deeds" (AP D2,7). Yet boredom that may become productive of new experience becomes increasingly rare in modern, bustling, ever-busy cities, and thus literally has no place in them: "Boredom is the dream bird that hatches the egg of experience. A rustling in the leaves drives her away. Her nesting places—the activities that are intimately associated with boredom—are already extinct in the cities and are declining in the country as well."[3]

However, protected from rain, the streets lose their natural cleanser and get covered in dust: "As dust, rain takes revenge on the arcades" (AP D1a,1). Dust enters every single pore of the lush colors, penetrates every surface ("Plush as dust collector" [AP D1a,3]). The cheerful appearance of the city changes to a monotonous and dull one, and the work of cleaning the invisible, all-pervasive particles that only rarely show themselves dancing in a ray of (artificial) light, becomes the epitome to the monotony of the city life, matched only by work on a conveyor belt. The modern cosmos finds a way to retaliate against the brave and bright new world of consumerism. The new cosmos is a rotating mechanism, repeating its movements with the startling necessity of natural law. As a mirror of nature, the social world also becomes a sociological reflection of abstract mathematical principles. This reflection, however, in the words of Proust, is incurably imperfect (AP D2a,1), not because it is irregular but precisely because it is too regular and always the same, functioning according to established rules, patterns, and tastes.

The modern social world is boring because it follows and imitates the new mechanistic world. Speaking about Blanqui's last work, *L'Éternité par les astres*, written in prison—the book of the rebel who tried to escape the monotonous injustices of the bourgeois world by turning to science—Benjamin writes to Horkheimer:

> The cosmic vision of the world which Blanqui lays out, taking his data from the mechanistic natural science of bourgeois society, is an infernal vision. At the same time, it is a complement to the society to which Blanqui, in his old age, was forced to concede victory.... It is an unconditional surrender, but simultaneously the most terrible indictment of a society that projects this image of the cosmos—understood as an image of itself—across the heavens. (AP D5a,6)

Still, the entire city cannot cover itself with glassed ceilings, which remains a utopian vision and aspiration for the future. Devoid of the glassed-roof protection, city dwellers need to use umbrellas, which become one of the most ubiquitous carry-along items in modern city life, statements of fashion and prestige, often depicted in late nineteenth-century French painting. According to a piece on the climate of Paris from 1845, by one Victor Méry, serene nature showing itself in clear skies and fine weather is alien to French literature, where Corneille mentions the stars only once, and the sun in Racine is equally a hapax, being introduced into literature by Chateaubriand, who discovered it in America (AP D1a,5).[4] Only occasionally, when escaping the boredom of the rainy or dusty life of the city, a *parapluie* can turn into a parasol: umbrellas can also protect from the sun—a favorite topic in Renoir. But the umbrella's cousin, the fan, was never a protection against the force of nature—heat—in Paris. Rather, it was used to reveal seductive beauty by intentionally hiding it. For the power of erotic attraction is always in the lack of transparency. But now, in modernity, even in lascivious pictures and appearances, the fan becomes substituted by the umbrella, which now fans erotic fantasies by providing an intentionally small, discreet refuge beyond which the city dweller wants to throw an indiscreet look (AP D1a,6).

Inevitably, one needs to leave the cozy streets of the covered arcades and the snug salons, where the whirl of commotion and conversation results in the nothing of boredom, and go out into the streets. There, again, one is met with the inevitable gray and the rain. The capital of the nineteenth-century world is a rainy and foggy place. For when the rain stops, it does not recede altogether but gets sublimated—into the fog. In Baudelaire, the fog is spleen (AP D1,4), which linguistically feels like an untranslatable borrowing that epitomizes the eternal fog from another great city across the English Channel. The fog, which tends to turn into haze, and, in modern industrial society, into smog, is the embodiment of boredom. The colors, which the city tries to scale up, turn inevitably into the ubiquitous gray, and life gets back on its monotonous track.

This modern perception of rain as the epitome of "natural" boredom is opposed to that present in the famous print by Hiroshige, which depicts seven people on a bridge and one boatman caught by an evening shower, who keep on walking and rowing under the protection of hats, umbrellas, and a straw mat. There is no hint at boredom but rather the expression of feeling an exalting sorrow brought about by the perception of the world's transience. The picture of the fleeting scene is taken at dusk, which will last for a short—not long—while, and then will disappear forever. The people will pass, the shower will stop, and the day will fade away—and will never repeat but stay in its momentary, transient, and utterly nonboring fascination.[5]

(2) *The boredom of waiting.* The inward side of boredom, however, is waiting (AP D9a,4). Again, Benjamin does not provide an argument for the claim—only

a thesis, which is then supported and justified with reference to other theses and quotations. He continues, in parentheses: "Boredom waits for death [*Die Langeweile wartet auf den Tod*]" (AP D9a,4). And a further quote, from Victor Hugo: "Waiting is life [*Attendre c'est la vie*]" (AP D10a,3). Therefore, one should conclude from this seemingly unpretentious sorites that boredom is life that waits for death.

Yet death is never a given for us. It is never a part of our experience, since experience can only be lived through by a living being. Death is not a purpose or telos of our existence, although life can be looked at as being toward death, because death is the limit of all aspirations in life. However, there is something odd in this modern attitude to death: death is not frightful, but boring. As frightful, death is still meaningful. But as boring, it is just an indefinitely postponed event, which neither has meaning by itself nor is able to give meaning to life.

Therefore, boredom is waiting for that which one cannot know and yet still keeps waiting for.[6] Such a waiting is a very peculiar kind of anticipation and search. If life is waiting for that which it cannot possibly grasp or attain, we come back to the Socratic paradox of knowledge: if we are looking for something that we do not yet know, how do we know what we are looking for? And if we come across that which we have been looking for, we should have known it all along, and therefore should not have been looking for it.[7]

This appears to be a paradoxical and enigmatic situation. For Benjamin, "We have boredom when we do not know what we are waiting for" (AP D2,7; see also D4,6). Hence, boredom is a uniquely *negative* expression of looking for knowledge as waiting for that which we do not know, and which is thus marked as death. This modern attitude to knowledge is radically different from the ancient one: for Socrates, it has an insuperably erotic, attractive character, so that one cannot oppose the unavoidable—and very engaging—gravitational pull of knowledge. However, in modernity—and this is what its most acute critics perceive and express—knowledge becomes a burden, a tedious responsibility, a bore. Modern knowledge is never a revelation of the what is, but a long-winded, superficial, and boring construction of what should be. This is well grasped by Benjamin: "That we know or believe we know, is almost always nothing other than the expression of our superficiality or distraction" (AP D2,7). The *what is* is apparently there, veiled but waiting to be revealed in an act of knowledge. It is the ultimate triumph of the life of the mind. The *what should be* is never yet there but always needs to be achieved, though never in a final and finalized way. As such, it is boring, the unattainable, repulsive, and yet unavoidable waiting for death.

Modern knowledge, built piece by piece and accumulated with the constantly renewed effort of its scholarly artisans, is the product of a factory of knowledge (in Bacon and Descartes).[8] It should eventually take the shape of a *system* of knowledge, which will be complete, comprehensive, and exhaustive. But the system signifies the end of effort and the death of knowledge in the making. A system is to be expected and therefore boring, in contradistinction to a seemingly isolated insight—which is always sudden and unexpected. One should fill in every single entry that the system demands. Philosophical systems are fascinating in their grandiosity but are boring (in Proclus or Hegel). A system is meant to achieve a final and ultimate transparency of all things and processes, both in nature and history. Understanding is thus deadly, whereas misunderstanding, or not yet understanding, is productive and alive. It is a wonder that cannot be classified or fit within a system. But modern systematic knowledge welcomes the wonder of the not yet formulated and deductively justified but nevertheless anticipated, knowledge. And if the productive misunderstanding abandons us moderns to the tedious job of systematic knowledge production, it can only be substituted by an artificial and intentional "strong misreading" of a problem or a text. Building a system is thus difficult, and the difficult is boring, because it is not the challenge of solving a particular problem but a big and long task, which needs waiting. In the end, a system turns out to be the death of the mind.

Knowledge is transparency. Solving a problem may be a challenging task, but the process of the solution may be engaging, because the unknown but aspired for is erotic, insofar as it attracts by its not yet full transparency. But when we come to know, the life of the mind comes to an end, which in the ancient search for knowledge is the purpose of the mind, but in modernity is flatly an unexciting ending. In this sense, the search for knowledge is life, while knowledge itself is death. The *new* knowledge is engaging in its novelty. And novelty is never boring, because it is an interruption to and a seeming end to waiting.[9] But novelty for novelty's sake is boring, because it itself is never new but always repetitive. The search for novelty as a means for getting excited, and thus for overcoming the modern boredom of waiting, becomes a distinguished trait of modern life.

As Benjamin observes, modern bourgeois society intends to become more and more bureaucratically organized by increasing the extent and grasp of administrative norms. The necessity of following the network of these self-proliferating norms makes people wait even more. Caught in the bureaucratic web, people find escape and liberation in games of chance (AP D10a,2). Gambling, then, becomes the expression of modernity: as the preferred distraction, gaming seemingly liberates, but does not really save people from the superfluous stifling regulations that they anonymously impose on themselves without their own proper consent or even willingness. Gambling becomes the main functional principle of modern financial capitalism, which is entirely based on the concept of chance and luck—the Calvinist expression of the predestination for winning as salvation. Salvation, that is, from boredom. A further rational support for gambling is found in an entirely new mathematical apparatus, which in Pascal introduces the study of probability as the *exact* science of modernity.

Entranced by boredom, modern society perceives it as a collectively shared phenomenon. In parallel with Durkheim's collective perception and Halbwachs's collective memory, we can introduce the concept of *collective boredom*, in which everyone inevitably participates.[10] Unlike Heidegger's Stimmung, collective boredom is the mood that is not rooted in the constitution of human being and is not its ontological predicament or destiny. Boredom is not a collectively shared phenomenon in antiquity, since there is not even a concept of it. The "epidemic" of boredom (AP D3a,4) is a very modern "disease," precisely as that which puts people collectively out of their ease in society. For Benjamin, boredom is a clear expression of *collective dreaming*, the "indication of the participation in the sleep of the collective [*Index für die Teilnahme am Schlaf des Kollektivs*]" (AP D3,7).

In a dream, many things happen simultaneously yet haphazardly and without a clearly established plot. One could say that dream functions according to the principle *post hoc sed non propter hoc*. In this sense, dreams are plotless. As Ágnes Heller has suggested, dreams are organized according to the modern logic of contingency. The demand of constant growth as the purpose of the modern capitalist economy is set off by the jumps and deviations of gambling with the market, which grip everyone's attention—but, as in a dream, without any resolution or meaning. Boredom as waiting, then, is the situation in which much is going on and yet nothing really happens. Such a waiting is not even a constant return to and of the same, but an unavoidable (neurotic) repetition of a different other as another in the absence of the same, which keeps repeating in a game without an ultimate meaning or end to the plot. There is no plot in gambling, just a limitless variety of distractions, which are infinitely entertaining but ultimately contingent and boring.

(3) *The boredom of repetition: the eternal return of the other.* The first form of boredom in Benjamin (in my reconstruction) comes from and with the mechanistic structure of the world as the repetition of the same. Repetition brings melancholy as exhaustion, tiredness, and fatigue. And from antiquity through the middle ages, melancholy was considered a malaise, a weariness caused by repetitive action or the complete lack of action, as either a somatic sickness or a mood that paralyzes moral and physical action and is akin to depression.[11] In modernity, though, melancholy "implies a longing for a (lost) state of wholeness. . . . tied up with the traditional vision of leisure that had been rendered obsolete by the new valorization of work and individual achievement."[12]

One should note, however, that boredom is consistently distinguished from depression in psychology, not only for the reason that, unlike for depression, there is no medical prescription for boredom and the two are distinct in their psychophysiological symptoms, but also for conceptual reasons. In McWelling Todman's formulation, the distinction comes from the corresponding underlying false beliefs: that in boredom the achievement and preservation of the positive state is never sustainable, while in depression the negative state is forever unpredictable, uncontrollable, and inescapable.[13]

The embodiment of repetition is *rain*, from which the modern city wants to protect itself with glassed roofs. This repetition is perceived as mechanical and as such is countered by mechanical means. The mechanism is always repeating the same as the same, according to a firmly established set of natural laws and in accordance with the task—or a multiplicity of tasks—that it is meant to perform and that becomes its efficient and *as if* final cause. A quotation from Blanqui's *L'Éternité par les astres*: "The universe repeats itself without an end and paws in place. In infinity, eternity imperturbably impersonates the same representations" (AP D7a).[14] In early modern science, *the* mechanism that becomes the model and the image of the world is the clock, which either needs constant or periodic rewinding by its maker, or is set to run once and for all according to its mechanic design.

Yet, for Benjamin, in the mechanistically repeating world, it is rain that exemplifies the repetition without an end. Such nature, translated into social second nature, has no end—only an accidental ending without purpose. Rain is nothing but monotony and repetition, where same does not meet other. The rain that was sent by nature or by gods to nourish the living is nothing but a nuisance for the modern city. It only indicates "the decreasing magical power of rain" (AP D1,7).

The second form of boredom is *waiting*. We only wait for the rain to stop, in order to be able to go about our business. But rain has no purpose in its monotonous persistence of the same. Rain is the recurrent eternal other. It is the eternal repetition, the return of the other. Waiting is the unending eternal same. While rain is the other without the same, waiting is the same without the other.

Both the other and the same come together, without a synthesis or interaction, in *repetition*, the third form of boredom. This is repetition without repetition, a pure monotony. It is one repeating tone, one and the same theme without variations. It is the monotony of serialism without a chance for polyphony or even a simple melody.

The "eternity" of the same and other, however, is not the eternity that would be an eternal presence of the other in the same, a *nunc stans* or αἰών. In modernity, the eternal is just an embellishment, reduced to a parergon, a fashionable, suggestive, yet ultimately insignificant detail, a "ruffle of a dress" (AP B3,7). Modern eternity is eternal repetition, boring and monotonous.

Monotony "feeds on the new" (a quote from Jean Vaudal [AP D5,6]). It is waiting for the new that turns out to be eternally the same, and thus is forever old, or rather is without past and future, yet is not in the present. The monotony of repetition is ahistorical. Repetition is thus neither a process nor an act but is their coincidence without identity.

Repetition is the eternal avoidance of death without a possibility of asserting life: "In order to grasp the significance of nouveauté, one should go back to novelty in everyday life. Why does everyone share the newest with others? Probably, in order to triumph over death. This only where there is nothing really new" (AP D5a,5).

One can say that the boredom of the cosmos as reflected in rain is the repetition of the other as the *discrete*, of the units as the monads of number. It is ... The boredom of waiting is the continuation of the same as the *continuous*, of the extension of line or magnitude, which cannot be reduced to the discrete.[15] It is —. This distinction reproduces that which is between the peak and the breadth in Heidegger's profound boredom. Repetition, then, is a nonsynthetic binding and bringing together of the same and the other into a cycle or circle, where the same and other remain mere opposites without any mediation. It is O.

The mechanistic repeating universe of Laplace, where the position of everything can be calculated and predicted with absolute certainty at any moment in the past and future, is the world devoid of any extra meaning except for the cognition of its mechanical-mathematical laws. In such a world, the idea of any being transcending the existing repeating established order of things is obsolete. The world that endlessly repeats itself does not have an end as a meaning or purpose. This is the Nietzschean world where existence (*das Dasein*) is "without meaning and purpose, but inevitably recurring without any finale into nothing: *the eternal return [die ewige Wiederkehr]*" (AP D8,1).[16] This is the world that feeds on itself, the world without will, without a goal—unless one finds consolation in the "the luck of the circle" (AP D8,4; D8,5). Yet Nietzsche attempts to avoid positing the idea of eternal recurrence as a new myth and is thus obliged to provide an argument in favor of the unavoidability of the eternal recurrence, thereby paradoxically making, or assigning, sense to his construction of the nonsensical and boringly self-repeating world of the eternal same. This mechanistic world is determined by a finite quantity of force and its bearers; therefore, in infinite time, all of the possible combinations should be repeated, and the world will inevitably come to the same state where it once was (AP D8a,1; see also D6a,1).[17] The world, however, does not consist of a finite number of constituents. Moreover, finite irrational numbers, such as π, play a central role in the constitution and description of the world. Yet, in the infinite decimal transcription of π, no finite combination of numbers ever repeats itself.

Therefore, Nietzsche's eternal return of the same into the same is ungrounded and impossible, as is the world which it regulates. In the very last fragment dedicated to boredom and eternal return, Benjamin greets the eternal recurrence as undermining the very idea of progress, which for him is the belief in "an infinite perfectibility understood as an infinite task in morality" (AP D10a,5). For him, the two

> are complementary. They are the indissoluble antinomies in the face of which the dialectical conception of historical time must be developed. In this conception, the idea of eternal return appears precisely as that "shallow rationalism" which the belief in progress is accused of being, while faith in progress seems no less to belong to the mythic mode of thought than does the idea of eternal return. (AP D10a,5)

Progress as an infinite moral task and the infinite return to the same are opposites, and yet both are false, and hence do not present a real antinomy. Each one is a myth. Myth is supposed to liberate us from boredom. But the myth of eternal reiteration is profoundly boring, and such is also the myth of infinite perfectibility without perfection and so without any meaning except the repetition of the very process of perfectibility. Both are the myths of the modern monological subject that keeps reaffirming and reiterating itself with a hope of getting rid of itself in the boring, recurring repetition of the same.

Imperfection. Benjamin mentions Proust's perception of "*imperfection incurable*," which lies in the very essence of human communication and sociability (*Geselligkeit* [AP D2a,5]). Plato would agree with this assessment, since for him imperfection is inextricably linked with the transience, *genesis*, of things, which is the result of their materiality and the inability to *be*. Being is ever unchangeable, intelligible, and transcends things, which get their formal properties by causal connection or "participation" in being. Being for Plato is never boring, because there is no repetition or temporality associated with it, so there is no term for boredom. The modern universal subject, however, constructs the world—the physical (in Kant) and the social (in Vico and Rousseau). But that the modern world is *incurably* imperfect means that imperfection is perceived as sickness and malady, and thus lies in the very subject itself. Benjamin and Proust diagnose the modern subject as an incurably ill patient, sick with itself, unable to cure itself. The imperfection, then, coincides with Kant's "unsocial sociability" (*ungesellige Geselligkeit*), which is the source of ongoing social and political conflicts, and of human development throughout history.[18] For Kant, one should be able to cure humans from the historical illness of war by reaching the permanent health of eternal peace and a state of social equilibrium. And for Hegel, the absolute subject is capable of building and finally achieving itself as perfectly and forever healthy, healing itself through history and logic into the shining utopia of the state. Yet for the contemporary subject who loses any connection with the transcendent, imperfection is inevitable in its unalienable presence to itself in the absence of others. The *incurability of being*, then, is another expression of the modern human condition. One can temporarily and indefinitely—but never ultimately—dodge from imperfection, easing its dull pain, which is the ache of boredom. But one can never cure it. One can put an umbrella or a glass roof above one's head as a temporary protection from rain, but the rain will never stop.

But imperfection does not need to be perceived as a sickness: in the aesthetics of the Hagi pottery, imperfection is the source of infinite fascination with the world, including socially shared gatherings. Such a fascination comes precisely from the realization of the transience of the world and the insufficiency of human relations, and yet is not perceived as a malaise but as a blessing. For in the very lack of uniformity, symmetry, and perfection, which are reflected in the irregularity of a diligently produced thing or in a fluent poetic inscription, one can forefeel the beauty of the world, perceived in its visible but sometimes almost imperceptible imperfection.[19] The visible deficiency of a thing at hand—a cup—can be seen as always different and new, precisely because of its apparent incompleteness, which creates an infinite number of combinations, details, and fractal, imperceptible deviations in rhythm and order, which, however, neither result in the eternal repetition of the same, nor shatter into a sheer multiplicity of unconnected fragments—but are held together by the unity of purpose and the simplicity of design. The ever-different same of a simple, rough, rustic thing becomes the embodiment of the ungraspable beauty through and in its everyday use, which can always be seen from a different perspective and shared with others. The infinite abundance of such "incurable imperfection" generates unfinalizable relations with oneself and others, each of which is always unique, engaging, and never boring.

The ideological boredom of the ruling class. Most of Benjamin's reflections on boredom bear on literary and cultural criticism and history. Apparently, Adorno encouraged him to write more on political issues, and Benjamin's voluminous convolutes, with multiple extracts from Saint-Simon, Fourier, and Marx, reflect Benjamin's socialist sympathies.

In the process of the worker's self-alienation, according to the young Marx, "the worker produces capital; capital produces him—hence, he produces himself, and...his human qualities exist only insofar as they exist for capital *alien* to him.... Production... produce[s] man as a... dehumanized human being" (AP X1a,1).[20] Capital, then, regulates the production and produces—reproduces—itself by the labor of the workers who are dehumanized to the extent that they are—always in plural—the inorganic organ, the tool of such production.[21] In this way, the producer—the capital—that stands behind the production as its ruling principle produces without working, by the sheer will of the modern economic embodiment of the quasi-divine omnipotent being. The modern subject, then, as a fully autonomous, self-legislating, willing intellect, considers the other—others—as part of the external, mechanistic world. Therefore, the workers are mechanical, lifeless extensions of the body of the res extensa of the universal res cogitans, whose pure thought is translated into financial capital. The workers as lifeless limbs are considered tools and instruments, which are hence inevitably alienated, not only from the product they produce but also from their very humanity, because humanity now belongs to the universal subject. This modern subject *is* capital, the soul of the world of modern exploitation behind the production, and it is socially constituted by the economic ruling class of the owners who use the labor of dehumanized workers.

Yet, something strange happens to such a subject: instead of either physically enjoying the fruits of the others' labor that it unduly appropriates and considers its own production, or morally suffering from the realization of the injustice of such distribution, the modern subject is *bored*. Benjamin astutely notes that factory work is "the economic foundation of the ideological boredom of the higher classes" (AP D2a,4). The ruling class, which is the economic embodiment of the modern subject as pure same, cannot even enjoy what it produces, because the autonomous subject is the ultimate loner that dooms itself to the inescapable and eternal repetition of the same. It is others who really produce the goods by their work, and yet, being reduced to nonhuman organs—reduced to instruments—they are unable to use and enjoy the product of their labor. Modern capitalism is driven by the boredom of the repetition of the same cycle of the forced growth, inevitable recession, growth—all for the sake of repeating it again and again, which becomes a self-contained game that profits only a few, leaving many in misery. Neoliberalism is the ultimate state of boredom, which it in vain tries to get rid of by constant, ever more refined entertainment. The dull pain of the boredom of the repetition of the same is epitomized in ongoing and ever-increasing consumption, which becomes entertainment and which has no other end except for distracting the subject—the ruling consuming class—from itself, which it is unable to do, incapable of moving beyond its self-imposed solitary confinement of self-isolation, which amounts to inevitable self-punishment.

Modern bourgeois ideological boredom is thus associated with production and consumption, in stark contrast to the premodern boredom of ceremonies (still present in grand academic ceremonies), which was opposed to the engagement, immersion, and involvement in battles and tournaments (that Benjamin notices in the depiction of the *dolce far niente* of battle scenes [AP D2a,8]). Consumption becomes utterly boring and dull, bringing excitement but never satisfaction.[22] The inescapability of such consumption results in modern (Romantic) abdication from the struggle, which results in boredom, from which one seeks relief in a "poetry of refuge and escape" (D4a,2).[23] For the modern bourgeois ruling class spends its life on production without creation, and consumption without enjoyment. Such a life is marked off by the inevitable "ideological" boredom, which becomes the agony of the constant unavoidable repetition of the same by the same in the absence of the other.

The pain resulting from the self-isolation of the modern subject and the mechanistic repetition of the same is well spotted by Engels in the myth of Sisyphus, as quoted by Marx in *Capital*: "The bleak routine of endless torture of work (*Arbeitsqual*) in which the same mechanical process is repeated again and again is like the work or labor of Sisyphus; the burden of work, like the rock, always keeps falling back on the worn-down worker" (AP D2a,4).[24] In the Greek myth, however, Sisyphus is punished to the eternal repetition of the same meaningless boring labor for his dreadful wrongdoing by gods—who are many, just, and enjoy their eternal life shared with others.[25] In the modern rendition and appropriation of the myth by the universal subject, Sisyphus becomes the working class that is punished without having committed any crime, and has to suffer unjustly for being excluded from the same of the modern subject, being considered as a mere instrumental extension of the subject's bourgeois embodiment, clad in capital. In his historical materialist project, Marx wants to return the alienated workers back to humanity by making them *the* subject of history, the makers and producers of the just history based on equal and fair distribution of the produced. And yet, he does it still within the paradigm of modern universal subjectivity, which is why the substitution of one class for another within the same subject does not make it less isolated and does not create sisterhood with the other oppressed. Modern Sisyphus is punished without guilt, and thus without a real punishment. Sisyphus has to suffer, but so does the one who makes him suffer unjustly. The ruling class assumes the position of the gods who punish the humans—the workers, the poor, the dispossessed. But in doing so, the owners, the rich, the possessors, in fact assimilate themselves to the modern, self-sufficient, autonomous subject, who usurps all legislation and justice. In the modern reversal of the myth, Sisyphus suffers the physical pain of destitution. But the real torture and ultimate punishment is the self-inflicted pain of boredom, from which the modern consumerist ruling class, the embodiment of the modern subject, can never escape.

Who is bored? If the modern subject is inexorably bored, how is boredom translated into ordinary life? For, in the end, the subject is a philosophical and historical construction and does not walk the streets of the modern city.

Produced by and within the project of modernity with its multiple facets of humanism, the social state, liberal democracy, anticlericalism, modern science, art, but also colonialism, imperialism, and nationalism, the modern subject in turn produces cultural and historical commonalities or types embodied in us humans who walk the earth, reproducing themselves as cultural types and sometimes disappearing, only to later reemerge under a different guise.

In Heidegger, the bored subject appears as the bored mystic, oracle, or prophet who discloses the truth of boredom hidden in plain sight as the essence of our own Dasein, which is most intimate in temporality and ever present to us and yet never noticed. Everyone is bored—but not properly. Only a few philosophers chosen by Dasein are capable of understanding and of properly and authentically embracing profound boredom. In Kracauer, the entire society—everybody—is bored. There is no escape from boredom, and therefore one has to face it. But again, the proper embracing and understanding of boredom is only accessible to an intellectual grounded on the sofa.

The modern universal bored subject is personified for Benjamin in three types of the bored: (1) the gambler, (2) the flâneur, and (3) the one who waits. "One must not pass the time—one must invite it to oneself. To pass the time (to kill time, drive it away): the gambler. Time spills from all of his pores.—To store time, as a battery stores energy: the flâneur. Finally, the third: he invites the time and releases it in altered form—in that of expectation: the one who waits" (AP D3,4).[26]

In a sense, all three are the hypostases of the same bored subject. Facing boredom, in the "beginning" one is the gambler who drives the time away in his inability to manage time and come to terms with it. No matter whether one wins or loses, one gambles away one's life as free time and is thus always a loser. In the "end," the one who waits appears to be the real winner, since that person copes with and through time by expectation, although not in an ultimate achievement of an end where everything would fit together. One keeps expecting the unexpected—a sight, a sigh, an insight, always partial, dug out in an unexpected place—a showcase, an exhibition, an occasional conversation, a tree on one's way—which one always shares with another, in order to fully appreciate it, abandon it, and keep waiting in expectation of the always partial but always fascinating new thought. The alleviation of boredom as annoyance and discontent comes in and from random thoughts, casual reading from meticulously selected books, unintended conversations with friends about seemingly haphazard topics, and playing with literary genres, expressing itself in aphorisms, fragments, journalistic essays, anthologies, and collections of thoughts.[27] But the one in the "middle," the flâneur, the troubled seeker of elusive mundane wisdom, is the one who left the annoying flight from the undistinguished single to the distinct singularity.

Perhaps one could say that each of the three types experiences boredom differently as repetition—of the discrete units of the same (the gambler), of the duration of one single same (the flâneur), and of the duration wrapped into a circle and thus reproducing itself as the same (the one who waits).

At this point, we might make a brief digression: where does the number three come from and why does it keep coming back in the analysis of boredom? Perhaps it comes from the necessity to structure any narrative as having a beginning, a middle, and an end (ἀρχή-μέσον-τέλος, Aristotle, *Poet.* 1450b26–27)? Or from the need to begin with making a distinction between different kinds of the subject under discussion? The minimal distinction is between two, which, however, easily turn into opposites that might resist mediation. A simple act of discrimination of and by the modern subject into same-other as I–not-I (in Fichte), turns into both the narcissistic enjoyment of the thus constructed self and its suffering of utter loneliness in the impossibility of connecting with the other who is external to the self and so forever out of the limits of communication. This logic of binary opposition and the exclusion of the third is at work in the (self-)construction of the modern subject that reflects and perceives itself as autonomous. The attempt at mediation inevitably brings in a third. Yet in both Heidegger and especially Benjamin, it is not the Hegelian triad of thesis-antithesis-synthesis. Rather, the third comes as the Aristotelian alogical syllogistic "middle term" that has to be excluded, in order to properly connect the subject (modern subject) and its predicate (boredom) in the conclusion.

The flâneur. The "middleman" of the three (cultural and historical) types of the bored is an intriguing and fascinating figure that energetically accumulates and distributes the experience of boredom.[28] The flâneur is a wanderer, a viator who walks around and hangs about without a perceptible aim. In a sense, the flâneur is a *planet*, which literally means a "wandering star," circling forward in retrograde loops around its central sun. The flâneur is a monotonous vagrant who is roaming around without having left his home, to which he always returns. The star that keeps him gravitating always toward the same in its seemingly infinite facets is the city. There is a certain monotony to the stars (AP D6a,1), not only because of their dim, repetitive, yet irregular expansion among the lights of the city but also because they form the visible representation of the melancholy of eternity (AP D7; D7a), where everything always returns to the same and nothing changes in the perennial repetition and waiting, only rarely interrupted by the rain of the falling stars. This is why the flâneur traverses his grounds along the familiar routes while making occasional loops not only during the day but also at night in fits of noctambulism (AP M6a,2).[29] The flâneur is primarily and mostly a pedestrian who wanders around for a *long time*. Walking, as Kant suggests, makes it easier to enjoy oneself, allowing one to leave behind the monotony and emptiness of everyday life (APH 7:164). The flâneur is thus a *walker* who spends hours wandering around a *big city* (the paradigm of which in the nineteenth century is Paris, and then New York, but which now increasingly has become the global virtual city).

The city, and especially the big city, is an artificially produced place, according to a plan, visible or invisible, regulated by human needs for shelter and the exchange of goods. As such, the big city is full of remembrances and reminiscences, which the flâneur is capable of extracting from its places by walking and observing them. For this reason, he is not only a connoisseur but also a kind of historian of the city, which is always *his* city. Unlike the tourist, who gravitates toward recognizably significant places about which one can read, the flâneur knows seemingly random places by paying his respect to minute details inaccessible to others, by frequenting subreptive corners and just-above-ground places. Every street, then, is "precipitous" (AP M1,2), leading him right down into the underground, hidden past.

One could say that the tourist is a historiographer who studiously works on the *adequatio* of the bookish written guide with what she observes in travels all over the world, thereby elevating her experience into a systematic historical knowledge. The flâneur, on the contrary, is an *antiquarian* who stays in one big city but prefers to get his knowledge of its places in pieces and keeps it as a collection of precious yet disconnected fragments, urban myths, and the minutiae of colorful splinters of small details that might add up to a whole mosaic if there is one who would bother to collect them all and put them into a coherent picture. But that would be a task for the tourist as historiographer, whose concern is generalization rather than attention to particulars. As the antiquarian, the flâneur prefers to attend to his favorite places by personal evidence, hearsay, and anecdotes, rather than through a comprehensive narrative.[30]

Memory, city, landscape. Walking down memory lane, the flâneur appropriates the nonprivate and thus owns it. "His soles remember" (AP M1,1). Meandering through the city, the flâneur walks his grounds "without definite attachment to anything" (AP M2a,1, a quote from Proust's *Du côté de chez Swann*), driven only by curiosity and the pleasure of recognizing familiar places, which are now his own—in his memory and reminiscence. Each place is populated by people and events from the past and present, each becomes a place for the inner theater, where the drama of city life unfolds in its multiple independent yet often intersecting novellas. The walked city is not a geographical map superimposed onto bricks and stones and occasional trees, but is the animated *landscape* in which every place is unique, has a strong individuality, and is loaded with an antiquarian historical account.

Embodied in the Romantic "ideal landscape," in which imaginary groves are inevitably complemented by grottoes and a "malerische Ruine," landscape is the place for *imaginary* wanderings where one can realize one's longing for the ideal that always only partially, or perhaps never at all, is translated into the real.[31] But the flâneur transmits and transfers the live Romantic landscape into the living organism of the city. As Benjamin notes, "the old Romantic sentiment for landscape dissolves and a new Romantic conception of landscape emerges—of landscape [*Landschaft*] that seems, rather, to be a cityscape [*Stadtschaft*], if it is true that the city is the properly sacred ground of flânerie" (AP M2a,1). In this sense, the flâneur is a new Romantic who lives in his own intimate world created and guided by his imagination (AP M17a,1), populated and kept alive by frequent walks through memorable places. The flâneur turns the site of the city into a cityscape.

The flâneur is hence the creator of his own world, and as such translates and interprets the macrocosm of the city into the microcosm of his room. The room is now the contracted city, and the city is the expanded room. "So the flâneur goes for a walk in his room," as does Kierkegaard in his early work (AP M2a,2). "The city splits for him into its dialectical poles. It opens up to him as a landscape, even as it closes around him as a room" (AP M1,4). The boring "epic" *Voyage autour de ma chambre*, however, demonstrates the "dialectical" character of the flâneur's wanderings: creating the space for freedom in the city, he produces the prison of his own room, where he locks himself for life.[32] But the room as the isomorphic reflection of the city is more than just a physical rectangular space: it is the imaginary place for the walk in *memory places*. The *loci memoriae*, the invention of which is ascribed by Cicero and Quintilian to Simonides and that have been today reinterpreted by Pierre Nora, are imaginary places where one puts and stores images of the events and things to be remembered, located, and then retrieved when needed.³³

The flâneur lives in and off memory places, thus reproducing the collective city memory: "Just as every tried-and-true experience also includes its opposite, so... the perfected art of the *flâneur* includes a knowledge of 'dwelling.'" And since "images can inhabit a place, then we have an idea of what concerns the *flâneur* and what he looks for. Namely, images, wherever they lodge. The *flâneur* is the priest of the genius loci." In this way, the collective memory—now becoming anonymous and withered—lives on in images inscribed into the places visited by the flâneur.³⁴

The flâneur is therefore the bearer and interpreter of memory as inscribed into now live and living places. Memory is transformed by him from antiquarian into personal and autobiographical memory, which, when shared (for the flâneur is the one who *writes*), can also become part of collective memory. Both liberated and imprisoned in his imagination and memory that superimpose the remembered onto the places in the city and the room, the flâneur is permanently *drunk* and intoxicated by memory in his perambulations, where he now cannot distinguish the imaginary from the actual. In the self-induced state of "anamnestic intoxication in which the flâneur goes about the city" (AP M1,5), he experiences the permanent "intoxicating interpenetration of street and residence" (AP M3a,5; see also M1a,1; M2,3; M17a,5). Benjamin distinguishes between *Erinnerung*, "memory" broadly speaking, and *Eingedenken*, which, as he writes in response to Horkheimer, is a reconstructive form of remembrance capable of modifying the past and so constitutive of history itself (AP N8,1). In this respect, Eingedenken is similar to recollection that allows a reconstruction of the past in a step-by-step reasoning.³⁵ The Romantic translation, transformation, and identification of the unmediated dialectical poles of the ideal and the real is thus accomplished by the anamnestically inebriated flâneur, locked within the city room of his memories.

Yet, as a true Romantic, the flâneur is a bourgeois, and his very attitude (*Haltung*) is that of the comfortable middle class of urban dwellers who fantasize about idyllic rustic life (AP M2,5). He is not a bohemian, since he has a place of residence—his room—and not a vagabond, but rather an urban philistine.³⁶ The flâneur is originally a Parisian type, distinct from another cultural type, that of the dandy, which is a product of London, another big city where one might wander around without reaching one's starting point after hours of walking in the crowds (AP M1,4; M5a,1). According to Larousse's *Grand Universal Dictionary of the Nineteenth Century*, which knows all definitions, "the dandies are disdainful of pleasing.... The dandies pleased only in displeasing" (AP D4,1).[37] The dandy is an aristocratic reaction to, and a personal protest against, modern commercialized urban life, in which capital reigns supreme.[38] Being deeply antibourgeois, this protest is also targeted and directed against the modern city. Similar to ancient Cynicism and modern punk, the dandy destroys or at least suspends the triviality of the modern communicative attitude rooted in the exchange-value of things (seen through the glass of a showcase) rather than on the intrinsic dignity of each person.[39]

Unlike the flâneur, the dandy is an eccentric and otherworldly hero, a Don Quixote who fights the vulgarity of modern life, asserting the quality of intangible human relations by seemingly suspending them haughtily against the quantity of the universal yet faceless exchange-value provided by the means of exchange. In the words of Baudelaire, the dandy is an unemployed Heracles (*un Hercule sans emploi*), a hero who is out of work in the modern world, which does not offer a task or labor that would be up to his prowess and power (AP D5,2).

Flâneur as observer and consumer. The dandy is thus a profound yet unintentional cultural critic of modernity, whereas the flâneur is its acute observer and keen consumer, being a critic of modernity by tasting, swallowing, and digesting it and then producing a verdict in writing.[40] In this sense, the flâneur is distinct from the type of the "philosophical walker" (AP M1,6), who intends to provide a solid, serious, systematic, but abstruse critical reflection on the current state of social and political affairs with an extrapolation into the future. The flâneur is thus a peripatetic, an aporetic dialectician, capable of thinking through the intricate puzzles presented by the city: "In the flâneur ... is reborn the sort of idler that Socrates picked out of the Athenian marketplace to be his interlocutor."[41]

The flâneur belongs to the modern ruling class of gods who exploit the destitute and dehumanized producers, those who constitute the contemporary, desperate conjoint Sisyphus, rather than the self-governed, dreadful Leviathan. Therefore, the flâneur is a *consumer* who spends and enjoys the producers' work, and relishes and appreciates its display in the department store, his ultimate ambit and terrain. As Benjamin perspicaciously notes, the flâneur's "empathy [*Einfühlung*] with the commodity is fundamentally empathy with exchange-value itself. The flâneur is the virtuoso of this empathy. He takes the concept of marketability itself for a walk" (AP M17a,2). Therefore, the flâneur is the *observer* of the market (AP M5,6).

In the arcades, the imaginary lived world of the flâneur is all covered with glass, from ceiling to the walls, which allows him to look on, to get engaged in one of his preferred activities, which is staring into shop-windows (AP M18a,3), providing a seductive transparency without possession.[42] The one who is bored can see without possessing what is seen. Observation through and under the glass regulates consumption without consummation, since full transparency incapacitates desire and kills eroticism. But in the shop-window world the object of desire is not fully seen to the extent that it is deliberately and artfully veiled, withdrawn from sight, inviting the onlooker to be made fully transparent in the imagination, as the end result and prize of the work of practical and theoretical cognition. The flâneur is thus the opposite of the ancient (Athenian) philosopher driven by the erotic desire to know and discover the true things behind the appearances. In his ongoing investigative observation, the flâneur becomes an unwilling private *detective* who couples "criminological sagacity...with the pleasant nonchalance,"[43] unraveling and restoring innumerable stories behind the things seen in the streets and arcades. As I will argue in what follows, the detective is a major comic figure who is also a walking philosopher capable of thinking through the current entanglement toward a resolution of the conflict in a good ending. Yet the modern (Parisian) philosopher is the flâneur who desires without desire, consumes without enjoyment, and claims the impossibility of getting to the truth of things, since there is nothing behind the shop windows' appearances but the appearances themselves, multiplied in the reflections through the glass.

The flâneur is the spectator of boulevards, cafés, shops, and photographers' studios behind the glass: visible but not touchable, they are like the stars or that absolute past of epic events that one cannot change but only see or tell about. Yet this absolute past is now made into the absolute present of the market behind the glass cases.

As *the* observer of modern city life, the flâneur is a leisurely figure: he reaps without sowing and consumes without having produced. Unlike the dandy, who has means of his own, the flâneur, in order to justify his social existence, has to market and sell himself by displaying himself on this side of the show windows in public. Yet what can he offer, the one who belongs to the leisurely nonproducing class?

The flâneur is the one who *writes*. He can write about his strolls for his diary, but for the public he can only make himself appear useful and interesting by writing for the newspaper, which is the mouthpiece and the critic of the marketplace.

> The social base of flâneur is journalism. As flâneur, the literary intellectual [*der Literat*] ventures into the marketplace to sell himself.…"We know," says Marx, "that the value of each commodity is determined by the quantity of labor materialized in its use value, by the working-time socially necessary for its production."[44] … [The flâneur is] in the privileged position of making the work time necessary for the production of his use value available to a general and public review by passing that time on the boulevard and thus, as it were, exhibiting it. (AP M16,4)

Journalism (and now, blogging and tweeting) is constitutive of the modern marketplace, where people discuss the latest news and establish and defend political programs. The journalist is an intellectual who is the critic of the life of their time who uses not elaborate philosophical theories but rather the clichés of the day. Yet, they are a critic nonetheless. In the words of Benjamin, "The intellectual is the sworn enemy of the petty bourgeoisie, because he must constantly overcome the petty bourgeois in himself."[45] And the bourgeois is utterly boring. The flâneur's amateurish journalistic critique comes as a posture against the boredom of mass production: "Boredom in the production process arises as the process accelerates (through machinery). The flâneur protests against the production process with his ostentatious nonchalance."[46] In this way, the flâneur's passing the time in public becomes the justification of his use-value. Leisure in modernity thus becomes indistinguishable from work, and gods as bourgeois intellectuals impose the Sisyphean labor of self-commodification on themselves, in order to justify their observant and consumerist boring existence.

Looking at wares in the shop windows, the flâneur inevitably looks at his own reflection. Maybe he looks for it in the first place. So the flâneur is a narcissist, more so than the dandy who intentionally creates the appearance of being a narcissist. The flâneur enjoys showing himself off to others and to himself in the streets, publicly reflected in the glass of show-windows, and privately in the mirrors of his own room. Yet he does it in solitude, alone among others, "abandoned in the crowd."[47] And yet he is fascinated with the masses, in which he sees his own reflection, multiplied and enhanced. People *en masse* inhabit the city as their own dwelling place: "Streets are the apartment of the collective. The collective is an eternally unquiet, eternally agitated being that—in the space between the building fronts—experiences, learns, understands, and invents as much as individuals do within the privacy of their own four walls" (AP M3a,4). Setting himself apart from the masses as solitary, the flâneur is nevertheless part of them, without even noticing it, since he is always busy with his own image and reflections. This inevitable inclusion in the masses further enhances his constant inebriation and delirium with the city.[48] Being the staunch spectator and critic of modernity, the flâneur is fascinated and drunk with the motion of great masses in the city, which proves to be a sweeping revolutionary force, as Eisenstein makes visible in his "Battleship Potemkin." Benjamin notes that the great construction projects of the nineteenth century—"railroad stations, exhibition halls, department stores"—all have been of great collective importance and were built for the masses. "The flâneur feels drawn to these 'despised, everyday' structures.... In these constructions, the appearance of great masses on the stage of history was already foreseen" (AP M21a,2; see also K1a,5). The flâneur is the first to detect the looming contours of the history that will soon befall the city, unwilling to recognize its dangers and consequences, still busy with his own glass mirror reflections.

In this way, there is a certain dialectic to the flâneur's existence, since he is *both visible* and *invisible*: he walks the streets of the city and writes about it as an individual. And yet he is variously present in manifold reflections in glass windows (today, on CCTV cameras) but is ultimately lost in, and dissolved into, the masses. The flâneur is thus "on the one side, the man who feels himself viewed by all, altogether a suspect and, on the other side, fully elusive, the concealed one" (AP M2,8). He thus turns into "the werewolf restlessly roaming a social wilderness" (AP M1,6). As the social werewolf, the flâneur is seen and not seen; is both conspicuous and anonymous; mixes with the crowd and yet keeps apart from it; is the perceptive observer of modern social and political life and yet is its most complicit bourgeois supporter and participant; is permanently drunk with the excitement of the city life and yet is utterly bored with it; is replete in his writings with the premonition of coming disasters and yet is incapable of averting any of them.

An antithesis of boredom? "Now, it would be important to know," asks Benjamin, "What is the dialectical antithesis to boredom?" (AP D2,7). Indeed. The knowledge of a thing might come from various and heterogeneous sources: from logical investigation, empirical research (driven by an explicit or implicit theoretical scheme), historical sources and comparisons (always made from a particular historical vantage point, which is often deliberately ignored and taken to be ahistorical), from its causes, or from the understanding of what it is not by opposition. The antithesis to boredom might not be singular and unique but rather each time *an* antithesis to a particular form of boredom, but it might be helpful to cast a brief glance at the opposite of boredom and see if it is really not (that) boring. If it is not found, then perhaps the very search might be the antithesis and overcoming of boredom.

An antithesis is the opposite that can be taken either as *contradiction*, which has no intermediate, or as *contrariety*, which allows for mediation.[49] If we are looking for a contradictory opposite to boredom, then it has to be exclusive of boredom; and if for a contrariety, then such an opposite might point to a state in which boredom and its opposite are overcome and yet are still somehow present. And "dialectical" in the "dialectical antithesis" may mean either the Platonic questioning that leads to the proper understanding of the subject, or the Hegelian "sublation" of the opposites that is meant to disclose a new category produced out of the "struggle" of the unmediated opposites.

(1) In the case of the boredom of *rain*, its antithesis is unmistakably obvious and self-evident: it is sun and sunshine (AP D1a,9). Instead of bleak and monotonous shades of ubiquitous gray, one is exposed to bright colors that are meant to enliven the flâneur's ambience. Yet, such colors provide a distraction and entertainment but not an overcoming of boredom. The alluring promise of happiness, as embodied in the blissful landscape of the beach, is a figment of the consumerist imagination, which dreams of a world that has hardly a connection with the repetitive, inescapable reality of rain, where the opposite of pouring— drizzling—is even more boring.

(2) The antithesis to *waiting* can show itself in multiple ways. Against killing the time, it appears as *play* that has no particular purpose and is thus the opposite of gambling (see AP D3,4), whose aim is profit—the goal of the modern market economy—which makes it utterly boring. The play (chess or basketball) does not have any purpose other than itself and is a self-sustaining activity that can be repeated without repetition and hence without being boring.[50]

Another antithesis to boredom as waiting is *battle*. Battle, which stops or transforms time from long, dull, waiting to the momentous anticipation of immortality in the moment of death, is disruptive of the lengthy time of the Langeweile. The momentous battle scene is captivating in its momentary messiness and unpredictability, and as such is opposed to lengthy ceremonial scenes (see AP D2a,8), to the boredom of the ritual, and to the purely formal and the solemn.

And a further antithesis to boredom as waiting is the *search for knowledge* as the life of the mind opposed to the deadening and finalized knowledge as a *fait accompli*. Knowledge can be reinterpreted, rethought, and even rejected, if the scientific community switches to a new paradigm, but as a given and accepted system of thoughts, statements, and facts, it is boring. Knowledge is repletion with and repetition of the same, whereas the search for knowledge is the anticipation of and waiting for a discovery of radical novelty. This radical novelty of the other never is, but always will be meaningful only within the same of the existing knowledge that no one has ever achieved up to now. Yet all these three antitheses to boredom as waiting—play, battle, and the search for knowledge—can themselves be boring, tiresome, and exhausting, and thus do not represent a clear opposite of waiting, because each one does involve waiting and anticipation and cannot be understood apart from them.

(3) Finally, what would be antithetical to boredom as *repetition*? It might be *reading*, impossible without the repetition of the discursive operation of going over parts of syntactic structures, gathering letters into syllables into words into paragraphs into chapters into a book—eventually into a whole, restoring and squeezing a meaning out of and into a text. No doubt, reading can be a pleasurable experience. But "le plaisir du texte" is more often a torture of boredom, accompanied by the narcissistic pleasure of self-immortalization through the incessant repetition of writing and rewriting, reading and rereading.[51]

Another possible candidate for the antithesis of boredom as repetition is *travel*, an old remedy for spleen. A journey presupposes the change of places that do not repeat themselves, and are different from the familiar, from the places seen before. From visiting such places, one would expect to learn something, which connects travel with the search for (antiquarian or historiographic) knowledge. Yet the downside of travel is fatigue, which comes from the repetition of the same and distraction from the familiar which itself is (too) familiar. The hoped for *far niente* of travel often does not bring the refreshment of the novelty of the other but returns to the well-known same, where distraction and entertainment substitute for the search of well-being.

It is therefore difficult to find a clear-cut antithesis to boredom in any of its appearances, the one that would be either exclusive and complementary to boredom or would allow for a nonboring mediation. Each time, boredom is still lurking in what might appear to be its opposite. The problem is really ontological, for boredom is neither a subject (there is only one subject, that of the self-reflective and self-aware cogito) nor a predicate. Nothing is opposite to the subject, and boredom is not a predicate of the (modern) subject.[52] The difficulty of finding an—or the—opposite to boredom is that boredom inevitably accompanies the modern subject, which is very much its own construction. As self-constituting, the modern subject cannot get rid of itself and thus cannot escape boredom as its own unavoidable proper, and hence cannot establish itself as nonboring to itself in its own activity. Therefore, one needs to look for a being that would allow for subjectivity and yet be nonboring. But this means finding a *different* kind of subject.

Ennui: between restlessness and diversion. I will end the genealogy of boredom with where it might have started: "It does not matter where I start, for I will come back there again."[53] The move is not circular, nor is it reverse nor opposite; rather, the move, prominent in Romanticism, is from temporality to inwardness, in which temporality resides, or which, in any case, it regulates.[54]

Being the expression of the modern condition, boredom is pervasive in contemporary life and appears under different guises: as the incessant monotonous duration of the Langeweile—and as the inextinguishable tedious dullness of the *ennui*.

Etymologically, "ennui" comes from Latin *odi*, "to hate" (in Catullus's "Odi et amo," "I love and I hate" [*Carm.* 85]), *inodiare*, "to annoy," and the further related *taedium*, "weariness," or "disgust," related to Latin *odor*, "smell," or "stench." Of the same origin is Homer's ὀδύσσασθαι, "to hate," which derives respectively from Greek ὄζω, "smell," or "stink." Modern "boredom," however, comes from "bore": hurting with the action of boring, allegorically piercing a whole, or cutting one's body. *Odium*, then, is the poisonous hatefulness that makes it impossible for us to enjoy *otium*, our leisure. Ennui marks the passage from the freedom to be on our own with ourselves in free time, the time free of care—to the unbearable burden of being at the same time in the same place, which becomes a prison, a solitary self-confinement that we cannot escape and that is built by ourselves around ourselves, sealed off from others.

Pascal, the thinker of ennui. Pascal is one of the first and most prominent singers of boredom in the long and illustrious French tradition, from Baudelaire to

Sartre and Simone de Beauvoir, who pick up the meaning of boredom derived from odium as hatefulness of one's own being.[55] It is an inevitable dull mental pain that accompanies us in all actions in our life and cannot be ultimately relieved by our own effort. For Pascal, this means that we can be delivered from this inescapably tedious (in the original etymological meaning) suffering only by grace, which comes as divine salvation. Ennui, therefore, is to be taken gravely and seriously. The negation of this radically negative position leads to an equally negative suggestion that the only meaning of life is its being utterly meaningless and absurd. In fact, the severe seriousness itself is the expression of our modern tragic condition of being nauseously bored, rather than living in a state of comic, joyful elation.[56]

Boredom is followed by inconstancy and misery, and pride and vanity, which are all distinctive signs of human corruption and wretchedness, *bassesse* and *misère*.[57] Bordering on disgust with ourselves and with existence itself, the unrest of boredom is an inexorable, protracted agony accompanied by a fear whose cause we cannot understand unless we accept that it is an expression of our very human condition.[58]

Remarkably, Descartes too identifies boredom with disgust (*l'Ennuy, ou le Degoust*), although he relates it to temporality, as a reaction or "passion" that can be caused by the *duration of the good* (*la durée du bien*). In this respect, boredom is opposite to regret (*le Regret*), which is caused by a past, but now absent, good.[59] In other words, the good in its persistence is boring! Hence, as Pascal famously proclaims, the human condition is: "Inconstancy, boredom, disquietude" (PE 58).[60] Once understood as a fundamental and inescapable predicament of human existence, ennui, "this glib and pathetic despondency," becomes a strong—perhaps the strongest—incentive for us to escape the inescapable in our life.[61] For Pascal, this is salvation. But, for Camus, it is suicide.[62]

Boredom is thus a sign of the radical inconstancy, imperfection, and fortuitousness that underlie our existence, both mentally and physically. It is not by chance, then, that Pascal is the first modern thinker to think about chance, paying close attention not only to boredom but also to establishing the foundations of modern probability theory, which describes accidental events with precision.

Being always dependent on the accidental, on chance, we nevertheless always want to be in full control of ourselves and events. Such an attitude is implied in the ideal of the autonomy of the modern subject, which we unwillingly and unwittingly have produced, in which we all participate, and which makes us desire to fulfill the desire for independence. In Pascal's formulaic diction: "Description of man. Dependence, desire for independence, needs [Dépendence, désir d'indépendance, besoins]" (PE 113; PF 73).

Yet our contingency—which is differently expressed as finitude, mortality, historicity—means dependency on our needs, both physical and mental. In fact, their very existence is the expression of our insufficiency or, in Pascal's words, "wretchedness." The human being is thus a span between necessity and contingency. The elementary example of a need is hunger. Being hungry suggests that we are *not* physically autonomous and self-sufficient, but ultimately depend on the world, our other, to sustain us in physical existence. One needs to eat in order to keep living. But eating, like sleeping, is never boring. Propelled by the needs, the incessant movement of desire for independence or rest leads to a momentary rest—satisfaction, satiety, sleep—which we always inevitably abandon, only to be moved again by the desire for independence or rest. In exactly the same way, our spiritual life goes from a momentary rest of satiety to perennial restlessness in our search for the next stop, which we will then leave, driven by spiritual hunger. It is this spiritual hunger that is boredom or ennui, which for Pascal is no less than the hunger for justice (PF 731).

Hunger is similar to boredom in that, as Kant has told us, boredom allows for the renewal and continuation of life. Both are the devices planted in us by nature to keep us alive, to ensure our continuous subsistence in a safe body and sane mind. But being alive, for Pascal, does not mean—and in fact excludes—being happy. Life without redemption and even without a hope of redemption is the sign of our gloomy condition. And this is ennui.

Becoming satisfied, fulfilling the desire for independence—for a *short* while—is the *long* while of boredom. When we get satisfied, we get bored. When we get bored, we move on, so our needs, and primarily the need for independence, never get satisfied in the end. Rest as perfect tranquility is now the expression of death, of nothing, of being without a possibility of changing, of the impossibility of becoming and being different. Boredom, then, is the reaction to *rest* and the lack of activity, which results in the perception of being exposed to *nothing*. Ennui inevitably has *goût du néant*, the "taste of nothingness," of vacuity, and hence is to be understood as the "monumental struggle against the power of nothingness."[63]

Says Pascal: "Boredom. Nothing is so intolerable for man as to be in a state of complete tranquility, without passions, without business, without diversion, without effort. Then he feels his nothingness, his abandonment, his inadequacy, his dependence, his helplessness, his emptiness. At once from the depth of his soul arises boredom, gloom, sadness, grief, vexation, despair" (PE 515).[64]

If thinking is motion from one thought to another, then thinking is restlessness, which makes life without thinking, or without striving toward thinking, unbearable and utterly boring. One gets bored if one does not think. If one does not think, one forgets, because recollection always requires a reconstructive thinking process. Oblivion is a burden in that it obliterates us from the things past, both lived through and learned and imagined, with which we associate our being as being-remembered. But oblivion can also be a blessing not only in that it might save us from the burden of a trauma but also from the boredom of the repetition of the same, and thus allow us to (re)discover the previously known but forgotten anew and as new.

Yet the autonomous self-thinking subject puts itself to sleep and rest because it does not need to think any more once it has thought and thereby has assured its own existence in moral uprightness, once it has arrived at independence and stands on its own, not relying on the approval of others, on heteronomously established and accepted norms. This is the death of thought, the sleep and rest of reason, from which it is awoken and put into motion by grief, vexation, and despair. Ennui is the desire for rest as independence, accompanied by the inability to achieve it.

One might observe that in contemporary psychological research, boredom is often taken as "the unfulfilled desire for satisfying activity." As such, it can be interpreted as a longing for something that mostly cannot be clearly formulated and distinctly defined, lurking behind a passive expectation of the desired, and a hope for its achievement.[65] The desire without enjoyment can result in enjoyment without desire—or the desire of desire.

Besides, boredom in psychology is always associated with temporality and comes up once time is perceived to stand still or move unbearably slowly, thus causing either impatience or desperation, depending on whether the desired goal is considered achievable or not. Psychological boredom thus appears to replicate the distinction of the desperate dullness of ennui and the indefinite duration of Langeweile.

So both our mind and body are driven by mental and bodily hunger in their desire for independence. Both our mind and body are restless in restlessly seeking for rest. The universal expression of the endless movement in physical nature is the fundamental law of motion that Galileo, Descartes, and Newton describe as the inertial infinite movement.[66] It is an infinite movement similar to ennui in being endless, without a purpose or a stop. It embodies the infinite in the finite and unites the impossible—movement and rest—at the same time and in the same thing. Movement, which can only be finite for Aristotle in the well-ordered, finite cosmos, becomes infinite, embodying the impossible, the coincidence of the opposites of movement and rest—the restless movement, the deeply paradoxical *status movendi*. The Aristotelian rest is substituted by modern inertia, in which motion and rest are indistinguishable. The impossible becomes possible for the autonomous subject who produces the law out of itself, making the partless—a point—fill everything by having moved to the infinite distance. The infinite becomes the pointless embodiment of the point, making the infinite actual and complete, the impossible possible, and the unnecessary necessary.[67]

Human life itself is a fragile balance between the opposites as extremities, both of which are infinite and hence frightening in their incomprehensibility: the infinitely great, the actual infinity of the world—and the infinitely small, the *nihil* of the indivisible, the point. We are in the *middle* ("Deux infinis, milieu" [PF 38; see also PF 185]), staying there in motion without ever having chosen what we choose. Being alive means being left to chance, oscillating in uncertainty between the frightening, unreachable, and infinitely removed extremes. In the deeply pessimistic and gloomy picture of our wretched and bored being, sketched by Pascal fragmentarily yet with a ruthless precision, we cannot escape being abandoned between the extremes of these two.

The coincidence of the opposites is unfathomable for us, thrown as we are into the middle. Everything is one, yet everything is different ("Tout est un, tout est divers" [F 120]). Everything desires to be independent, yet everything is dependent on the other. Everything is at rest—ever for a while—yet everything remains in infinite, incessant motion, being always at inertial rest. In the Orwellian world, war is peace. In the Pascalian universe, imperfection is perfection. Imperfection is not imperfection, and thus is perfection. Driven by hunger and ennui, dependence is freedom. This is the boring and startling predicament of modern subjectivity that marks its efforts to achieve independence in thought and action.

The impossibility of physical rest in the infinite inertial motion is paralleled by the impossibility of mental rest. Rest is difficult and boring, because it exposes ourselves to ourselves. One should dare to embrace being with oneself, alone but not lonely, being by and with oneself as the other with whom one can—and perhaps should—engage in conversation. This is what Kracauer's ascetic exercise of being on one's own, lying on a sofa in one's small room, seems to suggest. Perhaps not accidentally—for Tolstoy, also, lying on a sofa is a spiritual exercise of doing nothing that becomes an alternative to doing evil.[68] For Pascal, the impossibility of being at rest and peace with oneself shows itself as restlessness. Here, he agrees with Tolstoy and Kracauer that all our troubles come from our "incapacity to stay in one room" (PE 168; PF 126). Staying in one place feels like punishment and incarceration, so our own room, which is meant to be the place of freedom, turns instead into prison or even a (self-)torture chamber. It is thus utterly paradoxical but not entirely unexpected that modern society spends so much effort on guarding and closing off private space from others, where one can apparently be free in one's own place, and yet gets agonizingly bored in it. One thus both yearns for one's private room and abhors it.

For Pascal, one should get engaged in the concentrated ascetic meditation about our miserable condition and the possible way out; for Kracauer, we should just let ourselves go with the flow of the reverie without a distinct purpose. But either way we should be able to be "saved," to get out of the self-imposed monastic staying in one place and time that threatens to last long—longer than any thinkable time—yet can be condensed into an instant. We should be able to overcome the literal mental inertia of the infinite unaffected motion in our mind until we liberate ourselves from drifting away from ourselves. Being afraid to be left alone with ourselves, we remain utterly miserable, unable to reach out to ourselves and others, locked within a monological autonomous subjectivity.

Not being able to "stay in one room," at a rest that cancels inertia, we are inevitably looking for diversion and distraction. Unable to embrace and enjoy rest—our day off at our place—we go out looking for entertainment. In modernity, restless entertainment substitutes for rest but never gives repose. We are constantly looking for rest, but once we obtain it, "it becomes unbearable, because of the boredom it engenders" (PE 168; PF 126). Entertainment becomes our modern curse and damnation. Rather than bringing amusement and rest, entertainment amounts to the death of the subject that cannot achieve death, infinitely running from itself in the hope of reaching itself. Pascal expresses it bitterly:

> The only thing that consoles us for our miseries is distraction [*le divertissement*], yet it is the greatest of our wretchednesses. Because that is what mainly prevents us from thinking about ourselves and leads us imperceptibly to lose and forget ourselves. Without it we should be bored, and boredom would force us to search for a surer way out, but distraction entertains us and leads us imperceptibly to death. (PE 33, trans. mod.; PF 393)

Distraction amounts to vain curiosity (PE 112; PF 72; see also PE 114; PF 74), yet without distraction and entertainment, we get utterly bored, "wither from boredom" (PE 70; PF 33). Therefore, boredom, ennui, is the call to arms that might save us from the damnation of the inertia of standing still while constantly running away and around in our mind, and thus liberate us from desolation. Pascal and Kant agree in this, although ennui for Pascal is a supernatural force, while for Kant it is the call of nature.

Our modern condition, which is that of dependence, of looking for independence, and the inability to achieve it, is thus expressed in our inevitable restlessness or mental inertia, on the one hand, and in our dependence on entertainment, on the other hand. Distraction, which is the purpose of entertainment, is meant to save us from our miserable condition, yet it never achieves its aim, and we are left forever miserable in the inescapable loneliness imposed on us by the modern universal subjectivity that becomes our destiny. Yet this modern subject is not predetermined in its necessity but is historically our own construction. The hope, then, is that we can overcome it by daring to be left exposed to ourselves in our "small room."

CHAPTER 3

Critique of Bored Reason

The conclusion we have reached so far is that boredom is a specifically modern phenomenon, ubiquitous under the guise of the vexing ennui or unbearable duration. We cannot reject being bored or overcome it by entertainment; and yet if we look deeper into boredom, we might come to understand our own condition better and the missed opportunities that it might offer to us.

My main claim here is that boredom is the proprium of the modern subject. Modern subjectivity is deeply bored. This means that in order to understand boredom systematically, we should look into the historical construction of the modern subject. In recent decades, there has been an extensive critical debate around the modern subject and its role in the formation of the specifically modern modes of cognition and moral practice.[1] So we need to turn to the discussion of the main constitutive features of the modern subject, which I take to be its (1) singularity and uniqueness, (2) autonomy, and (3) reflexivity.

(1) *Loneliness and aloneness.* The most salient trait of the modern subject is its uniqueness and aloneness: it is the lonely *ego* that thinks itself in and as the first-person singular. Establishing its being as existence assured by an act of thinking, the subject is indeed singular in that it is alone and the only thinking thing, res cogitans, that thinks itself as thinking. The other, then, is by exclusion a non-thinking, or extended thing, which is the world. The other of others who might be equally thinking is/are not there, nor here, since they are singled out by the singular act of the first-person singular thought. The modern subject is exclusive of the other. In order to think itself as the other, the subject has to split and think itself, the *ego/I*, as *non-ego/not-I*. If the modern subject is one and unique, it is thereby inevitably lonely and alone. Being desperately and forever the *same*

and impersonal, it attempts to generate—or recognize—the other in an act of thought that ultimately targets and reaches out only for itself. The modern subject persuades itself to be its other. There is no one to date except for itself. The other remains forever an unreachable goal for the lonely subject who starts and ends with itself.[2]

Loneliness is being-*without*-the other: the other is longed for but is never found, remaining a task to be achieved, at best only a being-*toward*-the other. Any action of the self-enclosed subject takes the community of others only as an abstraction, as oneself (one self, one's self) imagined, multiplied, and extended to the many.[3]

Such a solitary and isolated subject comes to realize that its loneliness is a self-limitation translated into finitude. The only other that is established from within the act of finite thought is the infinite thinking subject, the radical, equally unattainable other of the finite self.[4] Lonely and lonesome, the modern subject succumbs to finitude, which becomes the decisive moment in its constitution and self-definition, in the way it sees, understands, imagines, depicts, and realizes itself. Finitude in cognition is translated into *reflectivity*, which is the act of thinking that targets the only available limitation of thought by *itself*. And finitude as temporal is translated into the realization of mortality, although not of the subject, who is atemporal and thus immortal—but of the individual, who is a concrete conceptual realization and historical embodiment of the modern subject.

In this situation, the negative basic passions that are (or should be) involved in the realization of finitude and mortality, and that are culturally interpreted as conditioned emotions, remain *unmediated* and therefore practiced in solitude. Thus, fear can be understood as the rejection and nonacceptance of the other, directed at the self; anger as the rejection of the self, directed to the other; shame as the rejection of the self, in presence of the other; and disgust as the rejection of the other, in presence of the self. And yet, in its solitude and loneliness, the modern subject does not have a proper other, and hence does not have a proper self as interacting with others, which is why it cannot properly perceive and benefit from any of these fundamental emotions as shared with others.

In a genealogical sense, the modern subject is itself a genre of the publicly staged and enacted drama. As such, it is a system of rules and conventions, which are made explicit through reflection but remain mostly implicit, and define publicly shareable practical (moral and political) action and theoretical cognition and investigation. And this genre is *tragedy*. Indeed, dramatically, finitude and mortality are realized as the tragic condition, insofar as tragedy is the celebration of finitude and mortality, where one has to accept the finitude of one's existence, the inevitability of undeserved suffering, and the inescapability of death. The modern subject is therefore *tragic*. It is unavoidably and "fatally" (since it is its own *fatum*) attracted to tragedy, which is a modern fantasy on the theme of the classical ancient Greek tragedy, transmitted via Seneca, and tamed to the bourgeois play by the Romantics. Such a tragedy allows the modern subject to narcissistically enjoy the sublimity of its self-imposed loneliness, moral uprightness, and heroic suffering in the seclusion of solitude.

Yet since the other only remains an artful construction of the self, even death cannot be achieved. Death might be a beginning for the subject in defining its self-understanding as the mortal one, but it is not the end: there is no end in and to the solitary thinking except for itself. Death cannot be achieved in and as the end. This is probably the most tragic in the situation of the lonely subject: forever terrified by the understanding of its mortality, facing the inevitable and unable to get rid of the fear of death, the modern subject *cannot die*. It remains forever immortal and cannot even commit philosophical, social, and political "suicide," in order to get rid of itself—either by claiming the "death of the author," by the critique of foundationalism, by distilling itself into a highly specialized logical debate of the boring minutiae of reason, by perpetuating self-suspicion, by turning toward intersubjectivity, rendering philosophical problems meaningless, denying ontology in favor of hermeneutics, and the like. The modern subject is thus doomed to remain in the eternal present, in the inescapable presence to itself, to its regal and annoyingly unavoidable self.

(2) *Against autonomy*. The loneliness of the modern subject is translated into uniqueness and singularity, which the modern subject reflectively perceives and presents to itself as its own *universality*. Along with this universality comes *autonomy*. Both universality and autonomy are understood as the features of pure reason, which primarily thinks itself as capable of establishing the law for nature as theoretical reason, and the universal moral law for itself as practical reason.

Autonomy is self-constitution through self-legislation that establishes a normatively binding law, or a set of laws, grounded solely in the authority of the legislator, independent of any other authority. In modernity, political autonomy is translated into sovereignty that is then identified with freedom, as independence from others and ruling over oneself as a body politic.[5] But political autonomy can also mean democratic and thus *autarchic* self-governance, once people act as one legislative body that establishes a commonly accepted law either through public democratic deliberation or through a body of elected representatives. Yet the autonomy of the modern subject is that of a lonely (overly) reflective pure reason that needs and recognizes no other except for itself, whom it has to follow and whose prescriptions it now has to accept as obligatory, insofar as they are its own rationally justified precepts and norms. Norms are often transcribed as rules, yet norms cover more than rules. Following rules and rituals as customs makes life ordered and possibly free from unpredictability, yet monotonous and boring. The legislative autonomous authority of the modern subject, therefore, is meant to establish and assert the universally binding laws, norms, and rules that are meant to be obligatory for others while effectively asserting the legislating subject as independent from others in the absence of the other.

The autonomy of the modern subject appears as both theoretical and practical. In its autonomy, the modern subject presents itself as the "for itself" of reason as solitary and monological reason that translates itself into the precision of acting and the punctuality of being as being-there-on-time. Social and political practical being becomes regulated by a precise calculable measure that is further translated into the regulation of financial capital. Yet punctuality overregulates life and makes it utterly boring and vexing. As Evelyn Waugh puts it, "Punctuality is the virtue of the bored."[6] But if one is always punctually late, can it still be considered punctuality?

The theoretical autonomy of the subject is based on its self-exclusion from, and opposition to, nature. The modern subject does not tolerate the other except for itself, which the subject considers as its own other, who is never a given but is produced by the subject on its way to eventually achieve the full rational self-transparency.

The concept of the unconscious in Eduard von Hartmann, Freud, and their followers, is a philosophical reaction to the allegedly rational autonomous self-disclosure. The unconscious is a metaphysical construction that intends to limit the rational reflective hubris of the modern subject that asserts itself as purely rational and capable of giving an account of its legislative autonomous act. The subject's very being is, if not produced, then at least assured and justified by the act of reflection.

The universal modern subject thus fails to recognize the other of nature and the other of real others who might be involved in an egalitarian dialogical exchange. The other and others become only a task to be realized, as epitomized in the Cartesian cogito, which is the subject's construction of the other (thought) as its own self (thinking).

Moral autonomy: freedom against nature. In the absence of mediation between the thinking subject as res cogitans and the res extensa of nature as complementary to it, the other of nature is lost as a residue of "naïve metaphysical realism." Therefore, the other of nature, of the world, also becomes a task to be achieved. Locked within its loneliness, the modern subject can only reach out to the other of nature by *construction*, by producing it from within itself in its law-like regularities. Nature as the other remains a mystery—the thing in itself—yet it is demystified by rational construction, which is an imposition of rational laws onto the nonrational other, which makes sure that nature will never misbehave but will always move and act according to the subject-given laws. The subject thus becomes the *pantokrator*, the all-powerful legislator and ruler of nature. The truth of nature, then, is *verum factum*, or is *made*, produced according to the cognitive structures imposed on the known by the modern subject. The theoretical subject excludes the world to the extent that thought excludes extension.[7] Because there is nothing mediating between the I and the world, the subject is worldless, which means that the world remains irrational and unordered until the subject gets its hold of nature and constructs it as regular, according to the subject's own precepts of sensibility and understanding.

Such an approach is epitomized by Kant in the *Critique of Pure Reason*, which assumes that natural laws do not exist in nature but are only recognized in it to the extent that they are produced and put into it by the cognizing subject. For the modern subject, this amounts to no less than a scientific revolution, which swaps the places of nature (which was formerly independent of the subject) and the cognizing subject (formerly, as dependent on nature). It is now the subject as lonely and fully transparent to reason that subjugates nature and makes it its own. This radical reversion is a modern scandal, which I will discuss below.

For Kant, as for Descartes, nature is both complementary to and exclusive of its other, which in Kant's practical philosophy is rational free will, since the law of nature is opposed to the law of freedom.[8] Nature manifests itself in natural events, while free will manifests itself in moral action. Nothing can come in between and interfere with the two, except for the capacity of judgment, which conveniently bridges the gap between the theoretical and the practical. Nothing can cognitively mediate between the subject and the world, which thus becomes *its* world, spun out of, enlivened, and made meaningful by the subject. By elevating its sensibility and discursive logical reason (understanding) to universal *a priori* capacities, the modern subject gives the law to nature, where everything is bound by necessity. But breaking away and opposing itself to nature, which is now its construction and product, the modern subject imagines itself free and sovereign in the realm of objectively given moral ends, which the solitary subject inhabits as its only citizen and hence the monarch, shared with other imaginary citizen-monarchs who are the projections of lonely moral reason.

As autonomous, self-reflective, and thus admittedly fully rational and self-transparent, the modern subject has to establish itself as reigning supreme—as the absolute autocrat—in the moral kingdom of ends, where moral action is determined by the rationally rectified will. However, in order to act morally, the modern subject does not need others, even if it might want to have them as the addressees of its moral prescriptions. The deep unfulfilled desire of the lonely monological subject to reach out for others and even to get rid of itself in favor of intersubjectivity—where the other is always presupposed—is a powerful motive and driving force behind the discourse ethics of Apel and Habermas. Bored with itself, such a monological subject wants to generously lend its voice to others, to the poor and dispossessed, yet it is its own lonely, autonomously established, and disciplined voice that substitutes for the polyphonic and messy richness of others' mutually interrupting voices, making them redundant and obsolete.

Yet intersubjectivity is a pure relation that is still constructed by the same lonely subject. The utter loneliness and the (four) hundred years of solitude of the modern practical subject transpire in the construction of moral autonomy that makes moral action not collective but a matter of the lonely monological deliberation that the secluded subject exercises vis-à-vis itself as its other.

Moral autonomy, as it is presented in Kant, can be described by the following three features: (i) as the capacity (*Vermögen*) of practical reason to will and *establish* moral norms and the moral law itself according to (supersensible) purposes.[9] This is the expression of the subject's *legislative* authority, insofar as moral law is established freely and autonomously by the subject as universally valid, in an act of self-legislation by its rational free will. The modern subject establishes the law that it itself has to follow as binding, since such a law is of its own making. As Korsgaard puts it, "the source of the normativity of moral claims must be found in the agent's own will, in particular in the fact that the laws of morality are the laws of the agent's own will and that its claims are ones she is prepared to make on herself. The capacity for self-conscious reflection about our own actions confers on us a kind of authority over ourselves, and it is this authority which gives normativity to moral claims."[10] This self-established authority wants and hopes for, but does not need, the other.

Moreover, (ii) moral autonomy comes with an incentive or motive to follow what the subject has freely established as moral, since otherwise the subject would lose self-esteem and admiration for what it has produced. In this capacity, the subject exercises *executive* authority over itself.

Finally, (iii) moral autonomy requires an act of *judgment* that understands the established law as moral and rules that the law should and has been followed rightly and justly. In this capacity, the subject exercises *judicial* authority. The first two aspects of moral autonomy presuppose acts of will understood as rational and as such as moral. The third one implies an act of reason that directs and justifies the exercise of will as rational by and in an act of judgment, which thus can be considered self-autonomy (*Heautonomie*).[11] The universal pure and self-regulating rational autonomous will can be considered self-intentional. The *will-of* is the *will-for* itself as the universally legislating rational will.

And yet, the modern subject inevitably and paradoxically deceives itself, when it cannot tell lies but cannot tell the truth either. For this reason, when it wants to be upright, truthful, and moral, which it achieves by establishing the very moral law itself, its straightness with itself is inevitably a lie and an unavoidably missed opportunity. For the modern subject intends to establish moral maxims as universally valid, but in the end they are meant for and directed to itself qua universal. Yet, quite simply, morality is the way to reach out and treat *others*. Rather than being a law directed to oneself as the other, a moral claim in its normative demand can be a nonoppressive gift to the other, *omnibus non sibi*. But for the modern lonely self-isolated subject there is no other, except for the reflectively established self, and thus no others.[12] No wonder, then, that all the maxims of the (moral) will in Kant are formulated in the first-person singular, and all the formulations of the moral imperative are in second-person singular as the constructed other of the self—but never in the first-person plural. So if freedom and moral autonomy presuppose each other, the very act of establishing such an autonomy is a lonely enterprise exercised by a solitary reflective reason that carefully protects primarily itself from the *logical* mistake of giving the moral law as not universalizable. Universalizability, then, is the extension of the universal lonely subject over itself into an imaginary community of rational and volitional beings.

Autonomy is the expression of the freedom of will against nature, and thereby becoming the ground for the dignity of a rational being.[13] As such, moral autonomy needs only strict and responsible rational thinking guarding itself against a doubtful fantasy of imagination. Understood by itself as autonomous, the proud pure reason becomes *autocratic*, self-ruling, being in full self-possession and self-control, where the ruler and the ruled, the police and the policed, the oppressor and the oppressed, the liberator and the liberated, the playwright and the actor, are—or is—one and the same.[14] In the absence of the other, autonomy is both self-control and self-oppression. Autonomous moral reason is thus the true sovereign who both separates and unites the legislative, the executive, and the judicial moral powers.

And yet, the self-legislating, self-governing, and self-judging reason leads to the paradox of voluntary and free self-enslavement, because now the subject is subdued to the unconditional command of itself over itself, from which there is no escape. Because no mediation is possible for the lonely reason, it can only find comfort in a self-consolation that embraces the opposites of freedom and unfreedom in a freely self-inflicted suffering. The corresponding imperative addressed to itself, then, is: "You must suffer!" This unconditioned command is addressed to oneself as the other ("you"), but in the absence of the other it is the lonely self that becomes the origin and the subject of the imperative. Severed from others, the one has to represent the imaginary and inaccessible humankind in a single person of the first-person singular that projects itself into the first-person plural.

One of the formulations of the categorical imperative in Kant demands to act in such a way as to treat and represent humanity in one's person as the ultimate end in itself.[15] The imperative, then, can be reformulated as: "You should act in such a way as to represent all of the imaginary and inaccessible others as humankind in your single person as autonomous, suffering, and lonely." But the other is detached from the lonely subject and is only a construction or imaginary extension of the self. Boredom, then, is precisely the expression of this incapacity to reach out, represent, and substitute for humankind in one's single persona.

In the realm of moral autonomy, only *one* is free—the one autocratic reason that becomes an unbending rational will. Pure autonomous reason is (all too) serious and almost divine, although it discontentedly realizes its finitude, which it takes to be the tragic intimation of mortality. Free and rational, the modern solitary autonomous subject is inevitably suffering. Pure reason is thus boringly tragic reason.

Comic reason, on the contrary, is not autonomous, for it always thinks with and against others and reflects on the life shared with others. Comic reason is critical and discerning with others. Autonomy brings about *loneliness*, being *without* the other: the other is longed for but is never found, remaining a task to be achieved, which, however, can never be completed. Any action that follows from autonomy treats the community only as an abstraction, as oneself (one self) abstracted, multiplied, and extended to the many. Since the autonomous self-confident subject acts entirely on its own, being its own foundation and establishing its moral law that it universalizes, the subject persuades itself to be its other, which makes a collective action meaningless and redundant. The modern subject legislates autonomously, by itself (and in itself)–but only for itself, hence negating and destroying the possibility of having reason and being shared with others, which it could rethink and from which, as its own history, it could learn. The solitary exercise of rational autonomy is utterly boring because it directs the same toward the same, repetitively without repetition, so once and for all, in the absence of others who are only an imaginary projection of the same self without other.

Yet again, in a simple sense, the point of morality is the capacity for reaching out and living with others as equals, when *all* are—or become—free and thus share well-being with everyone. The morality of autonomy is the absolute monarchy of the regal solitary subject in the realm of final and ultimate ends, established by a tragic *act* of its rational will. On the contrary, the morality of shared thinking and deliberation of the nonexclusive plurality of nonautonomous beings is the comic democratic *process*, which might not always be rational but which allows for reaching the nonfinal but always renewable end of well-being and the good life shared with others.

One could say that the will becomes rational and fully transparent when it is accompanied by an account of the *that*, the *why*, and the *what* of its volition.[16] But it is very difficult to find a situation where all the three aspects of will–the act, the cause, and the object–can be precisely and unambiguously distinguished. If properly established, they can become fully transparent only *after* the act of will. Moreover, the full transparency of the *that*, the *why*, and the *what* might utterly incapacitate the will. Yet rational will is supposed to be fully aware of the three aspects *before* its act, while in fact it institutes the three by the very act of its volition as autonomous. Autonomy, then, is an inevitable illusion and the wound that the rational will of the modern subject willfully inflicts upon itself.

Deontology. In the absence of others who could testify to the being of oneself, the "is" ("am") of the lonely thinking reason becomes not only its duty but also its right.[17] Being, in the act of monological and tragic pure reason, has to be achieved by the very same reason devoid of any empirical concerns and considerations. Since the other is not there but is a task of reason, the existence of oneself can be assured only in a rationally justifiable way. The achievement of the lonely being becomes a moral duty. For without a reason, there is neither a moral law nor are there the laws of nature.

This means that the self of the subject has to universalize itself, which amounts to the modern subject becoming the regal legislator in the realm of moral ends. Because such a legislator is the only and lonely one, it cannot but think of itself as universal, and thus becomes the embodiment of the idea of all of *humanity* as "the purpose in itself."[18] The universal humanity as represented in the fully transparent reflective self-directed thought is an abstraction made real by the rational effort of the modern subject, in order to justify its autocratic claim and respect for itself, which it portrays to itself as respect for moral law.[19]

The ethics that mostly suits the self-righteous autonomous subject is the deontological ethics of duty, norms, and obligations established and exercised by the autonomous singular self-centered tragic subject, as opposed to teleological ethics as the ethics of shared well-being of the nonautonomous pluralistically decentered comic subject. Yet if philosophy might afford being nonproductive—of new truths or new norms and their justifications—it might be a form of ontology and ethics of being with others. The decentered comic subject, then, can be considered neither as autonomous nor as autocratic, and does not unite or usurp the legislative, executive, and judicial powers. Instead, it shares them with others. Comedy does not recognize the ultimate autonomy of the subject. The comic moral and political subject always comes only in the plural and is always a being with and toward others. The comic subject is unapologetically neither lonely nor autocratic. For comedy is not an imitation of action: comedy is the very being of the moral and the political.

Abandoning the hope of achieving the other and thus the good life as the life shared with others, the tragic subject can only hope for a nonadversarial outcome of its actions according to a universal principle of moral action ("categorical imperative"), which should assure that any action coming out of such a principle and done according to it will not be morally (and politically) disastrous.

Deontological ethics affirms the superiority of the rational autonomous "ought" over "is," *Soll* over *Sein*. Yet, in doing so, the modern subject's solitary Soll becomes—*is*—its Sein. The rational duty of the straightened lonely thinking that thinks—or furtively imagines—itself as pure moral reason *is* its very being. But such a being needs to be *asserted*, which can be done only by an act of will that coincides with that of reason. In being moral and self-legislative, the pure reason of the modern subject has to become, or make itself, identical with its *will*. Therefore, there is nothing more to its being than the dutiful, rational self-asserting will.

Will. The relationship between will and reason is an uneasy one throughout the history of philosophy, and is still not well understood. Aristotle recognizes the capacity of choice that has to follow rational deliberation, in order to be translated into moral action.[20] Yet ancient philosophy does not have or recognize the concept of will as autonomous or free will. The concept of will that does not follow any other prescriptions except for its own comes only with the understanding of being as produced by an act of such will. The will that is not compelled or constrained by anything else is not defined by the other and thus becomes infinite or divine. Translated into human action, it becomes the striving of the not-impelled soul in its effort to keep or acquire something to which it aspires to as an object of desire.[21] As a capacity of free volition, will testifies to human freedom as striving toward the ends that are freely chosen and rationally ascertained by will.

One can say that the entire "project of modernity" is based on *the primacy of will*, which, as fully rational, becomes self-legislative and thus autonomous, imposing the universal moral law onto itself. Autonomy *is* the freedom of the will and is the only principle of all moral laws and of the corresponding duties.[22] This is what will is and how it is epitomized by Kant: as the principle of universal legislation.[23] As legislating, the self-accountable will establishes the rationally approved moral law (universal categorical imperative), which is the law of freedom, and opposes it to the law of nature, which is the law of necessity.

The relationship between will and reason, however, is the source of conflict in and for the modern subject, which wants to keep its identity, uniqueness, and self-respect as the only legitimate source of the law. Yet, strictly speaking, the two capacities are not identical: reason is the source of cognition, while will is the origin of moral action. This leads to the separation of the "is" from the "ought," of the theoretical philosophy of the necessity of reason from the practical philosophy of the freedom of will.

One can say that the modern subject establishes itself in an act of will. In order to justify its claim to the supreme legislative authority, such a will makes itself rational, or coincidental with pure, now practical, reason. However, modern will can exist and establish itself as autonomous apart from reason, whereas modern reason cannot exist without will. For reason needs to legislate in a pragmatic act of *asserting* what it has thought of as rational and universal, and thus *impose* the thought onto itself. This means that the solitary modern subject has an irrepressible propensity toward voluntarism, when its "pure" will comes to deny or at least suspend reason by absorbing the rational.

An act of pure will is an act of faith. Says Kierkegaard: "faith begins precisely where thought stops."[24] Salvation as reaching the kingdom of moral ends, then, can only be achieved through a nonrational pure and purified will in an act of faith, by Luther's *sola fide*. Reason becomes an accomplice suspected of the worst thought and deed. No wonder, then, that for Luther, "reason is a whore [*Hur*],"[25] and for Dostoevsky "reason is a scoundrel, whereas foolishness is direct and honest,"[26] as the expression of pure will. At best, the will of the modern subject can be identical with pure reason by making itself rational and therefore pure, which the will does by justifying its claim to autonomy and universality.

Even if will and reason are different in their action, they are virtually identical in their being, insofar as they come from the same source in the autonomous universal (self-)legislative modern subject. The emphasis on autonomy and independence from the "external" or the other of reason that would make it heteronomous makes the modern subject submit and subjugate reason to the power of will. As theoretical, reason becomes the dictator of and over nature, imposing the constructed law onto it without nature's consent, which is not needed from something that is pure res extensa, devoid of life. But as practical, reason makes itself into pure moral and thus free rational will that subjects itself qua reason to itself qua will.

Tragic will and Willkür. The will of the modern subject is thus the will for selfautonomy (Kant's *Heautonomie*), the autocratic ruling over itself in the absence of others, making itself both the legislator and its own other as the subject of its universal exceptional legislation. But such a will is *tragic*, insofar as it is lonely and alone, legislating for itself as the only other. And it is also the tragic *will-toward-death*, for although it legislates universally, it still does so for a finite being corruptible by inclinations that lead it away from the pure kingdom of moral ends.

The manifestation of this tragic condition expressed in finitude and mortality is modern *Willkür*, sometimes translated as "the power of choice." Willkür stands for arbitrariness, for the capacity to choose, or freedom of choice as unrestrained by reason.[27] The will of the modern subject voluntarily puts a yoke of moral law on itself, subjugates itself to itself in its imputed self-autonomy, forcing itself to follow reason as practical and moral. Willkür is the other side of the same will as the capacity to say "no" to the very best reasons that reason may present to itself. Willkür, therefore, testifies to the ultimate lack of transparency in the modern subject, to which the subject aspires in an act of reflexivity devoid of doubt. Willkür is something opaque and even evil in the absolute autocrat of the moral kingdom and is hence the expression of the subject's tragic incapacity to *be* pure, moral, rational, infinite, and immortal, and indeed to be free will, the *liberum arbitrium*.

The modern subject runs into its finitude by discovering, to its chagrin, its "impure" sensual sensible inclinations (*Antriebe, stimulus*). In Kant's account, only animals incapable of morality follow their sensual inclinations and thus succumb to the unfreedom of their Willkür (*arbitrium brutum*), whereas the moral being should be *affected but not determined* by Willkür, which is only possible when such Willkür is free, that is, determined by pure reason. The negative concept of free Willkür—its independence of sensible inclinations—is then complemented by the positive concept, which is no less than the Willkür's capacity to make pure reason practical for itself![28] In other words, the will's tendency to be weakened by sensible inclinations and therefore yield to finitude is willfully ordered and overcome by the will itself, which in this way becomes pure and free and allows for reason to be such. Only the arbitrary suspension of arbitrariness, the definite choice for definiteness, and the austere ascesis aimed at disinterestedness can guarantee the modern subject's purity of reason as the legislator of the supreme moral law.

Fact of reason and the boredom of the will. The freedom of reason is thus inscribed into, and coincides with, the freedom of will, insofar as a self-chastising and self-disciplining act of the will acts on itself and against itself as Willkür. The free will has already punished itself before committing any trespass against its universality and the purity of its intentions. Only in this way can the freedom of the (self-)legislating will as pure practical reason be guaranteed. The moral law that the will establishes as universal, then, gains an a priori apodictic givenness of the pure practical moral reason as (supremely) legislative—an undisputed givenness that reason cannot reject. The pure will suspends its own arbitrariness by having already and forever established the universal moral law, in which reason becomes pure and ultimately coincides with the free will. The presence of the moral law in us is the strange "*fact of reason*." The fact of reason is nonempirical but rather "thrusts itself upon us" as given, as something that pure reason discovers in itself with astonishment as "the sole fact of pure reason, which thereby announces itself as originally legislative," thus making reason majestically recognize itself as the source of moral purity, untainted by any sensible inclinations or empirical interests.[29]

The universal moral law legislated by the free will as pure practical reason is realized as an inexplicable fact that does not follow from any experience and cannot be deduced from empirically verifiable premises but is rather an a priori given that universal legislative reason cannot possibly miss, ignore, or reject. Strangely enough, the same pure universal legislative reason that has *established* the moral law at the same time realizes and becomes aware of its act of legislation and of the moral law that now "is given as a fact, as it were, of pure reason of which we are conscious a priori and which is apodeictically certain."[30]

The reason that makes itself pure, rational, and autonomous by legislating the universal moral law discovers what it has established as free will to be a *fact*! But such a "fact" is actually made by reason within itself, and reason can now recognize this fact as "given" to itself without acknowledging that it is the same reason that has produced the "fact of reason" that reason imposes onto itself—without recognizing this fact as its own act. This is what "factum" originally means in Latin: something that is made (up) or produced. In this sense, the *factum rationis* is in fact *verum factum*, that is, the (moral) truth *made* universal by being *produced* by that very reason that *then* recognizes it as its own *factum*. The modern autonomous subject thus acts entirely on its own, that is to say, is the foundation and source of its own (moral) law that it universalizes by constituting it.

Yet the unbending rational moral will is utterly tiresome and boring, because it acts always in the same way and legislates the same. Boredom thus has the structure of *pure will* that always establishes and repeats the same, without any "empirical" or "sensible" distraction, elevating its own making into the produced "fact" of reason imposed onto reason by the same autonomous universal lonely will. Boredom signifies the eternal return of the modern subject to itself in the renewed act of self-legislation, which it takes to be rational, moral, and universal.

In defense of impure reason. Pure reason is the legislating, ruling, and judging reason as the supreme instance of establishing the law, acting out of the law, and judging on the basis of the law. Pure reason is the reason that dominates the other according to the law that it establishes. But since the other is inaccessible to the fully autonomous self-sufficient reason, domination turns into the domination of itself, which reason cannot get rid of. The idea of autonomy suggests learning how to internalize the prescriptions of the imputed pure reason and to carry them along at all times. Being exposed to the stern gaze of the pure unbending reason that judges one's every move becomes the source of modern anxiety and the neurotic fear of making a misstep. Everyone becomes an instance of the universal pure reason. In this way, everyone issues the supreme natural and moral law, carries it within oneself, acts according to it, and judges and punishes oneself for any of its trespassing. The legislator, the executive, and the judge are now the outcrops of one single pure reason, inescapably present in every person, who therefore do not need others. The criminal court and the prison are now conveniently within each of us. Each one is the judge and the criminal at the same time.

Since everyone is the same personification of the universal autonomous theoretical, practical, and aesthetic reason, everyone is equal. However, since the other is unreachable and anonymous, this is equality to oneself as identity with oneself. Yet, since the other is not there, the one's self is not thematizable or reachable either. The other is only a fictitious projection of oneself, one's extension into an imaginary community and its institutions. The best political model that reflects the equality of all the members of society is democracy. Yet democracy is the equality of equals as robust and real others, not reducible to instantiations of one abstract pure reason. Pure autonomous reason is exclusive of the other and is thus monological. Therefore, reason that is radically inclusive of others has to be *impure* and heteronomous. Hence, democracy in modernity remains an ideal to aspire to, a regulative idea that can hardly be reached and realized. In contradistinction to the ordered, tragic, and autonomous self-legislation, a radically democratic politics can be considered comic in that it is messy and incomplete at any given moment, although it maintains an unflinching intention of reaching its end: well-being shared with everyone.

Comic democratic reason, then, is the reason that is shared with others, suspiciously heterogeneous and heteronomous, decentered, and often mistaken. It is a nonautonomous reason that does not follow a presumed universal practical self-legislated sublime and tragic reason by establishing an imaginary moral law. The ultimate law produced by pure reason is mortifying in its being eternal, universal, unshakable, and exclusive of others. It is the comic dialogical reason that allows people—real others—to be with each other and work together toward a resolution of a conflict, moving in a number of steps toward its reasoned resolution and thus reaching jointly shared well-being.

Allonomy. Heteronomy is the feared and hated slip of reason that fails to live up to its own expectations of being pure and autonomous, universally representative of an imaginary humanity in its lonely existence. A better way to characterize the impure, multifocal, distributed, comic, and potentially democratic reason might be through the concept of *allonomy*. In ancient Greek, "other" might mean the exclusive other, one of the two, *heteros*/ἕτερος (Latin *alter*), or the inclusive other, one of a number, *allos*/ἄλλος (Latin *alius*). In comic communication generated by heteronomous reasoning, everyone interacts with the other and is oriented toward the other in what one is and does. The other of such dialogical communication is both the other of and within oneself and the other of the fellow actor, who are not mutually exclusive but whose interaction is incomplete at any moment, moving toward the fulfillment of the end of mutually shared and distributed well-being. Such interaction may not be easy and not reach a full agreement, yet it is not utterly dissensual or antagonistic, because everyone strives for and shares the not yet achieved common good. In this sense, the dialogically decentered interaction is based on *allosensus*, which allows for the continuation of acting together, often taking a detour and being mistaken.

Allonomy means the dependence on the plurality of others, on the nonerasable difference with the other that allows for the dialogically interactive legislation of moral prescriptions as teleologically necessary for achieving the common, publicly shareable good. As I will argue in more detail in what follows, since comedy does not recognize the ultimate autonomy of the subject, comedy allows for a different subject who is always integrated with others in a nonautonomous thinking and (inter)action. Therefore, such a subject is allonomous and pluralistic, capable of achieving freedom, where everyone becomes free as a result of a (not always immediately transparent but ultimately meaningful) *process of* interaction with others, and not by an *act* of the self-legislating unique will that aims at an unchangeable end established for and by the lonely pure reason.

Pure reason is thus a myth created by the modern subject that it makes its own credo. This makes truly democratic politics impossible: in the absence of the real other, one cannot be equal to another, so equality remains a normative yet unrealizable demand. This is the tragic condition of the modern subject obsessed with the purity of its theoretical reason, which legislates over nature and thus reduces its law-like regularities to the inner structures of sensibility and thinking within the subject, and of its practical reason, which legislates over moral actions in an apparently universal legislation driven by the desire for universal equality.

Yet this desire remains unfulfilled in the exclusion and absence of the other. The ensuing impossibility of a meaningful democratic politics is tragic. Democratic politics can only be based on heteronomous comic reason that accepts the premise of unconditional equality while recognizing the uncertainty of moral action that reaches out for the other while relying on the other in making wellbeing with others possible. Autonomy is the domination of the subject over itself as an imaginary other, which leads to the unavoidable, fatal, and tragic self-repression that becomes further translated into the oppression of others who do not fit. The purity of reason is the fate that the modern subject imposed onto itself in its lonely and boring autonomy.

(3) *Reflexivity*. Finally, the third distinctive feature of the modern subject is its reflexivity. In an attempt to get rid of doubt about anything that can be doubted—ultimately, about *itself*—the Cartesian subject is capable of suspending everything except its own thinking about its thinking at the moment of thinking. The only undoubtedly certain thing, then, is the very existence of thinking once it cathartically purifies itself, becoming devoid of any content and thus exposed to an empty act of thought, which cannot be exercised without the existence of the thinking subject. What is important in and for the Cartesian cogito is *that* it thinks, and not *what* it thinks. It may be mistaken in the *what* it thinks but it cannot miss the *is* of its thinking. Therefore, cogito asserts being: *existentia*, not *essentia*, because for the thinking lonely subject it is impossible to think without existing, which becomes the precondition for the lonely reflexive thinking that presents its act to itself in the first-person singular (cogito, sum).[31]

The modern subject thus establishes its loneliness and aloneness since it excludes any other as doubtful and hence nonexistent. In this way, the subject asserts itself as fundamentally reflexive, for its very existence is made certain by its turning to itself, by a reflective self-identification of the one and only with itself. Speaking about Kierkegaard, who in many ways encapsulates the main features and trends of modernity, William McDonald observes that "the modern age... has disconnected reflection from passion. Reflection alone is unable to transform a self which is narcissistically preoccupied with self-image."[32]

Reflection therefore comes as identification, affirmation, and recognition of the identity of the singular and solitary subject with itself, S≡S. In an act of (noetic) thinking, it amounts to simple positing, or asserting S. But in a discursive act of (dianoetic) thinking, or understanding, it amounts to asserting the S as S, and thus as not only identical but also numerically distinct from itself, as not-S, ~S, because in the act of reflection, S makes itself into its own object or puts itself in the position of the predicate. As its own predicate, S is fully included in S, not analytically but productively, in the sense that S reflexively generates its own predicate that coincides with itself as the subject S. In this way, the Aristotelian subject of the *subiectum*, the logical, grammatical, and rhetorical ὑποκείμενον, the S of P, becomes the direct object of the cognition, construction, and invention of the modern subject, as not-S, ~S. Therefore, S thinks itself not as S but as something else. Hence, S≡S means S≡~S at the same time.

Yet asserting both S≡S and S≡~S is impossible without a contradiction if, as the law of noncontradiction suggests (i) it is the same S, (ii) S is taken in one and the same respect and (iii) at one and the same time.[33] (i) S might not be the same or self-identical, since S becomes different as the result of its own reflexive thinking, which both identifies S with itself—and splits and opposes itself to itself as not-S, ~S, as the mirrored image of itself. Moreover, (ii) the respect in which S is taken might not be the same or identical, since S's understanding of itself changes in an act of reflection, in (ii.a) the cognition of both its "what" and its "is," and in (ii.b) establishing itself as the other, which S was not before the act of reflection. Finally, (iii) S might not be the same or identical over time, since, although it is discursive, reflexivity as thinking of itself might be considered not temporal but setting the very structure of temporality, understood as a sequence of acts or the process of discursive thinking. Therefore, while reflexively thinking itself, S can be, and think itself, as both identical and nonidentical to itself without a formal logical contradiction. But this does not yet produce, create, or generate the real other of and from the isolated, lonely, and monological thinking subject—the other of itself as nonreflexive (prereflexive) personal being; the other of another person, which shows itself as pluralistic and comic being in dialogue with equal others; and the other of the world, which resists attempts to subjugate it to the laws of the modern subject's thinking and perception, which the subject imposes onto the owned world and thus dissolves nature in the act of lonely reflection.

Reflexivity as malaise. The act of reflection establishes the understanding of one's self as seen—reflected—in the mirror of the other. Yet in the absence of the other, the modern subject cannot be but self-reflexive, insofar as it does not have anything or anywhere else to turn. The modern subject is thus doomed (by itself) to return to itself seen through itself as alienated, nonidentical, and different from itself. The modern, lonely subject always comes back to itself without ever having left itself, in an attempt to assert itself as capable of universally valid theoretical claims and of practical norms based on universalizable rational grounds. The true is the trued. And yet, it can only address itself as the other that is invented by the act of reflection, who is the same same, directing its norms and prescriptions to itself as a constructed imaginary plurality of others. There is no other to and of the modern subject, only the repetitive eternal same. All the books of introspection that express the rich and variegated inner world of a thinker are written by the same author—just under different names. Meaningless repetition makes life, work, and thinking unbearably dull and boring.

The modern subject thus always faces the possibility of solipsism, which it tries to avoid by promoting intersubjectivity (in Apel), which, however, becomes a normative demand and a postulate of the same self-centered modern subject who decides to take itself as communal and even a priori, as a community of communication, a "we" that is meant to precede any "I."[34] This postulated "we," however, still remains split into the I and not-I by the same act of reflection of the unitary subject, which means that the not-I is not a real other of the I but its imaginary projection. Setting itself as one's own other is schizophrenic, which is an inevitable act of the lonely subject in the original sense of "schizophrenia," which means "splitting the mind."

Such a lonely and solitary reflection is thus thoroughly narcissistic and cannot be suspended or overcome. The inescapability of reflexivity inevitably leads to its redundancy, for it never reaches its aim. In its unavoidability and excessiveness, reflexivity is a malaise.[35] Reflexive narcissism is not enjoyable, because the modern subject is concerned with the universality of its claims, norms, and institutions, which it wants to get to the other, whom it denies or cancels by its overly reflexive stance toward itself in the first place.

Being inexorably reflexive, the modern subject is once again tragic, insofar as it realizes—and carefully cultivates—its sublime tragic suffering, doing so consciously and reflexively, remaining utterly solemn and serious about itself and its own self-inflicted suffering. In this way, the modern subject *cannot escape itself*, its own overwhelming and boring presence. The best it can do is to take itself not as a given but as something to achieve, and finally and ultimately to reflexively clarify. Hence, the modern subject goes to great lengths in explaining how the whole of the logical, natural, psychological, social, and historical come out of itself, which is initially devoid of any determinations and even of being (e.g., in Hegel's *Encyclopaedia*).

The modern subject *cannot even forget* itself, although it does not remember itself from and in its beginning, since it has no beginning and denies itself any *arkhē*. For recollection requires the other that can be recalled. The modern subject thus cannot stop thinking and reflecting on itself, including this very reflection in which I am now engaged: in this sense, it instrumentalizes every thinker who (even occasionally) thinks about it, denying the aspiration to well-being with others, both to itself and to everyone who thinks with and struggles against the modern subject. The overcoming of excessive reflexivity can only come with the overcoming of the modern subject, which differs from the epistemological task of switching the point of view from subjectivity to intersubjectivity, the latter being still inscribed into the subject. Rather, it requires a dramatic change in the dramatic attitude—from monologically tragic to dialogically comic action and interaction.

Lie as a paradox. The modern subject is the subject who seeks and establishes the truth about itself and the world. In doing so, it establishes, first, the moral universal truth, which is the truth about itself as universal, and second, the truth about nature to the extent that the very law of nature is given by itself, which it thus takes as necessary and universally true. It appears, then, that having constructed the moral and physical truths, the modern subject cannot lie. And yet, lying is paradoxically inevitable to it, so that the subject has to keep unveiling itself to itself in the indefinitely renewable set of acts of positing itself as identical to and with itself, continuously splitting and distancing from itself, identifying again with itself as this newly posited other, and reflexively splitting again. Et cetera.

There is a deep paradox implied in the subject's revealing the truth to itself, which necessarily implies a lie that the subject wants to but cannot overcome. In order to lie and be able to deceive, one needs the other as others, so it seems that the modern subject is incapable of lying, because there is no real other, and the practical and theoretical truth is established in the absence of the other of others and of the world, which are only implied by the universal truth. And yet, the modern subject inevitably lies to itself in its inescapable reflexivity, since it takes itself to be the (only) other, which is not only a logical mistake or a metaphysical illusion but is also an unavoidable lie.

The paradoxical inevitability of the lie of the lonely monological subject can be seen in what we could call here the "rhetorical subject." Rhetoric, whose invention is attributed to Corax from Syracuse (5th century BCE), is originally meant to describe the "concealed art" (ἀποκεκρυμμένη τέχνη, Plato, *Phaedr.* 273c) of the use of logical arguments and fallacies in court that would help to persuade the judges, affect the judgment, and win the case. As such, rhetoric refers and appeals to the same binary opposites that appear in logical propositions and thus always uses the S-P, subject-predicate structure. Apparently, Corax had a student Tisias, although "Corax" (κόραξ, "raven") might be Tisias's nickname, in which case these two are in fact one person, which perfectly represents the situation with the modern subject who splits itself into the same self and its other, so that the self can never remain the same.[36]

This preserved story illustrates the paradox of the inevitability of lying for the "rhetorical subject." Corax took Tisias as a disciple and agreed to take the fee that Tisias would win in his first court case as tuition. However, having learned the rhetorical use of arguments, Tisias evaded going to court, thus avoiding paying his teacher. Corax then took the case to the court, arguing that if he won, he would get his fee as awarded by the court, and if he lost, then he would get his original contractual fee from Tisias. But Tisias retorted that if he were to win the case, he would get the money granted by the court, and if he were to lose, he would not have to pay as per the original agreement with Corax, which presupposed paying the fee only if Tisias won his first case.[37] In any case, both Corax and Tisias would have won, and the fee would have been both paid *and* not paid.

The modern subject is thus both Corax and Tisias at the same time, both the plaintiff and the defendant, the accuser and the accused (and also, unlike in the Sicilian court, the judge), who must win and lose and who cannot win and lose. The modern subject has to lie to itself. In doing so, it makes the pact with itself and sues itself reflexively against itself, both unavoidably winning and losing and being incapable of winning and losing, at the same time. The rhetorical subject, who accuses itself and is thus also the accused, who presents the argument in defense of an accusation of itself, thus cannot refer to itself—sue itself—without falling into a contradictory lie, which is the result of the subject's inevitable, excessive split reflexivity in the absence of the other.

Proprium: the "idiotic" gaze of the modern subject. Being always reflexively exposed to itself and having to return to itself as the eternal same in the absence of the other makes the modern subject inevitably bored and boring. Boredom is thus the *conditio humana moderna* as the expression of the modern reflexive solitary subject—the self-appointed universal subject of theoretical meanings and practical judgments. But what is the logical and ontological status of boredom? As I have argued, boredom appears under many different guises yet is neither a subject nor a predicate. My thesis is that boredom is not a sentiment, feeling, mood, or mode—but a symptom, or rather, the intrinsic inalienable property, proprium, the proper of the modern subject.

At this point, it might be helpful to turn to Aristotle, who dedicates the entire fifth book of the *Topics* and a number of passages in the *Analytics* to the consideration of the ἴδιον, or proprium. In ancient Greek, ἴδιον stands for "private" as opposed to the "public."[38] But in logic, Aristotle distinguishes four kinds of the *predicabilia* or the ways to state and express the subject, according to their mutual substitutability (when subject and predicate can exchange places) and essentiality (when the term defines what the subject is). Among the *predicabilia*, the nonsubstitutable essential one is genus, the nonsubstitutable nonessential one is the accidental, the substitutable essential one is definition, and substitutable nonessential one is *proprium*, property or the proper. In this sense, one can speak of the proper as double: the one that expresses the essence (τὸ τί ἦν εἶναι) of a thing, and the other that does not. The proper that expresses the essence is definition (ὅρος), which tells what a thing is (*Top.* 101b19-23, 39, 109b9-10, 132a11-13). And the properly proper is that which is mutually convertible or substitutable with the subject but does not express its essence or its "what."

In Aristotle's account, then, the proper is that which, although it does *not* express, show, or demonstrate the essence of a thing or what a thing is by itself, belongs only to that thing and is mutually substitutable or replaceable with that thing in the sense that both are predicable of each other.³⁹ Here, the logical mutual convertibility or the capacity to stand for each other as expressed in speech and thought is crucial. When Aristotle speaks about the essence as τὸ τί ἦν εἶναι, he uses the term "ἀντικατηγορεῖται," and when he speaks about the essence as τί ἐστιν, he uses "ἀντιστρέφειν." The former verb means "to be mutually convertible," "to reciprocate," or "to accuse in turn, recriminate upon." And the latter means "to be convertible" or "to be conversely predicable," but also "to be interdependent" and "to stand in reciprocal relation."

The proper and the thing of which it is the proper thus properly "accuse" each other of being what they are and nothing more than that, or "call" each other in the public space of the agora by mutually appealing to each other in shared speech.

The proper by itself, then, is that which always belongs to all things or instances in a species, or, as Porphyry says, is "alone and all and always" (*Isag.* 12.13-22).⁴⁰ A famous example of Aristotle's is that for the human, proper is the ability to learn grammar (γραμματική), or, for Porphyry, laughing (τὸ γελαστικόν, *Isag.* 12.18; 22.5-6).⁴¹ The proper, then, cannot be the proper of any other subject (*Isag.* 20.18). And it is impossible for the same to be the proper for many different things, so that in every species there is a proper, and different species have different *propria* or ἴδια.⁴² In other words, each thing has *its own* proper, its proper proper. However, there can be several different mutually unrelated *propria*, as, for example, designing and sailing for humans.⁴³ The proper "converts" (ἀντιστρέφει) or is counterpredicated, mutually predicated, or said (ἀντικατηγορεῖται) with every thing in its species, so that the two can be substituted for each other logically and in speech: "if human, laughing; and if laughing, human" (*Isag.* 20.12); or "if horse, neighing; and if neighing, horse" (*Isag.* 12.21-22).

Without its proprium, the species and every item in it do not even subsist (οὐκ ὑφίσταται, *Isag.* 21.22-22.1) and are not properly thinkable. The difference is that the proper, as Porphyry explains, is logically and ontologically posterior, and the species is prior. Species exist or subsist before (προϋφέστηκεν) the proper, and the proper comes into being after (ἐπιγίνεται) species, "for there must be a human in order for there to be something laughing" (*Isag.* 20.18-20). In this sense, "species are always *actually* present in their subjects, whereas properties are something so *potentially*. For Socrates is always actually a human whereas he does not always laugh (even though he is always of a nature such as to be laughing)" (*Isag.* 20.20-22).

In the discussion of boredom, we need to stress two moments. First, the proprium and the subject are convertible or mutually substitutable, and thus stand in the reciprocal relation of pointing at and uniquely presupposing each other. If the proprium indeed does not refer to the essence or the "what" of the subject but still shows itself through that which cannot be ascribed to or thought in anything else, then we are each time playing the game of guessing "what is that that Xs?" What is it that laughs? Neighs? Is bored? We need to guess and disclose the only thing or subject that has this proprium as its unique property, without necessarily even knowing the essence of that subject. Writing books apparently does not belong to what we are as humans, but only we seem to be capable of it. We can say, thus, that boredom is the proper, the proprium, of the modern subject. If modern subject, bored; and if bored, modern subject.

And second, proprium does not properly express what its subject is. This is particularly relevant to the discussion of the modern subject, which *does not have any essence beyond that which it autonomously establishes or assigns to itself*. The modern subject that fights against "essentialism" and any attempts to objectivize itself, constructs itself as capable of establishing meanings and values that it finds appropriate at a particular moment of its historical presence. In this sense, nothing is essential to the modern subject, and everything is boring. As the proprium or ἴδιον, boredom is the expression of the "idiotism" of the modern subject, its proper "idiotic one's own." The *improper* is that which does not fit the subject's grandiose self-picture and is thus scandalous. In what follows, I will discuss the modern scandal, or rather scandals, in an attempt to show that it is *comedy* with its lack and disregard of autonomy that is capable of providing a viable alternative to the boring stiffness of the modern subject. It is the nonautonomous distributed and shared comic subject that is the properly improper "idiot," a fully private subject without the possibility of reaching out to others in the public, the critic of modern self-centeredness and exclusion of the other that pushes us to embrace boredom, the only excuse for which is its apparently being "proper" or most "profound."

The impossibility of mediation. Since the modern subject is always exposed to itself by itself and faces itself—and only itself—as its other in the mirror of its act of reflection, there is *no mediation* between S and S as ~S. The act of reflection establishes the identity of the identical to itself, which is not really an identity, because identity needs the distinction of the same and the same, which then becomes its other. In the absence of the other, the modern reflexive subject is incapable of mediation. The "≡" is itself not a mediation, a mediator, or an act of mediating but the expression of the modern subject's desperation over the inability to get through to the other.

Without mediation, the opposites have to coincide, because this amounts to being coming directly out of nonbeing, which is epistemologically, logically, and ontologically impossible. The critique of the absence of mediation as implied by the postulated but unthinkable coincidence of opposites is already waged by Aristotle against Plato.[44] The Platonic tradition of allowing for the immediate interaction of the opposites and their unmediated coincidence originates in the *dialectical* debate that searches for the understanding of a thing by reference to the opposites, which are taken not as mediated but rather as pointing toward a pass through the argument to the conclusion or the right definition.[45]

In Aristotle's logic, an opposite (ἀντικείμενον or ἀντίθεσις in Greek; *oppositum* in Latin) may mean either a *contrariety* (ἐναντίον; *contrarium*), which allows for mediation because it has an intermediate (μεταξύ) and is referable to an intermediate, that is, to an opposition-neutral substrate; or an opposite may also mean a *contradiction* (ἀντιφατικόν or ἀντίφασις; *contradictio*), which has no intermediate and allows for no mediation, that is, it arises when the opposites meet immediately.[46] Aristotle himself looks for the mediating and opposition-free (natural) substrate (ὑποκείμενον or *substratum*) or substance (οὐσία or *substantia*), which does not have an opposite. As a substrate, such a substance acts as a "third" that mediates between two opposites without, however, allowing them to merge.

The immediate coincidence of opposites amounts to the violation of the law of noncontradiction, which for Aristotle is unthinkable and impossible, and destroys being and thinking. Thus, the opposites cannot coexist as actual and should be thought of as *contrarieties* in relation to that which is.[47] But Plato and his followers (such as Nicolas of Cusa, Alexander Baumgarten, and Hegel) reject a third principle as the opposition-free substrate and thus think the unthinkable—the coincidence of opposites—is possible. However, such a coincidence is found only in nondiscursive reason and is invalid for discursive thinking, for which the logical laws and principles remain valid.

In ancient dialectical debate, the lack of mediation can still be considered a dialogical or eristic device that can either lead to the truth of the debated question or to the skeptical suspension of it. Yet in modernity the coincidence of the opposites becomes the prevalent tactic of the modern subject. In order to overcome the potential contradiction implied by the nonmediated identification of the opposites, one needs to overcome the finite point of view of the finite reason and identify it with the infinite reason, thus moving the perspective to infinity, where the impossible becomes possible. Then the infinite is the finite, the other is nonentity, *non-ens* (Baumgarten); the circle is the straight line (Nicolas of Cusa);[48] being is nothing (Hegel); war is peace (George Orwell). *Nothing*—which is not a thing but the lack of the other—stands between self and self as not-self. Nothing is between the modern subject and its reflected thought that becomes the law of the moral and physical world. Caught within the inexorable reflexivity, which becomes a sickness, the modern subject remains inescapably lonely, singular, and alone.

The impossibility of mediating the opposites within the overly reflexive, dialectically oriented thinking of the modern subject leads to their being perceived as unbridgeable, mutually exclusive, and complementary, and thus contradictory. In Nietzsche, the opposites become redressed and famously personified as Apollo and Dionysus, which oppose each other as the serene divinity of light to the ecstatic divinity of destruction. And yet, astonishingly, Nietzsche does not notice, or does not want to notice, that each one comprises the other within itself and thus possesses a dual nature. Apollo, then, is the keeper of harmony and the leader of the Muses; he is identified with the Sun, the source of life, and is also the protector of herds and a skilled physician capable of curing disease.[49] But the very same Sun can burn and be pernicious. When turning to the world with his other side, Apollo appears as "night-like," and turns into a destroyer who can also cause disease and put terror in people, and is capable of atrocious acts, such as flaying Marsyas.[50] He is also an arrow-shooter and a killer: he kills Python in Delphi, the sons of Niobe, cyclopes, and even his own lovers—Coronis and (accidentally) Hyacinth.[51] Dionysus, in turn, is ecstatic and can cause insanity, which is why he is associated with inebriation and always appears in the presence of wine and vine. But he also shows his other side, gentle and playful: as a child, Dionysus is often depicted as cheerfully playing with a satyr.[52]

Any attempt to overcome the same by the same without the mediation of the other only leads back to the same that has not even abandoned itself. The modern subject's attempt at a mediating way inevitably and tragically fails. The revolutionary burst of the *tiers état* does not mediate between the other two but annihilates and abolishes them. Boredom, then, can be understood as the rejected intermediate third of the tragic, unbridgeable opposition between the right and the wrong in the absence of the lost comic triad of the good, the bad, and the ugly boring that mediates between the two.

No place for imagination as mediating. Modern philosophy—in Descartes, Leibniz, Christian Wolff, Baumgarten, and Kant—still operates with mental faculties when it comes to cognition. The lack of mediation makes the modern subject conceive of its own cognition in terms of opposites—those between reason and sensation or rationalism and empiricism—and deny and abolish any faculty or operation(s) that would mediate, stand, or officiate between the two. In ancient philosophy, it was *imagination* that mediated between reason and sense perception, but the modern subject leaves no place for an in-between faculty, and hence does not really know where to place the imagination, looking in the most unexpected places for it, including the anonymous collective, social, and institutional imaginary.[53]

Aristotle already claims that imagination differs from both sense perception and discursive thinking.[54] Imagination is understood by Aristotle as a mental faculty or ability that is capable of discerning and telling the right from the wrong. Sensations and the thoughts that are properly thought are always true, because they show what they show and tell what they tell, so that error arises only in their (mis)interpretation or wrong connection. But the images of imagination are mostly false.[55] And yet, as Aristotle famously claims, one cannot even think without an image produced by the imagination.[56]

As a faculty, imagination is not just different from sensation and discursive reason or understanding—it is *intermediate* between the two. For Aristotle, imagination has its origin in sensation, which provides the model for inner imaginary visualization. At the same time, thinking is impossible without imagination, because imagination provides a kind of pictorial diagram in which thinking can then distinguish certain properties.[57] Imagination is thus not only different from sensation and thinking but also connects them, both separating and uniting the two.

Perhaps the best and most original illustration of the intermediate position of imagination is found in Proclus's commentary on the first book of Euclid. Following Aristotle, Proclus argues that imagination (φαντασία) is the intermediate cognitive faculty between sense perception (αἴσθησις) and discursive thinking (διάνοια). As for Aristotle, every faculty for Proclus is defined by its specific object. The objects of the highest cognitive faculty or reason (νοῦς) are the indivisible intelligible concepts (νοητά); the objects of διάνοια are discursive representations of the concepts, or definitions (λόγοι); and the objects of sense perception are the sense perceptions (αἰσθητά). The objects of imagination are images or φαντάσματα, which make the thinkable mentally representable or visualizable for the inner gaze of the mind. If we take the circle as an example, it is present for νοῦς as the indivisible concept, for διάνοια—as the definition ("the place of all the points equidistant from a given one"), and for the senses—as a physical circle drawn on a material surface. It is the circle in and for the imagination that is the perfectly round figure existing and "seen" as imaginary, for neither the concept nor the definition are circular and round (they do not have the property they describe), and the sensible representation is not round but is of an irregular shape that only resembles the circle. Therefore, the imaginary object is *intermediate* between the logical definition of the circle and its sensible representation.[58] This is why Proclus says that "mathematical being necessarily belongs neither among the first nor among the last and least simple of the kinds of being, but occupies the middle ground between the realities that are partless, simple, incomposite, and indivisible—and entities endowed with parts, and characterized by every variety of composition and division."[59] The intermediate imaginable (mathematical) objects are thus situated "in between" the thinkable entities and the physical things, insofar as the intermediate objects are more complex than the former but more precise than the latter. Contrary to Kant, for whom imagination works from the "bottom up," submitting the manifold sensible data to the bondage of the understanding, in Proclus imagination acts "top down," transmitting the concepts of discursive reason to the sensible representations.

In Proclus's account, like the thinkable and unlike the physical, the imaginable does not change over time, because its properties are univocally inscribed into its concept (εἶδος) and definition (λόγος). Yet like the physical and unlike the thinkable, the imaginary has parts and constituents and can be represented as a multiplicity of objects of the same kind (many circles); moreover, it can be mentally visualized as quasi-extended (as a circle). For this reason, Proclus even characterizes imagination as being a specific, "intelligible" matter, which is a sort of "screen" onto which discursive reasoning "projects" an abstract definition—λόγος, where it becomes visualized and "unfolded" and can be understood through a kind of picture (of the circle) "seen" or "drawn" in the imagination.[60]

As the middle between the faculties, imagination thus puts them in touch, mediating their otherwise broken and interrupted communication and facilitating their striving for knowledge, even if what we come to know still remains within pure appearances that are constructed according to the conceptual lawfulness of the modern subject's understanding.

The Cartesian treatment of imagination is exemplary of its modern fate. Hesitant about whether to locate the imaginable in the res extensa or in the res cogitans, Descartes cannot find a proper place for imagination. In the *Discourse*, imagination is portrayed as a "way of thinking"; in the *Meditations*, as an "ability to visualize inwardly"; and in the *Rules*, as a "mode of thinking involved in processing images of extended things."[61] And yet, there is a fundamental difficulty with Descartes's understanding of the imagination: if imagination represents a geometrical object, as it does in Proclus, then, as an object with immutable properties, it should belong to the res cogitans; but as an extended object, it should belong to the res extensa. Imagination, therefore, is at a complete loss and cannot be univocally located either in the thinkable (the nonextended) or the material (the extended). Imagination, then, has to be split in Descartes into the mental imagination as "imaginatio" and the corporeal imagination as "phantasia," but there is no explanation of their connection and interaction—no more than the interaction of the res cogitans and the res extensa. As a result, imagination is denied the mediating position within the order of cognitive faculties, cognition, and being.

Wolff and Baumgarten also deny imagination the mediating role in cognition, considering imagination, together with sensation, an "inferior" cognitive faculty, opposed to the "superior" faculty of understanding.[62] Kant still attempts to find a position for imagination in his theoretical philosophy as a pure transcendental scheme mediating between sensation ("intuition") and understanding ("spontaneity").[63] On this interpretation, imagination is a pure synthesis that binds plurality of sensation with the unity of thinking.[64] While sensation is an a priori manifold of pure intuition (many), imagination is the synthesis of this manifold (one-many), and only the concept of understanding gives this synthesis unity (one), which results in cognition and knowledge.[65] Because our intuitions are sensible for Kant, imagination belongs to sensibility; but because synthesis is an exercise of spontaneity, imagination as an a priori synthesis (figurative synthesis, *synthesis speciosa*) is also the expression of understanding. This is the imagination as transcendental, which has affinity with sensation (intuition) on the one hand, and with understanding on the other.[66]

However, imagination has no place whatsoever in Kant's practical philosophy and action, which epitomizes the role of the modern subject as sovereign and autonomous. For being within our power, "up to us" (ἐφ' ἡμῖν),[67] imagination might decide to declare itself free in representing the past as the (temporal) present, by making the absent the (ontological) present, and in this way imagine itself autonomous and independent of the supreme rule of the modern reason that, by legislating universally binding rational laws, carefully guards and defends its royal autonomy in the kingdom of (moral) ends against incursions of its subordinate.[68] The modern subject wants to determine and identify itself as pure reason in the absence of the mediating acts and faculties. Such reason is an imaginative and productive fantasy of the modern subject in the Kantian sense: it is a priori (is purely rational and not empirical) and spontaneous (follows the logic and prescriptions of reason itself as discursive understanding). Yet both the a priori quality and spontaneity of productive imagination are creatively productive inventions of the reason that imagines itself to be pure. This is the autonomous, self-legislating, bored reason.

Being a moralist, for whom freedom consists in following the strict rules that modern autonomous reason establishes for itself, Kant is afraid of the unrestricted freedom to do what one wants, even within the virtual reality of the imagination. For when the imagination disobeys the rational laws, it cannot function properly, and thus destroys the conditions of the possibility of cognition. Therefore, one has to discipline and punish the productive imagination, and let it be productive or spontaneous only within the limits of cognition.

Hence, the entirely unrestricted productive imagination is suspect not only because it is *cognitively impossible*—but because it is also *morally suspicious*. Such an imagination can—and inevitably will—go askew and become willful, following and exemplifying Willkür, the capacity to act against *any* reasons, however strong and rational they might be, and thus against moral rational will. In fact, to the extent that the productive imagination always acts according to the concepts of understanding, it does *not* act at will.[69] Productive imagination as entirely independent of understanding is not only cognitively useless but also morally doubtful.

In moral matters there is thus no place for the playful imagination: "We play with the imagination frequently and gladly," says Kant, "but imagination (as fantasy) plays just as frequently with us, and sometimes very inconveniently."[70] Kant is wary of morally unacceptable consequences of unrestrained play that could represent and imagine reprehensible behavior and unwanted examples. The stern moral censor in Kant, which he takes to be the autonomous and rational self-established law, shies away from the public display of any morally suspect patterns of behavior.

Kant speaks about the *free play* of imagination and understanding, which produces the pleasure of experiencing a beautiful thing but which, however, should always be bound by rational norms, because, again, imagination has an intrinsic affinity with understanding.[71] But in the game with and against the understanding, imagination can seem to play freely and creatively but always by the book written by its opponent, who is the main player and the judge at the same time.

Moreover, imagination can easily produce seductive erotic images, of which Kant is apparently scared, because they bring an unlawful enjoyment. One should deter and hide this illegitimate imagining behind the veil of rational norms. Kant is afraid that imagination can produce something attractive yet embarrassing, which might shake the world of ends, well built on the firm foundation of moralistic prescriptions. Such an imagination can easily go beyond the norms and become seductive and tainted by an illicit enjoyment—particularly by representations of sexual love where imagination "enjoys walking in the dark."[72] A way out, then, is to play with subtle hints and innuendos, the response to which in modest and polite bourgeois society should be "[bringing] out a smile" and hiding the inappropriate behind the hypocritical cultivated acting.[73] The possibility of having erotic phantasies and colorful dreams is deeply troubling to the modern subject, who, as universal and transcendental, should not have any such deviations.[74] This is why Kant speaks about the necessity of the culture of imagination, for the uncultivated uncontrolled imagination is dangerous.[75] Kant thus keeps struggling with the freedom of imagination, which he perceives as unwarranted and seductive, trying to put the productive imagination under the yoke of the rational (understanding) and the moral (will).

... Bored by the necessity of staying in his room under house arrest and hence confined to *imaginary* epic travel across a very limited space, Xavier de Maistre says that the best remedy from boredom is books, writing, and above all, poking the fire: "A good fire, a few books, some quills—what excellent antidotes to boredom! And what a pleasure then to forget your books and quills and to poke the fire relinquishing your thoughts to some pleasant meditation—or composing some rhymes to amuse your friends: the hours slide over you and fall silently into eternity, and you do not even feel their melancholy passing."[76] Being alone in a solitary confinement inevitably causes boredom in all of its avatars: of duration, repetition, and odium. Reading and writing are the distractions that can ease the pain of boredom for a while, but even they are eventually abandoned as artificial and artful yet inefficient remedies. This is exactly what Descartes also does in his *Meditations*: abandoning reading and writing, which are abundant in doubtful transmitted opinions, he turns to the spontaneity of thought, which, however, eventually also falls prey to boredom and is suspended. The presence of nature as the only other with which one can communicate by poking it remains the last resort against boredom. But the fire is eventually extinguished, and one is left in complete darkness in silent solitary meditation where the only other is the *imaginary* other of oneself who cannot but think its own thinking while thinking itself.

No other is really there. As de Maistre notes, the *other* in Plato is said to be matter (*Tim.* 48e–53b). The other of the nonboring communication with the flame comes to an end, and the only other that is left, as de Maistre ironically observes, is the beast (*bête*) of our body that is

> accused of I know not of how many dreadful things, quite inappropriately I am sure, since it is as incapable of feeling as it is of thinking. The real culprit is the beast, that sentient being utterly distinct from the soul, the veritable *individual* that has its own separate existence, tastes, inclinations and will, and is superior to other animals only because it happens to be a little more well-bred and endowed with more perfect organs.[77]

Body as the sleeping, but more often wakeful, beast makes its repetitive claims and troubling incursions onto our allegedly independent autonomous self and "pesters us in the most distressing manner." And yet matter and nature are now mere constructions of the regal self. So the beast of the body is quickly bound and put under full rational and volitional control, becoming a rather boring residue of the imaginary res extensa under the full command of the legislative autonomous subjectivity.

Thus, from the point of view of the modern subject, imagination is highly suspect and is denied the role of a mediator, for it does not fit within the dichotomies of thought/sensibility or freedom/nature. Since imagination does not provide knowledge and does not pertain to moral action, and since it can imagine the nonexistent and make the absent present, imagination is doomed to be "impure" and deceptive. With the modern loss of mediation between the opposites, imagination as a mediating faculty is forever gone. From now on, in science, politics, and art, the modern subject can think what it cannot imagine.[78]

Boredom and the lack of mediation. The lack of mediation induces boredom. Indeed, the unmediated opposites appear as the other of each other, and yet for the modern subject there is no real other but only the perennial same of itself. Being always the same as the unmediated reflexive same of itself, the lonely modern subject, S, appears in the form of the other, ~S, who is reflexively the nonother, ~ ~S or the same same S. The unmediated opposites, therefore, are the *same* to each other and hence to themselves.

The mediation between the opposites can be established in many different and fruitful ways, which could generate a diversity of thought, and of cultural, social, political, and artistic life. As such, the mediation is nonboring, because it allows one to avoid the monotonous repetition of the same in the inescapable reflection of the same lonely subject who takes itself (seriously and tragically) as the other while still remaining the same, making boredom an inevitable proprium of itself.[79]

Hence, in the logic of the unmediated opposites, their struggle does not lead to the eventual elimination of the domination of one over the other but to the reversal of the roles in such domination. Marx detects this in his analysis of pauperism in nineteenth-century England, where the two opposing parties try to blame each other and offer opposite solutions to the problem of the poor, none of which really work. The solution, then, would be building a completely classless society in which the poor will cease to exist, but this would suggest the elimination of the power based on unmediated opposites by the same kind of power.

Philosophically and politically, this would amount to the suicide of the modern subject, which, as said, it tries to commit by staging a deliberate revolt or rebellion against itself.[80]

The lonely, autonomous, overly reflective subject, devoid of imagination that could mediate between sense-perception and reason, is deeply bored and thus attempts to get rid of itself and the social and natural world it has produced. Yet each time the attempt at self-elimination fails, because the modern subject does not even have the other from whose standpoint it could ultimately banish itself.

CHAPTER 4

Being and Boredom

After a historical reconstruction and a critical digression, it is now the right moment for a "theory" of boredom and its primary categories, which might allow us to come up with a more nuanced understanding of boredom, its different forms, and their mutual relations.

In order to be able to speak about something and somehow think of it, we need to make distinctions. The very basic one is setting a this against a that. The act of such setting generates the basic primitive opposition that then can be mediated by a third term, which, in turn, can get distinguished from another one that can be taken as its opposite. The newly produced opposites can be mediated again, opposed to a new term, mediated, and so on. The repeated process of opposition and mediation can lead to a complex system of (mythological) entities, or to a beautifully and impeccably organized, yet rather boring, system of studiously arranged (philosophical) categories that all follow from one source and do not miss anything that can be possibly thought.[1]

Historically, this basic initial opposition has been variously described as the distinction of the two hands ("on the one hand—and on the other hand"), as the left and right, right and wrong, even and odd, etc. Philosophically, the distinction has been set in various ways in terms of opposites: as one (ἕν) (identity, positive, affirmation, finite, limited, same) and as many (πολλά) (difference, negative, negation, indefinite, unlimited, other).

Since every surviving philosophical term has already been much used, is heavily historically loaded, and comes with a pedigree, often changing its meaning depending on the context of a discussion at a particular period and subtext that mostly remains undetected, it is difficult and perhaps even impossible to appropriate it for one's own purposes. The alternative is to invent a new term and introduce it into the debate. This seems possible, and yet even such apparently newborn concepts always unwittingly bear the heritage of the entire tradition that generates them. In this sense, it is never possible to disentangle new notions entirely from their tradition. We cannot get consent from other thinkers from different epochs and should not go along with the consensus of the current philosophical community that has influence but no ultimate authority over our thinking. Making something one's own that belongs to somebody else without the other's permission is theft. This could also be said of concepts. The quotation marks do not really help, because no thinking can move within the quotation limits, and instead needs to obliterate them if it wants to liberate itself and be original, that is, to go to a simple truth of things, rather than to that of quotes and the infinite rebound of reflections, which inevitably distort beyond recognition the unpretentious and simple, and thus original, thought. Therefore, even a quotation is theft. Every appropriation, and not only that of Proudhonian private property, is thus a theft, and hence every appropriation is misappropriation, not (only) on moral but also on hermeneutical and systematic grounds.[2]

In particular, "identity" and "difference" have been appropriated by Deleuze, who has argued that difference always already precedes identity.[3] His intention might be motivated by the desire to see things as different, anew, and in a strange kind of way, which, however, was already suggested by Viktor Shklovsky's concept of estrangement.[4] Estrangement or defamiliarization (остранение) allows us to see reality differently, the familiar things in an unfamiliar way (which, for Shklovsky, is the main move of modernism), rather than seeing unfamiliar, new, and invented things, which can also be new concepts, in a familiar way. The one and many, the limited and unlimited, and the finite and the infinite have a strong affinity with the Platonic tradition, which is helpful in thinking about ontology, especially the ontology based in mathematical thought.[5]

Yet I will not be using the concept of identity and difference, because, with Aristotle and against Deleuze, I take identity to be a *relation*, πρός τι.[6] There should be something that will be thought and described as identical to itself in the relation to itself. Identity as ταὐτόν is the equality of S to S, S=S, which is a relation between S and S as itself. The difference comes once S is considered not only identical to itself but also different to itself in the act of the identification or relation to itself as itself, αὐτό. While S is identical to itself in relation to itself, it can be the same without a relation to itself. As Heidegger observes, "The formula A=A speaks of equality. It doesn't define A as the same."[7] Identity is the narcissism of the relational identification of S≡S without assuming the equation of identification ≡ as the mediating term. Identity is an *immediate* reflectivity without the possibility of mediation. A not yet clarified "itself" has to predate identity, which is thus not an originary term. This is what the modern subject is: a pure identity before identity that searches for a difference that the subject establishes as *the* difference to itself from within itself. Only then can the modern autonomous subject be satisfied in considering itself an unmediated reflective being that has now assured its being as identity.

In this sense, difference is not a pair category or an opposite of identity. Identity *is*, insofar as it is established or affirmed by the subject in an act of "pure" thought (unblemished by the other) that coincides with an act of rational will. Identity is its own difference. Or, rather, the identity of the modern subject is *indifference*, since it is not different from itself in the absence of the other. All of its differences are indifferent. Hence, the identity of the modern subject is established by nondistinction as not-other, which is thus indefinite. As the indefinite not-other of any other, it has an unrestricted propensity to understand itself as infinite, as *non aliud*.[8] In this sense, Descartes's insistence on the distinction between the finite human ego and the infinite divine thinking is just a further unmediated self-reflective "othering" of the self that has no ground besides its initial unmediated identity, which is maintained and safeguarded with much effort and great care.

Same and other. I will go down the trodden path of using the concepts of "same" and "other," which have been much used, perhaps overused and even abused up to the point of making many of their nuances almost obliterated. We thus need to begin with some further distinctions.

(A) Same and other are mutually related as *opposites*. As such, they may be taken either as unmediated, and thus mutually exclusive, antiphatic contradictories—or as enantiatic mediated contrarieties. The possibility of mediation is fundamental for the discussion of boredom. Because, as I have argued, modernity expels the mediating structures in being and cognition, the same and other have to be mutually exclusive. The modern subject is same without other, an other which it takes to be pure externality, assigned to the world and the other self, the existence of which still needs to be assured from within the same. There is no place left for the other of either another person or of nature, which become a pure construction of the same self of the subject. The otherness or alterity is a task to be accomplished by the subject, which nevertheless always remains within the pure sameness. The monological, lonely, tragic subject always faces the prison of itself, of its own owned and appropriated autonomous self, the self-imposed bondage translated into and expressed as its proprium, or boredom.

(B) "Other," as was said, can be taken in two different ways: as the exclusive other, one of the two (*heteros*/ἕτερος/*alter*), or as the inclusive other, one of a number (*allos*/ἄλλος/*alius*). Depending on whether we take other as heteros or as allos, the resulting ontological, ethical, and political picture differs substantially.

(C) In contradistinction to identity and difference, which are set in relation to each other, I take same and other not as relational but as terms that can be considered on their own yet still capable of being in relation to each other as circumscribed by *mediation*. However, the mediation of same and other is not an additional term but the one that is determined by same and other in their relatedness. I will establish the relation between same and other in three steps, which will show the relatedness between same and other as necessarily *reflective*.

Other of the other of the other. (1) Let us begin with one term. No relation can be established here. Same : same is tautologically same. S≡S, and there is no other to it. The modern subject is pure same. Yet, without other, same is not reflective and is undistinguishable from itself and hence is nothing.

Other: other is just other with nothing other than it. But nothing is nothing. O≡O. There is no same and no other to nothing. Hence, nothing is not unique and not singular. There can be no identity and no distinction to nothing, as there can be no identity and no distinction to other. In this sense, pure other is nothing.

Since the modern subject is exclusive of any other, the (Levinasian) Other in its absolute otherness is transcendent to the same—it cannot be reached or communicated with. For it cannot be related to the same as equal, to other as another, but only as constituted through an unconditioned ethical obligation in the face of the unseen and unthinkable, the superabundant radical Other. In fact, this Other coincides with, and is indistinguishable from, the same, and is the same same but only redressed, since such Other is also a construction of the modern subject, although now not in the realm of nature but in ethics, where the radical Other is constituted through an ethical call in the face of the unseen and unthinkable, the transcendent radical Other.[9]

(2) Two terms arise when we recognize the possibility of a not yet mediated relation to itself. This is the *unmediated reflection* that establishes the primary difference that can be first thought as a kind of intentionality or belonging. Similar

to the distinction between being and being-something, or being and being-of, it is same and same-of, and other and other-of. Grammatically, it is expressed by the distinction between nominative and genitive cases. This is same of the same. But same of the same is still same.

Similarly, we can establish an other of other. Yet, an other of other is not other—but same. Therefore, the unmediated reflection of same of same and other of other is not symmetrical. But it establishes for the first time the oppositional relation of same and other. They are mutually related and can be translated into each other: same into other, and other into same.

(3) Finally, three terms come together in the full *mediated reflection*: same of the same of the same. Since same of the same is same, then same of the same of the same is still same. Same here reflectively mediates itself by implicit reference to other. With the other as its opposite, it is exactly the same: other of the other of the other. Since other of the other is same, then other of the other of the other is other. Thus, other, too, reflectively mediates itself by implicit reference to same. The mediated reflection of three terms thus leads back to its original term by implicit reference to its opposite.

In this way, we have established the mediated reflected connection between same and other in three movements: (1) Same. Other. (2) Same of the same. Other of the other. (3) Same of the same of the same. Other of the other of the other.

Corollary on being. Thus, same is never isolated from other, but the two are always related. However, it is important to note that in the unmediated reflection same *can* be reached from, and thought of as, other (as other of the other), but other *cannot* be reached from same (same of the same is still same). In this respect, although same and other imply, need, and presuppose each other, and are dependent on and mediated by each other in the mutual reflective relation, the two are *not symmetrical*. For same can be thought as other of the other—but other cannot be thought as same of the same. In this respect, other takes precedence in this relation. The other can be considered to represent the primary negativity, which allows for the other of the other that is not other. The negativity of the other suffices in order to establish and reach both same as other of the other—and itself as other of the other of the other. Yet the positivity of the same cannot achieve the same.

In this sense, one can say that the primary negativity is inextricably inherent in and bound to other. Other, then, is constitutive (as other) and generative (as other-of), not only of *what can be thought* but also of *what is*. If being is a mediated reflective synthesis of same and other, then it is fully determined and constituted by the mediated reflection. If being *is*, it is reflectively mediated. Being, then, *is* other of the other of the other.

With the third step, same of the same of the same, and other of the other of the other, we have reached the end of the mediated reflective constitution of what can be thought and what is. This end is also the beginning of the whole structure of (1)–(3), so it can be understood and completed as fully reflective and mediated within itself with reference to same and other. Having reached this end, we do not need to go any further, since any continuation of same of the same of the same of the same . . . , and other of the other of the other of the other . . . leads back, as it is easy to see, to either (2) or (3). Three terms of the same or other suffice to constitute the full mediated reflective completion in the constitution of being, of what is and what can be thought. In "same of the same of the same," same is its own mediation and an implicit reference to other. And in "other of the other of the other," other is its own mediation and an implicit reference to same.

Therefore, one should not start (and end) with the isolated same, which is what the modern subject is. Such same is always and inevitably the same without other that can only come as a normative demand of the same, which does not really produce the other. The three movements of the reflective relation between same and other show that the same cannot be without its other. The two have to be mediated by, and be inclusive of, each other. Yet the modern subject is one and unique, and thus has no other, in the absence of which it is exclusive of anything or anyone else, and hence is forever the same. The other is then just the same, and not the same with others (who always come in the plural), because others are absent from the singular self-producing and self-legislating same. It is the modern subject's inevitable destiny to be and remain the same that wants to produce or establish the other by its alleged power of negativity, which, in fact, is the power of productive imagination. Being inevitably only the same, the modern subject does not allow for the mediation of itself by itself in thinking, and thus is the same of the same, which is the same. The same of the same is boredom, which means that the modern subject is in boredom, boring, bored. This same without other is prison, where everything is always and inescapably the same for life, is the same same, has to repeat itself again and again. In the absence of reflective mediation, same of the modern subject finds its proper expression through its proprium—boredom. In the absence of other, the third step of the fully mediated reflection cannot be achieved.

For the modern subject it is therefore always meaningful to continue the chain of boring iterative genitives of "same of the same of the same of the same..." This is the recursive *repetition* that never ends, constructing and reproducing itself according to a self-established rule, starting from a self-posited origin or basis. Such a perpetually reproduced calculable repetition is only possible because the modern subject in its "pure thinking" always takes interest in itself as the other in the hope of generating something new. Yet in the absence of other who is only an imaginary projection of the same without other, it only produces the same, which is same of the same, indistinguishable from same of the same of the same, etc. In this unrelenting repetition, the same is not mediating between the same and the same, because there is only the same without the other. Repetition is the inevitable predicament of the modern subject and is translated into boredom. Without other, repetition is always repetition (is always repetition ... etc.). But, in fact, repetition is never a repetition because in order to be recognized as such, repetition should at least implicitly refer to and presuppose other. In the absence of other, repetition is not-same, which is not yet the other. In the absence of other, there is no same, and repetition is just the same of the same of the same of the same ... which is not same. In the absence of other, the modern subject faces its inescapable tragic condition of self-abandonment to itself and of its unrecognized inability to come to an end and even commit suicide. Such repetition without an end is boredom. Boredom, then, is the absence of the mediated reflection of same and other.

Repetition thus becomes constitutive of the modern subject.[10] Since the modern subject cannot achieve other, it is doomed to always neurotically recur to repetition, which, however, is never the same, for it is other without the same, and thus other to the other that is not the same but other to other to the other to the other ... etc. Hence, the modern subject is same without not same, and thus not same, because for same to be same it needs to be reflectively mediated by the other. Therefore, always being in violation of the principle of noncontradiction, the modern subject *both* is and is not what it thinks it is.[11] Its *sum*, then, is established by its thinking as its other, which is not the other, and thus as *nonsum*. What it has ultimately achieved, is *cogito ergo sum sed simul non sum*.

Negativity as productive. As we have seen, same and other are equal in their ontological standing, insofar as being is a synthesis of same and other. Yet they are not symmetrical, because other implies and refers to same, while same only repeatedly returns to itself. For this reason, same can be associated with positivity, while other with negativity. It is then the negativity of other that is productive, bringing same out of its status quo. It is because of this negativity that there is something rather than nothing.[12]

Here, we can go back to the distinction between *heteros*, the exclusive one of the two, and *allos*, the inclusive one of many, which has been introduced in the discussion of allonomy. In its negativity, other splits itself into the other and another. And while the other of *heteros* is the same of other, an other of *allos* is not (quite) the same and is thus "slightly" other.

The otherness within other itself allows not just for the two concepts of same and other but for a whole plurality of *many* others. As the other other to itself, as *heteros*, other constitutes the mediated reflective system of same and other, which constitute being. But it is as another other, as *allos*, that other allows for the nonboring well-being in the allonomy with others who are integrated in a shared comic activity, and thus for various forms of moral and political interaction and constitution (see "Allonomy," chapter 3).

Derivation of same and other. But where does the necessity of the distinction and of the relationship between same and other come from? One could say that it is established, as Aristotle already understood, by the structure of *logos*, both as language and as reasoning. This relation can be determined in three ways: first, *affirmatively*, insofar as the *logos* presupposes the S-P, subject-predicate distinction, which can be taken as the P of S in terms of "other (P) of the same (S)" and "same (P) of the other (S)."

Second, the relation between same and other is established *negatively*, from the described triple reflective motion of mediation: of other of the other of the other as same—and of same of the same of the same as other, which was discussed above.

And third, the relation can be established *interrogatively*, insofar as the *logos* implies the question "What is the P of S?," which can be understood as a logical version of the primordial question "What is it?" In a distilled philosophical form, the question presupposes the essence ("what") / existence ("is") distinction, and the pragmatic reference to that which contains them ("it").[13] Interrogatively, in the simple original question we are not yet committed to any theoretical and practical position, but both same and other are already implicit in the very act of questioning. One can say that the fundamental ontological categories of the other and the same are already present in the act of not-understanding of a this, which results in questioning the this and reference to that, and the subsequent establishing of a manifold (theoretical, practical, productive) relation, a synthesis, between the other and the same.

In this sense, modern philosophy comes not out of wondering but out of the sense of marvel: not from "to wonder" but from "I wonder."[14] Not "I doubt, therefore I am" (Augustine) or "I think, therefore I am" (Descartes)—but "I wonder, therefore I am."[15] "I wonder" establishes the possibility and in fact the necessity of the question, "What is it?," where "what" comes with "I wonder that," and "is" comes with "I wonder if."

Thus, both other and same as its other are buried in *logos*. Despite their simplicity, same and other are irritating to the modern subject who rids itself of the other by inventing new idiosyncratic logics where either the subject is itself deduced from the other (of the indefinite being) and is thus claimed to be the embodiment of the inherent negativity (in Hegel), or by getting rid of *logos* altogether (in Heidegger). It is Frege and the contemporary analytic tradition that come to (re)introduce various forms of logic based on same and other—from formal (in Frege) to modal (in Plantinga)—back into philosophy as its very core.

Three forms of boredom. So far, I have outlined a conceptual history of boredom (how it has been thought of), established its relation to the modern subject as its proprium (what boredom is), and introduced the categories of same and other (by which boredom can be thought). Now, we can finally have a closer look at what boredom is and how it can be understood.

Besides Heidegger's and Benjamin's accounts of the types of boredom, there are a number of typologies of boredom, both in philosophy and psychology. Most of them follow the Prodican-Aristotelian program of classification, which is based on the distinction of various ways in which a concept or a phenomenon is mentioned and used, or "said in many ways," without, however, giving an account of why there are exactly as many different meanings to it and without attempting to derive these meanings from a common ground.[16] Such are, for example, the kinds of boredom based on the distinction of its cognitive causes of inattention, hyperactivity, impulsivity, and executive dysfunction;[17] the distinction between agitated boredom (once every attempt to get rid of it fails) and apathetic boredom (once one has no desire to change one's dull and monotonous environment);[18] trait boredom (as chronic propensity to experience boredom) and state boredom (as the actual experience of boredom);[19] the types of boredom corresponding to different degrees of valence and arousal, such as indifferent, calibrating, searching, reactant, and apathetic boredom;[20] or situative, satiated, existential, and creative boredom;[21] and others. In what follows, I will also offer an account of different types of boredom, which, however, I will try to explain by reference to the fundamental ontological categories of same and other that underlie the discussion and the very existence of boredom.

Boredom changes our experience of the world, of the other, and of ourselves (of our thinking, perception, and imagination). We can distinguish *three* forms of boredom: as same without other; as other without same; and as same and other as both present to each other yet ultimately incapable of a mutual relation or communication.

(I) *Boredom as same without other: long while and duration.* The boredom of same without other (let's call it boredom I) is the expression of the modern subject in its solitude and isolation as the exclusion of the other and another. This is the boredom of pure duration without end and without an end that the isolated "pure" thought could happen to achieve. This is the *long while*. This is the unhurried but not leisurely *Langeweile*, the geological *longue durée*. As such, it embraces all three of Heidegger's kinds of boredom, including the "deep" boredom as the most intimate and fundamental expression of our fundamental "mood" in which we are called by being itself as time and which we thus have to embrace. However, I take the Heideggerian "deep boredom" to be the expression of the same same of the modern subject that wants to get rid of itself in listening to the "call" of other-as-being. Yet this other that summons us to attend to it is still a wishful projection and invention of the modern subject that intends to suspend itself by glorifying and accepting itself as the unreachable other, who indeed cannot be reached.

The long while of boredom I is duration as the endless present of the same, which is eternity without change.[22] It is the eternal boring present, an utter stillness where nothing happens. As pure duration, boredom I is the unbearableness of waiting—for anything and thus for nothing. The duration has to be endured, since it makes everything unendurably slow by stopping life. The short time is long, yet the long time passes in the blink of an eye.[23] One of the main preoccupations of modern culture, then, is to unslow this duration, which leads, as Koselleck has argued, to the equally repugnant constant acceleration of modern life.[24]

In the absence of other, this enduring anticipation is the never-fulfilled waiting for Godot, the promised yet never accomplished Heideggerian search for the meaning of temporality, which is that of being itself. Boredom I is the death of the modern subject in the long while, while the subject is still and forever alive. It signifies the simultaneous necessity and impossibility of death in the absence of the other, which makes the boring endurance of the incessant duration of life profoundly tragic.[25]

The boredom of same without other as uninterrupted (long, tiresome, unceasing) duration is translated into weariness, uneasiness, and tragic suffering that come out of the modern subject's incapacity for reaching out for the other. Here, boredom comes out of a constraint, which is perceived as external: no freedom to leave in the absence of other. Paradoxically, the utter loneliness brought about by the exclusion of other results at the same time in seclusion, which comes as a sense of absolute security, which results in the serious but utterly boring business of guarding and protecting oneself from and against oneself. Boredom I is the indication of the self-imposed exile and self-isolation in the castle of the royal self, which is the prison of same without other, which makes the intended security of self-preservation forever insecure. Such a self is not only utterly boring but also unachievable, because in the absence of the other it is always the same and yet not the same, since same can be the same only in (at the very least, an implicit) relation to other.

Yet boredom I differs from tiredness, because one can be bored without being tired and tired without being bored. And the physiological reaction to being tired or stressed is expressed in all kinds of animals as *yawning*, which is also social and communicative at the same time, being "contagious" even between the species and thus expressing and communicating one's state to others at a bodily level.[26] As such, yawning contrasts and complements equally communicative and "contagious" ways of expressing well-being—smiling and laughter. But these forms of communication are only meaningful for beings that are not lonely—that communicate and live in a constantly renewable dialogue with each other, with themselves, and with the world.

In a different sense, boredom I is "contagious" too: it gets passed around very quickly. As Friedrich Schlegel observes, boredom is akin to stuffy air: both build up very quickly once we get stuck in a confined space with no ventilation provided by the flux of new and fresh air.[27] However, the contagiousness of boredom is of a different kind: it separates us from others and makes one confined to the prison of the modern ego, in which everyone is locked up in a noncommunicative space that we still share, and in which we contaminate each other with boredom.

Boredom I testifies to the modern incapacity of being as being in dialogue, to the extent that dialogue presupposes and needs others. This is always a conversation with oneself, which means the impossibility of dialogue in the absence of a real other. Moreover, if dialogue is based on interruption, the boredom of self-isolation is a painful monotony of the same uninterrupted enduring sound produced by the isolated self.

Once same is posited without other, the modern subject can only perceive itself as "pure" and "untainted" by the other, which gets translated into "pure" thought that wills itself as pure autonomous rational will. But such "pure" reason remains unreachable and transcendent to itself, insofar as it originally arises out of the unmediated reflection; while in order to be able to think anything at all, to "anythink," thinking has to start with establishing differences by mediation. The inability, and at the same time the necessity, of differentiation, leads to the introduction of bizarre neologisms, which, however, still do not release the solitary tragic thinking from the anxiety and pain of the boredom of the eternal recurrence of the same. The inevitable narcissism of "pure" thought is not even enjoyable but is altogether boring, because the isolated lonely subject cannot even perceive itself or have an image of itself, insofar as such an image would require mediated reflection: the mirror of the other and the mediation of the "look" of the thought that thinks itself as other, and thereby different. The monotonous same without other remains forever tragically inaccessible to itself, which the lonely subject takes very seriously—all too seriously. Seriousness is a fundamental flaw of modern philosophy. But we should not take ourselves too seriously. Solemn seriousness is ultimately ridiculous in its being: not only utterly boring but also deeply (unnoticeably) ironic in the subject's narcissistic incapacity for (self-)irony, which requires distancing from oneself by a mediated reflection in the other.

The boredom of immortality. As I have argued, the modern Cartesian subjectivity is tragic in its loneliness, even if Descartes intends to provide a proof of the immortality of the soul, thus establishing a comic good ending to life. Yet such an immortality is the immortality of utter boring loneliness and thus of eternal suffering.

As Erich Fromm observed, boredom is "one of the greatest tortures." This means that hell, the place of suffering and torture, *is* boredom, from which there is no escape in modern society.[28] If hell is the place of the eternity of infinite duration in which the same Sisyphian events return, again and again in the eternal recurrence and repetition of the same, then the boredom of the unending enduring same is infernal. But the unending duration is immortality. Therefore, one should wish to get rid of immortality. In hell, one wishes for death, but one cannot die. This, as we have seen, is precisely the situation of the modern subject who immortalizes itself in its universality and autonomy.

Referring to Karel Čapek's play *Věc Makropulos*, in which the main character becomes immortal by taking an elixir of life, Bernard Williams has suggested that immortality would be utterly boring, because of its utter repetitiveness.[29] Yet, unlike the modern subject, Čapek's character is still capable of achieving death by refusing to take the elixir of life and destroying its formula, which makes the play into a comedy (which Čapek claims it to be), since the termination of unending suffering from the boredom of immortality is indeed a good ending. Since its publication, Williams's argument provoked quite a bit of commentary and debate.[30] Hans Jonas, too, has forcefully argued against the indefinite prolongation of life, stressing the blessing of mortality allowing for the growth of the young and the new.[31] Before Williams, the same claim was made by Schelling who, together with the Romantics, could not miss the centrality of boredom in the project of modernity. As Schelling observes, the angel is the most bored of all beings, because there is nothing really new for the angel who already knows everything that has happened in history.[32] The eternal knowledge of all things is perennially boring. No wonder that for Nietzsche even the gods cannot overcome boredom.[33] This suggests that not only hell but also paradise is utterly boring, in which nothing changes and everything stands still in its constant frozen inertial motion, because the eternal life is ever repeating and provides nothing new, nothing that could make its inhabitants engaged with each other. There is no change of seasons either in hell or in paradise.

In Mitchell Leisen's and Rod Serling's short film, *Escape Clause*, a hypochondriac man makes a pact with the devil to exchange his soul for immortality and indestructibility, with a clause that, if he asks for it, he can voluntarily die a quick and painless death.[34] When the man is bored, he tries everything as a distraction, yet nothing works and nothing hurts him. When his wife accidentally falls from the roof, he reports to the police that he has killed her, hoping to get executed by the electric chair. Yet the judge gives him life in prison without parole, which means eternal and inescapable boredom. After this, the man quickly summons the devil and then dies: boredom made him immortal and then killed him.

However, immortality is boring only from the perspective of the modern subject who wishes for death but cannot find it, because it cannot reach out for the other and is thus incapable of being as being in dialogue. This is the modern understanding of life, and of immortality as autonomous seclusion that makes life boring in separation from the other. But if life is being as communication and exchange with others, it is immortal to the extent that it keeps going and reproducing itself dialogically and unfinalizably, without repetition, and thus never getting bored.

(II) *Boredom as other without same: repetition and privation.* The boredom of other without same, or boredom II, comes out of the modern subject's inability to get to the other. The other, then, cannot be thought or communicated with but only postulated or required as a (or the) moral unconditional claim at best. The other falls apart and can never be grasped as the other of the same in their mutual relation, because there is no such relation. While the modern subject names itself in the first-person singular—always the first and only singular, the other cannot even be named. The other is anonymous.

Other is absent in its presence. We can put a face on the other but the other still remains elusive, nameless, and excluded from any narrative, and thus is ahistorical. In its solitude and isolation, the modern subject is same that positively excludes the other as negativity and becomes its own negation. Hence, other is a negation and exclusion of same, but not in the same way. Other without same is a *privation* of same, a negative exclusion as the *privation of inclusion*.

Contrary to boredom I, which was characterized as a long while, boredom II is a *short while*. In its shortness, which cannot even be detected or properly determined, because it would then need to be referred to the other of the other as the same, this "while" can only be considered a *repetition* of the indistinguishable others as another and another and another.... The boredom of other without same, then, is pure repetition: that it *is* repetition that can be understood, but not of *what* it is the repetition. In the absence of same, it cannot be considered neurotic, because this would be the repetition of the same, while in the short while there is no same. Metaphorically, it is not even a heap, which is one out of many, but rather a congestion or squeeze of the undistinguished and undistinguishable repetitive others that are not others in the absence of same.

Boredom II is the expression of the flight from the same that cannot be stopped or fixed. It is translated into the homelessness of the modern subject that cannot find a proper place or time for itself anymore and anywhere in the world in the very absence of the world, which requires both same and other in their diverse and multiple connections and interactions. Repetition becomes a common modernistic trope for the expression of profound boredom. No wonder, then, that modernism in literature and philosophy pays particular attention to repetition as a way of "estrangement," of disclosing by unfamiliar means the boring familiar same as other without same.[35] Heidegger seems to have understood this, since he keeps repeating the formula "it is boring," "*es ist einem langeweilig*," again and again in his analysis of boredom (GM 224 et al.). Yet he never explains the significance of repetition, since he is bound to his program of the explication of time as a mysterious and deep underlying essence of our existence.

Similar to boredom I, in boredom II there is no security of being in one's place, for there is no place to be, and the change of other to another is not a travel but an indistinguishably repetitive floating in the undetermined. This is other of the other of the other of the other ... repeated indefinitely without repetition.

If boredom I is unmediated reflection, boredom II is the lack of any reflection whatsoever, because there is no same that could be the mirror of and for oneself, so that no mediation of same and other can be established.

Entertainment. As endless repetition without a meaning and an end, boredom II expresses itself in and as *entertainment*, constant in its inconstancy. Incidentally, "short while" in German is *Kurzweil*, which means "entertainment," and is explicitly mentioned by Kant in opposition to boredom as "long while" or *Langeweile*. In fact, as Kant rightly observes, entertainment as incessant amusement becomes the cause of boredom: "The constant occupation with amusements eventually causes disgust at all amusements and thereby boredom."[36] And as Jean-Baptiste Dubos has noted, one needs constant spectacles in order to keep off boredom and avoid "heaviness": "The soul hath its wants no less than the body; and one of the greatest wants of man is to have his mind incessantly occupied. The heaviness which quickly attends the inactivity of the mind, is a situation so very disagreeable to man, that he frequently choses to expose himself to the most painful exercises, rather than be troubled with it."[37] Inextricably linked to boredom, entertainment becomes a clear sign and expression of modernity.

The modern subject is incapable of being satisfied with a simple same and thus resting, because simplicity presupposes a definite relationship and interaction between same and other, and rest is defined in contradistinction to work as its other. The only option left is to flee away from oneself, which can never achieve itself in the absence of same, and hence has to succumb to the change without change, to nonuniform uniformity of the seemingly variegated, to perennial repetitive progression of another and another that is never other. This is modern entertainment, an inescapable, restless dissipation, diagnosed by Pascal as damnation and by Benjamin as distraction.[38] It is a repetitive entrancement without a stop and does not end in the absence of a meaningful end, and is therefore utterly boring.[39]

Entertainment is the expression of boredom II as the repetition of other without same in seemingly different yet ultimately indistinguishable forms. In the absence of same, entertainment does not absolve itself of boredom and thus cannot be properly enjoyed, not even as a narcissistic enjoyment with oneself, because in the absence of same, narcissism is meaningless and impossible. Such a repetition does not discover or invent the nonboring novel, but is always driven by a futile hope of its achievement. The monotonous repetition without same only generates the new as another and another. Repetition as entertainment cannot even be absurd, for absurdity as unexpected can bring about a radically novel other that might hurt or question the recognized and established norms perceived as unjust or boring. The embodiment of boredom as the repetition of other without same can be exemplified as the unrealizable attempt to count all natural numbers to infinity, which only demonstrates the tragic despair of the isolated modern subject who decides to assert itself by demonstrating and enjoying the suffering of the self-imposed fateful effort to do the impossible.[40] This is boredom II: it is void. It is nothing but the repetition of indistinguishable other that cannot be distinguished from another in the absence of same. It is the privation of same.

A note on privation. When Aristotle discusses the first principles (ἀρχαί) in the *Physics*, he comes to the conclusion that the principles should be opposites, one positively expressing what a thing is, which is its definition (λόγος), and the other negatively denying the λόγος as its lack or privation (στέρησις). However, contrary to Plato, the opposites for Aristotle cannot coexist or interact without mediation, because this would amount to the violation of the principle of noncontradiction.[41] For this reason, nothing is or can be contrary or opposite to substance as either substrate or the subject of predication. Therefore, as Aristotle argues, one needs to assume the third, opposite-neutral, principle, which is a substrate (ὑποκείμενον) capable of mediating the opposites.[42] This is why privation differs from negation (ἀφαίρεσις), which is a mere absence (ἀπουσία), because privation always refers to a substrate that can be deprived of something.[43] One could consider this a distinction between nonbeing and not-being.

For this reason, privation is the opposite (ἐναντία), either of definition, or of being. As the opposite of being, privation is absolute nonbeing, *nonbeing as such* (καθ' αὑτήν), which is not anything that can exist on its own and have active or final causality. Rather, privation stands for the indeterminateness of nonbeing in the absence of the same, which is why privation is the being of the infinite or indefinite.[44] In the *Physics*, privation comes as the opposite of matter, as nonbeing as such, opposite to accidental nonbeing. However, Aristotle also speaks of the privation of form (εἶδος; cold is the privation of the form of warm) and of substance (οὐσίας στέρησις).[45] As such, privation can be opposite to substance, although not qua substrate or subject of predication, but as the opposite of definition or of genus.[46] Privation as the absence of being is not an active act but a lack, a shadow that happens to "be," or rather not be, there where the light does not penetrate.

Yet, every concept for Aristotle is said or used in many ways, and the same category can have various characterizations, depending on a particular task he has to address, which also explains why the central category of privation receives a different treatment in different works. In the *Categories*, Aristotle distinguishes the category of the opposite (ἀντικεῖσθαι) into four kinds: relation (τὰ πρός τι); contrarieties (τὰ ἐναντία); privation and having (or disposition, στέρησις καὶ ἕξις); and assertion and negation (κατάφασις καὶ ἀπόφασις). The paradigmatic examples of these four kinds of opposites are: the double and the half; good and evil; blindness and sight; and "sitting"-"not sitting." Aristotle agrees, then, that evil is the opposite (ἐναντίον) of good, even if sometimes evil is opposite to another evil.[47] However, privation as not-having appears in a different kind of opposition than that of good and evil, and thus, strictly speaking, is not applicable to the description and understanding of evil. Privation is thus opposite to *being* (as having a disposition to act in a certain way), and not to the good.

But in the modern subject, privation is realized as its proprium in the form of boredom II, which is the boredom of other without same. This is the privation of inclusion, the lack of difference as the nondifferentiation and nondistinction of other in the absence of same. In this sense, boredom as privation is the privation of being, if being is being in dialogue with others, and also the privation of good, if good is that of the shared comic life with others.

(III) *Boredom as the rupture of same and other: odium and incapacity*. Finally, boredom III, the boredom of same and other as incapable of communication—that is, the inability of same to reach out to other, and other as cut off from same—is the expression or proprium of the modern subject in its incapacity *to be*, if being is a synthetic unity as the interaction of same and other. In this sense, the utterly bored modern subject *does not exist*, but is a historical imaginary construction, a fantasy with a particular pedigree and genealogy that still has a profound grip on us who participate in the universal autonomy of the lonely tragic subject.

In this kind of boredom, same and other remain separate and separated in a profound rupture constitutive of the modern subject in its imaginary but nonthinkable nonbeing, which is the privation of being in the dialogical communication of same-and-other. Here, boredom comes out of a constraint, which is perceived as internal and self-imposed: a duty to do something, which is socially and morally obliging, which, however, is perceived as fully autonomous and in separation from others.

The "and" of the complete severance of same *and* other, however, is of a peculiar kind. It is not the inclusive and binding "-and-" of the interactive and mutually codependent same and other. This "and" is neither of inclusion nor of separation that sets off two equal but opposite constitutives of being. Rather, it is the contradictory opposition of "and" and of "and-not." In this "and," same and other are contradictories that do not interact or reach out for each other in any way. Same and other are deprived of each other. Boredom III is the boredom of *rupture*, of the unsurpassable break between same and other, same— —other, same // other, the two of which should be intrinsically bound and dialogically interact with each other in being.

This type of boredom comes as the deep abysmal break within the modern subject itself, which it cannot notice in an act of reflection, because now same and other exclude each other and thus deny themselves. This is the exclusion of the noninclusion of same *and* other that results in disrupted singular isolated beings, each of which is a unique exemplification of the modern self-universalizing subject. This is a broken collection of indifferent and undifferentiated shards of what could be being as the dialogical interaction of same-and-other. Same is never same and other is never other in their inability to come together and communicate even as opposed and struggling. Same "and" other are there without being. They are neither reflected nor mediated by, in and for itself or other. Neither is a singularity, which negatively or privatively presupposes the reference to a totality of functionally connected sets. The same never does return to itself as its same other, and other is never reached in any of its three different forms—as the other of the world, of another person, and of oneself.[48]

Boredom III, then, is primarily expressed as odium, as self-hatred, and ennui, which signifies the modern subject's incapacity for an ontological synthesis as mediated reflection, while boredom I is caused by the incapacity for unmediated reflection, and boredom II by the refusal of reflection. Boredom III comes with the recognition of the impossibility of reflection that would represent others and oneself as one's self enriched by interaction with others. This ultimate form of boredom is an unreflected and unmediated assembly of accidental fragments and dispersed fractions.

Boredom III is the recognition of the modern subject's impotence, of its incapacity to reach out for others, who should be there but are rendered indistinguishable in the absence of a meaningful manifold relation of same and other, which, due to the power of the creative negativity of other, can be always novel and surprising. It is the incapacity for mediation and reflection, that is, for the synthesis of being. It is the incapacity for the inclusion of others who always appear to be there but are always missed. It is the incapacity to communicate with others, and therefore for being, if to be is to be in dialogue, in which same and other can unfinalizably communicate.

This always failed attempt of reaching out to others results in *violence* against oneself and others as projections of oneself, in an attempt to secure one's *right to boredom*.

In a now famous experiment, Wilson et al. showed that, when asked to be left alone with their thoughts even for a short while, people preferred to do anything at all, and many even chose to electrocute themselves rather than do nothing.[49] Being exposed to oneself inflicts the odium of facing nothing, since, in the situation of the rupture with the other, our own thoughts do not constitute a real dialogue.

The very rupture between same and other, however, suggests that the other somehow should be there. And yet, incapable of communicating with the other and thus of connecting same and other, the modern subject postulates the other as the justification of its normative claims. Within the rupture of same and other, the other of the self cannot be reflected; the other of nature is constructed and regulated by the subject's rationally imposed laws; and the other of another person is established by the act of the autonomous will. But the real other—the other of and in the dialogical relation with the same—escapes and resists the attempts at being assimilated and forcefully included into the modern subject's kingdom of ends.

The incapacity for being with others, which first appears in boredom I, in boredom III now comes with the pain of the odium, the dull self-hatred whose cause the subject cannot realize and determine. But its self-imputed autonomy gives the modern subject the right to what it has established, even if it does not fully understand what it has produced in the absence of the other as *alius*. In this sense, the modern subject has a *right to boredom*, which it is determined to realize by accepting the pain of boredom as ultimately inescapable yet liberating (in Kracauer and Heidegger).

This self-hatred immanent to boredom III is translated into *humiliation* (which can also be considered another fundamental mood), which comes with the anonymity of *guilt*. The acceptance of guilt while not having committed anything morally wrong seems to have no cause, and yet it persistently follows self-purified moral thought as *bad conscience*, the source of which is the subject's inability to be moral, since morality presupposes reaching out for the other for the sake of the other.[50] The persistent and importunate sense of guilt comes from the fundamental indifference as the *incapacity to differentiate* between same and other, and thus include the other into moral considerations.

Guilt is then translated into responsibility for the other who is not (and never) there—the unreachable other of another person, the future not yet existing generations, et cetera—but should still be recognized as unconditional in the moral demand. Humiliated by itself, the modern subject inflicts the sense of guilt onto itself yet, having established itself as morally autonomous and thus upright, tends to blame another, somebody or something else, which appears as aggression toward a form of activity or a group deemed to be responsible and guilty, a scapegoat that cannot be chased away. The one who blames is the one who is to be blamed, yet cannot be blamed, because it cannot perceive itself as other. Needless to say, the inescapability of guilt without having intentionally trespassed the autonomously self-established rules is the tragic condition.

The boredom of symmetry and the loss of spontaneity. The rupture of same and other is akin to a self-inflicted wound that does not heal but always hurts, which is perceived as the boredom of ennui or odium. When we repeatedly attempt to overcome boredom III, we always fail to do so, because we moderns recognize ourselves as the realization of the modern subject, which reigns supreme in its self-established moral and natural world.

In the odium, this failure transpires as the loss of spontaneity. Originally, spontaneity refers to a free act that follows one's own intention, accord, and authority (*sua sponte*). Spontaneity also belongs to nature as φύσις, yet in modern philosophy it is appropriated by Kant as the characteristic of the mind taken as the faculty of cognition, which produces order, or synthesis, out of apparently disorganized sensible data.[51] As spontaneous, the modern mind does not act out of its own free accord with itself but rather out of its own necessity perceived as a tiresome and boring burden to bring order to the initial chaos of undistinguished perception, and thus to produce uniformity out of multiplicity.

Facing the inevitability of the rupture of same and other and yet the necessity to overcome it, the response of the modern subject attempts to heal it by establishing a rules-based method (*mathesis universalis*, in Descartes and Leibniz) that would allow one to get to a necessary logical truth by way of calculation. Such a method should get the answer to a question as always, invariably, and univocally right. Everything in thought and action needs to be carefully regulated, as calculated and described in as much detail as possible. This is the new "algebraic" Cartesian method of putting down long detailed lists of necessary steps in an algorithm that is meant to provide a new truth and solve an existing problem. Such a method is based on "order and measure" and is meant to bring *symmetry* and *regularity* into the solitary cognition. The new method ousts and replaces the live rhythmic pulsing interaction with others, who are capable of solving theoretical and practical problems at hand in a seemingly chaotic, mutually interruptive, sometimes erroneous, inexplicably comic, and yet rationally shared way.

The modern scientific method is meant to render the difficult and variegated into the simplified and univocal, to make one and many into a strict and ordered knowledge. To think the simple is simple and yet, at the same time, is difficult, because the simple is neither simplified nor given but needs to be achieved as the result of a complex and often meandering reasoning. Indeed, on the one hand, one needs to think simple things or concepts as clear and distinct ideas. But, on the other hand, one needs to combine these simples into formulations and propositions, that make one (conclusion) out of many (concepts, premises, and steps of deduction or reasoning). Therefore, one needs one universal method, which, on the one hand, needs to be rational, unambiguous, and thus unique.

On the other hand, it should be simple and *easy to use*, almost effortlessly leading to the understanding of the world and its properties (in Bacon's *Novum Organum*, Descartes, and Leibniz).[52] However, since the world (or at least the scientific ideal substitution of the world) is complex in its phenomena yet simple in its underlying principles and constituents, or is one-and-many, the complexity should be reduced to simple constituents, from which true propositions should then be deduced. The two operations of the mind that make the method work are intuition and deduction.[53] Intuition allows for understanding and grasping the multiple simple constituents or ideas, which themselves are not propositions; and deduction allows one to connect and combine or—to use Plato's metaphor[54]— weave them together by means of the method's rules into chains of reasoning arranged by "*ordo et mesura*," order and measure, which lead, through divisions, arrangements, and enumerations, to true propositions and knowledge.[55] Complex phenomena thus should be analyzable down to simple notions, and complex theories should be then constructible out of these simples, which are *sui generis* mathematical atoms or elementary building blocks. The two constituents of the method therefore are reductive analysis, for which the paradigm is the "algebra of the moderns," and deductive synthesis, for which the pattern is the "geometry of the ancients."[56] The modern scientific method, therefore, is meant to bring order, regularity, and intelligibility into the seemingly chaotic, unordered, and irrational things.

But perfect symmetry, reproducible regularity, and reasoned lawfulness that are set forever in place as unchangeably the same cannot be but boring. In the absence of life as a renewable and complex interaction of same and other, boredom III is (literally) deadly boring and signifies the death of the mind and action, which exist and unravel only in (sometimes uneasy) interaction with others.

In the situation of the utter rupture of same-other, under the guise of individuality and pretense of uniqueness, the modern subject promotes and causes *atomization*: there are *many* dialogically disconnected others (as individuums or social and political atoms), existing but not bound into *one* (social and political space of indifference). Modern individuality thus signifies the tragic incapacity for the synthesis, interaction between, or reaching out to others who mutually rely on each other. Trust in others gets substituted by the *fear* of others, who do not appear, act, or look exactly the same as prescribed by the autonomous act of will. The self-imposed autonomous law that expresses same without, and severed from, other, has to punish any deviation from strict sameness. Boredom III, then, is the incapacity to reach, represent, and stand for humankind in one's solitary person.

Socially, the irreparable break between same and other is translated into extreme *professionalization* and *specialization* of knowledge and of social and professional skills. Even people who work in related areas (e.g., in science), often do not understand each other's language and problems, which become highly segmented and fractioned. The unity of social communication is now largely provided by the anonymous sphere of the media, where one cannot really understand the problem and find a solution, but where a nonsolution and ever-repeating patterns of distraction from urgent social and political problems are perpetuated under the guise of the new, which is ever the same without other. The epitome of this inseparable separation between same and other in the form of extreme fragmentation within the anonymous space of unreasons is modern social media, where atomized autonomous individuals seem to communicate—but in fact, inevitably miss each other—with a plethora of anonymous users, who use each other as a means of self-promotion and self-assertion in one virtual space of unreality, where one same is securely severed off from the other. This makes the modern surrogate sociality of virtual communication inevitably boring.

Hypocrisy and boredom: politeness and pretense. The ultimate form of boredom is the odium of self-hatred that comes with the incapacity of the modern subject for the ontologically mediated reflection of being with others. A way to counter this is by establishing and following a *habit*. To be sure, humans are habitual beings: habits play a major role in establishing social customs and in the constitution of most cultural, social, practical, and political action. In Aristotle, habit as ἕξις is the foundation of moral life, since one can be a moral person only if one is habituated to perform virtuous acts and make right decisions.[57] Yet habit, as the expression of the modern subject's incapacity to reach not only for the other but also for the same of itself, is a well-ordered routine that is imposed unreflectively on oneself by oneself in order to convince oneself of the propriety of one's actions as appropriate and moral. Yet, as argued, morality is primarily exercised toward and with others, which is now not an option for the tragic modern loner. Therefore, one should pretend that others are routinely there in social and societal communication, which, however, because of the rupture of same and other, is only a habitually imaginary and virtual communication.

The boredom III of odium is of the atomistic individualized same with indefinite variations, seemingly refined yet ultimately boring and lacking in subtlety. Habit, then, is established to tame and address the always changing variety of meanings and possible situations. Habit is the nonrepetitive repetition that attempts to overcome and suspend the boredom of repetition by coming to a same that cannot be reached as the same of the other of the other.

In modernity, it is *politeness* that becomes a major visible and conventional virtue that is meant to testify to the presence of other in its absence, and to the moral uprightness of oneself, hiding the inescapable self-hatred of the lonely moralistic attire. Politeness is the modern testimony to the autonomy and atomization of people as individuals. It seemingly allows us to avoid the humiliation of utter loneliness and thus both the exclusion of other and of the self-exclusion from others and from the self that cannot properly *be*, that is, be in dialogue with others. One can endure hardships but not humiliation, and the humiliation of being excluded—in this case, self-excluded—is one of the worst.

"Politeness" comes from Latin *polire*, "to polish," and is thus meant to be a civic ability to communicate with others in a cramped civil societal (city) space without rubbing each other the wrong way or stepping on each other's toes on the narrow streets of a polis. Politeness is therefore "political" from the start, as an expression of the recognition of the equality and value of those with whom one is to communicate. It is also gallant and is meant to make communication pleasant rather than boorish, to value smiles and occasional laughter over aggression and insult. But politeness can also be hypocritical and pretentious, inhibiting our capacity to get to the other. It can veil the anxiety of being rejected and excluded, not accepted into the rigid social ranks. And it can express the recognition of one's inability to reach out for others and for oneself. Politeness thus becomes the form of an inevitable, strangely pleasing estrangement amid the crowd where no one can be reached or properly addressed, the expression of being alone behind a mask among other masks. The punk or leftist straightforwardness as the expression of disdain for bourgeois formality in (mis)communication is then a reaction to the hypocrisy of politeness that is meant to retrieve the abandoned *sincerity* and *equality* of being with others.

Politeness is hence the expression of the modern atomization of socially and politically isolated individuals who are unable to communicate but only bump into each other in stochastic Brownian movement within the confines of a lifeless extended world. Such atomic, disconnected, self-annoying monads do not see into the other or into oneself, for, as Leibniz puts it, they have no "windows" opening onto each other or onto the world.[58]

Under the pretense of uniqueness and individuality, politeness, then, is the convention that is meant to allow for an action in the utterly departmentalized yet insecure world in which interaction is impossible. In their atomization and dispersal, people do not interact but keep moving in a seemingly changing yet deeply boring repetitive way, acting as actors in a self-staged drama, where the only outcome is loneliness and inevitable death. For Kant, politeness allows for the "appearance of the good," publicly promoted through pretense, hypocrisy, and (self-)deception. Yet, the more cultivated people are, the more they are actors.[59] Everyone is then the actor-*hypocritēs*, the director and the spectator of the self-staged and self-directed tragedy of the autonomous, utterly boring moral life, where same and other can never come together, interact, or meet each other. Being all about the appearance of the same, and the severance of the other from moral life, politeness presupposes rigidly repetitive, uniformly accepted, but utterly conventional manners, which cannot be but ultimately boring. Observant Byron cannot miss that "Society is smooth'd to that excess, / That manners hardly differ more than dress.... Society is now one polish'd horde, / Form'd of two mighty tribes, the *Bores* and *Bored*."[60] But politeness also excludes everyone who does not fit and attempts not to be a hypocrite, thus running against the idea of a moral life as shared with others as equals.

Three forms of boredom, compared. To sum up, boredom I is the boredom of same without other and is paradigmatically represented as the duration of the "long while." Boredom II is the boredom of other without same and shows itself as repetition and privation. Finally, boredom III is the boredom of the complete rupture of same and other and appears as the odium of ennui in the incapacity for communication between same and other.

Now, a brief comparison of the three forms of boredom might further clarify each one, and their mutual distinctions. If one can philosophize in prepositions, since each preposition expresses a different set of relations, then one might perhaps distinguish between boredom-with, boredom-by, and boredom-of. *Boredom-with*, then, would be boredom I as expressing the boredom with the unending duration without an end. Here, one is bored with everything. *Boredom-by*, on the contrary, would be boredom II, where one is bored by constant inevitable repetition without an end. Finally, *boredom-of* would be boredom III, where one recognizes one's incapacity simply to be, making one bored, tired, and hateful of one's very being, if being is a dialogical interaction of same and other. Yet any preposition can be used differently and in many ways with multiple cases. For this reason, the prepositional distinction between three kinds of boredom can in principle always be rethought.

Let us now look at how three kinds of boredom transpire in different concepts and metaphors.

(1) *Infinity.* Boredom I appears under the guise of actual infinity, which is complete and is there all at once, indivisible and preceding anything finite. This is the appearance of same without other as not-other, Cusanus's *non aliud*, which, in the absence of other, is infinite and thus cannot be perceived, imagined, or thought. This is the new modern infinite that appears as Descartes's mathematical and theological *infini* primary to any finite magnitude, which is a negation of the infinite; as the infinite space that famously caused fear in Pascal and became the foundation of Newton's mechanics as absolute space; and as infinitesimal difference in Leibniz and Newton.[61] Boredom II, on the contrary, is present in potential infinity in a pure repetition of one or a unit that is not one, insofar as for one to be a unit or numerical monad it should relate to other as many. The potential infinite is that of other without same as exemplified in the Pythagorean "indefinite dyad" or ἀόριστος δυάς, the Aristotelian infinite of "another and another,"[62] Descartes's *indéfini*, and Hegel's "bad infinity," always incomplete, where one can always make another step.[63] Potential infinity generates the boredom of indefinite repetition. Finally, boredom III as the odium of the incapacity of being is represented as infinity broken into unrelated subsets, where same does not hold or contain other, and other does not add up to same. This is the infinite in which the cardinal number of the infinite set does not amount to the cardinal number of all the subsets of the set, so that C is *not* equal to $2^{\aleph_0}$, or to the set of all finite subsets of the natural numbers.

(2) *Moral attitude.* Three kinds of boredom appear in different moral attitudes. Boredom I presents itself in the moral uprightness of the autonomous moral subject and the resulting self-aggrandizement. It transpires in moral indifference as nondifference and the lack of concern for others who are not there because, in the absence of other, differentiation and (moral) judgment are impossible. Boredom II appears in moralism as the repetition of the same in the form of a rigidly established set of moral prescriptions that never converge and fit a concrete case. And boredom III comes to the fore as hypocrisy in an attempt to disguise oneself through appropriate manners in front of imaginary others

who cannot be communicated with, which results in the rupture of proper social relations with others and the realization of the futility of any such attempt leading to the inevitable odium of self-hatred.

(3) *Sound*. Acoustic variations can be considered as a metaphor for the bored monological autonomous subject reigning supreme over itself in the absence of others. One could say that boredom I is represented as the monotony of the same sound and pitch, where another sound is not a sound but a foundation or background established by one single dominant sound. Boredom II appears as multisound yet without distinct voices, which are all complementary only as lacking in each other: each one is the privation of the other, incapable of generating a resounding polyphonic texture. And boredom III is the metaphor for sounds that do not interact or interpenetrate. In the absence of any gradation, the resulting acoustic picture is not a whole but breaks down into a bleak rumble and indistinct clatter, in which the sounds cannot intermix or interact.

(4) *Poverty*. Modernity is the time of simplification, which is translates into poverty. In ontology, we have at best two mutually exclusive substances. Modern poetry knows only a handful of genres, which nowadays are practically reduced to only one genre of vers libre as the expression of the autonomous monological subject, written in a few basic meters, while Greek lyric has a great variety of genres and meters. In politics, the one and only modern nation-state reigns supreme, while in Greek antiquity, Aristotle alone described about two hundred different constitutions. In antiquity, democracy is the engaging, nonboring, and comic rule of the poor,[64] in stark contrast to the solitary ruling of the self-universalized subject, which is translated into the unitary power of the modern nation-state that institutes democracy as the rule of disconnected equal abstract political units in the situation of the rupture of same and other. One can associate boredom I, then, with the self-realization and self-fulfillment according to a plan one has established for oneself, which, in the absence of others, is utterly boring. This attitude translates into the attempt to accumulate as much material possession and wealth as possible in order to sustain oneself, since one cannot rely on help from others in their absence. The modern autonomous nation is the embodiment of the autonomous liberal subject as a boringly long political and cultural soliloquy not addressed to anyone but oneself, which thus cannot really be delivered or heard in the absence of interlocutors. Boredom II follows poverty as privation, where everyone is inevitably and repetitively deprived of any possession, of anything that one could call one's own. And boredom III deeply

permeates the degrading incapacity for political and cultural wealth to be equally distributed and shared with others. In the situation of complete atomization and the deep rupture of personal, social, and political ties, the self- and mutually enriching communication becomes impossible and is substituted by the meaningless accumulation of wealth against, and at the expense of, others, who cannot even be registered as others but remain only abstract statistical and sociological units.

(5) *Home/dwelling.* If we take the metaphor of home, boredom I can be considered as the accompanying proprium of a fortress—a fantasy palace for the modern subject as the one and only monarch, the claim to the ownership of which is justified by being the autocrat in the kingdom of ends (no wonder that the size of an average house has considerably grown in the last two generations in America, while the size of the household has shrunk). Yet in fact, this is the boredom of suffering in a self-built prison cell, which the modern subject inevitably imposes onto itself and into which it encloses itself as a rescue from an other who is not there anyway. Boredom II is the mark of the escape from same that appears as homelessness and wordlessness, where one cannot find a proper place for oneself anywhere in the world in the very absence of the world. Finally, boredom III signifies the rupture of human communications and is the proprium of those dwelling and drowsing in isolated apartments in enormous high-rises, in detached houses where people pass by each other as faceless incommunicable shadows without ever having to talk.

In the experiment of Wilson et al., it is important to mention that people were not allowed to leave their *place*, and hence many preferred to voluntarily inflict pain on themselves in order to get rid of the excruciating boredom, which could not be endured even for several minutes. Being in the same place or room without the other and a possibility of dialogical communication with them is perceived as a cruel and unusual punishment, a prison confinement, which the flâneur in vain tries to get rid of by restless motion from one place to the other in the still confined imperceptible prison of the modern city. It is utterly paradoxical but not entirely unexpected, then, that modern society spends so much effort on guarding and closing off private space or place from others, where one can apparently be free in one's place, and yet gets agonizingly bored in it. One thus both yearns for the Pascalian room and abhors it.

(6) *Exclusion.* Different kinds of boredom stand for different types of exclusion, which translate into a whole range of social and political practices of

discrimination. Since boredom I is the expression of the modern subject's solitude and self-isolation resulting from its inability to reach out for the other, it signifies the exclusion of the other in the long while of duration that never comes to an end and can never receive a meaning as a result. Socially and politically, it translates into the exclusion of the dispossessed in being dislodged into the indefinite waiting for the fulfillment of promises that will never be realized. The modern subject's elimination of the other results in ugly modern forms of exclusion such as colonialism, imperialism, nationalism, racism, gender exclusion, and so on, which deserve a separate study. Since boredom II is the proprium of other without same as the privation of same, it implies a negative exclusion as the privation of inclusion. In other words, this is the privative noninclusion of the same that is too familiar and repetitively boring. This is the painfully repetitive boredom of the social and political inability to include those who do not fit the sameness of the norms and standards imposed onto them socially and politically—those who come from elsewhere, speak and look differently, and bring other customs. And boredom III comes out of exclusion as the incapacity for inclusion, as noninclusion of the self as same and other—of oneself, of another person, and of the world. This is the noninclusion of same and other as mutually indifferent and undifferentiated—broken, dissociated, and dislocated splinters of being as an interactive whole of same-and-other. This is the ultimate form of boredom of the atomized society that hopes for something else, but, being stuck in the disrupted being and thinking brought about by the historical construction of the modern subject, is ultimately incapable of any real social and political changes.

CHAPTER 5

The Nonboring Well-Being

Contrary to modern thinkers of boredom, who are locked in the inescapable grasp of the modern subject and thus claim that we cannot escape boredom, but in fact that we only live to the full when we allow ourselves to be deeply bored, I want to argue that a nonboring world is possible. If boredom is so pervasive in its various forms and appearances and is inextricably linked with the modern subject as its proprium, then in order to be capable of being a nonboring being, we need to rethink the very concept of the acting subject as inscribed into a different understanding of being. If another world is possible, then it should be the one that is not enacted by the monological, tragic, and lonely subject. Therefore, the other subject should be dialogical, comic, and allow for being with others. Only then can such a subject cease to be boring and bored. Only then can we—who enact and participate in such a subject—hope to realize a nonboring social and political life that, while oftentimes messy and unpredictable, might allow for a nonboring well-being as being with others.

(1) *Well-being as being in dialogue*. As I have argued elsewhere, the alternative to monological thinking and the exemplifying same in the exclusion of the other can be found in *dialogue*. In dialogical communication, everyone is integrated as an equal and recognized partner in shared *unfinalizable* communication, which can always be meaningfully carried on further without a repetition of contents. In this respect, dialogue fundamentally differs from an exchange and sharing of information, which is conveyed in a finite number of steps, after which it becomes repetitive. Because dialogue can always be meaningfully continued *without repetition*, it is live and engaging, so that same and other are never severed from each other. Everyone can participate in dialogue and is thus an equal and free dialogical partner.

Instead of autonomous self-sufficiency, dialogue requires mutual dependency and dependability. As such, dialogue is based on what I called *allonomy*, which allows for establishing and exercising morally binding action together with others in dialogical interaction. Hence, dialogue is never boring.

It is here in dialogue that the spontaneity of being in shared action is realized without repetition and without being forced. Every person in dialogue is present as the "personal other," which cannot be expressed in traditional ontological and logical terms; that is, it cannot be considered a subject or predicate; it thus differs from the modern subject. The "personal other" is a synthetic unity of same and other as definite yet never fully expressible and extinguishable, so that every person can continue the dialogue, always disclosing themselves yet never in a finalizing and objectifying way. One is never either same or other, but is always "not unlike" oneself while still being oneself, thus tying together same and other in an ongoing and engaging dialogical interaction.

Following the distinction of same, other, and same-and-other as bound together in dialogical interaction, one can distinguish three kinds of dialogical others that have already been mentioned: the other of oneself (the "personal other"), the other of another person, and the other of the world. With each one, we can establish dialogical communication that should allow us to fundamentally rethink personal being, social and political being, and the philosophy of nature. In each of its hypostases, the other is an intimate partner in dialogue who transcends the abyssal gap to the other produced by the modern subject: the same and other as dialogically bound together is more than the sum of mutually unreachable same and other.

If this is the case, then the modern monological and monoconscious subject as exclusive of the other should be replaced by a shared personal dialogical being that is capable of bringing together same and other in a dialogical synthesis. Ontology thus also has to be fundamentally rethought, for on this interpretation *to be is to be in dialogue*.

For this reason, dialogue is *nonproductive*, because being as being in dialogue together with others does not—and does not have to—produce anything. Being in dialogue cannot be produced: it happens with others. In a dialogue, one can come to, or produce, a conclusion, a decision, or an answer to a question, but this is accidental to dialogue, because one can very well perform the same proposition outside of dialogue in a solitary meditation, to which the modern lonely subject is particularly inclined.

Locked in its autonomous and monological boring loneliness, the modern subject has no choice but to proudly take its solitude as aesthetically sublime and morally uplifting.[1] In its self-inflicted isolation and in the absence of others, the modern monological subject is incapable of communication and therefore inevitably has to suffer in its miserable and boring being without others—with no prospect, chance, or even a hope (since it is the moral subject and thus has to be honest with itself) for well-being. The monosubjective lonely being cannot be a shared well-being, which is why the vocabulary of happiness (in ethics) and beauty (in aesthetics) is eventually wiped out of the modern philosophical discourse and substituted by the satisfaction of following one's moral duty and obligations. In short, autonomy is utterly boring in its loneliness and self-sufficiency.

Being as dialogical allows for well-being, if well-being means sharing being with others as free participants in dialogue. Such a dialogical life is moral, if it is realized as the actual participating in and promoting of the common and thus public good; and it is political, if political life is the exercise of commonality as the free communication of equals.[2]

However, being in dialogue does not mean easy being: it is not and cannot be an unconcerned being together regulated by the ideal of consensus in communication. Steering between a flat consensus and an uneven dissensus, dialogue allows for *allosensus*, the creative tension of being with others who keep disclosing themselves in an unfinalizable dialogical interaction. On the one hand, this tension transpires as a constant lack of consensus: a final agreement brings dialogue to an end, since there is no point in continuing the discussion any further. However, allosensus is to be distinguished from mere dissensus or antagonism where interlocutors remain at their point of view without attending to the other's. The allosensual difference is never erased in dialogue but allows the speakers to stay in a meaningful conversation and communication. On the other hand, the dynamic tension in dialogue appears in the necessity of mutual interruption, without which a meaningful dialogue is equally impossible.[3]

Understood this way, dialogue counters all three hypostases of boredom—of waiting caused by the indefinite duration, of repetition, and of the rupture of same and other. (1) Dialogue presupposes waiting for the other's response at the opportune moment, yet such waiting is brief and not boring, since dialogue is based on mutual interruption. (2) Dialogue is the repetition of communicative acts without, however, repeating their contents. It is thus not boring, because the dialogical situation is never the same yet is capable of bringing out the new as the other at any point. And (3) dialogue overcomes the rupture in being and in human relations, because the intimate interaction between same and other is the precondition for dialogical communication. Without it, dialogue is impossible. Same and other are constitutive of the interaction with another person, with oneself, and with the world. In the situation of the complete rupture of same and other in boredom, each one is fixated as such without the possibility of becoming other and reaching out for the other. Yet in dialogue, same and other are closely connected in and through interaction and, while being the same person, one is always inscribed into one's personal other. One is therefore also another as different and not rigidly socially objectified—but as personally inextinguishable. In dialogue, everyone is free in being, action, and thinking in responding to the other(s). This is the freedom of the dialogical spontaneity that is translated into the creativity of everyone who is engaged in an ever-different and renewed dialogical situation in which one is capable of real novelty. Such renewed and unfinalizable interaction allows for well-being as being with others in a nonboring but engaging communication. It is thus in dialogue that one can properly be and exercise well-being.

Dialogical well-being is engaging and nonboring, and thus *interesting*. Here one might recall Kolnai's discussion of the "interesting," which he finds in aesthetics but which can be equally traced in dialogue. If, paraphrasing Kant's famous dictum on the beautiful, the interesting is that which evokes interest "without appealing to one's interests,"[4] then dialogue as being with others constitutes the public communicative forum where one exercises one's being as dialogical without any particular or private interest. For nothing can be gained or lost in a dialogue as being with others. In its manifoldness and nonextinguishability, dialogue is interesting in that it wards off monotony and boredom.

At this point, one might recall Benjamin's "rain" as the embodiment of modern boredom, which is the manifestation of the grip of nature on the city's inhabitants. Dialogue takes place in a concrete, contingent, and often bleak conversational environment, which, however, ceases to be boring once it is lit up and enlivened by the dialogical exchange. One can say, then, that the nonboring appears, first, in the everydayness of the setting of the dialogue; second, in the suspension of everydayness in an act of dialogical creativity, rather than a heroic struggling with everydayness within solitary monological subjectivity; and third, in making interaction meaningful through dialogical acceptance of the other as capable of novelty and surprise—of oneself, of the unfamiliarly familiar other, and of the world, which always show themselves anew. People are often weary of everydayness, and in an attempt to escape its apparent boredom turn to the extremes of entertainment or to the search for transcendence. And yet, the everydayness with the other is not boring: quite to the contrary. Hence, dialogue is never boring, because it allows for real novelty as coming out in the nonfinalizable interaction of same with the other of the nonextinguishable personal other of the dialogical participants.

However, in my interpretation of well-being as (nonboring) being in dialogue, the relation of well-being (W) is *symmetrical* (aWb iff bWa) and *transitive* (if aWb and bWc, then aWc), but *not reflective* (~aWa). Rather, W is only *conditionally reflective*: one can be well with oneself only to the extent that one exercises and shares well-being with others. Reflectivity is therefore realized as transitivity with oneself through the other as a consequence of well-being's transitivity and symmetry (if aWb and bWa, then aWa). Yet boredom *is* reflective, since, shaped by the construction of the modern, lone, and monological subject, one is invariably bored with oneself. Hence, well-being is *not an equivalence relation*, which is defined by being reflective, symmetrical, and transitive, and thus does not split the community of dialogical partners into mutually sealed off classes of equivalence, but rather makes everyone capable of sharing and participating in well-being as an equal.

Hence, dialogue allows for well-being as dialogical being with the other of oneself, others, and the world, and not the other that the modern monosubject invents and produces for itself out of and from within itself as the imaginary other of its narcissistic self-observing self. To be well, one needs to be, that is, to be in dialogue.

Dialogue is thus never boring. In a dialogue, one is an actor in a drama with not just one singular protagonist but with many diverse and independent actors, all involved in staging the drama of mutually shared well-being, where everyone is the protagonist, the supporting actor, the dramatist, and the director at the same time. Such a drama has to be able to enact the common well-being that is not a given or guaranteed but can be reached at and as the end of the common shared and mutually enhanced dialogical effort.

(2) *Well-being as comedy*. This brings us to the second determination of well-being that stands against the exclusion of the other. As was said, the modern subject is both the author and the director of its own tragic drama, in which it is

both the protagonist and the sole actor in the absence of the chorus of others. The modern subject is tragic, because it inevitably faces its finitude and loneliness, and is thus being toward death—which is precisely the tragic condition.[5]

Contrary to the tragic autonomous understanding of the modern moral and political subject, comedy establishes commonly accepted patterns for public political interaction, for the structuring and transmitting of social practices, and hence for the constitution of an entirely *different subject* of morality and politics. This is the subject who is not a function of a shared pattern of interaction but is a real robust other person who establishes moral and political norms in concert with real and equal others on the chaotic public stage of democratic political action. There is no place for solitary action or thinking in comedy. The comic moral and political subject always comes in the plural—*pluralia tantum*—as subject(s), and is (are) already oriented toward others. Yet, at the same time, such an actor is a unique person present in the comic exchange, which does not exclude either same or other but allows for their interactive dialogical unity to be reestablished and renegotiated at each point. Unlike the modern tragic subject who is lonely and isolated, for whom the other is only a task to achieve, the comic subject is neither isolated nor lonely and is already bound with and by the other who is inseparable from the comic self as the bearer of comic reason exemplified in the commonly distributed action. Every comic political actor is collectively integrated with others and as such has to act with and against others toward the solution of the current (moral or political) problem or crisis. Such a solution is never guaranteed but is possible in and through shared action and collective deliberation.

The modern tragic subject neither understands nor tolerates comedy, which is suspiciously unruly, seemingly messy, and dangerously unpredictable action by and for all.[6] Comic action depends on a plurality of actors, each one being not an imaginary projection of oneself but a real, robust, rigid other who can disagree with and stand up and against oneself, yet on whom one eventually depends. Together, comic actors advance the plot toward the achievement of the resolution of a current conflict.

In contradistinction to tragedy, comedy celebrates (1) not death but *life*, which can be enjoyed, renewed, and is oriented toward the common good that can be mutually shared and in which the desired becomes possible. We always face the possibility of death, which might bring meaning to the whole of life as its completion. Yet in modernity, the isolated, lonely, and single subject is incapable of achieving a "we" and remains the singular "I" that cannot find the end as established to its life otherwise than by itself as universal and universalized. Tragic death is the ultimate end of the modern subject as giving its existence meaning and fulfillment. In this monographical life story, death is aspired for but is never achievable, becoming the very condition of the possibility of the subject's autonomous self-realization. The autonomous subject constitutes itself in the face of death but never dies and cannot even commit (philosophical or literary) suicide. Unlike tragic death, life is never terminal or complete but keeps renewing itself and goes its way, a way that cannot be fully anticipated. Comedy is constituted by shared action as interaction with others that is meant to come to the resolution of a current conflict and achieve the desired end. Yet this end is never ultimate or terminal, and so one needs to live on, which ties together same in life's renewal and continuation with other of its constant dissipation. In this way, life strives to the infinite as the overcoming of the nihil of nonbeing and oblivion—and yet it cannot become infinite, because it always needs to renew itself in concrete and finite ways. Life is hence indefinite: it is more than finite but less than infinite. This gives the comic subject the character of indefiniteness, which irritates the modern subject that is intent on making everything that autonomously defines its action normatively predictable and clearly defined.

The modern tragic subject is propelled by the mood (translated into the feeling) of *fear*—of the unavoidable loneliness inscribed into the impossibility of getting through to the other, which thus precludes a good life as the life shared with others. It is the fear of death as the ultimate failure. It is the fear of the inevitability of the same. On the contrary, the mood of the comic subject is *joy*—not only of the anticipation of a good life but also of the not yet complete and completed, often messy and chaotic, but joyful being with others. It is the joy of life as a possibility of accomplishing something new and other.[7] One could perhaps say that while the lonely suffering subject is tragically sublime, the messy joyful subject is comically beautiful.

Moreover, (2) comedy allows its participants—comic subjects—to affirm not the exclusiveness of others that is translated into tragic nobility and class distinctions, but *equality*, inclusivity, and the possibility of communicating across divides. And finally, (3) comedy depicts not the subjugation to the power of the fate or an inevitable social malaise and historical evil, but is the affirmation of the comic subjects' *freedom*, which is neither a given nor a right, nor is guaranteed, but should and can be achieved as the result of comic action, which brings liberation from injustice and oppression in an action, shared and codirected with others. In this respect, comedy anticipates not the worst, as does tragedy, but the best, the common good life and shared *nonboring* well-being. If well-being means being with others, then the solitary modern subject is tragically incapable of well-being.

Being lonely and exclusive of others, the modern subject is also utterly *monological*. If being is being in dialogue, then well-being is the realization of such being in interaction as dialogue with others, equal and equally involved in the ongoing conversation. Such well-being is comic dialogical being with others, contrary to the lonely suffering existence of the modern secluded and tragic subject. Unlike the tragic subject that is inevitably monological, because the other for it is only a task to achieve, the comic subject is *dialogical* and as such is closely connected with the other in a commonly distributed action. Every comic actor on the stage of moral and political action is collectively integrated with others and has to act allosensually with and against others toward the solution of the current (moral or political) problem, which is not guaranteed but is possible through mutual action and collective deliberation. Instead of strict laws that are established in advance and even a priori as determined norms of public, moral, and political engagement, comedy allows for reestablishing and renegotiating them. Comedy allows for the *transgression* of the rules without harm to others and to oneself, allowing everyone to join in the shared action. For this reason, comedy is never boring.

If the comic subject's dialogical thinking is translated into action, then drama is particularly helpful as a form of its critical depiction, since it shows not by narration but through action and dialogue. As I have argued elsewhere, of all the dramatic genres, the most appropriate genre that characterizes our joint action, well-being, and in fact the very *conditio humana*, is New Comedy. It originates as Greek New Comedy in Philemon and Menander, is converted into Latin by Plautus and Terence, survives right into the Renaissance and, through its appropriation in Shakespeare and Molière, still flourishes today, despite being downplayed and ridiculed by modern tragedy-fixated thinkers, such as Hegel, August Schlegel, and Nietzsche, who only see in New Comedy the banality of everydayness as opposed to the sublimity of tragic heroism.[8]

In comedy, well-being is exercised by a different kind of subject that comes in the plural, and yet, one is never dissolved into a uniform many but is integrated as a person into the dramatic dialogical action shared with others. In comedy, no one can usurp the action, which means that the comic subject is *decentered* or eccentric. There is no single center in comic dialogical communication and interaction.

Everyone equally participates and is included into comic action, which thus can be considered the precondition for dialogue. Everyone can be liberated and become free through comic action, although freedom is never guaranteed but is always possible. It is therefore in comedy that equality and freedom can be realized as the result of such interaction. The achievement of freedom, however, is not the result of an autonomous moral act of the lonely modern subject that allots freedom to itself and possibly to others as its own projections. On the contrary, equality and freedom can and should be enacted as the result of comic dialogical action and are made possible by comedy's plot carried out by allonomous comic characters.

Comic plot and comic reason. Political action finds both its criticism and justification through theoretical reflection, which follows and reproduces the ways of thinking that are used, transmitted, and perpetuated by the modern universal subject, who reflects on its actions in the absence of the other and thus inevitably distorts the understanding of itself, presenting itself in highly sophisticated yet odd historical and systematic accounts. But modern political action is also depicted narratively through historical and dramatic means. Drama is a particularly effective way of representing and thinking about our actions, since it represents them not by mere (theoretical) narration but also by (practical) actions. The question, then, is what kind of drama is the proper portrayal of shared moral and political action, or democracy, that shows its truth by and in *acting*, "in-acting," and enacting, rather than by a disengaged theoretical demonstration.

The importance of comedy as both describing and prescribing moral and political norms that are based not on the exclusion of the other but on the interaction of same and other is determined primarily by its structure. New Comedy is defined not by the presence of jokes or laughter, which have their place outside comedy, but rather by its *plot*. Comic plot displays a striking similarity and structural analogy to a philosophical argument. Comic plot moves through the initial complication that begins with a wrongdoing and trespassing to a seemingly daunting, unpredictable, and irresolvable complication, and achieves the resolution or "good ending" in a number of steps, by means of shared agonistic action and allosensual debate. The resolution of conflict at the end of a comedy, which appears irresolvable in the beginning, requires great dramatic and philosophical skill in reasoning and the construction of the plot. Similarly, a sound philosophical argument starts with premises, moves through a number of (often difficult) deductive steps, and arrives at the conclusion. The ways of achieving the desired conclusion may differ widely in philosophical reasoning and comedy (and political action, as a translation of the comic one): one can arrive at the same end by many different means and methods, various plots and forms of action. Both comic plot and philosophical argument are understandable at every step of their development, yet both are intricate and hence difficult to grasp and trace in their entirety, due to their complexity and abundance of subtle yet important details, which is why the two need to be carefully preserved in writing.

Comedy is thus the dramatization of reasoning on stage that is carried out not just by the lonely autonomous protagonist but also by the interaction of a number of independent yet mutually interdependent actors. The action of comedy is driven by *cooperation*, which is at times uneasy and allosensual, rather than by the competition that characterizes the neoliberal world of relations promoted by the single modern subject that has already and forever outcompeted all of its competitors and rivals who, however, are only its own imaginary projections.

Comedy promotes a particular kind of reason that exemplifies comic dialogical being as a synthetic unity of the plurality of actors, of same and other. Comedy, therefore, is a rational enterprise meant to promote well-being that comes with an account of ways to achieve it through interaction together and in solidarity with others.[9] What comedy accomplishes through dramatic action, philosophy does through arguments.[10] If shared (democratic political) activity presupposes a weighed solution, which is not given but can be achieved through a number of (oftentimes wrongly taken, mis-taken) steps of publicly staged, participatory dramatic action aspiring at freedom, equality, and the common good, then comedy both prescribes and describes the pattern of such action. In this sense, comedy is philosophical and political, and politics and philosophy are comic. We might even say that comedy is born out of the spirit of philosophically mediated political action as the allosensual action shared with others, and that it bears certain features that are understandable and explicable only through its initial proximity to philosophy and public democratic politics. In opposition to the "goat's song" of tragedy, comedy is the philosopher's political song.

Comic character. Contrary to the fate-driven and death-saturated, but ultimately boring entertainment of tragedy, which is the expression of the single, modern, autonomous, narcissistic subject, comedy is never boring in that it advances by the mutually responsive action in which all of its many participants are involved. One is never alone in the comic action but faces both the allosensual resistance and support of others. However, among all the actors one particular figure becomes (often unwillingly) the center of action and the mastermind behind the development of the comic political plot—the one who directs the performance, takes responsibility for tying together loose ends, and advances the common action toward the good end. In New Comedy, this is the figure of a slave, servant, or maid, of the poor and dispossessed, the wretched of the earth, who is in a socially disadvantaged position yet allows everyone, including themselves, to achieve liberation from oppression and the freedom of well-being and good life in and as dialogical comic being with others.

Already in the times of Greek New Comedy, and especially in the Roman cosmopolitan and multicultural world, there is an understanding of the contingency of class and social distinctions, which is rectified in and through comedy, where the deprived receive recognition and freedom.[11] Not only are they recognized as equal to others but they also become the embodiment of practical nonautonomous reason through which the poor can address and solve apparently unsolvable political problems, doing so by reasoning translated into action. In comedy, it is the slave, the poor, or the oppressed who is the thinker and the main actor. Only the dispossessed can transgress social differences and demonstrate through action that these conditions are only a matter of convention and have nothing to do with the human condition, which is both rational and comic, insofar as it always allows for a good ending and well-being achieved in interaction and deliberation with others.

The slave, the poor, or the dispossessed is thus the master of the comedy of life—its master dialectician, mastermind, and conductor and architect of its plot. And the master is the servant of comedy, since he is made to follow the dialectical development of the action, which often drags him along. Hence, the comedy of communal thinking on the stage of public politics is capable of restoring social justice. The central comic figure is isomorphic with that of a philosopher in the polis. As a comic figure, the (political) philosopher as a public practical thinker is often an object of ridicule: in the words of Plato, he is "the jest not only of Thracian handmaids but of the general herd, tumbling into wells and every sort of disaster through his inexperience."[12] Yet the comic thinker is capable not only of propelling the action but also of ironically reflecting on themselves and on the very limits of reflection, mockingly anticipating the modern solitary tragic Cartesian thinking of the lonely and tragic subject incapable of comic refinement. Both the (comedic) poor and the (political) thinker come under an ironic guise behind which we quickly discover a powerful and sophisticated mind. Both are master thinkers: the slave is a practical thinker, the one who leads us through the labyrinth of a plot toward a solution of the problem; and the (political) philosopher guides us through the maze of an argument toward a conclusion.

In comedy, it is the fool who is wise, which they demonstrate by enacting a "foolish wisdom" which shocks others, but from which we can learn about the good life and the ways of achieving it. This is the wisdom that allows us to recognize and know our ignorance.[13] The clever slave, servant, or maid is hence the mastermind behind the development of the argument and comic plot, the director of the intrigue who plans and stages a whole new dramatic frame in order to trick the seemingly wise and steer the action toward the good life.

In order to be taken seriously, the comic hero has to become a fool. In the search for simplicity and self-reliance, they suspend the serious norms of behavior and oftentimes even of thinking. The comic hero, who is poor and dispossessed, outsmarts everyone else, yet appears under the guise of a simpleton, fool, trickster, *alazon*, or buffoon. The fool is the one who fools around, who acts strangely and out of place, and seems to be mistaken, but in fact dares to tell the truth.

The comic hero stands out by being "the other" of everyone else. They look differently, speak differently, dress differently, and act differently. Already for the serious philosophical gaze of Plato, comedy is too base and ridiculous, and hence should be left to slaves and foreigners.[14] However, a foreigner or a slave is never a bore, exactly because they can see—and tell—things differently. In this sense, a philosopher is a comic figure and a foreigner to their own country because they despise the common sense that they lack, and is (or should be) ready and capable of thinking beyond the accepted social and political divides and cultural prejudices.[15]

In comedy, only a slave is capable of transgressing social and conventional differences and of driving action toward justice and equality. Personal, social, and political liberation is realized in the comic plot as a prized aim that can be accomplished in New Comedy. All those who were oppressed in the beginning—a slave, a mistreated and silenced woman, a person in a position of dependence, a stranger—are liberated in the end by their own effort, leading the others toward the same goal.[16]

Comedy can be thus taken as dramatic action that unfolds through its plot, which intends to resolve a complication through a mutually shared performance where one of the characters serves as a mastermind—or philosopher on stage—who moves action toward a resolution of the conflict and the fulfillment of the aspirations of all the participants. Comedy and philosophy, then, are capable of restoring social and political justice. We might say that the justice of comedy consists in the recovery of human equality and dignity, of well-being and freedom that are achieved in and as the end of (often difficult) action and free (and often dangerous) public deliberation with others in the exercise of free speech.

With the advent of the modern self-isolating subject who imposes its form of solitary thinking and action onto everyone who participates in it—no one can escape it—even the comic character becomes lonely, boring, bored.[17] This is ironic, but the modern subject is eager to wear irony because it is a thinly disguised pretense that shows off one's essence by seemingly withdrawing it, in a desperate and persistently boring attempt at constant self-assertion at the expense of the (absent) other.

The comic philosophical figure as the thinker who thinks with and sometimes against others on the public stage is best represented by the Cynic, an illegal "undocumented" immigrant to Athens from Paphlagonia, poor, dispossessed, and homeless, deprived of property and political rights, who deliberately and ironically appears simplistic, a Zanni, bumming around and provoking other citizens of the comic world, questioning oppressive everyday practices and commonly accepted thoughts, and eventually leading out of the impasse of the unresolved problem by pointing toward a solution.

However, ancient unselfish philosophical Cynicism, which intended to help promote the well-being of others, starkly differs from modern cynicism, popularized by Rousseau, Diderot, Wieland, and others, as the expression of the lonely, self-centered, vain, sarcastic, and ultimately tragic mind.[18] Many of the same features can be also seen in Aesop, a slave who composes fables that can be taken as abbreviated comic plots and who outsmarts, and thus rules, his master, and in Socrates, who speaks to the common people and fools around, ironically asserting his not knowing yet at the same time directing his interlocutors through the maze of a complex argument.[19] Both the comic poor figure who is the philosopher on scene and the philosopher who is the comic figure in life selflessly and nonautonomously promote the well-being of others.

It is not the tragic boring drama of the self-entertainment of the modern monological subject who desperately tries to find a way out of the self-imposed impasse of loneliness through entertainment—but comedy as the nonboring, engaging, dialogical interaction that allows for well-being with others as a nonbored actor in a dialogical comedy, rather than a tragic observer or bored flâneur.[20] Unlike the solitary unhappy observer who endlessly flâneurs around the city full of the silhouettes and shades of others, the comic observer always acts as a comic detective, who is capable of solving, together with others, a current, seemingly irresolvable (personal, social, or political) problem.[21]

Freedom and equality, then, are not given, guaranteed, or established by an act of a single autonomous subject but can and must be achieved in and through comic common action supported by shared thinking and deliberation, in which everyone is involved, yet in which the dispossessed—the public thinker on the political stage—guides everyone toward reaching the good ending. Comedy and (political) philosophy thus respectively establish plot and argument through a reflective, argumentative procedure that requires an actor as a thinker who advances, together with others, the resolution of a conflict, the conclusion of an argument, and the solution of a problem, as well as the resolution of a debate.

(3) *Ontology again: well-being as being with the other.* Finally, the third appearance of well-being overcomes the rupture of same and other, which characterizes boredom III as one's incapacity to act and be with others. In the severance of same and other, others get atomized and "swerve" at each one's inclination, which is interpreted as autonomous rational will, set within the indifferent social sphere where no personal communication or real political change is any more possible. Again, if to be is to be in dialogue, then this break constitutes the negation of personal being where each one is cut off not only from others but also from oneself and is thrown back to the odium of the lonely autonomous existence, which is not-being.

Well-being or good life, then, is the dialogical communication of same and nonexclusive other (*allos*) as others, where one is always already with others in being with others. In this respect, being and being with others are tautological. Within the boring rupture of the unsurpassable separation of same and other produced by the autonomous subject, one is always *among*, next to, and in the midst of others, who are unreachable and mutually exclusive only when postulated by the solitary moralistic reason, where one is always tragically *after* others, who are lost and gone forever. Yet being *with* others is being together in inclusive dialogical communication, which, however, is allosensual and unfinalizable, never settled once and for all, never afterwards but always renewable.

In well-being as being with others, one is not dissolved into or obliterated by others. For others are neither isolated atoms or individuums, nor a totality of representations or elements of one single function of the self-universalized autonomous subject, which can be variously represented as one single nation, state, language, literature, etc. Well-being as dialogical being with other-*allos* allows others to be together as unique, different, and inextinguishable others who deliberate on their actions and act together toward shared well-being. Well-being, then, is not being-without or being at the expense of others who are excluded from being well-off. Well-being is the commonly distributed being that is also political, is the being of *demos*, of the plurality of mutually irreducible equals who are engaged in the difficult yet realizable task of dialogical being with each other, liberated and free as the end of their action. In dialogical well-being everyone is responsible for, and always involved with, each other. Since no one is excluded from such renewable interaction of same and other, everyone is a free and equal participant in it, an actor in the comedy of well-being. Well-being as being with others might also return nature to us and bring us back to nature as the place of well-being, inhabited and habitable together with others, including other living beings.[22]

As I have argued, dialogical being is a synthesis of same and other, which means that same (of a person) and other (of others and one's personal other) always interact, to the extent that everyone is engaged in being as being in dialogue. But dialogical being is also a *mediated* being by everyone who is neither a function of the same nor is an abstractly asserted other of the same, but is a concrete person engaged in being as the unfinalizable dialogue. Every dialogical participant is the protagonist, the director, and the mediator of the dialogical being. The medium of being as being with other is dialogue, not the media of entertainment. Well-being, then, is nonboring being that brings together same and other as being with other mediated by and shared with others.

Productivity of boredom. If to be is to be in dialogue, dialogue is not productive. The well-being of being with others is neither a given nor guaranteed, but it can be achieved in and as the realization of the end of the comedy of human life in the joint effort of all the participants. As such, well-being is not produced, is not a product, and does not itself produce anything. Here, one might recall the Aristotelian distinction between the productive and the practical, making and doing, where the end of *poiēsis* lies outside of the productive action, whereas the end of *praxis* is within its activity. Comic dialogical being, then, is practical and not productive, because its end—well-being—lies within the shared activity of being with others.[23]

But while dialogue is not productive, boredom can be productive—not of well-being but of change that motivates us as guidance to act and move on toward well-being with others. We can think and discover new things because of boredom—but not any kind of boredom. As boredom I and II, it is not productive: in the absence of other and of same, it causes, and is translated into, stillness, consternation, stupor, self-denial, and flight from oneself which, in the absence of the dialogical other, is not there anyway. But boredom III can be productive, since it stands for the already always missed attempt of the modern subject to breach the gap between same and other and reach out for the other in dialogue with others—for the "and" in same-and-other. Boredom often does not allow us to ask the question and understand what that question might be. But being exposed to this inevitable form of boredom as odium, one misses oneself, others, and the world, but does so in productive and original ways. Once translated into *curiosity*, the boredom of the odium can become a major driving force in human inventiveness. Curiosity makes us vigilant to being as being-around. Looking attentively at something that appears new and unusual, curious and frightening, might seem useless and distracting, yet in the long run might teach us unexpected skills and help in solving unforeseen problems.

Besides, both misunderstanding and failure can be productive, to the extent that they motivate and enable one to try to understand the cause of the failure and to rectify it. Such is also boredom, which is the Kantian cunning of nature within us, an indication that something is not right, that we somehow have missed the possibility of well-being, yet the very possibility and the understanding of the good life are implicitly there in boredom. Boredom can enhance creativity.[24] According to a legend, Bach composed his *Well-Tempered Clavier* very quickly because he happened to be at a place with no harpsichord, where he was utterly bored.[25] Therefore, the critical analysis of boredom might give us a chance at understanding nonboring well-being and the way to live it.

Well-being as friendship. If well-being is dialogical comic being with others, then well-being is impossible without friendship and is itself a form of friendship. For being *with*—not in solitude among—others is the fundamental presupposition of and precondition for friendship, which is impossible without others. Being with others is analytically included into the concept of friendship.

Friend is famously "the other self," the *alter ego*, into whom one sees both the other and the reflection of oneself as the other, whom one follows and often imitates, and with whom one lives and acts not always in an easy but allosensual way, and does so toward the realization of well-being as good life with others.[26] Friend is the one who is capable of being, that is, of dialogical being with others. Therefore, in order to be able to exercise the activity of friendship as being with others, one also has to be a friend to and with oneself.[27]

Aristotle famously distinguished three kinds of friendship, those based on utility, pleasure, and the good, of which the last one is the highest form of friendship, practiced by people who share and exemplify moral attitudes toward each other.[28] But in any of its forms, friendship is always among *equals*. As the old Pythagorean proverb runs, "friends share everything in common": in order to be a friend, one has to be with others and treat others as equals.[29] By enacting the equality, one establishes a commonality, a communication between friends in which everyone participates, and which thus forms a community of common aspirations and interests.[30] Friendship is a being together with others that presupposes equality, reciprocity, and mutual responsibility as responsiveness to the other.[31] Such a communication is dialogical, because it is based on the unfinalizable disclosure of the other as a friend—as the other of oneself and others. Such a communication is also comic, because everyone is involved in achieving and practicing the good life as the end of their shared striving. The dialogical structure of friendship can be seen in that friendship, as Agnes Heller has observed; a structure that is based on the trinity of giving, receiving, and reciprocating, which can be understood in dialogue as speaking to others, being heard, and being answered. Friendship, therefore, is the allosensual dialogical and cooperative (rather than competitive) comic being with others, a concrete realization of the same and other in their interaction, and hence is well-being in its distilled form. As such, friendship is embodied well-being and thus can never be boring.

Sometimes we can tell more about a particular age—and retroactively think of it as an epoch—if we find out what is missing or excluded from its grand philosophical oeuvre, which can be taken as the age's attempt at self-reflection. It is important to see what remains subdued, suppressed, and is deemed unimportant.

For Aristotle's morally decent person (σπουδαῖος), friendship is absolutely fundamental as the way to relate to the other and not just care for one's own prosperity.[32] Friendship, then, is not a duty but an expression of moral goodness. Yet reflection on friendship is mostly absent in modern philosophy. Thus, there is no discussion of friendship in Descartes, whose main philosophical works move around the *ego*, while the *Passions of the Soul* describes the passions of a lonely soul who has no friends and suffers from unrequited love. Discussing moral duties toward others, Kant suggests that *moral* friendship is a *duty* and thus is very rare, while friendship as such is a pure yet necessary idea that cannot be reached at all.[33] And while Hegel speaks of just about anything and neatly arranges all possible logical, natural, moral, and political categories into a unified and coherent system, he remains strangely almost silent about friendship (as he is also about boredom), mentioning it only occasionally and in passing. To be sure, the omittance of friendship is not accidental: being lonely, secluded, and self-isolated, incapable of reaching out for the other, the modern subject is *incapable of friendship* as commonality and being with others. And without friendship as the embodiment of dialogical and comic being, the modern autonomous subject is incapable of well-being. It only produces the disconnected many individuals that live in seclusion among others but not with others.

If friendship is being together with others, as a commonality and communication in a community of friends, then its realization is a *political friendship* that promotes communal well-being. As a political friend, the human is a political being, πολιτικὸν ζῷον, who lives a shared life together with others as an equal, which in turn is the condition of democracy.[34] As being together, friendship is *acting together*, is the exercise in living together, and in sharing a particular form of (political) life. In this sense, (political) friendship is *ascetic* in the sense of ἄσκησις, the exercise of being-together with others, acting mindfully and thoughtfully toward the other, and hence dialogically and comically.[35] For this reason, the modern subject as incapable of friendship is also unable to engage in a proper politics. Instead of the dialogical politics of many, it perpetuates the autonomous ethics of the one. Therefore, in order to regain political life as action toward shared well-being, we need to transform the very understanding of ourselves as not atomistic embodiments of the modern, lonely, autonomous, and tragic subject and realize ourselves as political friends in comic dialogical communication, exercising well-being as being with others.

Well-being in flow? This understanding of well-being should be contrasted with the modern concept of happiness as "flow," as suggested by the psychologist Mihaly Csikszentmihalyi. According to this interpretation, the flow is "the positive optimal experience," which consists in "a self-contained activity, one that is done not with the expectation of some future benefit, but simply because the doing itself is the reward."[36] In Aristotle, this is the description of *praxis* as opposite to *poiēsis*, yet now it lumps the two together, suggesting that the productive activity can also be practical and exemplify well-being. Flow has to do primarily with the organization of the individual self as *consciousness* and has the goal of one's satisfaction and enjoyment, putting the stress on individual creativity.[37] As such, such an activity is individual, *self-directed*, and performed for the sake of one's enjoyment, rather than for the sake of others. The others come into the picture only as a pretext for the individual flow. Thus, teaching children can result in a flow if one enjoys doing it, whereas teaching children for the sake of their betterment without one's enjoyment does not qualify as flow. Happiness, then, is strictly individual and arises out of one's ability to use the environment, of which others are only a part, to creatively organize the proper enjoyable flow of one's life. Reaching flow apparently allows one to find a middle path between anxiety and boredom, and hence escape the pain of loneliness.[38] Flow is meant to avoid boredom, yet it equally avoids the other as a person, or rather is interested in them only as a means for easy flowing.

The concept of "flow" should be contrasted with the ancient Stoic concept of the "good or easy flow of life" (εὔροια βίου), which is life according to nature as rationally self-governed material being.[39] The flow with nature is the voluntary following of its universal law, which is reason or λόγος. Such a life is not, and cannot be, boring, because boredom cannot be meaningfully predicated of the self-contained rational life of nature. This comes in stark contrast to Kant's understanding of nature that has planted boredom in us for the purpose of productive life that eventually allows us to achieve the well-being of contentment with the consciousness of duty well-performed. In this sense, for Kant boredom *is* life according to nature. But this is the modern understanding of nature, which, in its rational regularity, is a construction of the modern autonomous monological subject. Although the flow experience is described as self-contained, it is not natural in the Stoic sense, but resides within individual consciousness, which is productive of the "flow" and the ensuing individual pleasure, not shareable with, and unattainable to, others.

In modernity, happiness comes into being as a *right* that needs to be secured by production, by labor, and especially by work, if one is to use Hannah Arendt's distinction.[40] In modernity, leisure is boring. The Reformation begins with considering Sunday, the day of rest, as a bore, because it interrupts and interferes with the "flow" of the regular work pattern. In the good life as achievable by mutual effort, one works in order to have rest, so that the purpose of the *vita activa* is the *vita contemplativa*.[41] But in modernity rest becomes utterly boring and almost unbearable, and is thus substituted by endless entertainment.[42] Yet modern entertainment is equally boring, for while everything appears different in its kaleidoscope, nothing really changes.

The personal freedom, the recognition of personal dignity, and the assertion of one's worth come only with and through socially significant and mutually inspiring work. As Sebastian de Grazia rightly observes, the concept of the "right to work" was first established only after 1848 (which coincides with the time of modern boredom's flourishing): "only through work, a new fundamental right, can men (all adult males and some females) pursue happiness. The original idea was the reverse: only through not having to work can men pursue happiness."[43] The problem of the liberation of work from its alienation and enslavement by private capital, of bringing work back to the equally shared sphere of public activity and practice, is a specifically modern problem, predicated on the understanding of well-being as individually tailored, productive, and produced. The artistic production as *poiēsis* may be difficult but it is not boring, being creative of the same in an (at least slightly) other new way. But modern work is boring, being stripped of creativity by invariably producing the same, where the other comes in the repetition of the indistinguishable another and another en masse, privately appropriated and owned in the interests of the few. Well-being or happiness in modernity is therefore associated with work, which now needs to be politically liberated. Making work once more engaging and nonboring, not through political struggle but rather by putting oneself into a trance-like state of flow is, then, a revisionist reaction to the seeming failure of such liberation.

In my interpretation, however, well-being is *nonproductive*: it does not produce anything, including enjoyment, which is included in being as dialogical. Well-being is not a *poiēsis*, because it is not produced but dialogically sustained and reproduced as a common practice. Personal well-being neither dissolves oneself into others nor makes others instrumental for one's being-well—it makes each one an indispensable and equal partner in the co-being with every other participant of shared being. One only needs to add that political liberation becomes a precondition for the possibility of nonboring well-being with others.

Anxiety. Anxiety, dread, or fear is the unsolicited yet inevitable and crucial response to our being rooted in the very construction of modern subjectivity, which, however, is different from boredom. The thinker of anxiety in modernity is Kierkegaard, from whom Heidegger takes the concept in *Being and Time*, in which anxiety, *Angst*, becomes the fundamental mood or attunement, and later, in *The Fundamental Concepts of Metaphysics*, turns into boredom.[44] In *The Concept of Anxiety*, Kierkegaard argues that anxiety is that which defines subjectivity: "anxiety is really the *discrimen* [distinction] of subjectivity."[45] Anxiety, *Angest*, is then the (psychological) state that responds to, and conditions the unconditional, which is the original sin (BA 179-80).

Original sin for Kierkegaard is not a state or disposition but the primary negativity itself, the "necessary other" (*nødvendige Andet*) that defines us both collectively and individually, and does so in a negative way: it is something that has to be accepted before we even know what it is. We have to agree to accept the negative before it can be known. The negative is "anxciting." Strictly speaking, sin does not take or have place; it has no place at all, which is its definition (BA 112-33), which means that the primary negativity is outside of time and place. The acceptance of the original sin, then, is a pure act of will and is done on the authority of volition that justifies its unfounded act by reference to that which is infallible and unprovable. This is the act of disobedience. For Luther, whom Kierkegaard is studiously following, the original sin cannot be known rationally (BA 123). Original sin is thus unthinkable, although it is most certain—for it is affirmed by an act of one's own will, just as is the autonomy of moral reason. In this sense, the original sin is *the other* of reason—the unfathomable, radical other. As such, the original sin is nothing, yet it is not the nothing of privation but the nothing that, in its absence, "is" the origin of our response to ourselves, others, and the world. This is the meaning of "original" in the original sin.

The transcendence of the negative, which defines our action, inaction, and the very attitude or mode of our being, makes its own origin inaccessible to reason and unexplainable to it. One cannot reach the origin in its negativity in a systematic argument by going, or running, through premises and the steps of reasoning toward the conclusion, and so one can only jump to it in a nondiscursive, and thus nonrational and noncomprehensible way. No wonder that modern philosophy of mind does not know or recognize nondiscursive thinking:

nondiscursivity is reserved for the will alone. Therefore, accessing the origin in its utter negativity—expressed as the original sin—becomes an act that can only be performed by the will. Modern reason runs, but the will jumps.

The acceptance of the negativity and the rational inaccessibility of the origin means that it can only be jumped to. And yet, since the leap of the will is sudden, unexpected, and does not follow from a previous, carefully ordered logical and systematic construction, it is atemporal and incomprehensible, and hence irrational. The jump to the alleged origin can be equally considered—in a nonthinkable way—as posited by the very act of will that is meant to recognize it. There is no gap or conceivable distance between the origin and that which is conditioned by it, that which it tries to get access to, or revert to, as its very origin. Hence, in the will that attempts to access the alleged origin of its action, the act of the recognition of that origin cannot be distinguished from the act of positing it. This is precisely the act of establishing the autonomy of will as free and unconditioned, which becomes the foundation for the constitution of the modern subject. This is the act of the free acceptance of the responsibility of the recognition of the origin in its negativity. The rejection of the origin makes it impossible for us to act and hence destroys the very possibility of action. In traditional terms, the rejection of the original sin is a sin. Accepting the unacceptable, a responsibility for something that is not our individual obligation—the original nontemporary and nonthinkable act of trespassing on the not yet posited—becomes our moral duty. This is the responsibility as answerability to the other that is not yet there and thus cannot answer back. Responsibility is the modern translation of guilt as the reaction to the original sin. Conditioned by the unconditional, this duty is the basis for responsibility as the expression of the autonomy of the will.

The negativity (sinfulness) of the origin of our being among the existent or beings defines the preeminent negativity of our response: from this perspective, our attitude is that of shame, guilt, sacrifice, and anxiety or fear (BA 159, 189-90). Negativity has already been posited even before temporality arises, because access to the other is precluded by taking the other of the origin to be inaccessible and unthinkable. Reaching out to the other can only be realized, therefore, in an incomprehensible "qualitative" jump (*Spring*; see, e.g., BA 127, 137, 141, 146, 152, 155, 168, 181), in which the self becomes posited, although in an incomprehensible way.

Nothing. Anxiety is a response and reaction to nothing. Anxiety is the fear of nothing, the dread we experience when we are confronted with nothing. But if nothing is nothing, then there is nothing to worry about. However, rather than experiencing calm or indifference in response to nothing, we experience anxiety.

As Dio Chrysostom says, for a tyrant the anticipation of troubles is worse than the troubles themselves.[46] Anxiety comes with the fear of an imagined trouble, the anticipation of something that is not there and might never materialize—of nothing. Nothing cannot be known, which is why not knowing is the nontemporal and nonhistorical state of *innocence*, where we do not yet know anything that might cause anxiety, because we do not know nothing—nothing cannot be known. By not knowing nothing, we know nothing. So it both is and is not the case that we know nothing—which cannot be known.

The innocence of not knowing can be abandoned only suddenly, in a jump, which is an act of will, and not as the result of a process, which is that of cognition. The realization that our being is not knowledgeable brings us deep concern, since nothing is not a thing, and knowing this amounts to the negation or suspension of knowing, which is the knowing that something is or is not the case.

Innocence, then, is the knowledge that stands for not knowing (BA 159). But the not yet known of not knowing is already something, and as such for Kierkegaard is a state (*Tilstand*, BA 132). Because it is the state of innocence, it should be the state of calm and quietude, but because there is nothing to encounter, nothing to resolve, nothing to struggle with, it causes uneasiness and uncertainty about the undeservedness of such innocence. Metaphorically speaking, this is the state of the dreaming spirit. Nothing can be opposed or grasped here. It is just nothing. The undisturbed dreaming of something out of nothing is not mediated by a reflection or reasoned decision. Nothing is nothing, and thus it does not cause or produce anything—and yet, in the dream-like opposition to nothing, it disturbs the dreaming spirit and generates anxiety or dread (BA 136). Nothing can become and be anything, with no reason at all for its being dreamed this way, always undeserved, contingent, and feared.

Since nothing is not a thing but nothing, it cannot be known. Yet one could still try to make some distinctions with respect to the indistinguishable. For one can say (1) "nothing" (N); (2) "nothing is" (N is); and (3) "nothing is nothing" (N is N).

In (1), "nothing" simply means positing or asserting nothing, yet, since nothing is not anything definite, it cannot be posited. Nothing does not even have a name, so "nothing" is an arbitrary expression. Hence nothing cannot be asserted or expressed. In (2), "nothing is" is an existential statement, yet, since nothing is not, it is contradictory and thus cannot be asserted either. In (3), "nothing is nothing" is a predicative statement of the kind "S is P." It is a tautology in which the subject and the predicate coincide, and which takes nothing as a subject with the essential predicate of being nothing. Yet since nothing is not anything that can be expressed in a positive way, it does not have an essence, and so the statement cannot be taken as true. Therefore, nothing cannot be expressed or asserted by way of thought or speech and does not have a name, essence, or existence. There is no way to nothing in and by thought. Peering into nothing does not lead anywhere, as the goddess already has warned us in Parmenides.[47] There is not even an "it" to nothing and no "is." Rather, using Heidegger's representation of being as graphically crossed out, ~~it is~~ not. Nothing "is" always in "is not" and thus is self-contradictory even before contradiction can be asserted or thought. Nothing is not a contrary to a "thing" or being. Nothing, therefore, is not a privation of anything but is not a positive thing either. It cannot be mediated in and by thought, which, again, means that it cannot be thought. Nothing can only be assumed or posited as preceding being, as a nontranscendental and nonthinkable precondition for the possibility of being that is not primary, originary, and utterly simple—for the absolutely simple is unthinkable—but being as a synthesis of the same and the other mediated in and by thought. Nothing is still incomprehensible and can only be posited by an act of will that then produces or creates something out of nothing.

Nothing, then, causes anxiety and fear. Yet, because it is nothing and cannot be thought, such causation itself cannot be expressed rationally but becomes an act of will. We thus create anxiety ourselves (BA 234).

Reflection. When we are bored, we know that we are bored, so we cannot miss it. Once we stop noticing that we are bored, boredom goes away, but anxiety stays. Therefore, once thinking becomes mediated by reflection (BA 153), the anxiety does not go, precisely because it has nothing for its nonexisting and nonobjective object. Rather, it is the fantasy of dreaming imagination that creates something out of nothing in its demiurgic act. The realization of this leads us to abandon the prereflexive and ahistorical state of innocence and become knowledgeable of being guilty of abandoning the original state, which still cannot be explained and thus can only be accessed in a leap of will. For knowing that we know nothing is the result of a sustained philosophical reflection, to which Socrates and Nicolas of Cusa come only after long deliberation. Yet, for the lonely self-aware subject, reflexivity does not provide liberation in thought but rather promotes guilt (BA 189–90), since reflexive thought is not able to rationally process and understand the jump from innocence, which becomes a leap of faith in an act of prereflexive and nonreflexive will.

Nothing as possibility. Nothing cannot be even said to be nothing because, by the act of identification with itself, it becomes something that is not a thing in which there might be recognized an "it" or a "self." Just nothing, then. But the nothing of dread is not a privation of something that has been there before (logically, and not temporally), the lack of which could cause anxiety. Nothing, therefore, is the pure potentiality of *anything* that has not, and has never, happened. It is not a universal capacity of actualizing anything and everything by dreaming it out or by willing it—but a pure potentiality that never becomes definite. Nothing "is" the potentiality of the not-yet and never-yet. It is thus the indefinite future of the eternity that coincides with the moment (BA 175, 232) in which nothing can yet be noticed or thought, but in which everything can be incomprehensibly transformed in a leap toward the actual.

Such a potentiality is not that of concrete possibilities that can be realized: it is not the capacity of thinking that becomes actual once we come to think something, but rather an indefinite *materia prima*, which is not a definite something that can take the shape of anything through the intention of will or by sheer chance.[48] The possibility of nothing is fearful and frightening. Only those who went all the way through the anxiety and fear of the indefinite possibility can come to not be afraid of any danger that life might bring. As such, possibility is heavy on us (BA 235). Fear is the fear of the infinitely and indefinitely possible. Possibility becomes actual only through anxiety, and yet, it is never realized, never becomes real and can never be known—because it is *nothing.*

Anxious freedom. Therefore, in anxiety one cannot choose between something and something, because something is not posited in and by an opposition to nothing, because nothing is nothing and hence is not opposite to anything. The possibility of nothing is the "possibility to can" (*Mulighed af at kunne*, BA 138), of being able to do anything and yet nothing, because of nothing's not-yet, its utter indefiniteness. Arising out of the confrontation with nothing, anxiety is the possibility of freedom (*Angesten er Friehedens Mulighed*, BA 234). As the never extinguishable range of possibilities, nothing yields or results in freedom. Nothing cannot be grasped or reached, and hence can only be jumped to. One can become free in the momentary leap toward the realization of the unrealizable, precisely because it cannot be realized or thought in its concreteness. Freedom, then, is the impossible choice out of the equally possible infinite number of choices.

Freedom can only be jumped toward in an unjustifiable act of will, beyond any reasoning that cannot grasp nothing but is always anxious of it. Freedom, then, cannot be a rationally justified choice but only an act of free will. If such a will does not want to consider itself contingent but necessary in its freedom, it has to become self-defining and thus autonomous, where an originally arbitrary and unjustified act of will becomes necessary and inevitable *after* such an act—the act of an incomprehensible leap of will.

Since freedom is the jump into the yet unknown, it extends the range of possibilities in ways that become possible and meaningful and can be explored only *after* the act of jumping. It is at this nontemporal moment that the prereflectively and autonomously established freedom first becomes possible and liberating. In Kierkegaard's account, evil is closedness, while liberation is openness and opening up, is that which widens and extends (*det Udvidende*, BA 207). Evil, therefore, is not a privation of the good but an unexpected and undeserved suddenness instead of continuity; closedness instead of openness for the other; muteness instead of conversation with the other that might liberate us from the original inaccessible negativity. The closed—evil—is mute, whereas the word, *logos*, is the liberative emptying into the openness of human possibilities. The word is first uttered into the void of nothing that only then becomes understood in its concreteness and all its meanings. This act of utterance is the leap of freedom. The opposite of evil is thus not the good but freedom, which lies in the sphere of volition and action.

The good is thinkable, yet thought is at its limit, *à bout de souffle*, in its attempt to grasp the radical beyond, which is nothing. Freedom, then, becomes separate from the good, which can be thought and understood. Even if one adopts the Platonic stance toward the good as situated beyond being, the good is still posited in the opposition to thought within thought.[49] Modern freedom, however, is exempt from thinking, which is clearly expressed by Kant, for whom freedom is realized by the act of will, which should become rational only after the act of an autonomous volition.

Anxiety is therefore opposed to boredom. For the anxiety about nothing implies the jump toward freedom that can—and ought to—become rational only after the solitary leap toward liberation. The reflective liberation of boredom, on the contrary, can open a way toward freedom in shared thought and distributed action with others. But this is something that modern thought, enwrapped with self-uplifting lonely suffering, badly misses. No wonder, then, that for Kierkegaard the boring is the "demonic," which stands for the gloomy emptiness of the contentless "continuity within nothing."[50] As Kierkegaard argues in the "Rotation of Crops," boredom is inescapable for human beings, because it comes out of nothingness that is inseparable from the existent. This is why all people are bores and all are bored. It is not idleness or laziness, then, but boredom that is the root of all evil.[51] If boredom is rooted so deeply in us, there is no escape from it, where admiration and indifference are indistinguishable. And yet, like a farmer who rotates the crops, we need to keep looking for something other, something else: always different, always new. Yet this new is not the new that can ultimately change our lives but is another and another: it is *arbitrary*. Therefore, we should marvel at nothing (*nil admirari*) but only cultivate the forgetting of the old.[52] Needless to say, it is a futile yet necessary attempt, since we cannot go beyond the self-established circle and limit of subjectivity.

For modern subjectivity, the boredom of continuity is expressed in the repetition of not dying, which is not immortality but being always the same, continuously repeating itself without a possibility of a radical break, without a liberating renovation or suddenness.[53] Death is tragic. It comes as a radical break that, due to the cultivation of the negativity of sin, might result in the hope of new life rather than life lived together with others, which is the aim of comedy. But the self-centered tragic subject, incapable of reaching out for the other and thus of friendship, takes the comic (*det Comiske*) as the continuity of the demonically perennial—or at least, endlessly long—same (BA 215). In this way, the modern subject inevitably misses, misunderstands, and demonizes the comic immortality of the renewal of life, love, and freedom as the boring not-dying. The inescapably anxious, self-divinizing modern subject, who finds its full expression in Kierkegaard's work, does not—and cannot—even notice that the boredom of the unending repetitive same without the other is its own self.

So it is the comic well-being that can liberate such a subject from itself, which, however, it inevitably misses in its autonomous, sublime tragic solitude and self-isolation.

CHAPTER 6

Scandal

We can break away from the spell of boredom in well-being as dialogical and comic being with others. In the absence of dialogical communication, entertainment as diversion from and substitution for well-being becomes the pointless and endless flight from boredom, which we can never escape and thus are advised to wholeheartedly embrace. Yet, within the life defined by the modern subject, a nonboring well-being is impossible because the modern subject does not recognize or tolerate the other of others, which is a precondition for well-being. So the subject desperately keeps staging a rebellion against itself in the most radical attempt at a breakaway from boredom, which is *scandal*. And if boredom is the rational calculation of the solitary monological thinking, scandal is its ecstatic autonomous will.

Scandal is an event that grasps everyone's attention and becomes the most discussed and referenced topic that enlivens the repetitive, measured, and steady flow of life. As such, scandal is always (1) *public*. Scandal is the public reaction to the violation of moral, legal, social, and political norms and customs, exacerbated once such breaching is perceived as intentional and deliberately provocative. Because scandal suspends and questions existing norms, it is indispensable in and for politics, where the norms are often implicit. Until these normative boundaries are transgressed in a scandal, they may not be clearly established or explicitly demarcated and understood by people. Scandal is only meaningful in the presence of others, among whom it becomes quickly spread, shared, and debated. It needs and involves other people, in order to understand the meaning and significance of a misdeed as misdoing in its semantic, syntactic, and pragmatic aspects.

The public space of scandal is the space of *spectacle*, which thus becomes *theater*. For this reason, scandal has the structure of a *theatrical act*: it needs spectators who are drawn into the discussion of the action and spread it further. Such theatrical performance is *conceptually written*, insofar as it involves an ordered philosophical or dialectical argument, which has a clear structure of premises, development, and conclusion. But *medially* this performance is *oral* and takes the form of public dialogical debate, often comic in its structure. On the scene of the public political performance, the spectators oftentimes themselves become (at least imaginary) actors of and in a scandal, who at the same time critically reflect on the activity and its implied norms that have been overstepped and, through reflection and discussion, publicly rehearsed, rejuvenated, restored, and reaffirmed. In this way, in the theater of political life, spectators can become actors, which is the intention of democracy. And yet, in a political scandal, the spectators are mostly not actors but are left to *publicly* discuss the meaning of the enacted event. A scandal, then, can trigger a series of important political actions that might lead to a change in moral, legal, and political norms and institutions. Hence, political life to a great extent lives off scandals and needs them as the means of rejuvenating public life. Scandal is always embarrassing, questioning and challenging existing moral, social, legal, and political norms and practices. For this reason, scandal is a *mediated* being with others where everyone is included in it as a participant. Oftentimes, the participation in a scandal is inadvertent, provoked by an unintentional blunder, omission, misquoting, or even misprint (Huxley's "vomedy"). Exclusive of the other, the modern subject is scandalously incapable of scandal, and yet yearns for it as a remedy from the inevitable, excruciating boredom. Scandal is therefore deeply political and is required in political life, which it refreshes, restates, and restarts.

Besides, scandal is (2) *dialogical*. For one needs others as dialogical partners in order to make *common* sense of a scandal. Dialogue engages others inadvertently as spectators, often as actors, and invariably as judges who attempt to grasp the meaning of an event. Scandal can be vicious, because it is a public display and testing of commonly shared moral, social, and political norms, which are now being suspended, judged, and performatively denied, or at least questioned. Scandal is a *sui generis* "border situation" in and for dialogue, when the latter is no longer possible and yet is absolutely needed. As I have argued, dialogue presupposes a certain creative and productive tension, or *allosensus*, which is not a dialectical tension but the one that constantly propels dialogue to move on. For dialogue requires interruption by others and is based on mutual interruption, which testifies to the life of the mind as being in dialogue and to the robust presence of the other who answers to one's call and rejoinder in unexpected ways. Scandal too brings tension into human interaction, but rather than disrupting it by exposing hypocrisy and pretense, scandal renews and revives communication by allowing for a new beginning and the rethinking of the interlocutors' positions and their very grounds, which often remain unthematized and not spelled out until the very moment and act of a scandal.

Scandal intensifies dialogue sometimes up to the point of its apparent (temporary) suspension. In this sense, (3) scandal is a *radical break* of dialogical communication to the point of its impossibility, and the rupture of dialogical relations that, however, can be then reflectively studied and restored as the result of a scandal. Insofar as scandal is radical, it allows for reflection on the possibility and the very root, rather than the origin, of shared dialogical action as interaction with others. This, as I have argued, is the ontological precondition of the possibility of dialogue, which is the unfinalizable and renewable communication with others that involves the personal other of the self and others in its inextinguishability. And insofar as scandal is a break, it is *critical* in its negativity, one that allows for novelty, for the rejuvenation of a stalled communication, and thus for rendering it dialogical again.

As theatrical, scandal (4) is *comic* (and as such is a staple in the comic repertoire), insofar as it often implies a hidden, and then suddenly revealed, physical altercation or illicit relationship for a (moral) double, which are all commonly explored in comedy. Scandal can degenerate into malicious gossip, as in Sheridan's "The School for Scandal."[1] But through a commonly shared critical reflection and reasoned action, comic scandal can also become a refreshing renewal of being with others, of a relationship that otherwise might go wrong and become stagnant, when the human enterprise of well-being becomes suffocating and boring.

Scandal (5) is characterized by *orality* and *loudness*: developing quickly in a vivid commotion, it propels and enhances itself through a loud bustle and noise.[2] The arresting attraction of scandal comes more from sound and hearing than from sight and vision. Sound can be frightening, whereas sight can be disgusting. Much more than a picture that is always abundant with excessive and often superfluous meanings, a loud unarticulated scream has the meaning of danger, of something going wrong that requires one's undivided attention, an unreflected and very quick response.[3]

Being dialogical, scandal is "conceptually" oral, since it is meant to be rehearsed, discussed, and processed in oral debate and (quick) transmission. The dialogical scandal is always mediated by the interaction with others, which constitutes being as dialogical being in public space. A good example of a modern productive scandal is punk music, which is conceptually oral (targeting and challenging the established written genres of poetry and music), intentionally loud, and challengingly public. Scandal has the structure of orality—not codified written literacy—and thus of myth, which always accompanies, or is created out of, a scandal. In this respect, prophecy is a scandal, and scandal is expected to have prophetic overtones that will set the crooked straight. Incapable of the proper scandal, the modern subject is a *loud* subject, crying out loud rather than whispering, warning itself of its superfluity and redundancy. Yet, at the same time, the modern subject is a silent one, remaining unheard and unreachable to itself and not properly understood by itself in its excessive lonely reflexivity.

Finally, in its blistering action, scandal (6) is *swift* and *spontaneous*. Unfolding very quickly, it cannot be held or controlled: it is an explosion, in which each one expresses themselves under the spell of necessity and yet freely communicates with others. One cannot choose whether to be in scandal or not, but one can choose how to behave and respond to its action, development, and challenges. Scandal is the expression of dialogical spontaneity, which testifies to live dialogical communication, not stifled by imposed prescriptions but rather following its own rules of engagement with the other. Unlike the solitary, unscandalous existence of the modern subject that preserves itself by the autonomous self-directed act of lonely volition, the messy scandal is *necessary* for dialogue and thus for our very being as being in dialogue, displaying its spontaneity and orality as the medium of the live dialogue, quick in its mutual, nondisruptive interruption. Being spontaneous, alive, and engaging, scandal is *never boring*. And if boredom comes with rational calculation that binds the will, scandal appears as an ecstatic spontaneous thinking shared with others that liberates the will.

The modern scandal and (lack of) mediation. There is, however, a specifically modern appropriation of scandal, which is an attempt of the modern, monological, tragic subject to regain the lost paradise of well-being as being with other. As I have argued, boredom is the proprium, the proper feature of the modern subject, its very ἴδιον—"idiotic one's own"—and nobody else's, since others are conspicuously absent from it. Scandal is always publicly improper: it is the *proper improper* of the modern subject.

The modern scandal (which, henceforth, I will be calling simply "scandal," in contradistinction to the dialogical scandal) is the inevitable and constantly repeated attempt of the modern subject to flee away and get rid of itself. As autonomous and moralistic, the modern subject intends to be critical of itself and hence constantly judges itself. In doing so, it scandalizes itself, which remains as futile and unsuccessful as its attempted suicide, because scandal is public in its nature and is therefore impossible in the absence of others. The modern scandal is both a response to and a distinct symptom of the modern subject's painful realization and unpublic recognition of the inaccessibility of being as being in dialogue, and of the impossibility of well-being. Such a lonely self-critical stance only creates—and constantly perpetuates—the crisis of self-understanding as the realization of being doomed (by itself) to boredom in the absence of the other.

As such, modern scandal is the embodiment of *unmediated negativity*, which does not allow for the reaching out to the other of oneself and the other of the world but rather denies such other. It is a Dionysian enterprise, where the other is never achieved in the chaotic celebration of life that ends in its utter negation. Returning to Benjamin's question of the opposite to boredom, one can say that the modern scandal stands in the unmediated contradictory opposition to boredom. Because of the absence of mediation by the other and the impossibility of well-being as well-being with the other, scandal can be considered the ethical *meson*, the mediating third between boredom and scandal. Perhaps, if being is being in dialogue and as such is well-being with others, then it can mediate between boredom and scandal. But the modern scandal is the expression of the modern subject's intolerance to mediation, which makes dialogue—and dialogical scandal—impossible, since it is supported and mediated by others. In this sense, scandal is opposed to boredom as the Dionysian to the Apollonian. Following Max Weber's distinction, one could say that the two ideal religious types of asceticism and mysticism correspond to the Apollonian boredom as unmediatingly opposed to the Dionysian scandal.[4] The very absence of mediation by the other *is* a modern scandal. If dialogical scandal is comic and sometimes carnivalesque, the modern scandal is downright tragic. If dialogical scandal lives off dialogue, the modern scandal is the condition of dialogue's impossibility. Hence, the tragic, lonely autonomy of the subject is itself a modern scandal. The modern subject is itself a scandal.

An illustration: Kant on scandal. A good illustration of the modern moralistic attitude toward scandal can be found in one of the major proponents of the idea of autonomy. In the *Metaphysics of Morals*, Kant argues that respect for the law is identical with the realization or consciousness of one's duty. In other words, one respects oneself for following the prescriptions that one has autonomously established for oneself as a universal representative of humankind and thereby for everyone, even if everyone remains inaccessible in this act of positing the moral law. The respect for the moral being—that is, for the legislator—is both a *duty* and a *right*. This for Kant is an undeniable claim that comes as the recognition of one's dignity and moral worth, the violation of which is infamy, disgrace—and a *scandal (Skandal)*. Scandal happens when vice becomes a publicly displayed example of the neglect of the strict laws of duty.[5] And although scandal is not legally punishable, it is an affront to morality. Hence, scandal should be prevented at all costs, and the *communication* that causes it should be arrested and *interrupted*.[6] Such an interruption, however, is not the mutual interruption that makes dialogue ongoing but the one that makes communication impossible.

The modern moral scandal is considered a trespassing of the rational self-constituting will of the autonomous legislator. Everyone who dares to disrespect and disregard this solemn sovereignty causes scandal and thus should be shunned, excluded from communication, and ostracized. The very discussion of scandal as the infringement and disrespect of the moral autonomy of reason becomes inevitably moralistic. Yet, since modern reason is lonely and tragic, always acting in the absence of the other and others, it cannot escape producing an imaginary scandal as a liberating thought experiment, in which the moralistic subject takes itself to be its own hypothetical other, making itself public and bringing its own autonomously self-prescribed moral law to its limit, in order to test its universal validity by violating, disregarding, and disrespecting the moral law and denying its strict moralistic prescriptions.

The scandal of plagiarism. When Plato and Alcidamas argue against writing, they repeat their argument almost verbatim.[7] We do not know who lifted the argument from whom, since neither refers to the other. But at the time it did not matter: everyone who read the texts knew both the references and the contexts and thus did not bother to establish the ownership of the original thought. Originality lay in the thought itself, not in its origin, so the very idea of owning a thought did not make sense. But since the modern subject owns and appropriates what it produces, everyone as its representative and embodiment is entitled not only to one's material product (which, however, is taken away from one under the modern capitalist system of production) but also to the results of one's will (moral judgments) and thought (intellectual products). Paradoxically, even though it is supposedly universal, the autonomously produced is owned as private. The work that is now considered the source of moral dignity is eventually appropriated by one owner and stored in the encampment of the private, and ultimately is owned by the modern subject under the guise of the universal and almighty—capital, state, law. The thought, written and published—made public—has to stand under, and be protected by, copyright. Plagiarism becomes a scandal. Even in an enthymeme, the omitted and the hinted at has to be properly referred to and acknowledged. Yet the quotation marks can produce a scandalous suspension of the said, in an ironic attempt to avoid scandal, when intentionally "quoting" the scandalous, abusive, or socially unacceptable phrase or word.

Medially, modern scandal becomes predictably inevitable and written, thus abandoning its spontaneity and orality. Without scandal, the dialogical life of the mind turns awry and loses the name of action. For the modern autonomous monological consciousness that wants to usurp, appropriate, and copyright even its own thought, it would be a scandal and a grave moral and legal trespass not to mention the source of each and every quotation, like the one in the previous sentence. I won't mention but rather scandalously plagiarize the quote, since its source is evident.

An etymological digression. A brief glimpse into the etymology of "scandal" might be helpful. Greek σκανδάλη originally means "stick in a trap on which the bait is placed, and which, when touched by the animal, springs up and shuts the trap" (LSJ). Metaphorically, it is used for "setting word-traps, i.e., throwing out words which one's adversary will catch at, and so be caught himself" (LSJ). In Aristophanes's *Acharnians* (687), σκανδάληθρον is used to characterize a trap of questions by which an old man is tricked in court by a skillful young orator. "Scandal," then, is a trick that makes weak speeches strong by planting scandalous, flawed rhetorical traps.[8] That a straight, simple thought or act can be bent and made crooked by a word snare is indeed a scandal, yet it suits the modern regal subject, who intends to win at any cost in any debate with itself in its own court, trapping itself intentionally against itself, and yet naively not noticing it. The related σκάνδαλον (Latin *scandalum*) appears in the Septuagint and the New Testament, where it stands for a trap for an enemy (LXX *Josh* 23.13, 1 *Kings* 18.21; *Rom.* 11.9). Metaphorically, it comes to signify a stumbling block or offense, and hence also temptation (*Matt.* 18.7; *Luke* 17.1), and as such acquires its contemporary meaning. The derived verb σκανδαλίζω means to cause to stumble, offend, disturb, and scandalize (*Matt.* 5:29, 17:27, 18:8).[9]

Therefore, "scandal" originally means provocation that is supposed to ensnare the other and perhaps display the truth (in court). But since the other remains inaccessible and just a task to be achieved, the modern subject scandalizes primarily and only itself, traps itself into an impasse with no way out. The modern subject remains a self-made immortal lonely thinker capable of inflicting the wound of self-scandalizing but incapable of death, juggling with logical constructions yet remaining an acrobat who performs on the tight rope of its own strung and straightened thought.[10]

Scandal in philosophy. Modern scandal is evident in philosophy itself, which is the transcription and expression of the modern subject as not a perennial being but a historical construction based on the appropriation of the idea of autonomy. As Kierkegaard observes, a single individual, as the embodiment of the modern subject, becomes more important than the universal, which becomes the scandal of the age.[11] But the modern subject is a lonely individual that makes itself a universal autonomous legislator.

One could say that from its very inception philosophy is a scandal: with Socrates and Diogenes, it is practiced and performed as dialogue with others in a public social and political setting.[12] A comic eccentric thinker creates a scandal that trespasses and suspends a norm of thinking and behavior but does not cancel it: by establishing a new norm, the action reaffirms the normativity of decentered commonly shared action. As dialogical, philosophy presupposes many interlocutors who often argue within the setting of a public allosensual scandal. As comic, philosophical debate is propelled by scandalous-thinking simpletons who walk the tightrope of dialectic, making others understand what and how things are and are not. By speaking in public and acting through personal example, the philosopher is not asserting an abstract true proposition or a rational theory but rather is engaged in truth-telling, and thus in a provocative, critical, and subversive act that challenges conventional codes of conduct. Philosophy is a scandalous affront to the common sense that suspends the unquestioned norms and rules of thinking and behavior and makes people reflect on their behavior and rethink it.

And yet, modern philosophy is a different kind of scandal, denying and upending the public, dialogical, comic, and radically critical offense of thought, which is the very condition of the possibility of philosophy. Rather, modern philosophical scandal becomes the condition of the impossibility of philosophy. Incapable of productive dialogical scandal, modern philosophy still always attempts not just to question but to entirely suspend and negate itself in a radical scandal. Levinas says that he is disturbed by the fact that, in order to leave a trace in contemporary philosophy, one has to make a scandal.[13] For him, this begins with Kierkegaard, but one can clearly see the radicality of unfulfilled scandal in Descartes, in Nietzsche, Heidegger, Foucault, and many others. Heidegger's interpretation of boredom as "deep" is scandalous in its suggestion to fully embrace boredom and not run from it. Hans Jonas, a careful and precise thinker who constantly converses with the philosophical tradition, begins his *Imperative of Responsibility* by saying that all previous ethical thought is wrong and that he is giving us a new one. And even Levinas himself intends to create a scandal through a radical break with the tradition that ignores and excludes the other. In other words, one has to be radical if one wants to think. One needs to eradicate, negate, and suspend the entire previous tradition, and establish oneself as a wholly new thinker. In modern philosophy, the unmediated negativity of thinking that negates the previous thought without sublating it becomes the norm. In order to be a philosopher, one has to assimilate oneself to the modern subject, become its sole ambassador and the current embodiment, and thus assume the role of the lonely autonomous tragic thinker.

Scandal, crisis, critique. Scandal comes with a swift and spontaneous judgment, without much deliberation and a properly established procedure, even though scandal has its plot, starting with an *observed* and *made public* violation, or negation, of implicit or explicit commonly accepted norms.[14] Because scandal suspends and questions the existing norms, it is indispensable in politics, where the existing norms are often implicit, and until their boundaries are transgressed in and by a scandal, they may not be clearly established, demarcated, or even understood. The violation of a norm trespasses the norm and suspends it but does not cancel it: by establishing a new norm, scandal is capable of reaffirming normativity, as in Kurosawa's *Scandal*.

Not every violation of a norm is scandal; only that which questions the existing norm and its validity. When Volkswagen cheated on emissions norms in the public scandal of 2015, apparently the directors of the corporation took these norms to be "guidelines" that can be secretly disregarded rather than as strict legal and moral rules meant to preserve public health.

Scandal is critical in its negativity. It questions the existent and makes the impossible possible, as with the concept of actual infinity, when we assign existence to that which cannot be thought—or dividing by zero. If indeed interruption is necessary for dialogue, then the dialogical scandal is crucial not only for a reevaluation of the existing norms but also for revitalizing communication that has become wilted and soured, boring and bored. Dialogical scandal, then, is an indispensable precondition for the public critical analysis of norms and their reimplementation in dialogical, shared well-being. Such a scandal involves others and also happens for the sake and benefit of others. But the scandal of the modern subject is a monological break, destruction, and demolition of the very possibility of being as being in dialogue, when the new is hoped for but the existing is never renewed and ever remains without instauration. Such an action is not only, or not so much, an action, as it is the state in which the modern subject unwillingly perpetuates itself.

The modern scandal of the critical reevaluation of all values establishes the domination of radical philosophy to which Levinas refers. Such a critical analysis, however, is not an argument of a lonely thinking that takes the form of judgment. Since Kant, judgment means establishing a mediating connection between the theoretical and the practical, between the realm of the pure construction of the modern subject and the sphere of moral and political action. Judgment thus means providing justification for lonely thinking and bringing justice to action based on the autonomously established moral law. Yet one might say that the modern scandal, as critical, creates *crisis* as anticipated (last) judgment.

"Crisis" comes from ancient Greek κρίσις, "separating," "distinguishing," which gives rise to "decision," "judgment" (also of a court), which is derived from the verb κρίνω, to "separate," "distinguish." Diligently exercised by the modern subject, judgment comes to mean distinguishing the right from the wrong, separating the wheat from the tares, and passing a verdict of moral judgment that is exercised, accepted, and followed by the same subject who ultimately judges itself, by itself, and for itself. Such a judgment is ultimately based on the self-passed, self-approved, and self-established moral law.

The autonomous, lonely, and monological modern subject is inevitably judgmental, because it needs the approval of what it has universally established and legislated—that is, by itself and for itself. In its self-constitution, the modern subject is inescapably (self-)critical. Therefore, it needs, keeps looking for, and always expects a crisis in order to keep sustaining itself. Crisis is ultimately the gloomy expression of the subject's tragic subsistence and hence cannot be avoided. And if a crisis is not there, it has to be produced: better crisis than stagnation, for crisis expresses the critical self-directed life of the lonely autonomous mind, whereas stagnation and stability is its death and self-annihilation. Paraphrasing Voltaire, one could say "si la crise n'existait pas, il faudrait l'inventer."

Since modernity is the expression, extension, and realization of the idea of the modern subject, crisis becomes the mode of our contemporary existence. Crisis is not only constantly recreated but is also recognized as inevitable: economic crisis (by Marx), financial crisis, ecological crisis, moral crisis, the crisis of traditional social and political institutions, and so on. Being modern, we are practically obligated to expect a crisis, create a crisis, and live from one crisis to another with an eschatological, yet critically reflected on, set of expectations.

Crisis can be destructive—of ourselves, the environment, and, most importantly, of the lives and ways of living of others who do not fit the Procrustean bed of the strict norms established by the moralistic autonomous subject. But crisis can also be destructive of old repressive forms and conditions of existence. Crisis can thus be productive of new ways of looking and dealing with the world and ourselves, in science, art, psychology, and politics, and of liberation and freedom—but only if taken and addressed in a dialogically integrative way that establishes a politically progressive shared thought in action.

If one ought to be radical, then one needs a radical, rigorously thought through, and carefully exercised break from the modern construction of the lonely autonomous subject. The pathological crisis could hopefully end not in a recovery or resurrection but in the death of the modern monological subject, which it could not achieve through repeated attempts at suicide. If one wants and hopes for a political life as living, acting, and being together toward the realization of the common good, then it can only be achieved by a common establishing and reconstitution of well-being as comic dialogical being with others.

Revolution and scandal. If we recall the three kinds of relation between same and other that constitute the three forms of boredom, we can say that modern scandal assumes three forms in three established realms of human activity in thought and action.

First, with relation to thinking and thought, it is the theoretical scandal of modern *science* in its interpretation of nature, which is considered the lifeless res extensa, the extension as the other-being of reason. Modern science is based on the assertion of same without other that leads to the loss of nature qua the world, as alive and a living place that we inhabit and of which we are a part. This is the nature of mathematical physics that assigns its measure and order to the lifeless extension that in this way acquires calculable laws. This is the nature of the abstract uniformly flowing Newtonian duration or "absolute, true, and mathematical" time.[15] This is the mathematical nature of the theory of relativity, which, in a modern scientific scandal, suspends the usual representations of space and time. Modern scientific revolution is then the expression of this scandal of modern science.

Second, with relation to beauty and the body, it is the productive or poietic scandal of modern *art* that is based on the assertion of other without same, as a repetition of another and another in the constant search for the new. In modernistic art and literature, it leads to the deliberate abandonment of form and to the fragmentation of the representation of whatever is left to represent after the loss of nature. Thus, Mondrian declares the *"abolition of all particular form,"* which should do away with figurative and imitative art that is oppressing the transparency of the simple whole, of life and beauty.[16] This should lead, then, to a "dynamic equilibrium" of *unmediated* opposites depicted as a pure *relation* of the right angle produced by perpendicular lines.[17] Mondrian believes that his art fights the oppression of the form by transforming our perception of reality, through carefully selecting new simple elements and representations of it.[18] And yet his balanced, rectilinear, simple, and colored vision of what reality is meant to be is in fact an unadulterated expression of the modern monological subject, which expresses itself in terms of constructed geometrical forms that represent pure relations devoid of any content beyond autonomous, self-referential reflective thinking. The scandal of the abolition of form celebrates and inaugurates itself in the modernistic revolution in art that overturns and surpasses the previous forms of artistic action and expression. Modern art intentionally strives to provoke a scandal by undermining existing artistic and literary norms. One cannot be a recognized artist without provoking a public scandal and creating a crisis in our perception of the world, which should testify to the unapologetic originality and radical novelty of the novel approach. But in doing so, the modern scandal of art pragmatically denies, or negates itself in and by its own action, eventually becoming repetitive and boring.

And third, with relation to shared life and action, it is the practical scandal of modern *politics*, which is rooted in the inability to connect same and other in a commonly shared life in which everyone can be involved as a political animal, exercising their political being as liberated, free, and equal members of political communication and community. The expression of this scandal is modern political bourgeois revolution, which is an extension of the modern subject's aspiration to autonomously assert itself and dominate the absent other.

The scientific scandal. Among the many facets of modernity, new science is undoubtedly one of its most important defining moments. Modernity is marked by a pronounced, intentional, and sought-after novelty, which amounts to revolution and which transpires both in the new understanding of the world and in our self-understanding as being humans who determine how and as what the world appears in thought and as what. The modern human capacity for thought is intentionally self-conscious, ruthlessly critical, and ceaselessly radical in the ultimate quest for the full transparency of both thinking itself and the world. This radical novelty amounts to revolution.

One might say that the "scientific revolution" of the sixteenth and seventeenth centuries is anachronistically named after the French Revolution at the end of the eighteenth. And yet, it is probably the other way around: the political and social revolution is made possible as a realization of the new understanding of the world and especially of the human being, which is meant to be a discovery but is in fact a construction of autonomous reason. Here, I am referring to Hans Jonas's analysis of scientific revolution, which predates and anticipates the extensive debate over the topic in the works of Kuhn, Feyerabend, Popper, Lakatos, and others.[19] For Jonas, "'*Revolution*' suggests a *sudden* event. What is commonly understood when revolution is applied to change? It has a certain *violence*, a *radical* nature, a *comprehensive* scope. It is a word applied to major, not minor changes" (OSR 3).[20]

Revolution is an event that has the same characteristics as scandal. It is (1) *unexpected* and unpredictable. However, in its reflective explanation and cultural appropriation, the revolution appears an unavoidable and necessary event that presumably has been prefigured by the entire previous historical development.

Furthermore, revolution is (2) *violent*, insofar as it intends to establish a break, a rupture with the past, and thus liberate itself from the deadening schemes of thought and action. This means that revolution also (3) occurs *quickly*, in a relatively short time span and (4) is *universal* in its appeal, and hence involves everyone, in one way or another, in revolutionary activity. No one can escape the grasp of the newly constituted modern revolutionary subject. However, one should notice, first, that the time of scientific or artistic revolution is usually spread across two or three generations, from the founders to their disciples. Second, revolution is collective action that brings about changes and transformations to the lives of many people, yet the active revolutionaries are themselves relatively few. And third, since the revolutionaries tend to critically distance themselves from existing institutions and practices, quite often they are not professionals but rather vocational amateurs. For this reason, the scientific revolutionaries, such as Francis Bacon, Descartes, Spinoza, and Leibniz, never held official academic positions.

Revolution is always (5) *radical*, which means that it always goes to the root, to the beginning, the principle, ἀρχή, uprooting the old and planting the new. And yet, similarly to the revolution—rotation—of the sky, the new might be thought of as the restoration of an original, simple, and true meaning of things that was later distorted or lost.[21] Revolution allows for a new vision—a *re*-vision—of the world and our place and action in it—political, social, artistic, and scientific. Therefore, revolution presupposes the understanding of our previous activity as outdated, prerevolutionary and oppressive, nonconforming to our current standards of thought and action, which are thus in need of a radical rethinking and change. Revolution, then, is the expression of the modern subject's attempts to get rid of itself by radical negation.

As such, revolution comes with (6) *novelty*, with a new foundation of thought based on the new self-confidence and distrust of authority, marked by that systematic doubt elevated by Descartes into the epistemological starting point that makes possible an entirely new knowledge. Modern revolution is a breakthrough to the new, whereas in antiquity *revolutio* means rotation, (re)turning in a circle to the original course.[22] The title of the revolutionary, then-new cosmological book by Copernicus was *De revolutionibus orbium coelestium—On the revolutions, or circuits, of heavenly spheres*. In antiquity, revolution is the *return of the same*. Modern revolution is a *break with the tradition* and the emergence of a radically new.

As Koselleck has argued, the very concept of the "revolution," which initially means rotation (turning around and returning to the initial point in the necessary natural cyclical change of the seasons or the position of stars), becomes a specifically political concept only in modernity.²³ As a pronounced modern phenomenon, it also displays a strong religious component of finality that brings about the realization of the purpose of history.²⁴ Revolution therefore becomes not only a—but *the*—historical event, inevitable and necessary, inscribed in the constitution of history and determining its flow, the collective singular occurrence that determines the beginning and the end of a universal teleological history, which is, however, an expression of the self-deception of the modern autonomous subject that takes the desired kingdom of ends as necessary in the flux and succession of historical events. In this sense, the modern revolution as the expression of the modern subject comes to substitute *nature* with its necessary rotation of cyclical events.²⁵

Modern revolution is thus marked by emphatic novelty as the searched for and asserted other of the habitual and customary, by radicalism and violence, and hence, by scandal. As such, revolution is a specifically modern response to boredom.

Scientific revolution. The modern scientific revolution is marked by a radically different understanding of the world, which makes it, at least for a while, an unusual place in which to observe and live. In Kuhn's interpretation, scientific revolution constitutes a radical break with the old ways of doing scientific research, which is then followed by "normal science" within the newly established and stabilized form of science that defines itself with reference to a number of spectacular and recognized achievements.²⁶ One could say that the "scandal" of the new science is defined by the novelty of its subject-matter and its method. The revolutionary scientific subject studies the new revolutionized object. In antiquity, it was a commonplace that one can only have a precise ordered knowledge of being but never of the world, which was transient and immersed in becoming-γένεσις. Hence, one could not have knowledge of nature-φύσις, but only (possibly, a right and correct) opinion that helped us both inhabit the world and set us apart from it by means of political institutions. This was Plato's approach, whereas Aristotle recognized the possibility of a science-ἐπιστήμη about nature, which, however, was based on qualitative, and not quantitative, distinctions. The modern scientific object is radically different. In order to be known, it has to become being: that is, fixed, stable, and inanimate, not living but dead. Therefore, the object of the scientific cognition (1) has to be devoid of any inner life or subjectivity, and thus be pure uniform extension, res extensa or a measurable thing in the uniformly measured absolute space.²⁷ This presupposes a new ontology best exemplified in Descartes, for whom the split between the two substances of living thought and lifeless matter is fundamental for the new type of scientific strict knowledge.

The model and measure for the precision of this kind of knowledge is established by *mathematics*.[28] Again, in Plato mathematics describes being—primarily, being as number—and thus cannot be applied to moving and fluent things, which for this reason remain outside any attempts to grasp them, nontranscendentally transcendent to rigorous knowledge. Only the cosmos as a finite eternal whole, which is an alive, well-ordered, structured, and beautiful finite being, can have mathematical proportions that underlie it—but not the things in it that are in a constant flux.[29]

On the contrary, the modern scientific revolution opens the possibility of proper knowledge of things, which (2) are, then, mathematically structured and ordered. Since physical things are always imprecise, since there are no perfect straight lines or circles in the world and no exact number of units to measure them, physical things should be mathematized or constructed as mathematical from the beginning, as Kant does in his *Critique of Pure Reason*. The measure and precision have to be put into things as the construction of the modern subject who then comes to discern and realize what it has built into the world as purely extended, mathematically measured, and ordered, and thus perfectly scientifically knowable according to the *verum factum* principle. The revolutionized world has to be devoid of any spontaneity or subjectivity, be dead, and as such it should be made up from extended and mathematical objects.

The scandal of the new world is that it comes to be devoid of life, produced and studied by the modern subject that cannot find its place in the world and instead puts itself into the position of its outworld scientific creator. As mathematized, ordered, and geometrical, this new scientific world calls for a new *aesthetics*: nature is strangely and scandalously beautiful in its lifeless extension, hinting at a purpose that we have put into it without recognition.[30]

New scientific aesthetics. The aesthetic aspect of the scientific revolution transpires in two of its features: in the *harmony* of celestial motions in Johannes Kepler, and in the *simplicity* of the constituents of both the world and knowledge in its mathematical description in Newton. Harmony attests to the either apparent or concealed beauty, and first becomes visible in Renaissance painting, which is a *sui generis* "revolution" of returning to the ancient ways of depicting beautiful bodies and their interactions. Harmony now appears to be an aesthetic criterion for the evaluation of the newly discovered and depicted world. In particular, the principle of harmony becomes for Kepler and Galileo not only an evaluative or descriptive principle but an *explanatory* heuristic one. Such a harmony is primarily present in proportions, which are both seen and thought in painting, as well as in the motion of the planets, and are describable mathematically.[31]

The other aesthetic constituent of new science is simplicity, which is both the simplicity of the world in its constituents and of the knowledge of this new world. Understanding nature as uniform and simple becomes fundamental for Galileo, as well as for Newton, who claims that "Nature does nothing in vain... for Nature is pleased with simplicity."[32] In describing such a nature, the thinkers of the newly constructed universe attempt to achieve utter simplicity. Complexity is perplexing but, once simplified by mathematical description, becomes beautiful. The achieved mathematical simplicity is that of both being and of the vision of this being.

For modern science, the being of the world *is* in becoming, which is why "the analysis of nature is ultimately the analysis of motions" (OSR 71; see also 68–71, 77, 173, 181). Moreover, the very terms in which motions can be conceived are quantifiable geometrical magnitudes and forces expressible in space, which can be known and described by new strictly mathematical means. The new simple components of nature are physical atoms or particles, represented as and studied by mathematical indivisibles, which are rethought as infinitesimals by Newton and Leibniz.[33] In cognition, these simple constituents are captured by simple ideas that allow for the reduction of the manifold complexity of phenomena to the (beautiful) simplicity of a few principles, elementary magnitudes, and basic forces that should be then accessible to analysis in thought. The simplicity of nature, then, becomes a postulate, which means that rather than being self-evident, it becomes a task to be achieved and accomplished by the productive efforts of modern scientists and philosophers.

Hence, the rethinking of being as including the simplified and mathematized, and lifeless and extended becoming is the ontological precondition for the possibility of the scientific revolution. This new ontology is most clearly expressed in Descartes, who asserts a split—both the opposition *and* complementarity—between the thinking, the mental, "subjective," "inner," or the knower—and the extended, the physical, "objective," "outer," or the known. It is this new ontological framework that allows us to see the world differently and anew, as well as to ask questions and stage the experiments that did not make sense and were impossible before.

Scientific method. The new simplicity of the known is also reflected in the simplicity of the knower and the known, represented in and as ideas. Unlike the Platonic idea, which is the real unchanging thing of which physical things are fluent and imprecise reproductions, the modern idea is a mental representation of a thing out there, and as such is something internal. Yet, since we can understand the world only in terms of and on the basis of ideas, some of them, which Descartes famously labels "clear and distinct," cannot be mistaken.[34] Clear and distinct ideas that are perceived in such a way that one cannot be mistaken about them, their object, and the very act of perception, then become a "certificate of truth" (OSR 155). In the fully self-transparent, self-reflective, and simple act of perceiving, which at the same time is the act of knowing, the fully intelligible comes to coincide with the real, and thus with the undeniably true. The ontological structure of the world, then, not only maps but also coincides with its epistemological reflection, both of which should be based on simple constituents. Therefore, clear and distinct ideas are themselves the elements of reality, and thus our knowledge of reality should be of the same kind and form as this reality is: clear, distinct, simple, and precise.

To think the simple is simple, and yet, at the same time, very difficult. For, on the one hand, one needs to think simple things: one needs ideas. But on the other hand, one needs to combine these things into formulations and propositions: one needs method. Since such a method is a further reflection of the postulated simplicity of the world and simple ideas, it should be, on the one hand, rational, unambiguous, and thus unique. The scientific method that is meant to provide exact knowledge about physical things in fact embraces a number of related methods, as did dialectic in antiquity (division/diairesis, definition, analysis, induction, and syllogistic), although modern science and philosophy of science keep looking for one unified method that would be applicable to *any* (sensibly perceivable, imaginable, and thinkable) object of study, provided that such a thing is reducible to a merely extended body expressed in space with all its characteristics expressible in terms of physics.[35] On the other hand, the method should be simple and *easy to use*, almost effortlessly leading to the understanding of the world and its properties (as in Bacon, Galileo, Descartes, and Leibniz). Says Descartes: "By a 'method' I mean reliable rules which are easy to apply, and such that if one follows them exactly, one never will take what is false to be true or fruitlessly expend one's mental efforts, but will gradually and constantly increase one's knowledge [*scientiam*] till one arrives at a true understanding of everything within one's capacity."[36] However, since the world (or at least the scientific ideal of the world) is complex in its phenomena yet simple in its principles and constituents, the complexity should be reduced to simple constituents, from which true propositions should then be deduced.

Meant to liberate the mind from a tiresome and often frustratingly haphazard search for truth, the method allows for producing new truths meticulously and precisely, systematically and surely, by following simple and easily performable procedures. And yet, by depriving us of the excitement of discovery and the search for the new, such a method does not bring liberation, but makes the life of the mind unbearably boring.

The two operations of the mind that make the method work are *intuition* and *deduction*.[37] Intuition allows for understanding and grasping simple ideas, which themselves are *not* propositional, and deduction allows us to connect and combine. Or—to use Plato's metaphor—it can weave them together by means of the method's rules into chains of reasoning arranged by *"order and measure,"* "*ordo et mesura*" that lead, through divisions, arrangements, and enumerations, to true propositions and knowledge, including that of the world.[38] Complex phenomena thus should be analyzable into simple notions, and then complex theories should be constructible out of these simples, which are sui generis mathematical atoms. The two constituents of the method are therefore the analysis, for which the paradigm is the "algebra of the moderns," and synthesis, for which the pattern is the "geometry of the ancients."[39] Descartes himself stresses the importance of analysis, because of its simplicity, although both constituents are an integral part of the method. Most important, however, is that the ideal of such a method is *mathematics*. But in order to be applicable universally to any problem that implies extended physical things, the new method of *mathesis universalis* should begin with the simplest terms, which serve as clear and distinct premises, divide problems into their simplest "atomic" parts, follow order in procession from simple to complex, and make enumerations.[40] In other words, physics is considered in terms of geometry, considered in terms of a new logic. This is the novel, revolutionary, and scandalous approach to the world.

The new logic and experiment. The new logic of scientific research starts by rejecting the Aristotelian syllogistic as a bare and merely formal way of drawing conclusions that are already contained in the premises, the veracity of which is either deceptively self-evident or based on a singular act of experience, rather than following from a scientifically established theory supported by experimentation. In new science, the observation of nature yields to experiments, which already in Galileo and Bacon becomes an interrogation, coercion, or even torture, putting nature under stress, in the conditions under which it is not normally seen but in which it starts confessing to what it usually does not do or say. Therefore, a scientist *already* needs to know, at least implicitly, what is meaningful to do and ask in order to extract knowledge from nature. In other words, we need either an explicitly or implicitly formulated program, or a conceptual framework that would function as a theoretical framework allowing for new knowledge.

The new logic transpires primarily through the analytic method that allows for incorporating and studying empirical phenomena and not just abstract logical propositions. In book 1 of Francis Bacon's *Novum Organum*, it takes the decisively negative form of the "purification of reason" by the radical critique of previous forms of knowledge as "Idols" that prevent us from making progress in the production of new knowledge. Such a catharsis should give way to providing new foundations of knowledge and science as the way in which the modern subject establishes certainty about the world. The new scientific knowledge that follows the new logic is not just deduced from pure reason: it appears from the conjunction of the rational and the empirical, where senses are directed by reason and reason is corrected by the senses; it is thus actively produced. It is the knowledge achieved by *making*, that is, by *construction*. The Cartesian method only further codifies the same intention to establish a new, revolutionary science-oriented logic, which is then rendered fully scientific as a mathematical method in Leibniz and Newton.

Modernity thus comes with a quest for a new logic. Logic becomes *the* expression of the modern subject, of the inviolable rules and laws that it autonomously establishes by itself for itself. As such, these logical laws have to be reflected in language, which gives rise to the "linguistic turn" in philosophy—and in thought, which gives rise to the enormous development in logic, including modal logic, and its pervasive use as *the* language of philosophy.

In his *Logic*, Hegel attempts to provide a new all-encompassing philosophical "dialectical" logic that would be universally applicable to all domains of human activity, including the science of nature, as well as social, political, and historical life. But if science is to be distinguished from philosophy as "metaphysics," then we need to establish a strict criterion for such a demarcation, or a properly scientific logic, which Popper famously finds in falsifiability, which comes out of his engagement with the scientific method, particularly the critique of induction. For if a scientific universal statement cannot be empirically verified, or supported by any finite number of empirical observations, then a scientific claim can only be that which can be possibly falsifiable, or refutable by experience.[41] But perhaps the most radical attempt at establishing the new scientific logic comes with the complete rejection and suspension of logic itself as a privileged human attitude toward the world in Feyerabend's philippics against method.[42] This is the logic of the scandal created by the modern subject in its attempt at self-assertion through self-annihilation.

Mathematization of the world. The new study of nature is ultimately defined by how nature is, and by what our mind is capable of knowing about it. In other words, we need a new understanding of *being* that would allow for a new knowledge of nature. We must be able to understand ontological shifts and changes in order to be able to understand the changes in the new picture of the world. The paradigm of the new science becomes the new physics as celestial mechanics. Its objects are now considered mathematically measurable and measured, thus allowing for the application of a new method. Therefore, one of the central scandalous features of the scientific revolution is the *mathematization* of the world. Mathematization means not only the acceptance of the underlying structures of the cosmos as mathematical, proportional, and beautiful, as they are perceived by the Pythagoreans and Plato, as well as by Kepler and Galileo, but aslo that the world is describable in its transformations and movements using mathematical terms.

The mathematization of the world suggests not only that we see mathematical objects as underlying natural phenomena or that the book of nature is written, as Galileo famously says, in the language of mathematics, of which the words are lines, triangles, and circles.[43] It much more means that we should be able to formulate the laws of nature as mathematically describable laws of motion, as Newton does (see OSR 77, 156–58, 167, 171ff). The presuppositions behind this new scientific mathematical description are: first, that only locomotion is considered motion, and not just any change, which was κίνησις for Aristotle.[44] And second, that *any* motion of *any* body—either cosmic or "sublunar," up there or down here—can be described by the same laws, method(s), and mathematical procedures. This had never been possible in ancient physics, which separated being from becoming or change, and therefore refused to apply mathematics to the study of ever-fluent things.

As motion through the uniform *res extensa*, considered as three-dimensional homogeneous Euclidean space, locomotion is best represented by the elementary act of drawing an imaginary line.[45] For modern science, including Galileo, Descartes, and Newton, the construction or drawing of such a line is best described not geometrically, as ancient mathematics does it, but algebraically, by establishing a purely *functional* relationship between two sets (of spatial locations and temporary moments). New mathematics is thus based on the concept of *relation*, rather than on nonrelational substance, which is now reserved to characterize both the knowing mind and the known medium in which the motion takes place. Indeed, substances are qualitative; only relations can be quantified. Rejecting the scholastic Aristotelian understanding of substance as a concrete *this*, τόδε τι, which logically can only be in the position of the subject and never that of the predicate, the very concept of substance in Descartes is produced by the thinking of the finite mind.[46] The new physically oriented mathematics allows for the description of quantities as related to each other, not as substantial units but as represented by mathematical functions in the process of their change, or in motion. The preference of algebra and functional analysis to geometry and substantial description, the rethinking of geometry as algebraic, constitutes an important premise that makes the mathematical formulation of kinematics possible.[47]

The early modern thinkers establish mathematics as the model for certainty in the cognition of the world. Despite the split between the two substances in Descartes, they are still the two complimentary elements of reality, which should be understandable and rationally known. This means that both mind and nature as substantial constituents of reality should be known essentially in the same way. And if the mind's knowledge is arranged according to the method that is modeled on mathematics, which in turn uses a new logic, then nature too should also be known mathematically and according to the same logic. In this way, *all* knowledge, including the knowledge of physical things, should be arranged and structured as mathematical.

The exemplary advantage of mathematics consists in the *simplicity* and *precision* of the knowledge it provides. For modern science, mathematics becomes the appropriate method of studying nature, because nature itself is constructed as utterly *simple* and hence rationally transparent in its foundations, but it appears extremely rich and complex in its phenomena. As Leibniz puts it, the world "is at the same time the simplest in hypotheses and the richest in phenomena, as might be a line in geometry whose construction is easy and whose properties and effects are extremely remarkable and widespread."[48] It is on the basis of simple mathematical concepts, elements, principles, and rules of deduction that the new science, beginning with Galileo, is capable of constructing scientific explanations of complex natural processes.[49]

Mathematics becomes *the* expression of the way two independent substances, mind and matter, are and can be known. The mind is essentially mathematical because it simplifies into the self-reflective and transparent res cogitans that thinks simply and precisely in terms and concepts that can be easily arranged mathematically by the mind's self-prescribed and self-extracted method. And matter is mathematical because it is constructed as an equally simple, uniform, and lifeless res extensa and thus can be taken as mathematically ordered Euclidean extension. Both mind and matter (or nature) are already "co-mathematical." Mathematics permeates both the mind and the world, yet the relation between the two is asymmetrical, because the one knows itself reflectively, and the other is known by its other. For this reason, mathematics can be considered not only as descriptive of the way things are but also as *prescriptive*: by looking at things scientifically, the mathematical mind *must* already see them as mathematical, as reflecting the same patterns and structures that the mind finds in itself. In this way, the mind intentionally and unwittingly constructs mathematical regularities into the world, as Kant famously argues in the *Critique of Pure Reason*.

The modern subject assumes the position of the autonomous creator of the world as the mathematician who constructs and prescribes the laws to the world, producing the world not in its *is* but in its *what*. This is the theoretical scandal in modern science, which is not nonsense, since it makes sense as a construction (rather, it is asense, upsense, downsence, onsense, unsense, insense, outsense). The mathematics of the mind is then disguised as the method, and the mathematics of the world appears as the laws of the ordered physical world. Mathematics, therefore, becomes the conceptual framework that allows Galileo and Newton to understand and mathematically formulate the laws of physical motion and the general mechanics and artifice of nature and, on the basis of this understanding and by following the new logic, to stage meaningful experiments that discover new truths about nature, all of which eventually paves the way for artificial intelligence.

The scandal of the infinite and the loss of the intermediate. The scandal of the new physics and cosmology only becomes possible in a new world, which is different from the old cosmos in that the mathematically measured and measurable universe is *infinite*, whereas the cosmos is finite. Ancient philosophy and science, both propelled and overwhelmed by the *horror infiniti*, recognize and accept only potential infinity or the infinite in which, according to Aristotle's definition, one can always take another and another, or that outside of which there is always something else.[50] The actual infinity, the infinite taken as a whole, as that outside of which there is nothing, comes first with the acceptance of the infinite omnipotent and omniscient creator of the world and of all things finite. This infinite remains outside of and transcendent to the world. The infinite, then, is ontologically and epistemologically primary, so that the finite is the negation of the infinite, rather than the infinite being the privation or removal of the finite.[51] The revolution in science occurs when the infinite is admitted into the world and the world becomes an infinite universe.[52] However, in the infinite there is no mediation of the opposites, which means that the opposites coincide in actual infinity. But then in the infinite anything is possible. As Cusanus already observes, in the actual infinite or "maximum," the impossible becomes possible and in fact necessary: the straight line coincides with the infinite circle and with the infinite triangle, and the minimum coincides with the maximum.[53] Therefore, in the infinite, *anything goes*, which becomes the modern scandal. The infinite inevitably generates paradox, which Descartes tries to avoid by setting apart the divine actual infinite, *infini*, from the indefinite extension of the world, *indéfini*.[54] Yet, the infinite remains a construction of the finite subject (who aspires to overcome its finitude through an imaginary aspiration to become the creator or constructor) and the infinite, mathematically precise universe (that comes to substitute for the finite ordered cosmos). Such a construction, however, is utopian in that it exiles the world into the no-place of mathematically arranged yet lifeless extension, and misplaces imagination from being the mediation and connection of thinking and perception in scientific cognition (see *No place for imagination as mediating*, ch. 3).

Therefore, the radicalism and scandal of the modern Cartesian ontological and scientific revolution comes with the acceptance of the actually infinite thinking substance as producing the unmediated finite substances of thought and extension. This leads to the expulsion of the intermediate from both ontology and cognition, which is an inadvertent yet necessary consequence of the rigid ontological split between the two finite substances. Being mutually exclusive and complementary, they do not need, and do not allow for, mediation. In this way, the intermediate is eliminated.

Besides, in the Platonic understanding of the order of being, the soul, which was the principle of life, was also intermediate between the ideal and the physical. But when the new ontology identifies the mind with abstract thinking modeled on mathematics and posits the essence of nature in geometry, it becomes incapable of providing an account for life as a reproduction of the same in the form of another and for the complexity and functioning of an organism. The new scientific world thus has no purpose (because the final cause has to be expurgated) and no life (which has been identified with abstract mathematical thinking).

Among the difficulties that the new science faces is the problem of exactitude or precision: while mathematical objects and calculations are precise, the physical phenomena—the bodies in their dimensions, forms, and motions—are not. Descartes is well aware of this problem, recognizing in his *Geometry* an insuperable gap between perfect geometrical figures and never precisely measurable and always irregular physical bodies, which these figures are meant to describe and represent.[55] In this case, the physical phenomena either cannot be really explained mathematically, or they only appear imprecise. Yet, Descartes is unable to explain why geometrical figures are precise, whereas physical bodies, represented by geometrical objects, are not.[56] For he cannot properly locate the mathematical qua geometrical objects: they have to belong *both* to the res extensa (as extended) *and* to the res cogitans (as precise and thinkable), and yet, the two are mutually exclusive. Because of the expulsion of the intermediate, Descartes cannot give a satisfactory answer as to where the mathematical (geometrical) properly belongs: in the physical, bodily, and extended—or in the mental, thinkable, and not extended. Therefore, the Cartesian attempt to think things clearly fails at its very foundational moment. The incapacity to explain the ontological status of geometrical objects becomes emblematic of modern science's inability to account for the mathematization of the new world in terms of nontheological realism, and to further explain why in the last instance we are actually able to see and study the world as mathematical. The revolution of mathematization, thus, expels the intermediate in ontology and science, and banishes the imagination in cognition.

The inevitable important consequence of the Cartesian ontological split is the suppression of the whole realm of intermediate entities, which in antiquity were associated with extended yet perfect geometrical figures, both thinkable and imaginable. This move enables not only the dichotomy of two complementary substances but also the *imposition* of one (geometrical as thinkable) onto the other (physical as extended and now also geometrical), as well as the identification of the thinkable nonextended numbers with the extended geometrical objects through the introduction of the system of coordinates. The physical, then, is *substituted* by the geometrical, which is then studied and described formally—algebraically and functionally. The identification or nondistinction of discrete numbers and continuous magnitudes, carefully differentiated in ancient science, particularly by Aristotle, becomes the major presupposition for the possibility of the scientific cognition of the world.[57] The physical, reduced to simple magnitudes and forces, is now seen, studied, and reduced to the geometrical. In this way, the new scientific world is *already* unwittingly built as mathematical.

The scandal of modern science is thus the construction of the world as mathematical, or the imposition of the mathematical structures of the mind and sensibility onto the physical. Paraphrasing Leibniz's dictum on music, one can say that the new science is "exercitium arithmeticae occultum nescientis se numerare animi [a hidden arithmetic exercise of the soul, which does not know that it is counting]."[58]

The aesthetic scandal. The scandal of the intended revolution in modern art—in painting, music, poetry, literature—comes with a search for new forms of language and presentation that go beyond representation, which could make the familiar transpire through the unfamiliar and thus allow us to have a distanced, renewed glance at our activities in life. Such a scandal is meant to *épater la bourgeoisie*. Duchamp was always looking for a scandal and was satisfied with the resulting *succès de scandal*.[59] Scandal is thus always based on provocation that does not stay within the aesthetic but often goes into the political, social, and moral.[60] The moralization of art scandal is precisely an expression of the moralistic attitude of the modern autonomous subject. Yet, oftentimes, art provocation stands for the search of the *novel* for the sake of the novel. This is an expression of the modern subject's profound boredom that it tries to overcome by the scandal that intends to allow an ever-deeper look into itself. But because the scandal is self-produced and self-directed by the modern subject, eventually it becomes usurped by the market and becomes entertainment.

Since I cannot go into a detailed discussion of the modern scandal in art, I will only provide a few examples of it, which otherwise are plentiful. In fact, the history of modern art *is* the history of scandal: in literature and the modernistic novel (Proust, Bely, Joyce, Kafka); drama (Mayakovsky, Beckett, Ionesco); poetry (Gertrude Stein, T. S. Eliot, Celan, Allen Ginsberg); film (Man Ray, Vertov, Buñuel, Cassavetes); painting (Malevich, Braque, Picasso, Lee Krasner, Pollock); photography (Rodchenko, Moholy-Nagy, Berenice Abbott); sculpture (Duchamp, Lipchitz, Moore, Louise Nevelson, Giacometti); architecture (Lloyd Wright, Gropius, Le Corbusier, Hundertwasser); and music (Schönberg, Berg, Cage, Boulez, pop, rock, and punk).[61] A different kind of scandal is created by attempts at the modern appropriation and (mis)interpretation of non-Western forms of music (sitar), painting (calligraphy), sculpture (Isamu Noguchi), and ceramics (the ceramics of Hagi, Oribe, Iga, Shigaraki, Shino, and Bizen). The list can be continued almost indefinitely, zooming in and out on each genre, subgenre, and period.

Just one example: for the 1964 World's Fair in Flushing Meadows, Queens, Andy Warhol created a mural for the exterior of the New York State Pavilion consisting of thirteen huge mug shots taken from a police brochure. Several days before the opening of the exhibition, Warhol's artwork was destroyed.[62] Apparently, the officials were scandalized and outraged by the provocative art and political critique.

One could say (leaving it here as a conjecture, since the full elaboration of the thesis goes well beyond the scope of the current discussion) that the general tendency of modern art toward (1) nonimitative and nonrepresentational depiction and (2) constructing the object rather than taking it to be imitative or representational of the existent, is the modern subject's attempt to reflectively externalize aesthetic meanings as the expressions of its sovereign autonomy. Thus, the premeditatedly constructed straight and streamlined streets and avenues of the modern city are boring, while medieval curvy ones are not, opening new vistas with every few steps and keeping publicly preserved memorial traces of the perhaps messy yet lively activity of their building and shared sociality of the past. Since it is not clear what is going on at the surface of modern nonrepresentational constructed art, one usually assumes that modern art has a deep hidden agenda, which one needs to decipher by using hints from the work itself, its title, the history of its production and reception, the account of the author's intentions and, above all, the smart narrative that the interpreter presents by showing off their erudition and interpretative skills.[63]

Genius as the creator of novelty. Thus, in order to be able to create, one has to produce something radically new, and be a scandalist. The scandal of the novel vision of the new world stripped of living nature and beauty is carried out by the specifically modern embodiment of the lonely morally self-constituting subject in another sphere of its action, which is neither theoretical (not natural), nor practical (not moral or political). This is the realm of art. The isolated modern subject imposes the model of tragedy even here, but follows the capacity or faculty that traditionally mediates between reason and sensation, which, as I have argued, is imagination. Having expelled the intermediate from ontology, the modern subject loses the imagination as a mediating cognitive capacity, but reinstates it as creative and productive. The figure of the sublime creator of the intentionally artificial as the embodiment of the modern lonely subject is the *genius*, the creator of art par excellence, who has to suffer and die in plain spectatorial view of itself but who also can't do precisely that.

The modern subject cannot escape, if not a possibility then a temptation of liberating itself from the self-imposed rational restrictions, on the one hand, and from natural sensible determinations, on the other, which it equally rationally produces and regulates. Its *maison de plaisance* is art, where the subject can practice its autonomous will and imagination as creative and independent (imaginarily autonomous), perhaps in the game of a "free play" with its own reason and sense-perception, thus escaping the watchful eye of its own thinking and eventually even itself as following empirical or logical laws and the guidance of rules.[64] It is the modern subject's willful imagination that both mediates between and separates reason and sensibility. This it does in art only, or in the aesthetic sphere, for the subject has eliminated imagination in the cognition of nature, where it has to belong both to the rational and the sensible—and to none at the same time, due to the insuperable separation of the mental and the physical, of mind and body. Such an imagination wants to achieve the impossible and thus the scandalous: to be free without any restrictions. In attempting to do so, it creates *another nature* and acts in a way that cannot even be fully determined by thinking, nor expressed in language. It becomes—or at least wants to become—what it unwillingly wills: the demiurge that produces its own virtual world, which goes far beyond what we can possibly perceive or express with a thought or word.

Reigning supreme, the modern subject as the artistic director of itself, others, nature, and art, takes itself to be the lonely and sublime, tragic and suffering genius. Genius assimilates itself to nature, and creates and produces the way nature does, in the apparently effortless effort of *sprezzatura*, which is the seemingly artless art of reproducing and replacing nature.[65] Yet, paradoxically, modern nature is itself the unintentional and unreflected construction of the modern subject (that is, until a modern philosopher notices and makes it explicit).

The possibility of the modern imagination breaking loose is inscribed into the power of negativity that is asserted and assumed by the modern subject. This negativity, on the one hand, is the source of the exclusion of the other, which amounts to obliterating the other different from oneself. And on the other hand, negativity is also the power of self-assertion over the now-absent and purely constructed forms of the other: of the self, of others, and of nature. The power of negativity allows the modern subject to make or depict the absent as present for itself as the only spectator. The modern productive imagination capable of creating a radical novelty as another—or the other—nature is only worthy of a divine-like creator, who is worshiped by the Romantics as the artistic genius and the mystagogue of art. Genius is the force of nature beyond nature.[66]

The concept of genius gets its proper elaboration in Kant's aesthetics: the genius is no less than "the talent for *discovering* that which cannot be taught or learned.... Genius, therefore, flashes as a momentary phenomenon, appearing at intervals and then disappearing again; it is not a light that can be kindled at will and kept burning for as long as one pleases, but an explosive flash that a happy impulse of the spirit lures from the productive power of imagination."[67] This enigmatic flash is the expression of the creative freedom of the productive imagination, which seems not to be that of free will. Yet because the modern subject constructs or produces nature as necessarily regular and law-like, and its freedom as the freedom of will is defined by its pure reason, the "flash" of the genius, in the last instance, is that of pure reason determined by its unwilling will pushed by imagination. And yet, even following the freedom of imagination, the genius still has to combine imagination and reason as understanding, where the imagination *freely* submits itself to the confinement of order and the lawfulness of the understanding by an act of will.[68] Such a "free" correspondence of the imagination to the lawful directives of reason produces "the unsought and unintentional subjective purposiveness" in the production of the genius, a work of art, and is only possible if one presupposes "a proportion and disposition of this faculty that cannot be produced by any following of rules, whether of science or of mechanical imitation, but that only the nature of the subject can produce."[69] It is this "originality of the power of imagination (not imitative production), when it harmonizes with concepts, [that] is called *genius*."[70] Otherwise, by not submitting itself to a rational concept and thus presenting an irrepresentable—unimaginable but only thinkable—the productive artistic imagination runs the risk of becoming fantastic or "enthusiastic," of being "possessed" by an irrational, seemingly divine power that produces deceptive images.

The genius thus produces freely and mysteriously by relying on their original, playful, productive, "free-willing" imagination that is, however, always inexplicably bound, limited, and disciplined by the immanent laws, and the lawfulness of thinking. Genius creates a scandal by producing a new model work of art. Genius is the creator of the original in art that goes against the existing rules of appropriate taste.[71] As Gadamer has argued, taste belongs to the eighteenth-century aesthetics that is rejected and replaced by the nineteenth-century Romantic aesthetics of the genius. Taste is superficial and shows itself through a univocal, self-identical, shallow, firmly established, sensible, and rational allegory, while genius delves into the abysmal depth of things, which it presents through an inextinguishable, "indentical" imaginary symbol.[72]

Originally, a symbol is a thing cut into two pieces that would authenticate the bearers, once they are able to match the parts. In a similar way, an "indentured" document was cut into parts along the serrated line, which would then prove the authenticity of the document confirming the voluntary servitude. The modern self-imposed servitude is the expression of the same self-identical autonomous reason that wants to become the other serving itself. In this sense, the modern subject is also "indentical," which is confirmed through the self-created scandal.

The radical novelty is thus deceptive because it does not correspond to anything that can be possibly perceived or thought. The unperceived and unthought, then, becomes perceived and thinkable for the first time due to the productive imagination of a genius. But even for the genius the radical novelty is ultimately impossible, because all the possibilities of the new are inscribed into the lawfulness of the understanding, which even the genius cannot upend and ignore. Even in its rational free will, the modern subject cannot go beyond itself to something really new, because it does not have the unexpected other, which the radical novelty is. The "other nature" is thus always only an *as-if* nature, present only in the imagination and hence not in the real thing (which for Kant is only accessible in moral action) but only in a fleeting beauty, which, once nature gets lost as independent from the subject, can only be artificial beauty—or, rather, its promise—in a work of art. Telling the truth by telling a lie, mystifying the spectator by the lure of an unachievable ultimate transparency of the purpose, is the scandal of modern art. And genius is the modern scandalist *par excellence*. For art, which is primarily produced by genius, shows the true by showing the false, by depicting what has not been, the fictional, the *as-if* real—the *voluntarily imaginary*—as universally valid.

The promise of the beautiful. Since nature becomes a scientific rational construction where the mathematical substitutes the physical and regulates it according to the rational mathematically formulated laws, nature as a self-regulating, self-contained, and living cosmos is lost. "Cosmos" by its very notion is a finite beautiful world. Rather than being Aristotelian *physis*, which is all that *is* and is the principle of motion, life, and growth, in early modernity nature becomes mathematized and thus is turned into a mere construction of the universal subject. That which exists by itself (*physis*) and that which is the matter of human positing as law (*nomos*), which were distinguished by the Sophists, now coincide in natural law as the construction of the modern subject.[73] Such an understanding of nature is already found in Galileo, Descartes, and Newton, and finds its apex in Kant's *Critique of Pure Reason*, which argues that all law-like regularities in this world are not found or discovered in, but are rather constructed into, the world by the subject, who then cognizes what it itself produces.[74] The infinite universe that comes to its place in a utopian nonplace devoid of beauty. The concept of beauty is therefore out of place in our contemporary world. The ancient understanding of the task of art as the imitation of nature becomes meaningless since nature is a product of the cognizing autonomous subject. Rather, life becomes an imitation of art.[75]

Here, my discussion will be turning around Ágnes Heller's narrative about the beautiful in *The Concept of the Beautiful*, which provides an account of the transformations of the concept of the beautiful throughout its history.[76] If the demise and self-canceling negativity is not analytically included in the concept of the beautiful, then one needs to provide a genealogical account that might explain its loss.

The common understanding of art in antiquity is that of the imitation (*mimēsis*) of nature. Hence, the better artist is the one who imitates nature better. Every imitation, however, is a deception. A famous anecdote relates the story of a competition between two famous painters, Zeuxis and Parrhasius: Parrhasius was declared a better artist because Zeuxis painted grapes so well that it deceived birds who took them to be real, whereas Parrhasius deceived a human by painting a curtain that Zeuxis demanded be removed in order to see the picture behind it.[77] Yet, if there is no longer any nature, then there is nothing to imitate. If the beautiful resides in nature and art does not imitate nature anymore, the beautiful eventually disappears from art. If, as Collingwood argues, beauty is the object of love, admiration, and desire, then it cannot be the object of aesthetic theory or art.[78] In modernity, art becomes an autonomous sphere of action and cognition (for some), and as such does not even need beauty anymore. If one of the purposes of artistic scandal is an "estrangement" that might help us look at the familiar anew and in an unfamiliar way, the new is not beautiful, since the beautiful as transmitted within the tradition is too familiar and boring. The radical novelty produced by the genius should go beyond anything that has been said and thought before and thus bring down any canon, destroy any system, and tear down any previous account. As radical reflection, philosophy becomes *a new form of art*, which finally suspends beauty and destroys art. Hegel's famous claim of the "end of art" means that in art, for Heller, "reflexivity is gained and creativity is lost" (CB 92; see also 125). We can only think about what geniuses have already created and in this way live in the "meager" time when reflection about beauty neither amounts to nor allows for the creation of new (beautiful) works of art. We observe and judge but do not create anymore.[79]

An account of the concept of the beautiful should therefore be inscribed into the critique of the modern subject that attempts to grasp and synthesize all the spheres of multifarious experience into a single whole, and thus to provide its coherent interpretation. And yet, because of the utter complexity of experience, the subject cannot capture the manifold of experience in its entirety, unless it autonomously produces this manifold itself. Therefore, the experience of the single solitary subject breaks up and becomes inevitably *fragmented*. Correspondingly, the experience of the beautiful becomes radically heterogeneous and negative, so that beauty can no longer be considered either as symmetry or proportion.

Plotinus occupies a prominent place in Heller's conceptual history of the beautiful: practicing radical philosophical thinking that goes beyond philosophy, he understands beauty as existing yet inexpressible. For Plotinus, beauty is everywhere and in everything—in nature, actions, virtues, characters, and theories. As such, beauty is both heterogeneous and ordinary but, not being identical with semblance, can be approached only apophatically and is thus beyond discursive logical distinctions or proportion.[80] Therefore, being both identical with and different from its appearance in beautiful things, actions, and thoughts, beauty remains a mystery and a secret.[81] In the last instance, beauty amounts to a revelation, which points toward the unspeakable beyond-being first mentioned by Plato in the *Republic* (509b). And although we already know *that* beauty is there, it is very difficult to grasp *what* it is. In order to understand beauty, we need to undergo a radical transformation: we need to carve our own inner "statue," thereby cutting ourselves off from everything that prevents our understanding and vision of beauty.

As a Platonic thinker, Plotinus realizes that the beauty of various heterogeneous phenomena can be explained through a particular kind of causation, that of "participation" of multiple things in one thinkable form. The forms themselves constitute a multiplicity of beings that are and cannot be otherwise. For this reason, they are beautiful (*kala*), and such is also the intellect that thinks them.[82] However, unlike Plato, Plotinus does not stop at formal beauty, which makes him a radical thinker of beauty. Instead, he affirms that the beautiful of and in thought is such because it strives toward the good, which is the source, principle, and cause of life, mind, and being, but is not itself being.[83] It is this ultimate beauty of the good that makes beautiful forms—and through them, things—beautiful.[84] Paradoxically, such beauty is present in an unthinkable way and is thus inconceivable because it is beyond being yet makes being beautiful. Since beauty is beyond being, we cannot even tell what it is: the "good" is a placeholder for the universal object of desire.[85] We recognize the ultimate beauty and testify to its existence in the whole heterogeneity of life, action, and thought without ever properly thinking beauty itself. The scandal of the beautiful in Plotinus is that it is and remains beyond comprehension and thought.

The claim to the universality and autonomy of the modern subject entails the rejection of the heterogeneity in the experience of the beautiful, which leads to the loss of the beautiful. Moreover, it also leads to the fragmentation of the beautiful, which is now claimed to reside only in one particular sphere and is thus reduced to just one singular form. In modernity, this happens to be the beauty of and in art. The modern subject, disappointed in itself, in its ability to incorporate and embrace various facets of beauty, turns against itself and becomes anti-metaphysical (see CB 27ff.). In my reconstruction, the philosophical drama of the loss of beauty unfolds in modernity in five classical acts,[86] which were required of a drama already by Horace: (1) in the Enlightenment and especially Romanticism, the experience of the beautiful is reduced to taste;[87] (2) in Kant, beauty can be meaningfully spoken of only in relation to the "inner," to the subject's judgment, rather than to an object, and thus to the interplay between cognitive faculties (of imagination and understanding);[88] (3) in Hegel, beauty is excluded from the fundamental logical categories, so that the beauty of and in nature becomes only a dim preliminary stage for the ideal of beauty; (4) after Hegel, beauty becomes solely the beauty of a work of art and thus drifts entirely to the domain of aesthetics; and (5) in contemporary philosophy, beauty, taken as a suspicious metaphysical concept, disappears altogether.

The demise of the beautiful thus has to do with the self-affirmation of the modern autonomous subject who constructs, produces, and determines the reasons and meanings for the world and society from within itself. In this way, the modern subject establishes itself as universal, purely rational, and necessary, and thereby expels the everyday and lived experience from metaphysics. With the demise of metaphysics, however, the lived experience, which was the locus for beauty in its multiple and heterogeneous expressions, does not come back, since the post-metaphysical scene is still the one of devastation, of a scorched landscape, of an empty, discolored stage devoid of decorations and any traces of beauty. The universal, lonely, and monological subject is extremely effective in leaving nothing in its trail, even if it has made a considerable (ineffective) effort in recent decades at a post-metaphysical "repentance," trying to get rid of itself by distilling itself into a highly specialized logical debate over the minutiae of reason.

The dominance of the modern subject is thus the main reason for the loss of the beautiful. If, as Heller argues, the beautiful in modernity can only be thought of as radically heterogeneous, the modern subject cannot tolerate its very concept, because it cannot be uniformly deduced from within the pure logical system of categories, as Hegel already realized. No wonder then, that the beautiful does not appear anywhere as a category in his *Logic*.

Beauty disappears from nature altogether. Although beautiful art for Kant is the product of genius, the beauty of nature still takes advantage and priority over the beauty of art, because the interest in the beauty of nature (the beautiful *forms* of nature) testifies to human goodness and the cultivation of moral feeling.[89] After Kant and Hegel, nobody even mentions nature when speaking about beauty. For Schelling, the absolute beauty is the truth expressed in art.[90] Beauty is lost in nature, because nature is not there: we do not know what nature is anymore.

Already in antiquity (in Plato and Vitruvius) and still in the early Renaissance (in Masaccio), the human body, rather than the autonomous spirit, establishes the measure and standard for the beautiful: the understanding and representation of the beautiful depends on our understanding of the body. Not surprisingly, Cicero relates that the gods for Epicurus are the most blessed and beautiful beings and thus should have bodies, because the human body is the most beautiful of all things.[91] In antiquity, the body is understood as an embodiment of a mathematical proportion, which can be studied and then represented in art. But in Kant the idea of the beautiful is seen through the prism of reflective judgment and not mathematical proportion, because mathematics is now the tool of the subject's construction of nature, which is purely phenomenal res extensa devoid of life and beauty. This leads to the suspension of attempts to consider universal regularities in the living body as expressible in terms of mathematical proportions. The living body is thus no longer mathematically measurable. It loses the canon of order and measure and becomes either amorphous or easily transformable in accordance with the current fashion. Because body sheds all mathematical form, and thus all proportion, it can be easily distorted, which ultimately leads to Kandinsky's and Pollock's loss of any comprehensible bodily form and to Picasso's disfiguration of the body, which cannot be meaningfully said to be beautiful. Cubism, which starts with an attempt to bring pure geometry into the description of the body, ends with representing it as unrecognizable and optologically dismembered. The modern autonomous subject makes itself into universal reason that, as res cogitans, becomes entirely disembodied and thus loses body—making itself embodied rather like an all-encompassing Leviathan of the modern pervasive state. Beauty, therefore, is an artful intellectual construction into a work of art, done by the genius, the epitome of autonomous tragic reason. Pure form that was formerly exemplified in the form of a living body is no longer beautiful but suspect: bodies of dead animals on display in an art gallery cannot be thought to exemplify beauty but rather an intentionally scandalous concept (e.g., Hirst's "the physical impossibility of death in the mind of someone living") produced by the lonely subject.

From its inception in Socrates and Plato, philosophy attempts to grasp the beautiful and define its concept. In a sense, this very attempt becomes defining for the activity and organization of thought called "philosophy" as a way of thinking about the beautiful, along with the true and the good. Historically, however, the three philosophical sisters, originally the universal normative ideas, face very different fates: the true is downgraded to the semantically true that is debated in various theories of truth; the good either disappears entirely or lurks in theology as the divine good and in politics as the (even more rarely accepted) public good; and the beautiful is abandoned by contemporary thought altogether.[92] But since the very distinction between "is" and "appears," or being and becoming is no longer meaningful, the concept of the beautiful as the ideal form is lost for and in contemporary thought.

One can agree with Hegel that the world is not destroyed by negation but rather grows through it: philosophy is itself the enterprise of critical reflexive thinking that advances by and through negation.[93] Yet contra Hegel, one can say that negation alone does not secure reaching the necessary and inevitable end of the universal subject's development (that of the Spirit) from within itself. Rather, negation allows for differentiation and otherness, and thus for heterogeneity of human experience, which might include the experience of the beautiful. Yet modern philosophy excludes the concept of the beautiful from the list of necessary logical categories, which means that no negativity is needed for understanding beauty, but only refinement and taste. The overreflective lonely reason prevents itself from understanding the beautiful and having a fulfilling experience of it.

The disappearance of beauty from the contemporary boring experience of thought implies that we can only wait for a Godot-like return of the beautiful, for which we are still waiting, but are never sure whether it will ever reappear or become thinkable. But we hope it will. We cannot predict its comeback and cannot force it, nor yet do we not want not to be absorbed in a melancholic mourning of the beautiful. Rather, we should stay awake and keep thinking and looking for the beautiful out of the profound boredom, which we cannot but accept. Currently, the beautiful still seems unthinkable and escapes our attempts at grasping or defining it. Yet nothing prevents its reappearance. As it stands now, the drama of the beautiful is a tragedy: the concept of the beautiful arises in antiquity, becomes fragmented in modernity, and dies in contemporaneity. Such an end, however, might not and should not be final but only provisional. It can contain within itself its own overcoming, which then could turn the drama of the beautiful into a comedy with a good ending. However, the return of the beautiful is never guaranteed, nor is it necessarily presupposed and inscribed into the history of its concept. Currently, beauty is only a *promise*, which, as Heller puts it, is the promise of happiness (CB 49, 62, 69-70, 142-43).[94] Such a promise might never be realized but it can be fulfilled, for the promise of the beautiful is realized in love.

This is the reason why Plato is the protagonist in Heller's philosophical drama of the beautiful: his dialogues are all propelled by the power of love or *erōs*.[95] Heller distinguishes between two opposing yet closely related currents in Plato's understanding of the beautiful, "warm" and "cold" (CB 1-19). Unlike in Kant, warm beauty does not just please without interest—it is the object of passionate desire and love that celebrates life becoming uncovered and displayed by and in such beauty. This beauty is dialogical, since it needs the other, and it presupposes a passionate striving realized as the ascent toward the good, which in Plato takes the form of sublimation and flight.[96] Warm beauty is the promise of happiness.

Cold beauty, on the contrary, is the beauty of thought and understanding, of poised methodical reasoning, of carefully and artfully calculated order. This beauty is dialectical and thus needs an art or *tekhnē* that may be shared with others yet is best practiced in the tranquility of solitude. It is sublimity without sublimation that strives toward perfection, transparency, and simplicity. It comes with the fear of flight, with the dread of chaos. It is beauty that needs an ordered step-by-step progression through the sciences and knowledge toward the eternal, which is the absence of rhythm, of excesses, and the repetitions of love.[97] Cold beauty is the promise of truth.

The distinction between cold and warm beauty in Plato clearly reproduces the Apollonian and Dionysian split in Nietzsche: as the divinity of light, Apollo is the embodiment of passivity, represented in and as the image and concept, of *what is*, which is contemplated in and by reason.

In Nietzsche's interpretation, Apollo, the divinity of light, is the foreteller and nunciate of the future, seen as a beautiful illusion in dreams. He is the embodiment of passivity, which is represented in and as the image and concept, of *what is*, contemplated in and by reason. Apollo, therefore, stands for cognition and self-cognition based on moderation and measure, which is the principle of individuation. Indeed, everyone has to apply and interpret the prophesized in dreams to oneself, and thus turn into a unique recipient and guardian of such knowledge. The uniqueness and self-deification become, then, the source of satisfaction and "cheerfulness."[98]

Dionysus, on the contrary, is the principle of life, insuperably powerful and joyful, displaying himself in intoxication, ecstasy, and sexuality. As such, Dionysus is represented as the sublime terror translated into the dissolute joy of the annihilation of the individual and the destruction of the principle of individuation. Instead of moderation and measure, exorbitance becomes the truth. Contrary to the Apollonian maxim "nothing in excess," the Dionysian precept is "everything in abundance." Reason and nature, then, are considered as opposites without reconciliation: in the modern understanding that is imposed onto antiquity, reason becomes disembodied in nature and nature becomes irrational, and thus can be known only to the extent that it is considered to be devoid of any thought. For Nietzsche, the Apollonian theoretical optimism of the cognition of being stands in stark contrast to the Dionysian practical pessimism of striving toward nonbeing. Rather than remaining an isolated individual who fasts eternally with water, one joyfully dissolves oneself into nothing, in a violent communal celebration with wine.[99] Hence, the picture of antiquity represented as the Apollonian "other" gets complicated by the original yet forgotten Dionysian, which appears as the not recognized "same" of modernity.

If beauty is indeed originally experienced as negative, then the beautiful is first perceived as the *ugly*, through the rejection of which we can first turn to and recognize the beautiful.[100] In the beginning is the Gorgon Medusa, who in ancient iconography often appears as joyous and smiling, as an affirmation of the beautiful through the ugly, disfigured, terrifying, horrible, and repulsive.[101] Already Hesiod speaks of evil beauty, καλὸν κακόν, which is deceptive yet appealing to humans.[102] Plato, in particular, first fell in love with the ugly—Socrates in his physical appearance—but because he could not stand it, he declared the ugly to be (inwardly) beautiful (CB 2). This trope of the encounter with the negative as the other of the beautiful, of its initial rejection and the subsequent acceptance as internalization and transformation into the beautiful, establishes philosophy as the way of seeing through things into what they actually are but do not appear to be any longer. The philosopher, then, is a seducer who tells the truth by hinting at an apparent lie and presents a live truth through its deadened fixture in writing, similar to an artist who shows the beauty of a live thing by deceiving us, presenting its dead semblance.

The modern scandal of the monological lonely subject is thus the tragic loss of the sight of beauty, since the subject itself regulates itself as self-ordered and reflectively transparent and thus cannot tolerate anything that cannot ultimately be rendered clear and distinct. Yet, beauty as the erotic appeals to the initial negativity of obscuring, veiling, and nontransparency, which can only eventually be revealed, become known, and lived with. One might only hope that the beautiful can be regained through the dialogical scandal as mutually shared and comically relived.

The political scandal. Modern politics lives off and thrives on scandal. Scandal can be important as a way of revealing, questioning, and transgressing the existing dubious and oppressive norms, rules, practices, and taboos in the hope of changing them to make communal political life engaging, not boring, and worth living. And yet, the criticism of scandal has to be publicly shared in common dialogical debate and action, whereas, as I have argued, the modern scandal is the expression of norms and practices instituted by the monological autonomous subject.

The scandal of modern politics becomes evident in that once the universal autonomous subject has anointed and appointed itself as the self-distilled spirit, as the supreme legislative, executive, and judging reason, a democratic politics is no longer possible. The modern rational normativity is set up in ethics and extended into politics, where political action and the political formation appropriate for such a subject—the centralized and self-centered modern state—follow the same pattern of autonomous legislation and decision-making. The utter loneliness and solitude of the modern practical subject transpires in the construction of moral autonomy translated into the political autonomy that the lonely autonomous subject exercises vis-à-vis itself as its own other, while imagining oneself to be the plurality of fellow citizens acting in the imaginary arena of public politics.[103] Only the scandal of nonautonomous morality and politics could shake the monolithic, self-sufficient autonomous subject.

It is worth noting that for Kant, with his cult of rational autonomy, there are two political opposites of the rationally organized autonomous modern state, both of which should be avoided. These are anarchism (political rule without masters), and the democratic monarchy (where everyone wants to be the master), in which everyone considers oneself the supreme ruler. For Kant, who acts within the eighteenth-century tradition of objectivating certain features in entire (predominantly European) peoples as the actors in the drama of world history (equally primarily European), with its inevitable taste of racist exclusion and schematic simplification of others, both types of political "deviations" have been historically embodied.[104]

As Aristotle has argued, democracy is the rule of the people (δῆμος, *plebs*) who are personally *free* yet are *deprived* (of means of subsistence and property), who are both denied of a fair distribution of wealth and political power.[105] Therefore, the *poor* (ἄποροι, *pauperes*) are primarily the people of democracy. As it was understood in late Roman times and in its later reception, the concept of *plebs* stands for all those who have to work to make their living (which includes artisans, doctors, teachers, workers, and laborers) and who are politically active in their striving and struggling for liberation from political domination and economic oppression. In Martin Breaugh's formulation, "The refusal to submit to political domination is the impulse at the core of the plebeian experience, and it opens onto the expression of a desire for liberty."[106]

The modern concept of democracy presupposes the elimination of the dispossessed by including them in a middle class. Yet, in ancient political thought the middle class was considered rather as a buffer between the haves and the have-nots, the cans and can-nots, and it was not inclined toward democracy, which the middle class feared and rejected as the rule of the poor, and hence was rather inclined to support oligarchy. Democracy is the rule of the dispossessed who, as Marx and Engels later note, have nothing (or not much) to lose. In the contemporary world, democracy as the rule of the poor can be rethought as the rule of the *dēmos* or *plebs*, or all those who have to work and labor in order to support themselves and yet are still dispossessed in comparison with the globalized neoliberal rich. One might also recall here the "new poverty," which for Benjamin is the poverty of our experience of the world, of our thinking, perception, and imagination, brought about by the superficiality and excess of everything that modernity has to offer—aesthetically, naturally, and politically.[107]

Modern political scandal is often based on the elimination of the middle, of the intermediary, once the "middle class" tends to usurp the dominating role of being the only and sovereign ruler, disregarding the poor and graciously forgiving the rich, assuming the powers inherent in the modern subject. In this way, the middle eliminates itself as middle. Yet, without mediation, the scandal turns into excess.

A radical democracy thus requires a radical rethinking of the very *subject of politics*—not as tragically self-centered and autonomous but as comic, pluralistic, and nonautonomous, or *allonomous*. The (explicit or more often implicit) understanding of the modern political subject, in turn, determines the understanding of politics. As Rancière observes, "Politics is not the exercise of power. Politics ought to be defined on its own terms, as a mode of acting put into practice by a specific kind of subject and deriving from a particular form of reason. It is the political relationship that allows one to think the possibility of a political subject(ivity) [*le sujet politique*], not the other way around."[108] So, to rethink politics, we need to rethink the concept of the modern subject.

Autarchy. The new political democratic subject thus can be only nonautonomous, or heteronomous—legislating by others, always in plural, establishing the laws not for *the* other but for others as equals, and thus for all. Only such a heteronomous, decentralized, and pluralistic subject is capable of establishing and maintaining political *autarchy* as self-governance and self-sufficiency, rather than modern autonomy. For Aristotle, αὐτάρκεια means self-sufficiency as independence that allows for well-being, which is the life that has all the necessary *material* means (including goods, possessions, and food in moderation) that make such life enjoyable and worth living.[109] Extended to the commonly shared life in the polis, self-sufficiency is the best way of living together and is thus the purpose that needs to be achieved.[110]

The concept of autarchy is closer to what Castoriadis calls "autonomy," which for him is "people's conscious direction of their own lives" or "people's conscious domination over what they do and what they produce," which is much broader than mere political autonomy and therefore should embrace all aspects of life.[111] The main difference is that Castoriadis still accepts and supports personal autonomy, which, however, is political and not moral for him. The dominant modern political and social system of capitalism, then, is the negation of autarchy, and is the result of the solitary domination of the modern subject, which does not allow for the recognized existence of others and thus does not grant them autarchy. Only a comic polyfocal decentered subject allows for the existence of equal and mutually dependent others who can be reciprocally equal and thus exercise the shared autarchy. Only such an autarchic subject can be free.

As Aristotle explains in his *Politics*, the principle of democracy is freedom. In particular, this means two things.

(i) Freedom presupposes freedom from domination, or from being ruled or governed by anyone (τὸ μὴ ἄρχεσθαι). Since, however, in a polity this does not seem to be altogether possible, the compromise is to govern (be the *principle* and the *origin* of political rule) and be governed in turn (ἐν μέρει ἄρχεσθαι καὶ ἄρχειν).[112] Therefore, freedom requires that one neither rules nor governs over others, nor is ruled nor governed by them, but governs and is governed at the same time through temporary participation in different institutions. In this way, everyone simultaneously has a share in power, and is the source of governance and the constituent of the law—and so, everyone is the subject of the law and governance at the same time. This is the principle of justice that brings about equality based on representation ("number") and not distinction.[113] In other words, the principle of "governing and being governed at the same time" makes everyone an *equal* and active citizen, irrespective of one's social standing or origin, which makes the democratic polity inclusive, rather than exclusive. This allows for the freedom of equals, and thus for political equality (κατὰ τὸ ἴσον).[114]

(ii) Freedom also means the freedom for each one *to live as one likes* (τὸ ζῆν ὡς βούλεταί τις): this is the life of a free citizen.[115] And this is the purpose and the outcome of power-sharing in democracy, which allows for deliberation and making decisions about how one wants to avoid domination and live one's life. Such a life is a good life in accordance with the common good, insofar as the good is universal and therefore publicly shareable or participable in democracy. The possibility of such a participation is not a given but should be and can be implemented through proper political, institutional, legal, and moral arrangements. Freedom is thus never guaranteed but should be achievable through a common recognized effort of politically shared (inter)action.

In other words, democracy is the polity in which the dispossessed and the oppressed are self-liberated and free, and in which every citizen is equal to any other one in both access to governance and in the establishment and constitution of laws, as well as in living a fulfilled and desired life. As such, democracy is radical in that it goes to the root of our existence as shared dialogical coexistence and codependence, and can be realized only as the politics of a nonautonomous plural comic subject. Comic political and moral heteronomy allows for the autarchy of self-organization not *a priori* but as a result of interaction with others.

The way to it does not go through a revolt against and a dictatorial power of the autonomous subject over itself but rather through the autarchic heteronomous and comic emancipation of the self with and among many. This is the revolution that brings people together as beings capable of dialogue, freedom, and equality that are never a given but are realized by their own effort as the result of the shared comic action.

Sovereignty and exception. The famous opening sentence of Carl Schmitt's *Political Theology* runs: "Sovereign is the one who decides on exception."[116] Although the suspension of the existing laws by making exception to them at the moment of a political crisis is already known to the Roman institution of dictatorship, the dictator was legally chosen only for a limited period, after which political life reverted to the usual legally prescribed normative boundaries.[117]

Scandal as the mode of modern existence creates crisis that lives off exception and thus has to constantly (re)create emergency. Emergency is therefore always a scandal and is translated into the defining moment of modern politics.[118] Exception points at *who* has the authority to make the decision in the situation of conflict, over which the sovereign has the monopoly.[119] Hence, exception is *the* expression of the autonomy of the modern subject, who is *the* sovereign that both establishes the (moral) law and is also capable of suspending it as its own maker. Autonomous reason establishes the law universally, which means that reason itself cannot violate or disobey the law, since it is its own authentic expression and is also willed universally by rational will. And yet, the suspension of the law equally belongs to its maker, even if the will is fully subdued and dominated by reason. This happens in the extreme moments of desperation, fear, angst, and profound boredom, when universal autonomous reason comes to the realization of its utter loneliness, the inability of reaching out for the other, the impossibility of death, and the incapacity of abiding in the kingdom of ends if it is founded on a single tear.

The exception is justified by extreme circumstances, by danger or "peril," which is precisely the situation of the modern subject's tragic condition, which is created by the subject and thus becomes its own inescapable predicament of being toward death. "It is precisely the exception that makes relevant the subject of sovereignty," as Schmitt observes.[120] This is how the modern subject exerts its moral autonomy as sovereign and translates it into the constitution of the political. In this way, the modern subject always finds itself in the precarious and paradoxical situation of the necessity of autonomously (re)founding and upholding the moral law—and the equally urgent necessity of its suspension as the expression of its autonomy and sovereignty, thereby constantly recreating the state of exception. Therefore, the modern subject always unwillingly and unnoticeably appoints itself the dictator over itself and its own needs, and yet cannot escape this dictatorship of its own reason and will by making it only provisional. Rather, the modern subject keeps, recreates, and reasserts sovereign self-rule as the permanent dictatorship, which it cannot avoid, and which thus becomes its tragic predicament. The state of exception that is meant to assure and preserve political freedom, safety, and well-being for all becomes the expression of the perpetual exclusionary being of the solitary reason and will, and of the unsafety of the modern subject.

Revolt, violence, civil war. As I have argued, scandal is always public; dialogical; a radical break that allows for a critical stance against existing, often oppressive, practices; comic; characterized by orality and loudness; and swift and spontaneous, and as such never boring. In antiquity, all these features are unmistakably present in and enacted by Diogenes. He is the master of the productive moral and political scandal, a revolutionary, and an embodiment of theoretical reflection in provocative practical action against oppression, hypocrisy, and boredom. He is the embodiment of the dialogical comic thinker who can act through public scandal with others toward the reasoned achievement of shared well-being. Because Diogenes is exiled from his hometown, he voluntarily "uproots," detaches himself from the inherited and the familiar, the traditional and the patriarchic.[121] Since Diogenes does not have a house, he does not have a private life. Every place, then, is his home, and thus the rigid opposition of public and private, which underlies the political, does not hold anymore. His house is the whole world, which is why he is a cosmopolitan (κοσμοπολίτης).[122] But Diogenes does not place himself outside of the political, nor does he deny its meaningfulness. Rather, he originates and hopes for a radically new politics, which is not the traditional politics of exclusion within the polis that also separates one political community from another and pitches the polis against nature, but the cosmopolitan politics of the radical inclusion of everyone into the world as *cosmos*, which from now on becomes the place for every living being, for humans and animals alike, and embraces both the *polis* and *physis*.[123] Citizenship in the entire co-shared world makes political and moral engagement in it never boring and exemplifies the opposite of the modern subject who is worldless and alone, not sharing its abandonment with anyone. Public and private thus become indistinguishable in the realm of the political.

Modernity loses the "what is"—of the other of nature, of the finite ordered cosmos, the place where we (can) flourish together with others in shared allosensual unfinalizable thinking, love, and action, and substitutes it with the uniform, politically indifferent universe. This causes the scandal, which is rendered as the three scandals of the revolutions in the understanding of nature, art, and politics as translations of the loss of nature in thinking, body, and action.

I have characterized revolution above as (1) unexpected and unpredictable, yet retrospectively necessary, (2) violent, (3) quick, (4) universal in its appeal, (5) radical, and (6) a novel event. Because the modern revolution expresses the aspiration of the modern subject to autonomously produce the radically new from within itself without the mediation of the other, the concept of revolution becomes extended from political (civil) to social and moral and other activities in which such a subject is active. It is only in modernity that one begins to speak about not only political but also moral, artistic, scientific, industrial (first mentioned in 1827 as *grande Révolution industrielle*), digital, and other revolutions.[124] So I turn finally to its political meaning.

The first political use of "revolution" comes in the middle of the 14th century to describe unrest in Florence.[125] This is the original meaning of the term, which stands for, and is first used interchangeably with, terms for discord, revolt, riot, and civil and political violence encompassed by the Greek στάσις and by the Latin *seditio*—and also by *coniuratio, conspiratio, turba, tumultatio, tumultus, factio, perturbatio,* and *rebellio*. Isidore of Seville defines "seditio" as *dissensio civium*, "the disagreement of citizens," and this is how the term is used in the middle ages.[126]

Seditio is a political discord, struggle, and rebellion *within* a polity, describing the struggle of one of its groups against another, or their mutual violence. Already in the middle ages, *seditio* comes to mean *civil war, bellum civile*.[127] This is the *inner war* of a polity, a discord and insurgency within and against itself, *bellum intestinum*, the "gut war," or *bellum domesticum*, where one part or party does not or cannot tolerate another.[128] Like στάσις, it is considered as a disaster already by Democritus, who saw it as inevitably detrimental to both the losers and the winners.[129] In a sense, all political thought in antiquity, whether in Plato's political projects of the *State* and the *Laws* or in Aristotle's *Politics*, attempts to establish a polity governed by laws and institutions that would exclude the possibility of στάσις. In the nineteenth century, civil war was commonly considered as the worst of all wars, political disasters, and social evils. Thomas Hobbes is quite categorical: civil war is the death of the state.[130] In a sense, once a civil war starts, it *never ends*, because it keeps generating civil disaccord, which, after the end of a military campaign, is perpetuated for generations by civic, political, and public means and is translated into institutionalized injustice, which was the origin of the civil war in the first place. The examples of China, Russia, USA, Spain, Chile, and other countries show the difficulty—almost the impossibility—of ending civil war, which becomes defining not only of the collective memory but also of political and social practices.

The inner discord brought about by the civil war is between the citizens of the same polity or state who fight against their own established and recognized moral and political institutions that now dissolve and crumble, when, as Hobbes says, we find "no one man so much as cohering to another,"[131] when the formerly accepted and familiar becomes foreign and strange, and when the division and conflict cut right through one's own familial and friendly ties, making even them painfully unfamiliar. A civil war might be caused by a commonly perceived injustice done to a part of the polity that wants to rectify it through a quick change in legal institutions or even moral arrangements in an often spontaneous uprising that expresses the indignation of the dissident and the oppressed.[132] This is why civil war is often perceived as devastating, which, however, might lead to the liberation of the poor and the rejected, which is perceived as a scandal by the wealthy and the powerful.

Not knowing who the enemy is in an internal civil conflict, one becomes the enemy of oneself. But in modernity, the discord of the modern subject with and within itself turns into an ongoing commotion, revolt, and war against itself. The subject's autonomy is at stake, and yet it cannot be gained in the unending strife in which there is no other and hence no real enemy. The subject becomes its own mortal enemy in the undeclared, ongoing, never-ending civil war fought against itself, in perennial self-devastation and boredom.

Yet modernity is the time not of revolutions as revolts but of *the* revolution. The modern revolution is the expression of the modern subject. As political revolution, it becomes meaningful only with the plenipotentiary representative of the modern subject: the bourgeoisie, who establish repressive institutions and exercise debilitating, repetitive, and often boring practices against its nonrecognized other (the poor, the workers, other races and genders) and turns against itself in self-hatred, while being unable and unwilling to change them. The modern-day liberatory anti-imperialist revolutions are the justified reaction to imperialism, which itself is the codification and expression of the modern autonomous subject, exclusionary and intolerant of others. Revolution is a *legitimate*, although not always legitimized, attempt of the dispossessed to achieve justice, to change the current oppressive network of legitimating social practices and the practices themselves.[133] Revolution is a public political scandal, a shared undertaking with the hope of achieving *liberation* by and for the wretched of the earth through the revolutionary uprising's "purgatorial thunderstorm."

Here, one can make the distinction between liberation and freedom, as discussed by Hannah Arendt. Liberation is *freedom-from*, the necessary negative moment of questioning and overthrowing the repressive habits and institutions, whereas freedom is *freedom-for*, the positive moment of establishing (or reestablishing) a proper political order, which, according to Arendt, can only be achieved in public.[134] Following this distinction, Arendt argues that the aim of revolution is freedom, rather than liberation.[135] And yet, the liberatory revolutionary impulse, often messy and violent, which might open a way to freedom, is often not followed by freedom but rather by reproducing the old, rejected practices upon which there has not been proper critical reflection, which remain unclarified and not understood, and thus reproduced differently as the same, under a different disguise.

Free speech. Among its other forms, freedom appears as free speech, which was practiced by παρρησία or *libertas loquendi* in antiquity.[136] For although one has control over speech in what one says, speech is a public phenomenon, because it is always addressed and needs an addressee, or the other. Free speech is the speech that questions and suspends the commonly accepted norms, conventions, and institutions. As such, (1) it is always *public* and unashamedly trespasses the limits between the private and the public, doing so often in a brusque and provocative manner, in challenging and often publicly offensive words, acts, and gestures. Free speech is both the sign and the moment of establishing a mutuality between oneself and others, between nonisolated persons and society, who not only can be liberated but also can be freely bound to each other in an act of free speech. Freedom of speech, then, is a most important—if not the major—political freedom (see the First Amendment), which has to be constantly reasserted and struggled for in public discourse. It is not by chance that Diogenes, a notable free speaker, claimed that παρρησία is the best in us.[137] In free speech, one becomes and asserts one's freedom and self-reliance in front of and together with others.

Free speech incorporates both the moments of liberation and freedom, for it is (2) always a *critique* of the existing (politically corrupt) morals, habits, and conventions. Such a critique is (2.1) rational but not theoretical, even if it aims at truth and intends to publicly disclose it.[138] Such a critique is also (2.2) performative, for it needs not only to be formulated in a thesis but also acted out. The truth of free speech is not an abstract theoretical but practical—moral and political— truth that resides in people and is exercised by and between people. Free speech is the mutual *practice* of truth. Therefore, free speech liberates and frees not only the others whom it targets—but also oneself. If free speech achieves its target, the free speaker or *parrēsiastēs* becomes the comic figure fighting for the liberation and freedom of all. Free speech presupposes and demands telling the truth to the best of one's abilities, with one's whole "might." Hence, paradoxically, although free speech does not lie, for it does not intend to lie, it does not necessarily always speak the truth but rather shows or hints at it.

Because the freedom-for (in autarchy) begins with the freedom-from (from the oppression of the unnecessary and abusive—of social prestige, convention, power, and wealth), free speech (3) is *dangerous*. One has to dare to speak truth against the seemingly unshakable social and political convention, or in the face of a dictator or tyrant, not only because of a possible backlash but also because, despite one's best intentions, one can be mistaken and should recognize one's fallibility. Therefore, speaking truth requires *courage*. If courage is indeed the originary virtue (both as the "archaic" virtue of the heroic age and the model for other virtues), then free speech is primarily virtuous, because it is courageous.[139] Yet the fear of saying—and knowing—the truth is mutual: both for the one who speaks, and for the one who listens, as one might never be the same after saying and hearing an uncomfortable truth. This is why free speech makes tyrants afraid. The courage to speak and the implied courage to listen and hear becomes liberating, insofar as it can lead to emancipation from the tyrannical repression in the soul.

Because free speech makes one free through liberation, it is (4) freedom from constraints imposed by an authority. The free speaker is not indebted to the authority of either the law (because it is a convention), or of the ruler (because the imposition of power is contingent and willful), or of entertainment (because it is endless repetition that does not liberate us from boredom). Free speech calls for the unconditional cancelation and abatement of all debts—economic, social, and political, and for starting anew in the revolution toward achieving the public good.

Revolution can lead to the creation of a new freedom, yet freedom is not inevitably inscribed into and rationally predetermined by the event of the revolution, the way it emerges in the totalizing motion of the Hegelian perennial reason as spirit progressing through the temporality of history. Modern bourgeois revolution is not a contingent event but the necessary realization of the *right* for self-liberation of the autonomous universal modern subject in the hope of achieving freedom. However, revolution as liberating is a collective practical embodiment of emancipatory *negativity*. As a break, a radical change that comes as the destruction of oppressive old ways, revolution is indispensable and unavoidable, even if historically contingent. It is a vital response to a social illness and a political crisis, which mostly occurs spontaneously, before being diagnosed by a learned philosophical doctor. As Benjamin puts it, revolution creates new space and gives fresh air to the city—to the polis that for far too long has been suffocated by the degrading, legally justified injustice of the *ancien régime*.[140]

Revolution and war, or civil unrest, are still closely connected and accompany each other in modern political life. With the advent of the nation-state, national revolution often follows national war, and the hoped-for world revolution should have followed the world war. Revolution is now thought (by Kautsky and Lenin) to be achieved at and as the end of a violent and devastating civil war.[141] Both revolution and war are expressions of utter negativity as violence and destruction. Yet modern revolution comes to the fore as *distinct* from revolt, embodied and exemplified in the French Revolution that without false modesty (still) presents itself as an exceptional and unique historical event, *the* event (*l'événement*) that represents all of humankind and becomes the paradigm for all such events that shape modernity in its political aspirations.[142] From now on, "revolution" becomes a *historical concept* that points not toward the past but anticipates a *new future*. The French Revolution, however, is a bourgeois revolution that becomes—and wants to be—*the* model for liberation in modernity, even for proletarian and decolonial revolutions, which end with the creation, rather than abolition, of a nation-state and of a nation. An important corrective and critical response to it is the Haitian Revolution, which has been entirely missed and misunderstood for a long time. For it is the revolution of the poor, the enslaved, and the dispossessed against the oppression of the power of the modern state, which turns into an oppressive, colonizing empire for those who are excluded from the nation.[143]

However, if we want to achieve liberation and freedom apart from the stifling, boring monotony of a universal monological subjectivity, we might look for a different kind of revolution, which would be the revolution for all against a dominant few. The Revolution is the embodiment of the negativity of Reason that inevitably progresses through the moments of negation and destruction in its constitution of history toward the end and the goal of the realization of freedom, which is the freedom of one single solitary and autonomous subject, rather than of the many of the dispossessed.

But is revolution a *reflective* enterprise? That is, should those who are engaged in an uprising realize that they are making a revolution—or should they fight for liberation and their vital interests and only later understand the importance of their undertaking? Since the modern subject constitutes itself as (over)reflective in the understanding of itself as immediately accessible to itself and as capable of actions that need to be rationally clarified, justified, and verified before they take place, the modern revolution is announced in its necessity even before it happens. If revolution is the expression of the modern subject, then it needs to be theoretically justified by the subject who then assumes the social and political role of the vanguard for the action in which the assigned revolutionary actor (a class or a people) has to act. But in the end, as I have argued, the playwright, the director, and the actor who acts against oneself is the one and the same universal monological autonomous subject who plans, stages, and lives through the self-prescribed discord or war with its self as a split self, in a necessary event of the imaginary universal history—in fact constructed by itself according to the *verum factum* principle. Yet the modern subject's capacity to generate and present its revolution as total and universal is undermined and challenged by the practice of the previous revolutions of the Gracchi, Arnold of Brescia, Cola di Rienzo, as well as of modern, collective liberatory anti-colonialist and anti-imperialist movements.

Revolution and mediation. Frightened by the violence of war that accompanies the revolution, and by the premonition of revolution's bringing an inevitable end to the comfortable yet unjust bourgeois life, conservative thought portrays revolution as evil and a "catastrophe," and hence as that which needs to be replaced with the slow, planned, and progressive movement of legal reforms. In the conservative outlook conditioned by the construction of modern subjectivity, belligerent revolution is opposed to peaceful evolution. Instead of a sudden, singular, and unpredictable event of revolution—comes a steady flow of the process of evolution, according to rationally established plans, as envisioned by Herder and Kant. Even Engels, later in his life, in an 1893 interview says: "We do not have a final end [*Endziel*]. We are evolutionists."[144]

Evolution might progress either according to a telos, or to a route that might have no finality but is suitable to the current needs. Depending on how revolutionary changes are understood—as inevitably inscribed in the logic of history or as addressing existing injustice—they might coincide in their intention with those of evolution. What distinguishes the two is the *speed* of such change: as I have argued, political revolution is desired and performed as a quick event. Koselleck's idea of the acceleration of history, then, is just another way to connect evolution and revolution without mediation, by claiming that the premodern evolution turns into modern revolution by the sheer intensification and shortening of the periods of changes.[145] Yet some modern revolutions—in science or art—continue for years and decades before being recognized as such and often do not have a clearly defined end, except for an emphatically and distinctively novel (re)description of the world and its appearance. Modern revolutions thus blur a clear-cut distinction between revolution and evolution.

Opposed to evolution, revolution is perceived as a rupture, a *radical break*, which as such needs *no mediation*. However, ironically, the opposition between revolution and evolution is itself radical and comes without mediation, and as such is itself revolutionary, undermining the intended substitution of revolution by evolution. The permanent revolution and the biological evolution both attempt to bridge and embrace the sudden singularity of the event and the perpetual continuity of the progression. Yet both do so by presupposing that nothing stands between singularity and continuity, and thus nothing mediates between revolution and evolution, where the former already presents itself as an unmediated event between past and future.

This brings us to the question of mediation in revolution, or rather the nonmediated negativity of the revolution. In modernity, revolution is considered a fight between *two unmediated* forces, two conflicting classes, which embody the abstract Hegelian unmediated contradictory opposites, the struggle between which propels the progress of universal world history toward its end.[146] The lack of mediation between the struggling opposites results in tragic terror, ending such a battle by establishing the dictatorship of the triumphant class, which becomes the embodiment of the modern lonely subject fighting the battle against itself.

The unmediated character of such adversarial opposition allows us to consider modern revolution as a civil war between two opposing forces: of the poor against the rich, of the proletariat against the wealthy bourgeois citizens. The lack of mediation makes it difficult to place other classes within the revolution, so that the large peasant class in the 1917 Russian revolution gets excluded, suppressed, and abandoned by both classes: by the bourgeoisie—as backward and patriarchal, and by the proletariat—as suspicious small-property owners who need to be stripped of their property and dekulakized. It is only in the nineteenth century that the internal, centuries-long *commocio innobilium contra nobiles*, the strife between the patricians and the plebeians, the aristocracy and the demos, is taken to be not between the citizens of the same polis but between *two parties* of the same state, where other parties get suppressed or sidelined. Modern revolution, as the scandal of the public fight between abstract unmediated embodiments of social forces, is then contrary to revolution as the struggle of all the oppressed, of all the people led by dispossessed comic thinkers against a small number of oppressors and the institutions that serve their interests.

The lack of mediation corresponds to the construction of the perennially self-dictatorial modern subject who does not tolerate the other and thus forecloses on its own access to a dialogical mediation in communication between a plurality of equals. Politically, this is reflected in the modern *monopoly of violence*: while knights traditionally had the right to wage their own wars, from around the seventeenth century on, only the king, the absolute monarch, and then the Leviathan of the nation-state as the embodiment of the modern autonomous subject reserves the legal and moral right to violence against other states and against its own citizens.

Revolution and the comic power. If, as I have argued, comedy indeed is the dramatic genre that describes the situation of the deprived and prescribes their publicly scandalous and rationally justified action toward liberation, then comedy also suggests a unique organization and *distribution of power.* The comic display of power is different from the depiction of power in modern philosophy, which is the reflection of the monological autonomous subject who exercises power as domination over the other of the self that is (and has no choice but to be) constructed as (self-)dominated. Modern political power is tragic, insofar as it is the expression of the sublime lonely sufferer who is punished by the fate of their own singular autonomous being, as the cause of their suffering that is beyond their power to change or control, even in the most scandalous and daring revolutionary act of self-rejection and transformation. The tragic power is based on the mentioned dualistic unmediated opposition: of the ruler and the ruled, of the two main struggling classes of the oppressors and the oppressed, of masters and slaves, patricians and plebeians, of *plebs urbana* and *plebs rustica* within the plebeians, of the bourgeois and proletarians, etc.

Within the logic of unmediated opposites, their struggle eventually leads not to the elimination of the domination of one over the other but to the reversal of the roles in such domination: in a revolutionary act, the oppressed, once they come to realize the possibility and necessity of their liberation, overthrow the oppressors, but in turn become oppressors themselves. Marx detects this tendency in his analysis of pauperism in nineteenth-century England, where the two opposing parties keep offering opposite solutions to the problem of the poor, none of which really work.[147] The solution, however, would require a radical restructuring of the society as classless, in order to exclude any renewed dualistic top-down distinction that might lead to further oppression. In such a society, oppression would no longer be possible and the poor would cease to exist—but this would suggest the elimination of tragic power based on unmediated opposites by an equally unmediated power. Philosophically, this would amount to the suicide of the modern subject, all attempts at which, as I have argued, remain futile. Yet, as I have further argued, each time the attempt at self-dissolution remains scandalously unsuccessful and futile because the modern subject does not even have the other, from whose point it could ultimately stab or banish itself.

In contradistinction to the unmediated power of the modern tragic subject, the comic revolutionary power is organized very differently, insofar as it presupposes not just one vertical relation between the dominators and the dominated but three distinct yet connected types of actors and their relations. New Comedy provides a good illustration and explanation of this distribution of power that becomes abandoned in modern political thought and practice. Contrary to the tragic power based on the duality of the oppressed and the oppressor, comedy is centered on the *triplicity*: of the oppressors (usually represented by parents), the oppressed (the children), and the poor and dispossessed (servants or slaves), who are further oppressed by the oppressed. Typically, the "high class" oppressors accumulate money and power and yet do not want to share with the "middle class" who want to be well off but cannot, and are liberated only with reasoned and clever help from the "lower class,"—those who are deprived of possession and social recognition. In comedy, children want to have access to the resources of their family and be with those they love but are prevented from doing so by the parents, and are helped only by the ingenious and inventive servants.[148]

The poor are in the worst social and political position and are the most deprived and unprivileged, and yet they help liberate others and themselves in and by the scandal of revolution, because they are thinkers educated through practice, by what they are doing, and can decide on the course of action. In comic action, the poor win over the rich not by the force of tragic destiny or by the inner necessity coming from the autonomous moralistic subject—but by the power of free, subtle, concrete thinking attuned to the current situation, which leads the dispossessed out of a political impasse and makes the political restoration of justice possible. Steering and directing the comedy, the slave becomes the master of comedy—the maître dialectician, the mastermind, the thinker who is the architect of its plot. And the master turns out to be the slave of comedy, insofar as he has to follow the twists and turns, the traps and clearings along the way of the action and the "argument" of the plot, which often drags him along. In comedy, the master is the slave of the slave and the slave is the master of the master.[149] The master's power, which tends to be tyrannical, is then illusory and a convention at best. The master/slave relationship establishes the pattern for the relationship between the ruler and the thinker, which becomes a trope for the relationship between power as the locus of the political and thought as the edifier of culture. In the end, the poor prevail not by sheer force but by organizing themselves and outsmarting their oppressors.

Comic, democratic plebeian power is thus constituted by three elements, rather than by two hierarchically arranged unmediated opposites. The role of the three constituent classes of society, of the rich, the poor, and those in the middle, was already stressed by Aristotle, for whom the middle functions as the measure in ethics, mediating between the extremes that should be avoided, so that the middle in the society should be capable of following the (right moral) reason.[150] Contemporary democracy is expected to be made for and by the middle class, *le tiers état*, the *third* social stratum that is originally situated *between* the upper and the lower social, economic, and political classes, which are taken to be the extremes or deviations from the middle class, who, through social and political revolution (or a series of reforms that hold the idea of revolution as a regulative principle) overwhelm the rich and incorporate the poor. And yet, the middle class does not incorporate but still opposes the poor, just as it opposes the rich.

In the comic triadic structure, however, no "class" can be considered "higher" than the other one, because the mutual distribution of power depends on its concrete constellation. The logic of the three power constituents is best represented in the ancient Chinese game of rock-paper-scissors, or Rochambeau, in which, depending on a particular combination, each one can prevail (rock over scissors, scissors over paper, paper over rock). This kind of power interaction, pervasive in New Comedy, places checks on domination and being dominated, shows the structure of oppression, and suggests a strategy for liberation. Thus, the parents rule over the children, the children prevail over the dispossessed (their servants), but the poor overpower the parents by outsmarting them, by thinking on the public stage of politics and making the decisions that steer the action toward the resolution of a current conflict and toward the liberation both of themselves and others. Here, all three are mutually dependent. The most oppressed are the destitute and poor, and yet they are neither subsumed under nor derived from the other two. The third order of the political actors here is neither a mediator between the other two nor a representative of the "sublation" of an uneasy relation between them as a kind of a "synthesis" of the "thesis" and "antithesis" of the opposites in political struggle. The triadic structure of comedy establishes an entirely different power distribution: it *prevents* the total domination of any one of its three constituents.

Even if the triadic power structure does not really cancel oppression and domination altogether, it allows for the spreading of opportunities for power evenly, giving everyone a chance to rule and be ruled, and ultimately allowing for a radical liberation. This means that the role of the dispossessed, who are the most oppressed and deprived, is crucial and central for comic political action, because, by tactically and strategically outsmarting their oppressors in the ongoing revolutionary struggle, the poor convert the vertical oppressive hierarchy into a Rochambeau triangle (or circle) that allows for the liberation of themselves and others, which comes at and as the *end*, as the result of a very complex and entangled comic political action that not only liberates the poor but also cancels the possibility of domination, and that can bring freedom.

It should be noted that the parallels with the tripartite comic distribution of power can be found, first, in contemporary politics in the three types of political approaches: conservative, liberal, and progressive, which stand for the three "generations" or "classes" of the "parents," the "children," and the "dispossessed." Such a distribution of political aspirations is better suited for the expression of the interests of various groups of people than the political system based on the opposition of only two parties. And second, the tripartition of the power distribution where the dispossessed and the poor can—and do—prevail over the powerful and the rich is also commonly found in nature, in the so-called trimorphism that has been observed in many different species of animals: in beetles, fish, lizards, and birds, where the (territorially) dispossessed can prevail over those who control most of the area by outsmarting them.[151]

In revolutionary political struggle, the dispossessed are thus the most progressive of the three orders. The poor are the most oppressed and yet are the directors of the comic political plot that aims at universal liberation and freedom. In comedy, the oppressed are fighting primarily for the liberation of others, but in this way they also gain their own freedom. Everyone seems to have a personal interest vested in action, but in the end the comic plot renders the common action selfless, since no one can be free until and unless everyone is free. The realization of the ideal of freedom, then, is impossible without the promotion of equality. The poor, who are the comic "practical" philosophers and thinkers-in-action, transgress, suspend, and eventually abolish social distinctions and privileges as merely conventional and in fact as depriving us of freedom and equality in sharing a common good as the end of comic political action and deliberation. By becoming free and equal, everyone should become politically "poor," which then cancels the very class distinctions and makes them meaningless. Whether this is a regulative principle or the achievable ideal of political revolutionary action remains to be seen, but if democracy as the power of the people can at all be enacted, then the trimorphism of the power distribution should become obsolete and redundant.

As the opposite of revolution, evolution can be considered as its contrary, as counterrevolution. Yet, because the modern revolutionary enterprise is a nonmediated struggle between two classes or parties that represent abstract unmediated contradictories, revolution always obtains its meaning in reference to, and is accompanied by, its opposite, counterrevolution. In the testimony of the counterrevolutionary Joseph De Maistre: "The counterrevolution will not be a revolution in reverse but the opposite of revolution."[152] The modern revolutionary subject necessarily bears counterrevolution right within itself.

As I have argued, modern bourgeois revolution is embedded in the negativity of the renewed scandal created by the modern subject in order to get rid of its excruciating boredom, which oppresses the subject and from which it wants to liberate itself without realizing that boredom is its own inalienable proprium. Hence, the ultimate revolution of the modern subject is the *counterrevolution against itself*, which, however, it cannot successfully carry through as the ultimate radical revolt of self-destruction, advocated by Blanqui and Bakunin. For the triumph of the self-inflicted counterrevolution would mean the subject's nonteleological end as death by suicide, which the subject wants but cannot commit, because its oppressor and oppressed are/is the same. The modern subject attempts to get rid of itself by a most radical negation, by waging a civil war within and against itself that it cannot end and cannot win—and cannot even lose—by the destruction, suspension, or sublation of revolution by revolution, by self-negating destruction without establishing a novel other.

In the end, the modern subject does not really want to dispose of itself, relishing the comfort of its autonomous self-sufficiency embellished with the repose of a bourgeois revolutionary struggling against itself. In this way, the modern subject keeps perpetuating itself under different guises—of neoliberal reforms, of conservative revolution, of reaction against direct action, of undermining the fight against racial injustice, of projectedly radical yet ever incomplete and inconsequential changes in various forms of modern individualistic expression and production.[153] The claimed and intended, but unachieved and betrayed revolution, does not bring power to the people, and instead only serves the purpose of the modern subject's narcissistic enjoyment of the tragic repetitive and unredeemable boredom of its suffering, which inevitably turns into a self-directed counterrevolution and makes it impossible to address the real suffering of the many dispossessed, not yet seen or heard.

The modern bourgeois revolution is thus the expression of the modern, monological, lonely, autonomous, tragic subject in its revolt against itself in the absence and thus exclusion of the other that does not fit, put in terms of the struggle of the socially and politically embodied unmediated opposites. As such, it should be distinguished from—but not considered a contrary to—the autarchic heteronomous and comic revolution that emancipates the many oppressed—the uprising against repressive political and social practices. The common, communal revolution is carried through by a liberating and decolonizing action, emancipatory dialogical interaction, and a realization of freedom and equality, which are never a given but can be realized in a mutually shared, oftentimes hectic, commonly reasoned action. This is the comic revolution fought by all the oppressed and dispossessed, led by comic thinkers toward the achievement of the nonboring well-being.

In Place of a Conclusion

On Method

After presenting the "elements" of the critique of bored reason, it is now appropriate to discuss its method, since to *use* a method is not the same as to *define* it.

The focus on method becomes central in modern philosophy and science, where, as I have argued, one searches for a single, rules-based, mathematically oriented, and logically formulable method for solving any problem that the modern universal self-reflective subject might pose about itself and its nonreflective other, the world. Yet there might be no need for one comprehensive method. For each method is defined by its use and purpose, and not by the requirement of systematicity for presenting an argument and formulating a thought. Each method is a *way* of solving a particular kind of problem, and as such is a *tool* that is appropriately and uniquely designed for it. Therefore, there may be *many* different methods for different objects and purposes, which means that no particular method is *the* method suitable for potentially solving all possible problems (as the *mathesis universalis* was intended to be), and from which all particular methods might be deduced. Thus, ancient dialectic embraces several (Alcinous counts six) related yet different and mutually independent methods and does not attempt to reduce them to a single overarching one.[1] Contemporary mathematics and science also use innumerable methods without attempting to subsume them under a general "scientific method."

The previous discussion was intended to show that, in its various activities as theoretical, practical, and productive, the autonomous modern subject tends to usurp thinking from others. Hence, the modern "methods" of critique might not be appropriate or applicable to the understanding of boredom as its proprium, since they are expressions of this same subject.

One such expression is *montage*. Lev Kuleshov, the practitioner and inventor (with Eisenstein) of montage, considered it to be "the essence of all art," and especially of the most synthetic modern art—film—which encompasses and unifies literature, architecture, painting, music, and drama.[2] According to the definition of Sergei Vasiliev, montage is "assembly" (*sborka*), assembling, the fitting together of various parts into a unified whole.[3] By means of montage, the assembled whole becomes the arrangement that expresses the main idea, theme, and content that the author wants to communicate in and through the final product. Montage is the method of creating the work by careful construction, by cutting and gluing multiple shots into a coherent whole, by interrupting the continuous, by unifying the multiple narratives and points of view into one single story and panoptical vision.[4] Montage is a choice made by a single director who builds a strongly historiographic account of events as guided by one dominant interpretation and the guiding idea that becomes elaborated as a logical sequence of steps within the action as a plot. In doing so, montage picks, cuts out, and joins only small fragments and frames that fit the grand unified vision of the director and suppresses and disregards and omits everything else as antiquarian and superfluous.

As I have argued, in modernity it is the same monological autonomous subject that appears under different disguises as the single director, playwright, and screenwriter, the protagonist and spectator who stages the drama of life and makes a film about it for itself. (Which is why, no matter what kind of public spectacle one tries to stage, in the end one still gets a tragic drama.) Montage within and between frames takes many different approaches to action seen from different perspectives and with different degrees of proximity, from a distant shot to a close-up; and, in constructing a frame, it puts the objects together in an arranged sequence that is meant to narrate what the sole author of modernity intends and wants to portray as the uniquely proper interpretation of the event. Many different acts and points of view are reduced to a single panoptic one, and various directions to one general direction.

Depending on the main task that the author has in mind and sets for themselves, one can cut separate episodes differently, assemble them in a different order, use slow or fast montage, assimilate a different rhythm, musical score, tempo, color, or light, and frame composition or "mise en cadre" (to use Eisenstein's term).[5] But the whole will still be the expression of the sole intention, "the main and the necessary," the plain plan and clear idea of the lonely subject, expressed by the laconic means of cutting and stitching together sequential frames, episodes, or acts.[6]

Montage is a break and a (deep surgical) cut that joins the broken together, which has been noted by Hitchcock. As such, it requires (1) breaking the continuity of the action of the plot, cutting it into pieces and inserting them within other, previously continuous and uncut pieces that oftentimes come from an entirely different context, which then gets reinterpreted by the act of montage. Moreover, (2) montage breaks the continuity of the action: the actors have to replay each episode several times over, although each time differently, remembering the psychological state, perceptions, the mood, the precise body position, and the arrangement of the objects on and around them.[7] Montage follows a preconceived, monological, and carefully established and thought through plot, which follows the reasoning and will of one single subject—of the film director and the surgeon who keeps operating on their own.

The montage script is thus a kind of a comic strip, filmstrip, diafilm, or a graphic novel with a carefully elaborated sequence of frames accompanied by the rejoinders of the actors in balloons and the commentary of the author. Alternatively, montage can also be conceived as an assemblage or a kind of puzzle in which the pieces are not prefabricated but are cut out by the author, in order to produce a completed whole that is meant to tell and display the prefabricated plan.[8]

The justification of the necessity of montage comes from the impossibility of seeing and following *all* the various multiple portrayals of the same event, which is why one needs to choose only the "essential" and the "important." But rather than getting engaged in a dialogical exchange with others as equals, each of whom might have a partial but independent perspective, in an attempt to establish a (or maybe even *the*) meaning of an event, the modern subject uses the single-person perspective to present the ultimate usurped meaning.

The idea behind montage is (i) to tell the story that the author wants to be told and heard, shown, and seen. If one puts all the long shots in one sequence, without assembling, cutting, and editing them, the told and shown would appear confused and long, and hence, boring. Therefore, frames and episodes should follow in a quick sequence, in which we mostly do not have time to pause, watch, and think. Therefore, (ii) (self-)entertainment is the other main purpose of montage. And yet, as I have argued throughout, the self-told and self-presented story of the monological subject is inevitably boring, precisely because it is the story of itself about itself told by itself to itself, always the same, no matter how creatively it uses the montage.

For this reason, montage is widely used in all arts and in modern literature. Thus, Tolstoy effectively used montage as a writer.[9] Modern systematic philosophical treatises are also the montage of a single-minded author, as is, for instance, Hegel's *Phenomenology of Spirit*. But since montage can be exercised in many different ways in order to achieve the same result, no philosophical system is unique but each one expresses the editorial, constructive self-reflective activity of the modern autonomous subject, assembling its thoughts into a whole by means of montage. By using montage, the director leaves out everything that is deemed superfluous and unnecessary, single-handedly deciding about the proper and the meaningful. By cutting and bringing together pieces of previously unified stories, the newly constructed narrative disrupts them, forcing them to say and show what the author-director wants to.

Montage is the production of *illusion*. All art is the creation of an illusion, of deliberate deception that intends to tell the truth about the depicted by telling a lie. In the case of montage, such an intentional deception works best when it is accompanied by an action or movement that continues from one frame into the other, and thus knits seemingly unrelated parts into a coherent, continuous episode.[10] As spectators, we are aware of the intended illusion as a convention, so we do not take it as morally wrong, because the intention to deceive and be deceived is implicitly agreed upon and in fact welcomed in art, insofar as it allows us to follow the unraveling of the action by means of productive imagination.

But the illusion created by the montage is an attempt to tell the truth not so much about the truth of the matter but much more about the author—the autonomous and sovereign director—who is the creator of the depicted matter. The illusion of the montage in film is taken to be true and objective, insofar as it is shown on the screen of imagination by the subject who takes to be true only that which it produces according to the *verum factum* principle. The reality is that which can be seen and portrayed as the result of the montage. The accepted becomes the story; the shown becomes being. The cut out, the redundant, is committed to oblivion as not anymore relevant, and thus nonexistent.

In this way, montage is *the* expression of the modern autonomous subject. Viktor Shklovsky and Kuleshov went as far as to suggest that *any* art is based on montage. At least, any kind of storytelling, such as literary or historiographic narrative, should imply montage. Through the illusory deception of montage we see and hear what we are shown, are meant to and indeed want to see and hear, to the extent that we follow certain, mostly implicit, means of making linear and nodal cohesions of individual episodes or frames that follow the author's preconceived and preestablished intention and the constructed plot. The montaged "infinite labyrinth of concatenations," then, results in the expected meaning.[11]

We then proudly accept such a meaning as our own, but in fact we are led to make it as an implied enthymeme. As an effective working illusion, montage is the realization of the logical fallacy of *post hoc, ergo propter hoc*, which creates a causal sequential connection by arranging one frame, episode, or scene to follow after another, thus producing a cause where one does not exist.

Montage is thus a powerful tool—*the* device of the modern subject—to produce and induce intended meanings. For Kuleshov, "montage has an enormous influence on semantic comprehension."[12] The semantic efficiency of montage becomes evident in the famous "Kuleshov effect": when the same frame (close-up of an actor attentively looking at something) is followed by two different frames (of food on the table and of a person sitting on the coach), the sequence acquires an entirely different meaning (craving for food and love-longing). Through montage, one can produce not only a new history but even a novel geography, making different disconnected places appear in one place, in the newly constructed yet increasingly familiar landscape of the memory theater.[13] Therefore, the choice of the succession of frames within montage determines the *meaning*. As such, montage also establishes the syntax of action, which brings together simple sentences/frames into a complex, compound one, in which acts follow and hold onto each other, unraveling the meaning of the spectacle of the modern tragic drama.

Demontage. In contradistinction to montage, throughout this book I have tried to use what one might call *demontage*, which is the way to restore the original, uncut multiple narratives told by the unedited voices of those tellers who are not professionally trained, the stories that might appear meaningless yet bear evidence of a simple story that communicates the meaning of an event shared in common action.

Demontage is a substitute for montage, for demolishing and breaking the original, always partial and incomplete, depiction of an event, which, although often muddled and prejudiced, still works within and in interaction with a plurality of alternative depictions. Demontage is the alternative to cutting and gluing together coherent episodes of what the modern subject stages as an auteur's tragic drama of and for itself where others are but produced imaginary appearances in a constructed world.

The partiality of each depiction and description does not imply relativism, where each point of view creates its own truth of an event. On the contrary, demontage intends to restore a meaning of the event by allowing every account to preserve its wholeness and speak for itself in interaction with other such accounts. No matter how unimpressive each account might appear, it is not boring because it is shared, discussed, and interpreted dialogically with others. For, again, boredom is the result of the historiographic interpretation of an event by the single monological subject who edits and redacts and cuts and joins the available accounts at hand into what it deems to be the correct, right, and true representation of the truth of the event, which, in the last instance, is the construction of the subject, who now is the director of the universal drama.

The distinction between montage and demontage differs from the Formalist distinction between *syuzhet* and *fabula*, that which is shown and said—and what and how we see and understand the shown and said—because in modernity both *syuzhet* and *fabula* are established and used by the same lonely subject who is the director, the actor, and the spectator of its spectacle.

As I have argued, scandal is the expression of the modern subject's desire to get rid of boredom, which, being its proprium, is inseparable from its boring self. Therefore, appearing under the guise of revolution in all possible spheres of the modern subject's action—in theory, practice, and productive creation—scandal signifies the subject's failed attempt at suicide, the impossibility of getting rid of itself by and through itself. Demontage, on the other hand, is also a scandal, but of a different kind: a productive crisis and a shared and corrigible judgment. The scandal of demontage is the spontaneous and natural action at which one sneakily peeks at (*podsmotrennoe deystvie*), disturbing the sovereign privacy and autonomy of the subject.[14] It is the action that does not ask for permission to look at and talk to the other but gets into direct dialogical interaction with them.

As such, demontage creatively dismantles the existing stifling rule and order of the modern subject. Demontage does not intend to reinterpret one single concept in an attempt to trace its various meanings, sometimes incompatible and incommensurable, by way of "genealogy," "deconstruction," or "conceptual history," which restore a meaning of a particular concept by singling it out of a complex conceptual network that itself is already a result and product of the montage. Thus, in the case of Hegel's *Phenomenology*, it might be the "master-slave" relation, "unhappy consciousness," "plasticity," or something else, taken as a magical key to open the entire complex conceptual system, reducing it to one simple, single denominator. Yet such a reconstructive reduction of a philosophical systematic montage is itself the montage and the expression of the sovereignty of the modern subject.

Demontage is not an attempt to demonstrate the cohesion of the acts of multiple actors in the middle of their actions. Rather, demontage allows for the meaning of an original narrative, the "fabula" of one of the multiple coexisting and coextensive histories, to be seen and heard through an often messy set of interacting accounts. Demontage is thus both a critique of the dictatorial position of the modern subject as the sole, forever-bored meaning-producer, the author of the theoretical, practical, and productive truth. Instead, demontage intends to understand the familiar as unfamiliar yet originary, restoring the continuity and the original multifaceted complexity of the course of events, depicted through the unpretentious simplicity of many different narratives. Demontage makes the obsolete indispensable, the unnecessary necessary, and the excluded welcome. It restores the order and the sequence of the frames into a single, long, uninterrupted, and unedited shot, which was creatively cut and rearranged by the universal autonomous subject to produce the sequence that would show its unique autonomous vision of the event.

Montage is the intentional rearrangement and distortion of the original flow of action, which is always episodic and is mostly in medias res, without a clear beginning or end. In doing so, montage provides a coherent narrative that presents the author's vision and interpretation of an event. Demontage attempts to let the original incomplete stories and actions be told and shown by their actors and narrators in interaction with other storytellers and interpreters, who are always in the middle of another action where the beginning is often lost and the end is not yet arrived at and indeed might never even be achieved. However, demontage does not aim at establishing a dominating interpretation, vision, or idea of an event, for otherwise it would become another case of montage or remontage. Rather, demontage intends to follow the structure of the already existing acts of the dramatic enactment of an event as they are told and acted out by the directors and the actors, in this way carefully and patiently trying to reverse the totalizing interpretation of the construction of montage.

Montage is the result of an intentional action that is meant to express a main idea of and about the event, propelled by the autonomous will that intends to establish a universal rule of such an action. Demontage is also an action, but its intention is to let every story be told and acted out on its own by multiple actors, often improvised and without an always evident purpose in mind. This purpose, however, may transpire in and as the end of the common effort of all the participants, in which everyone is the director, the playwriter, the actor, and the spectator at the same time.

It is never guaranteed that demontage will be able to restore the primary acts of multiple actors, to sort out the threads of the carefully interwoven texture into which we knit ourselves in ourselves. The originally incomplete and messy acts and narratives might again become mutually entangled. But by letting the stories be told without an apparent beginning or end, the interlocutors might be able to act them out together and come up with meaningful endings. Demontage aims not at a reduction but at a restoration of the told, thought, and acted in a simple shared narrative, thus attempting to preserve, repair, and tell as many lost, forgotten, and shattered details of actions as possible. The stories restored by demontage might not have immediately clear and distinct beginnings and endings, which is how the life stories of each of us mostly are. But if these stories might relate to a beginning and an end, ἀρχή and τέλος, of an event that everyone has witnessed, or the one in which everyone is participating, then the beginning and the end might come out in the middle—that is, in the dialogical and comic interaction of these uncut and unedited accounts that generate a simple story as the meaning of a shared history.

Notes

FOREWORD

1. Thus, Descartes distinguishes six basic or "primitive" passions: wonder, love, hatred, desire, joy, and sadness ("l'Admiration, l'Amour, la Haine, le Desir, la Ioye, and la Tristesse"). See René Descartes, *Les passions de l'âme* (1649), in *Oeuvres de Descartes*, ed. Charles Adam and Paul Tannery, XI 380 (§69), henceforth cited as AT; translated by John Cottingham, Robert Stoothoff, and Dugald Murdoch as *The Passions of the Soul*, in vol. 1 of *The Philosophical Writings of Descartes* (Cambridge: Cambridge University Press, 1985), 353. All references to Descartes's works in French are to the volume and page numbers of the standard Adam and Tannery edition of the *Oeuvres de Descartes*.
2. In Tolstoy's interpretation, тоска is the *desire for desires*, and is usually translated as "boredom": "[Vronsky] soon felt that desire for desires, boredom, rise in his soul [Он скоро почувствовал, что в душе его поднялись желания желаний, тоска]." Leo Tolstoy, *Anna Karenina*, part 5, ch. 8; *Polnoe sobranie sochinenii*, vol. 19, ed. V. D. Chertkov (Moscow: Khudozhestvennaia Literatura, 1949), 32.
3. See Roland Barthes, *Michelet* (1954; repr., Paris: Seuil, 1995), 57. The first use of "boredom" appears in Charles Dickens's *Bleak House* in 1852. See *Oxford Old English Dictionary*, 2nd ed. (1989), s.v. "boredom."
4. Curiously enough, Dostoevsky, Flaubert, and Baudelaire are all born in the same year—1821.
5. Henri Lefebvre, "What Is Possible," in vol. 1 of *Critique of Everyday Life*, trans. John Moore (London: Verso, 1991), 228. See also Patricia Meyer Spacks, *Boredom: The Literary History of a State of Mind* (Chicago: University of Chicago Press, 1995), 60ff.; Sara Crangle, *Prosaic Desires: Modernist Knowledge, Boredom, Laughter, and Anticipation* (Edinburgh: Edinburgh University Press, 2010), 71-103.
6. Seán Desmond Healy, *Boredom, Self, and Culture* (Rutherford, NJ: Fairleigh Dickinson University Press, 1984), 28-57.
7. Here one can mention the works of Stephen Vodanovich, W. L. Mikulas, Jerome Neu, Frederick Leong, Gregory Schneller, John Eastwood, Shelley A. Fahlman, McWelling Todman, and Timothy Wilson.

8. See, e.g., Elizabeth S. Goodstein, *Experience Without Qualities: Boredom and Modernity* (Stanford: Stanford University Press, 2005); Lars Svendsen, *A Philosophy of Boredom*, trans. John Irons (London: Reaktion, 2005); Peter Toohey, *Boredom: A Lively Story* (New Haven, CT: Yale University Press, 2011).

1. A CONCEPTUAL HISTORY OF BOREDOM

1. See Augustine, *De civ. Dei* XI.26.
2. "In Greek of the archaic, classical, and Hellenistic periods and in Classical Latin, references to boredom are very hard to find." Peter Toohey, *Melancholy, Love, and Time: Boundaries of the Self in Ancient Literature* (Ann Arbor: University of Michigan Press, 2004), 106; see also 104-57 (on *nausia* and *acedia*).
3. See Lars Svendsen, *A Philosophy of Boredom*, trans. John Irons (London: Reaktion, 2005), 21-22; Peter Toohey, *Boredom: A Lively Story* (New Haven, CT: Yale University Press), 145-46.
4. Empedocles, 31B136 DK, ap. Sextus Emp. IX.127.
5. Cicero, *ad Att.* XII.45.
6. LXX *Ps.* 60.3.
7. Cassian, *Inst.* X.1.
8. Euripides, *Medea*, 245.
9. Plato, *Prot.* 355a; *Gorg.* 477d.
10. Homer, *Od.* IX.398. As Aelian relates, the Persian king, "in order to avoid being distraught [ἵνα μὴ ἀλύῃ] while travelling, was carrying a knife and a piece of wood for whittling. For he did not have either a book to read about something important and sublime, nor the capacity to think about things noble and worthy of pondering" (Aelian, *Var. hist.* XIV.12). The physical work of creating a bagatelle substitutes for the lack of enjoyment of reading and thinking as silent conversations with the other.
11. Plutarch, *Eum.* 11.
12. Lucretius, *De rer. nat.* III.1053-69.
13. Seneca the Younger, *Epistles*, trans. Richard M. Gummere (Cambridge, MA: Harvard University Press, 1917), 1:181; *Ep.*, XXIV.26.
14. See Kristine Bruss, "Searching for Boredom in Ancient Greek Rhetoric: Clues in Isocrates," *Philosophy and Rhetoric* 45 (2012): 312-34.
15. Immanuel Kant, *Anthropologie in pragmatischer Hinsicht* 7:233-43 (§§61-66), henceforth cited as APH; translated by Robert B. Louden as *Anthropology from a Pragmatic Point of View*, in *Anthropology, History, and Education*, ed. Günter Zöller and Robert B. Louden (Cambridge: Cambridge University Press, 2007), 336-42. All references to Kant's works are to the volume and page number of the standard Academy edition (*Akademieausgabe*) of the *Gesammelte Schriften*, with the exception of the *Critique of Pure Reason*, which follows standard references to the A and B editions.
16. See also Immanuel Kant, *Vorlesungen über Anthropologie* 25:566, 25:1316; translated by Robert R. Clewis et al. as *Lectures on Anthropology*, ed. Allen W. Wood and Robert B. Louden (Cambridge: Cambridge University Press, 2012), 123, 425.

17. See Immanuel Kant, *Kritik der Urteilskraft* 5:242–43; translated by Paul Guyer and Eric Matthews as *Critique of the Power of Judgment* (Cambridge: Cambridge University Press, 2000), 124–25.
18. Johann Georg Sulzer, "Untersuchungen über den Ursprung der angenehmen und unangenehmen Empfindungen," in vol. 1 of *Vermischte philosophische Schriften*, 2 vols., (Leipzig: Weidmann, 1781–82), 4–23, esp. 21.
19. See Diogenes Laertius, *Vitae phil.* VI.85 = SVF III.178; Dio Chrysostom, *Disc.* 47.2-3.
20. "Simul atque natum sit animal . . . ipsum sibi conciliari et commendari ad se conservandum et ad suum statum eaque quae conservantia sunt eius status diligenda, alienari autem ab interitu iisque rebus quae interitum videantur afferre" (Cicero, *De fin.* III.16, trans. mod.). See also Seneca, who speaks about a "natural love for self-preservation [*naturali amore salutis suae*]" and about "the first tool that the nature granted them [living beings] for their preservation, self-attachment and self-care [*Primum hoc instrumentum in illa natura contulit ad permanendum, conciliationem et caritatem sui*]" (Seneca, *Ep.* CXXI.20, CXXI.24).
21. Boethius, *De consol. phil.* III. pros. 11.
22. See Descartes, *Meditations on First Philosophy*, trans. John. Cottingham, in vol. 2 of *The Philosophical Writings of Descartes* (Cambridge: Cambridge University Press, 1984), 56; AT VII 81. All references to Descartes's works are to the volume and page number of Adam and Tannery's *Oeuvres de Descartes*.
23. Immanuel Kant, "Idee zu einer allgemeinen Geschichte in weltbürgerlicher Absicht," 8:20; translated by Allen W. Wood as "Idea for Universal History with a Cosmopolitan Purpose," in *Anthropology, History, and Education*, ed. Günter Zöller and Robert B. Louden (Cambridge: Cambridge University Press, 2007), 111.
24. Bernard de Mandeville, *The Fable of Bees, or Private Vices, Publick Benefits* (London: Penguin, 1989; first published 1714).
25. Kant, "Idee zu einer allgemeinen Geschichte," 8:21.
26. For a critique of the modern paradigm of production that alone is supposed to establish human dignity and a defense of idleness as freedom, see Brian O'Connor, *Idleness: A Philosophical Essay* (Princeton, NJ: Princeton University Press, 2018), 3–11, 163–76.
27. Friedrich Nietzsche, *The Gay Science*, trans. Walter Kaufmann (New York: Vintage, 2010), 108 (§42).
28. Kant compares the enjoyment that comes as the result of initial unpleasantness and suffering to smoking, when the immediate irritation of the body results in the pleasure of new perceptions and even thoughts, even if such thoughts be only fleeting (APH 7:232).
29. Alfred North Whitehead, *Process and Reality*, ed. David Ray Griffin and Donald W. Sherburne (New York: Free Press, 1974), 259.
30. See Epictetus, *Disc.* 2.1-2.
31. See Immanuel Kant, *Die Religion innerhalb der Grenzen der blossen Vernunft*, 6:28–32; translated by George di Giovanni as *Religion Within the Bounds of Mere Reason* in *Religion and Rational Theology*, ed. Allen W. Wood and George di Giovanni (Cambridge: Cambridge University Press, 1996), 76–79.

32. See Epictetus, *Disc.* 2.11: "The beginning of philosophy... is the consciousness of one's weakness and impotence in the face of those things that are necessary and inevitable [ἀρχὴ φιλοσοφίας... συναίσθησις τῆς αὑτοῦ ἀσθενείας καὶ ἀδυναμίας περὶ τὰ ἀναγκαῖα]."
33. "Das Gebot: *du sollst... nicht lügen*, zum Grundsatz in die Philosophie als eine Weisheitslehre innigst aufgenommen, würde allein den ewigen Frieden in ihr nicht nur bewirken, sondern auch in alle Zukunft sichern können." Immanuel Kant, *Verkündigung des nahen Abschlusses eines Traktats zum ewigen Frieden in der Philosophie*, 8:422.
34. Kant, *Verkündigung des nahen Abschlusses*, 8:421.
35. See Aristotle, *Poet.* 1451b5-7.
36. See Ori Weisel and Shaul Shalvi, "The Cooperative Roots of Corruption," *Proceedings of the National Academy of Sciences* 112, no. 34 (2015), http://www.pnas.org/content/112/34/10651.full.
37. "L'hypocrisie est un hommage que le vice rend à la vertu." François de La Rochefoucauld, *Maximes*, in *Oeuvres complètes de La Rochefoucauld*, ed. Louis Martin-Chauffier (Paris: Gallimard, 1964), maxime 218.
38. Contrary to his argument in the *Anthropology*, however, Kant claims in *The Metaphysics of Morals* that the appearance of virtue *does not deceive* (*nicht betrügt*). See Immanuel Kant, *Die Metaphysik der Sitten*, 6:473; *The Metaphysics of Morals*, in *Practical Philosophy*, trans. and ed. Mary J. Gregor (Cambridge: Cambridge University Press, 1996), 588.
39. See Lawrence E. Klein, *Shaftesbury and the Culture of Politeness: Moral Discourse and Cultural Politics in Early Eighteenth-Century Europe* (Cambridge: Cambridge University Press, 1994), 86-90: one educates oneself about the meaning of words (e.g., fame) in a lonely, Stoic kind of discourse with oneself directed to oneself.
40. Kant, *Vorlesungen über Anthropologie*, 25:1336; *Lectures on Anthropology*, 441.
41. See Kant, APH 7:233: "The Englishmen hang themselves, just to pass the time."
42. See Dmitri Nikulin, *Dialectic and Dialogue* (Stanford: Stanford University Press, 2010), xii-xiii; see also Étienne Balibar, *Spinoza: From Individuality to Transindividuality* (Delft, Netherlands: Eburon, 1997), 3-36.
43. "Boredom strips away everything, even the courage to kill oneself." Stendhal, *Love*, trans. Gilbert Sale (New York: Penguin, 1975), 211).
44. Georg Simmel, "The Metropolis and Mental Life," in *The Sociology of Georg Simmel*, trans. and ed. Kurt H. Wolff (New York: Free Press, 1950), 409-24.
45. See Émile Durkheim, "Representations individuelles et representations collectives," *Revue de métaphysique et de morale* 6 (1898): 273-302. For Halbwachs, collective memory is related to collective consciousness as linked to collective beliefs and class consciousness. See Maurice Halbwachs, *On Collective Memory*, trans. and ed. Lewis A. Coser (Chicago: University of Chicago Press, 1992).
46. Elizabeth S. Goodstein, *Experience Without Qualities* (Stanford: Stanford University Press, 2005), 259; see also 26, 281ff., 398, 402. "'Boredom' is the name for the state in which the lived discrepancy between the involvement with transient means and their value in a larger vision of existence enters subjective awareness," 259.
47. Goodstein, *Experience Without Qualities*, 260, 399, 414. Goodstein follows Peter Sloterdijk, for whom modern skepticism is incapable of securing "a realistic foundation for philosophical knowledge of the world." Peter Sloterdijk, *Critique of Cynical Reason*, trans.

Michael Eldred (Minneapolis: University of Minnesota Press, 1987), 20; originally published as *Kritik der Zynischen Vernunft* (Frankfurt: Suhrkamp, 1983), 1:xxxiii.

48. Erich Fromm, *The Dogma of Christ: And Other Essays on Religion, Psychology, and Culture* (New York: Routledge, 2004, first published 1963), 144. See Svendsen, *A Philosophy of Boredom*, 70, 153–54.

49. Siegfried Kracauer, "Langeweile," in *Essays, Feuilletons, Rezensionen, 1924–1927*, pt. 2, ed. Inka Mülder-Bach, vol. 5 of *Werke* (Berlin: Suhrkamp, 2011), 161–64; henceforth cited as L, followed by page number; all translations are mine. The essay was originally published in *Frankfurter Zeitung* on November 11, 1924; see also Siegfried Kracauer, "Boredom," in *The Mass Ornament: Weimar Essays*, trans. and ed. Thomas Y. Levin (Cambridge, MA: Harvard University Press, 1995), 331–34.

50. Martin Heidegger, *The Fundamental Concepts of Metaphysics: World, Finitude, Solitude*, trans. William McNeill and Nicholas Walker (Bloomington: Indiana University Press, 1995), 5.

51. Walter Benjamin, "Ein Aussenseiter macht sich bemerkbar. Zu S. Kracauer, 'Die Angestellten,'" in *Gesammelte Schriften*, vol. 3, ed. Hella Tiedemann-Bartels (Frankfurt: Suhrkamp, 1972), 225.

52. See Gabriele Giannantoni, ed., *Socratis et Socraticorum Reliquiae*, 4 vols. (Naples: Bibliopolis, 1990), 2:227–509. See also vol. 1 of Dio Chrysostom, *Discourses*, trans. J. W. Cohoon et al. (Cambridge, MA: Harvard University Press, 1932); and Diogenes the Cynic, *Sayings and Anecdotes, with Other Popular Moralists*, trans. Robin Hard (Oxford: Oxford University Press, 2012). See also William Desmond, *Cynics* (Berkeley: University of California Press, 2008).

53. "Indessen: man will nichts tun, und man wird getan" (L 161). See also Miriam Hansen, *Cinema and Experience: Siegfried Kracauer, Walter Benjamin, and Theodor W. Adorno* (Berkeley: University of California Press, 2012), 18–19.

54. This is also Joseph Brodsky's didactic prescription: not to flee from boredom but to "go for it," for boredom opens the window on time as infinite opportunities, which cannot be embraced in their entirety and thus should be confronted to exercise humility in our attitude to life. See Joseph Brodsky, "In Praise of Boredom," in *On Grief and Reason: Essays* (New York: Farrar, Strauss, and Giroux, 1995), 108–9.

55. See Ludwig Tieck, *William Lovell* (Berlin: Carl August Nicolai, 1795; repr., Stuttgart: Philipp Reclam, 1986), 215, where the experience of the hellish suffering of boredom ("Langeweile ist gewiß die Qual der Hölle") is associated with passing the time in one's room on a sofa.

56. Kazimir Malevich, *Len' kak deystvitelnaya istina chelovechestva* (Moscow: Gilea, 1994), 13–25.

57. "Nichts weiter zu tun, als bei sich zu sein und nichts zu wissen, was man eigentlich tun solle" (L 164).

58. See Jean-Jacques Rousseau, *Reveries of the Solitary Walker*, trans. Russell Goulbourne (Oxford: Oxford University Press, 2011), 49–58. Dreaming at one's leisure, "to the attraction of an abstract and monotonous reverie, I am able to add charming images that enliven it. The objects of these images often eluded my senses in my ecstasies, and now, the deeper my reverie is, the more vividly it presents them to me. I am often more in their midst and more pleasantly so than I was when I was really there" (58).

59. See Erasmus, *Praise of Folly*, in *Praise of Folly and Letter to Maarten van Dorp, 1515*, trans. Betty Radice (London: Penguin, 1993).
60. Martin Heidegger, *The Fundamental Concepts of Metaphysics: World, Finitude, Solitude*, translated by William McNeill and Nicholas Walker (Bloomington: Indiana University Press, 1995), henceforth cited as FC, followed by page number; originally published as *Die Grundbegriffe der Metaphysik: Welt—Endlichkeit—Einsamkeit*, vols. 29-30 of *Gesamtausgabe* (Frankfurt: Vittorio Klostermann, 1983); henceforth cited as GM, followed by page number. In many cases I am retranslating the original text, without further notice.
61. See Martin Heidegger, *Being and Time*, trans. John Macquarrie and Edward Robinson (Oxford: Basil Blackwell, 1962), 26-27; originally published as *Sein und Zeit* (Tübingen, Germany: Max Niemeyer, 1993), 7; henceforth cited as SZ, followed by paragraph and page number. See also François Jaran and Christophe Perrin, *The Heidegger Concordance*, 3 vols. (London: Bloomsbury, 2013), 1:268-72.
62. "Stimmung" is etymologically related to "Stimme" (voice), "Einstimmung" (attunement), "bestimmen" (to determine, to appoint), and "stimmen" (to vote, but also to be correct and to tune). Heidegger's poetic ear is certainly well attuned to all the existing and possible meanings of the word. See FC 136; GM 205.
63. See SZ 134-39 (§29), 339-46 (§68), etc. "Mood represents the way in which I am always primarily the entity that has been thrown [Stimmung repräsentiert die Weise, in der ich je das geworfene Seiende primär bin]" (SZ 340 [§68]). See also *The Heidegger Concordance*, 2:437-38; and Miguel de Beistegui, "'Boredom: Between Existence and History': On Heidegger's Pivotal *The Fundamental Concepts of Metaphysics*," *Journal of the British Society for Phenomenology* 31 (2000): 147-52.
64. "das Wie unseres Miteinander-Daseins" (FC 66; see also SZ 117-25 [§26]).
65. See Xavier de Maistre, *Voyage Around My Room: Selected Works of Xavier de Maistre*, trans. Stephen Sartarelli (New York: New Direction, 1994), 49-50: "[In a dream] I say to myself: —What if suddenly a white bear, a philosopher, a tiger, or some other animal of that sort were to join this polite gathering . . . and shout out madly: 'Wretched humans! Harken to the truth that speaks through me: you are oppressed and tyrannized; you are unhappy; you are bored. —Rouse yourselves from your sleep.'"
66. The question of truth as unconcealment, *Unverborgenheit*, ἀ-λήθεια, occupies an important place in the first semester that Heidegger taught in Freiburg, in the 1928-29 lectures entitled "Introduction to Philosophy." He comes back again to the same topic in his lectures a year later, although in print the discussion of the unconcealment will appear only later, in the collection *Holzwege*. See Martin Heidegger, *Holzwege*, in vol. 5 of *Gesamtausgabe* (Frankfurt: Vittorio Klostermann, 1977; first published 1935-46), 15, 21, 37-69.
67. See "Не то, что мните вы, природа . . ." F. I. Tyutchev, *Lirika*, ed. K. V. Pigarev, 2 vols. (Moscow: Nauka, 1965), 1:81.
68. "Die Philosophie ist eigentlich Heimweh, ein Trieb überall zu Hause zu sein." Novalis, *Das Philosophische Werke I*, vol. 2 of *Schriften*, ed. J. Minor (Jena: Eugen Diederichs, 1923), frag. 21, p. 179.
69. Yet etymology can be deceptive in that it is not universal: in Dutch, which is linguistically closely related to German, "boredom" is "vervelding," which points to many or multiplication ("veel" is "many").

70. See Martin Heidegger, *Augustinus und der Neuplatonismus*, in vol. 60 of *Gesamtausgabe*, ed. Claudius Strube (Frankfurt: Vittorio Klostermann, 1995), 157-299. Heidegger ends these 1921 lectures on Augustine and Neoplatonism with a discussion of a similar yet different mood, *molestia*, "annoyance" (241-46), which he here takes to be the inalienable "how of the experience, a burden and menace of having-oneself [*ein Wie des Erfahrens, eine Beschwernis und Gefährdung des Sichselbsthabens*]" (244).
71. [Aristotle], *Problemata* 953a10-2.
72. See Espen Hammer, "Heidegger's Theory of Boredom," *Graduate Faculty Philosophy Journal* 29, no. 1 (2008): 199-225.
73. See Henri Bergson, *Laughter: An Essay on the Meaning of the Comic*, trans. Cloudesley Brereton and Fred Rothwell (Minneola, FL: Dover, 2005), 10, 50, 64.
74. I follow Heidegger's text in using Latin numerals to refer to the three forms of boredom (FC 130-31; GM 196-97).
75. On the mystical origin of *Gelassenheit* in Meister Eckhart, as coming out of the experience and practice of the "active passivity," see Thomas Strässle, *Gelassenheit: Über eine andere Haltung zur Welt* (Munich: Carl Hanser, 2001), 35-43.
76. For Bacon, Columbus in his "wonderful voyage across the Atlantic Sea ... gave reasons why he was confident that new lands and continents, beyond those previously known, could be found; reasons which were at first rejected but were afterwards proven by experience, and have been the causes and beginnings of great things." Francis Bacon, *The New Organon*, ed. Lisa Jardine and Michael Silverthorne (Cambridge: Cambridge University Press, 2000), 77.
77. See Walter Benjamin, "Theses on the Philosophy of History," in *Illuminations*, trans. Harry Zohn, ed. Hannah Arendt (New York: Schocken, 1968), 261.
78. Themistius, *Themistii in libros de anima paraphrasis*, vol. 5.3 of *Commentaria in Aristotelem Graeca*, ed. R. Heinze (Berlin: Georg Reimer, 1899). The concept of eternity as a timeless gatheredness that exists always "*already*" and at once is developed by Plotinus in his treatise *On Eternity and Time* (*Enn.* III.7 [45]). Here, he argues that time, with its flow, the succession of "nows," and the distinction between past and future, belongs to the life of the soul, which produces time and lives in it. The nondiscursive intellect, on the other hand, is atemporal and timeless, in which there is neither future nor past, neither "before" nor "after," because intellect *is* being that always *is*. As such, the intellect is eternal and originates eternity, and its very life is eternity (*Enn.* III.7.5.21-33, III.7.6.7-8, II.5.3.1-7, VI.6.18.4; see also Plato. *Tim.* 37d-38b). Plotinus uses the notion of "now" in the Aristotelian way, as the limit of and within the time at which "before" stops and "after" begins. The "now" thus primarily characterizes, for Plotinus, time rather than eternity (*Enn.* III.7.9.65; see also IV.3.13.21, VI.1.5.16, VI.3.19.22-23).
79. "If the present were always present, and would not pass into the past, it would no longer be time, but eternity." Augustine, *Confessions*, trans. John Ryan (Garden City, NY: Doubleday, 1960), X.14. See also Hannah Arendt, *Love and Saint Augustine*, ed. Joanna Vecchiarelli Scott and Judith Chelius Stark (Chicago: University of Chicago Press, 1996), 140, 159.
80. Here, Heidegger appears to be close to Pherecydes (7B1, A9 DK) who claims that those which have always been are Zas (Zeus, aether, the "height"), Chronos (being, time as defining the deep boredom of and in Dasein), and Chthonie (Earth, the "depth").

81. We already know from Kant that boredom is a painful gift that nature gives us for the advancement of a good life. Although Heidegger does not mention that etymologically Latin "to give" (dō, dare) and "gift" (dōnum) are closely related, as they are in many Indo-European languages, he could not have missed this relation between "geben" and "Gabe" (and "Gift" as "Begabung") in German. See Alfred Ernout and Antoine Meillet, *Dictionnaire étymologique de la langue latine* (Paris: Klincksieck, 2001), 179–80; Michel de Vaan, *Etymological Dictionary of Latin and the Other Italic Languages* (Leiden: Brill, 2008), 174–75, 179.
82. Martin Heidegger, *Zur Sache des Denkens*, in *Gesamtausgabe*, vol. 14 (Frankfurt: Vittorio Klostermann, 2007), 9–14.
83. As Neil Postman has argued, this is achieved by creating new media that define new forms of truth-telling and entertainment. See Neil Postman, *Amusing Ourselves to Death: Public Discourse in the Age of Show Business* (New York: Penguin, 1985), 27ff. In a sense, modern truth-telling *becomes* entertainment, because it creates scandal, the way the modern subject desperately and unsuccessfully fights boredom.
84. "Jedes Dasein als solches seine Zeit hat" (FC 127; GM 191).
85. Anonymous, *Liber Viginti Quattuor Philosophorum*, ed. Françoise Hudry (Turnhout, Belgium: Brepols, 1997), 2. See Nicolas of Cusa, *De docta ignorantia* II.11–12; Alexandre Koyré, *From the Closed World to the Infinite Universe* (Baltimore: Johns Hopkins University Press, 1957), 18; and Karsten Harries, "The Infinite Sphere: Comments on the History of a Metaphor," *Journal of the History of Philosophy* 13 (1975): 5–15.
86. See *Lexikon des Mittelalters*, ed. Robert Auty et al. (Stuttgart: Deutscher Taschenbuch, 2003), vol. 1, col. 1414–17. The so-called "Zwing und Bann" (constraint and ban) was practiced in Southern Germany (where Heidegger was from), where it stood for ruling and prohibition (forbidding) (*Gebot und Verbot*) both in the exercise of local village authority—usually by the village headman—and to communal rights (e.g., of pasture, *Trieb und Tratt* or *Tritt und Tratt*) (vol. 2, col. 735–36). In Heidegger, then, being stands in the position of a village elder/headman with respect to a particular Dasein.
87. See also Martin Heidegger, *Einführung in die Metaphysik* (Tübingen, Germany: Max Niemeyer, 1976; first published 1935), 14; "Brief über den 'Humanismus' (1946)," in vol. 9 of *Gesamtausgabe* (Frankfurt: Vittorio Klostermann, 1976), 328; *Nietzsche* (Stuttgart: Klett-Cotta, 2008), 1:366; and *The End of Philosophy*, trans. Joan Stambaugh (Chicago: University of Chicago Press, 2003), 3ff.
88. William James speaks about the will to believe, which can be understood as the formation of new habits that allow one to have new beliefs. See William James, "The Will to Believe," in *The Will to Believe and Other Essays in Popular Philosophy* (New York: Longmans Green, 1912), 11ff.
89. The language suggests in German and Danish the productive ambiguity of "Augenblick," which means "moment," and its constituents, "Auge," "øje" (eye), and "Blick," "blikket" (look).
90. The concept of *Augenblick*, which comes already in Heidegger's early works, is much discussed in *Being and Time*, and appears practically in all of his written works (especially in *Nietzsche I* and *II*) and the lectures. See *The Heidegger Concordance*, 1:109–10. See also SZ §34, 165; §36, 172; §52, 258; §68, 338, 347; §75, 391; §79, 410; §81, 427, etc. for *Augenblick* as the moment of the possibility of Dasein's authenticity. See also Koral

Ward, *Augenblick: The Concept of the "Decisive Moment" in 19th- and 20th-Century Western Philosophy* (Burlington, VT: Ashgate, 2008). Ward traces the history of the concept of *Augenblick* in Kierkegaard (øjeblikket), Nietzsche, Jaspers, and Heidegger, and argues that "Apocalyptic themes, first noted in Kierkegaard, pervade the philosophy of Heidegger in relation to the *Augenblick*. They are grounded in the idea that the social and political situation of a time is one of crisis, which appears to move inevitably toward total destruction. The culmination point of the state of crisis, the eschatological moment, cannot but give way to change and the instigation of a new order, as such it is, one might argue, the central concept of apocalypse" (98; see also 97-124). For the concept of *Augenblick* in Kierkegaard, see Søren Kierkegaard, *Der Augenblick* (Jena: Eugen Diederichs, 1923), 38-52ff.; and *Fear and Trembling*, in *Fear and Trembling; Repetition*, trans. and ed. Howard V. Hong and Edna Hong (Princeton, NJ: Princeton University Press, 1983), 74. See also Otto Pöggeler, "Destruction and Moment," in *Reading Heidegger from the Start: Essays in His Earliest Thought*, ed. Theodore Kisiel and John van Buren (Albany: SUNY Press, 1994), 137-56; William McNeill, *The Time of Life: Heidegger and Ethos* (Albany: SUNY Press, 2006), 110-13.

91. In this respect, the moment of vision is similar to the moment of the "sudden" (ἐξαίφνης) in Plato's *Parmenides* (156d-e), when the continuous activity (of motion) changes to its opposite, which happens not in time, but in the atemporal "sudden." It establishes the relationship between the continuous entity and a point: any point can be located geometrically on a continuous line, and yet there is no point "next" to it, that is, immediately adjacent to this point, because between any two points in a continuum there is always another one. The New Testament parallel, which attracts the attention of Kierkegaard, is 1 *Cor.* 15:51-52, which foretells that we all will change suddenly, in a blink of an eye (πάντες δὲ ἀλλαγησόμεθα, ἐν ἀτόμῳ, ἐν ριπῇ ὀφθαλμοῦ).

92. Martin Heidegger, *Parmenides*, vol. 54 of *Gesamtausgabe* (Frankfurt: Vittorio Klostermann, 1982), 219: "Das Wort Theorie meint, einfach bedacht, den vernehmenden Bezug des Menschen zum Sein, welchen Bezug nicht der Mensch herstellt, in welchen Bezug vielmehr das Sein selbst erst das Menschenwesen stellt." See also William McNeill, *The Glance of the Eye: Heidegger, Aristotle, and the Ends of Theory* (Albany: SUNY Press, 1999), 175, 303-19.

93. As Heidegger argues in *Being and Time*, in the *Augenblick* it is possible, "just for that moment," for Dasein to be "in a moment" (*augenblicklich*) "for its time" (Heidegger, *Being and Time*, 338; see also 187, 437, 479).

94. "Die Menschheit im Menschen befreien, die Menschheit des Menschen, d.h. das *Wesen* des Menschen befreien, *das Dasein in ihm wesentlich werden lassen*" (FC 166; GM 248).

2. BOREDOM AND THE FLÂNEUR

1. See Walter Benjamin, *The Arcades Project*, trans. Howard Eiland and Kevin McLaughlin, ed. Rolf Tiedemann (New York: Belknap, 2002); henceforth cited as AP, followed by convolute and fragment number; originally published as *Das Passagen-Werk*, vol. 5 of *Gesammelte Schriften*, ed. Rolf Tiedemann (Frankfurt: Suhrkamp, 1982).
2. See Fernand Braudel, *The Mediterranean and the Mediterranean World in the Age of Philip II*, trans. Siân Reynolds (New York: Harper & Row, 1972-73); first published 1949. See

Roberto Rossellini's film *Pa prise de pouvoir par Loius XIV*, which brilliantly shows that Louis's main instrument of imposing power onto his subjects was not sheer violence but the force of fashion, which he himself established and dictated single-handedly.

3. Walter Benjamin, "The Storyteller: Observations on the Works of Nikolai Leskov (1936)," in vol. 3 of *Selected Writings*, ed. Howard Eiland and Michael W. Jennings (Cambridge, MA: Belknap, 2002), 149.
4. Benjamin misquotes the author's name, which is Joseph: Joseph Méry, "Le Climat de Paris," in *Paris et les Parisiens*, vol. 1 of *Le Diable à Paris* (Paris: Hetzel, 1845), 245.
5. Andō Hiroshige, "Sudden Evening Shower Over Ohashi Bridge at Atake." This polychrome print (no. 58) from "One Hundred Views of Famous Places in Edo" depicts a shower over the wooden Ohashi Bridge that spans Sumida river, and was published in 1857, precisely at the time of the spread of the boredom epidemic in Europe.
6. See Andrew Benjamin, "Boredom and Distraction: The Moods of Modernity," in *Walter Benjamin and History*, ed. Andrew Benjamin (London: Continuum, 2005), 164–68; see also 168: "Boredom is an awaiting without an object." See also Carlo Salzani, "The Atrophy of Experience: Walter Benjamin and Boredom," in *Essays on Boredom and Modernity*, ed. Barbara Dalle Pezze and Carlo Salzani (Amsterdam: Rodopi, 2009), 127–54; and Eli Friedlander, *Walter Benjamin: A Philosophical Portrait* (Cambridge, MA: Harvard University Press, 2012), 98–99.
7. Plato, *Meno* 80d–e.
8. See Francis Bacon, *The New Atlantis*, in *The Major Works*, ed. Brian Vickers (Oxford: Oxford University Press, 2002), 457–89; and René Descartes, *Rules for the Direction of the Mind*, trans. Dugald Murdoch, in vol. 1 of *The Philosophical Writings of Descartes* (Cambridge: Cambridge University Press, 1985), 7–78; AT X 359–469.
9. Contrary to Andrew Benjamin, who argues that "repetition has to be understood in relation to a founding interruption; the interruption that founds" ("Boredom and Distraction," 168). On the role and importance of interruption as constitutive of dialogue, which in turn is constitutive of human being, see Dmitri Nikulin, *Dialectic and Dialogue* (Stanford: Stanford University Press, 2010), 95–118.
10. See Émile Durkheim, "Representations individuelles et representations collectives," *Revue de métaphysique et de morale* 6 (1898): 273–302; and Maurice Halbwachs, *On Collective Memory*, trans. and ed. Lewis A. Closer (Chicago: University of Chicago Press, 1992).
11. See Raymond Klibansky, Erwin Panofsky, and Fritz Saxl, *Saturn and Melancholy: Studies in the History of Natural Philosophy, Religion, and Art* (London: Thomas Nelson, 1964); Jean Starobinski, *History of the Treatment of Melancholy from the Earliest Times to 1900* (Basel: J. P. Geigy, 1962); Stanley W. Jackson, *Melancholia and Depression: From Hippocratic Times to Modern Times* (New Haven, CT: Yale University Press, 1986); and Martina Kessel, *Langeweile: Zum Umgang mit Zeit und Gefühlen in Deutschland vom späten 18. bis zum frühen 20. Jahrhundert* (Göttingen: Wallstein, 2001), 23–26.
12. Elizabeth S. Goodstein, *Experience Without Qualities* (Stanford: Stanford University Press, 2005), 95. See also Wolf Lepenies, *Melancholy and Society*, trans. Jeremy Gaines and Doris Jones (Cambridge, MA: Harvard University Press, 1992).
13. McWelling Todman, "Boredom and Psychotic Disorders: Cognitive and Motivational Issues," *Psychiatry* 66 (2003): 162.

14. "L'univers se répète sans fin et piaffe sur place. L'éternité joue imperturbablement dans l'infini les mêmes représentations." Auguste Blanqui, *L'Éternité par les Astres: Hypothèse Astronomique* (Paris: Librarie Germer Baillière, 1872), 76.
15. The distinction goes back to Aristotle, for whom the discrete cannot be infinitely divided, since its limit is the unit, the monad, which is the indivisible basis of numbers (see [Iamblichus], *Theol. arithm.* 1), but it can be infinitely expanded by repetition. The continuous, on the contrary, cannot be infinitely increased, because it will turn into a different continuous magnitude; however, it can be infinitely divided, since there is no limit to the division of the continuous. See Aristotle, *Phys.* 206a8-207a14.
16. Friedrich Nietzsche, *The Will to Power*, trans. Walter Kaufmann and R. J. Hollingdale (New York: Vintage, 1968), 35-36; originally published as *Der Wille zur Macht*, vols. 18-19 of *Gesammelte Werke*, ed. Richard Oehler, Max Oehler, and Friedrich Würzbach (Munich: Musarion, 1926), 18:46.
17. Nietzsche, *The Will to Power*, 548-50.
18. Kant, "Idee zur einer allgemeinen Geschichte," 8:20. All references to Kant's works are to the volume and page number of the standard Academy edition (*Akademieausgabe*) of the *Gesammelte Schriften*, with the exception of the *Critique of Pure Reason*, which follows standard references to the A and B editions.
19. See Yuriko Saito, "The Japanese Aesthetics of Imperfection and Insufficiency," *Journal of Aesthetics and Art Criticism* 55, no. 4 (1997): 377-85.
20. Karl Marx, *The Economic and Philosophic Manuscripts of 1844*, trans. Martin Milligan (New York: International, 1964), 120-21; originally published as *Der historische Materialismus: die Frühschriften*, ed. S. Landshut and J. P. Mayer, (Leipzig: A Kröner, 1932), 361-62.
21. Martin Heidegger, *The Fundamental Concepts of Metaphysics: World, Finitude, Solitude*, translated by William McNeill and Nicholas Walker (Bloomington: Indiana University Press, 1995), henceforth cited as FC, followed by page number; originally published as *Die Grundbegriffe der Metaphysik: Welt—Endlichkeit—Einsamkeit*, vols. 29-30 of *Gesamtausgabe* (Frankfurt: Vittorio Klostermann, 1983); henceforth cited as GM, followed by page number. See FC 212-26; GM 311-17.
22. See Martin Doehlemann, *Langeweile? Deutung eines verbreiteten Phänomens* (Frankfurt: Suhrkamp, 1991), 186-95.
23. A quote from Roger Caillois: "Romanticism ends in a theory of boredom (l'ennui), the characteristically *modern* sentiment (le sentiment *moderne*); that is, it ends in a theory of power.... Romanticism, in effect, makes the recognition by the individual of a bundle of instincts which society has a strong interest in repressing; but, for the most part, it manifests the abdication of the struggle (l'abandon de la lutte).... The Romantic writer... turns toward... a poetry of refuge and escape (une poésie de refuge et d'évasion)" (AP D4a,2).
24. Friedrich Engels, *Die Lage der arbeitenden Klasse in England* (Leipzig: O. Wigand, 1848), 217.
25. See Apollodorus, *Lib.* I.9.3.
26. Not quite as poetic as Heidegger in his play with words, their roots, prefixes and suffixes, Benjamin still discerns the three types of the one who is bored by distinguishing their relation to time: the gambler (*der Spieler*) is to pass and drive time away (*vertreiben*) by driving time out (*austreiben*); the flâneur (*der Flâneur*) is to store and (re)charge (*laden*)

time in the store of his memory; and the one who waits (*der Wartende*) is to both invite and load (*einladen*) time (AP D3,4).

27. For Benjamin, boredom is *Verstimmung* (AP D3a,4): a nuisance, misattunement, and as such is in stark contrast to Heidegger's *Stimmung*, mood, or attunement.
28. Benjamin dedicates the entire Convolute M to the flâneur. See AP 416-55. The flâneur is also a central character in Baudelaire, who himself is a flâneur: see Walter Benjamin, *Charles Baudelaire: A Lyric Poet in the Era of High Capitalism*, trans. Harry Zohn (London: Verso, 1997), 35-66, 69, 97, 128 passim; *The Writer of Modern Life: Essays on Charles Baudelaire*, ed. Michael W. Jennings, trans. Howard Eiland (Cambridge, MA: Belknap, 2006), 66-96, 187.
29. "The appearance of the street as an *intérieur* in which the phantasmagoria of the *flâneur* is concentrated is hard to separate from the gaslight." Benjamin, *Charles Baudelaire*, 50.
30. See Arnaldo Momigliano, "Ancient History and the Antiquarian (1950)," in *Studies in Historiography* (New York: Harper & Row, 1966), 1-39; and Dmitri Nikulin, *The Concept of History* (London: Bloomsbury, 2017), 67-71.
31. See Jacob Philipp Hackert's painting "Ideale Landschaft mit Motiven aus der Gegend von Tivoli" (1775) in the collection of the Goethe-Haus in Frankfurt.
32. *Voyage autour de ma chambre* is the French title of the 1794 book by Xavier de Maistre, where he describes his experience of imprisonment in his room: de Maistre, *Voyage Around My Room*, 3-78. See also AP 986 n.8.
33. Cicero, *De or.* 2.86.351-53; Quintilian, *Inst.* 11.2.11-15; Aristotle, *De mem.* 452a14. See Pierre Nora, *Realms of Memory*, trans. Arthur Goldhammer, ed. Lawrence D. Kritzman (New York: Columbia University Press, 1996-98).
34. Walter Benjamin, "The Return of the *Flâneur* (1929)," in vol. 2.1 of *Selected Writings*, 264. See Esther Leslie, "Ruins and Rubble in the Arcades," in *Walter Benjamin and the Arcades Project*, ed. Beatrice Hanssen (London: Continuum, 2006), 89-97; and Alison Ross, *Walter Benjamin's Concept of the Image* (London: Routledge, 2015), 79.
35. "History is not simply a science but also and not least a form of remembrance [*Eingedenken*]. What science has 'determined,' remembrance can modify" (AP N8,1). See Alexander Gelley, *Benjamin's Passages: Dreaming, Awakening* (Fordham: Fordham University Press, 2015), 177-78.
36. "By 'bohemians' I mean that class of individuals whose existence is a problem, condition a myth, and fortune an enigma, who have no permanent abode at all, no known place of refuge, who are not anywhere and whom one meets everywhere." Adolphe d'Ennery and Eugène Grangé, *Les bohémiens de Paris: drame en cinq actes et huit tableaux* (Paris: Dondey-Dupré, 1843), quoted in AP M5a,2.
37. A quote from Baudelaire, with whom Benjamin was utterly fascinated: "Dandyism is a mysterious institution, no less peculiar than the duel. It is of great antiquity, Caesar, Catiline, and Alcibiades providing us with dazzling examples; and very widespread, Chateaubriand having found it in the forests and by the lakes of the New World." Charles Baudelaire, "The Painter of Modern Life," in *The Painter of Modern Life and Other Essays*, trans. Jonathan Mayne (New York: Da Capo, 1986), 26; quoted in AP D4a,4.
38. See Friedrich Engels, *The Condition of the Working Class in England*, trans. Florence Wischnewetzky and V. G. Kierran (London: Penguin, 1987), 68-69; *Die Lage der arbeitenden Klasse in England*, 36-37; quoted in AP M5a,1.

39. Baudelaire, again: "[Dandies] are all representatives of that compelling need, alas only too rare today, for combatting and destroying triviality.... Dandyism is the last spark of heroism amid decadence [le dernier éclat d'héroïsme dans les décadences]." Baudelaire, "The Painter of Modern Life," 28-29; quoted in AP D5,1.
40. See Hannah Arendt, *The Life of the Mind* (San Diego: Harcourt Brace, 1978), 110-25.
41. Walter Benjamin, "Central Park," in *The Writer of Modern Life*, 163.
42. Benjamin, *Charles Baudelaire*, 37.
43. Benjamin, 41.
44. Karl Marx, *Capital: A Critique of Political Economy*, vol. 1, trans. Samuel Moore and Edward Aveling (New York: International, 1967), 181.
45. Walter Benjamin, "Review of Kracauer's *Die Angestellten*," in vol. 2.1 of *Selected Writings*, 356.
46. Benjamin, "Central Park," 157. See also: "His leisurely appearance as a personality is his protest against the division of labour which makes people into specialists. It is also his protest against their industriousness" (Benjamin, *Charles Baudelaire*, 54).
47. Benjamin, *Charles Baudelaire*, 55.
48. "The masses... stretch before the flâneur as a veil: they are the newest drug for the solitary.—Second, they efface all traces of the individual: they are the newest asylum for the reprobate and the proscript.—Finally, within the labyrinth of the city, the masses are the newest and most inscrutable labyrinth. Through them, previously unknown chthonic traits are imprinted on the image of the city" (AP M16,3). See Graeme Gilloch, *Myth and Metropolis: Walter Benjamin and the City* (Cambridge: Polity, 1996), 150-57.
49. See Aristotle, *An. post.* 72a12-14. See also Nikulin, *Dialectic and Dialogue*, 56-57.
50. See Hans-Georg Gadamer, *Truth and Method*, 2nd. ed., trans. W. Glen-Doepel, Joel Weinsheimer, and Donald G. Marshall (New York: Continuum, 2004), 102-10; originally published as *Wahrheit und Methode: Grundzüge einer philosophischen Hermeneutik*, vol. 1 of *Gesammelte Werke* (Tübingen, Germany: J. C. B Mohr [Paul Siebeck], 1990), 107-16.
51. For Barthes, "boredom is not far away from enjoyment: it is enjoyment seen from the shores of pleasure [L'ennui n'est pas loin de la jouissance: il est la jouissance vue des rives du plaisir]." Roland Barthes, *Le plaisir du texte* (Paris: Éditions du Seuil: 1973), 43; translation mine.
52. Aristotle, *Cat.* 3b24-27.
53. "ξυνόν δέ μοί ἐστιν, ὁππόθεν ἄρξομαι· τόθι γὰρ πάλιν ἵξομαι αὖθις" (Parmenides, 28B5 DK).
54. See Christopher Schwarz, *Langeweile und Identität. Eine Studie zur Entstehung und Krise des romantischen Selbstgefühls* (Heidelberg: Universitätsverlaf C. Winter, 1993), 60-211; and Lars Svendsen, *A Philosophy of Boredom*, trans. John Irons (London: Reaktion, 2005), 59-61, 139-42.
55. See Norbert Jonard, *L'ennui dans la litérature européenne: Des origins à l'aube du XXe siècle* (Paris: Honoré Champion Éditeur, 1997), 51-52, 155-80; Madeleine Bouchez, *L'ennui de Sénèque à Moravia* (Paris: Bordas, 1973). For de Beauvoir, boredom is the expression of the existence of "sub-man," who limits his possibilities to the readily available only and therefore refuses to be free: "The sub-man experiences the desert of the world in his boredom [C'est dans l'ennui que le sous-homme éprouve le désert du monde]." Simone

de Beauvoir, *The Ethics of Ambiguity*, trans. Bernard Frechtman (New York: Philosophical Library, 2015), 49; originally published as *Pour une morale de l'ambiguïté* (Paris: Gallimard, 2003), 59.
56. See Jean-Paul Sartre, *La Nausée* (Paris: Gallimard, 1972; first published 1938).
57. See Blaise Pascal, *Pensées and Other Writings*, trans. Honor Levi, ed. Anthony Levi (Oxford: Oxford University Press, 1995), frs. 86-88; *Pensées*, ed. Michel Le Guern (Paris: Gallimard, 1977), frs. 49-51. Henceforth cited as PE for the English edition, and PF for the French edition, followed by fragment numbers.
58. In a letter to Alexandre Kojève of June 3, 1934, Strauss suggests that with Hobbes, fear (of sudden violent death) comes to play a central role in modern morality through the opposition of vanity-fear, where vanity stands for the traditional Aristotelian virtue ethics based on honor, pride, and fame. See Leo Strauss, *On Tyranny*, ed. Victor Gourevitsch and Michael S. Roth (Chicago: University of Chicago Press, 2000), 228.
59. Descartes, *Les passions de l'âme*, §67, AT XI 378; *The Philosophical Writings of Descartes* (Cambridge: Cambridge University Press, 1985), 1:352.
60. "Condition de l'homme. Inconstance, ennui, inquiétude." Pascal, PF 22. See also Kessel, *Langeweile*, 21-23.
61. "Cette tristesse diserte et platte qu'on appelle l'ennui." Louis Veuillot, *Les odeurs de Paris* (Paris: G. Crés, 1914), 177; cited in Benjamin, AP D2,5.
62. Albert Camus, *Le mythe de Sisyphe* (Paris: Gallimard, 1965; first published 1942).
63. Reinhard Kuhn, *The Demon of Noontide: Ennui in Western Literature* (Princeton, NJ: Princeton University Press, 1976), 378. See Vladimir Jankélévitch, *L'aventure, l'ennui, le sérieux* (Paris: Aubier-Montaigne, 1963), 112-13.
64. "Ennui. Rien n'est si insupportable à l'homme que d'être dans un plein repos, sans passion, sans affaire, sans divertissement, sans application. Il sent alors son néant, son abandon, son insuffisance, sa dépendance, son impuissance, son vide. Incontinent il sortira du fond de son âme l'ennui, la noirceur, la tristesse, le chagrin, le dédit, le désespoir" (PF 529).
65. Cory J. Gerritsen, Maggie E. Toplak, Jessica Sciaraffa, and John Eastwood, "I Can't Get No Satisfaction: Potential Causes of Boredom," *Consciousness and Cognition* 27 (2014): 27-41; see also Charles A. De Leon, "The Special Significance of Boredom in Medical Students," *Journal of the National Medical Association* 50 (1958): 43-45.
66. Alan Gabbey, "Force and Inertia in the Seventeenth Century: Descartes and Newton," in *Descartes: Philosophy, Mathematics and Physics*, ed. S. Gaukroger (Sussex: Harvester, 1980), 230-320.
67. "Mouvement infini. Le movement infini, le point qui remplit tout, le movement est repos. Infini sans quantité, indivisible et infini" (Pascal, PF 576).
68. Speaking about *Crime and Punishment*, Tolstoy observes that Raskolnikov (who also lived in a small room) "did not live his true life when he murdered the old woman or her sister.... He acted like a machine, doing what he could not help doing—discharging the cartridge with which he had long been loaded.... He lived his true life when he was lying on the sofa in his room, deliberating not at all about the old woman.... when he was doing nothing and was only thinking, when only his consciousness was active: and in that consciousness tiny, tiny alterations were taking place." Leo Tolstoy, "Why Do Men Stupefy Themselves (1889)," in *Recollections and Essays*, trans. Aylmer Maude (London: Oxford University Press, 1937), 81-82.

3. CRITIQUE OF BORED REASON

1. See, e.g., Charles Taylor, *Sources of the Self: The Making of the Modern Identity* (Cambridge, MA: Harvard University Press, 1989), 139ff.
2. See Gottfried Wilhelm Leibniz, *Discourse on Metaphysics*, in *Discourse on Metaphysics and Other Essays*, trans. Daniel Garber and Roger Ariew (Indianapolis: Hackett, 1991), §13: everything that happens to one is fully included in one's individual notion and thus cannot be affected by others.
3. See also: "The gravest and the most painful testimony of the modern world...is the testimony of the dissolution...of community." Jean-Luc Nancy, *The Inoperative Community*, ed. Peter Connor (Minneapolis: University of Minnesota Press, 1991), 1.
4. Descartes, *Med*. III, AT VII 46.
5. See Hannah Arendt, "What Is Freedom?," in *Between Past and Future* (New York: Penguin, 1968), 164: the "identification of freedom with sovereignty is perhaps the most pernicious and dangerous consequence of the philosophical equation of freedom and free will."
6. Evelyn Waugh, *The Diaries of Evelyn Waugh*, ed. Michael Davie (Boston: Little, Brown, 1976), 782.
7. See Descartes, *Disc*. IV, AT 6:32; *Med*. III, AT 7:35; *Princ*. I 7, I 10, AT 8:7–8.
8. Immanuel Kant, *Critique of Practical Reason*, in *Practical Philosophy*, trans. and ed. Mary J. Gregor (Cambridge: Cambridge University Press, 1996); originally published as *Kritik der Praktischen Vernunft*, 5:69. All references to Kant's works are to the volume and page number of the standard Academy edition (*Akademieausgabe*) of the *Gesammelte Schriften*, with the exception of the *Critique of Pure Reason*, which follows standard references to the A and B editions. See also Immanuel Kant, "Idea for Universal History with a Cosmopolitan Purpose," trans. H. B. Nisbet, in *Political Writings*, ed. Hans Reiss (Cambridge: Cambridge University Press, 1991), 41; originally published as "Idee zu einer allgemeinen Geschichte in weltbürgerlicher Absicht," 8:17.
9. See Immanuel Kant, "Toward Perpetual Peace: A Philosophical Project," in *Practical Philosophy*, ed. Allen W. Wood (Cambridge: Cambridge University Press, 1996); originally published as *Zum ewigen Frieden: Ein philosophischer Entwurf*, 8:377; and *The Metaphysics of Morals*, trans. Mary J. Gregor, in *Practical Philosophy*, ed. Allen W. Wood (Cambridge: Cambridge University Press, 1996); originally published as *Die Metaphysik der Sitten* 6:480.
10. Christine M. Korsgaard, "The Normative Question," in *The Sources of Normativity* (Cambridge: Cambridge University Press, 1996), 19-20. On the reception and the development of the idea of autonomy, see Karl Ameriks, *Kant and the Problem of Autonomy: Problems of the Appropriation of the Critical Philosophy* (Cambridge: Cambridge University Press, 2000), 4–18.
11. See Immanuel Kant, *Critique of the Power of Judgment*, trans. Paul Guyer and Eric Matthews, ed. Paul Guyer (Cambridge: Cambridge University Press, 2000); originally published as *Kritik der Urteilskraft*, 5:185.
12. See Arendt's critique of the autonomy of the sovereign, self-sufficient subject: "If it were true that sovereignty and freedom are the same, then indeed no man could be free, because sovereignty, the ideal of uncompromising self-sufficiency and mastership,

3. Critique of Bored Reason

is contradictory to the very condition of plurality." Hannah Arendt, *The Human Condition* (Chicago: University of Chicago Press, 1998), 234.

13. See Immanuel Kant, *Groundwork of the Metaphysics of Morals*, in *Practical Philosophy*, trans. and ed. Mary J. Gregor (Cambridge: Cambridge University Press, 1996); *Grundlegung zur Metaphysik der Sitten* 4:433, 446–47; *Critique of Practical Reason* 5:33; *The Metaphysics of Morals* 6:480. See *Groundwork of the Metaphysics of Morals* 4:436: "Autonomy is . . . the ground of the dignity of human nature and of every rational nature [*Autonomie ist . . . der Grund der Würde der menschlichen und jeder vernünftigen Natur*]."
14. See Immanuel Kant, "What Real Progress Has Philosophy Made in Germany Since the Time of Leibniz and Wolff?," trans. Peter Heath, in *Theoretical Philosophy After 1781*, ed. Henry Allison and Peter Heath (Cambridge: Cambridge University Press, 2002), 20:259–351.
15. Kant, *Groundwork of the Metaphysics of Morals*, 4:428.
16. Similarly, speaking about justice, Nancy Fraser finds it necessary to define the "who," the "what," and the "how" of justice. See Nancy Fraser, *Scales of Justice* (New York: Columbia University Press, 2009), 5–8.
17. Kant, *The Metaphysics of Morals* 6:303-4.
18. Kant, *Groundwork of the Metaphysics of Morals*, 4:430.
19. Kant, *The Metaphysics of Morals*, 6:303-4.
20. Aristotle, *NE* 1111b4-1113b2.
21. "Voluntas est animi motus, cogente nullo, ad aliquid vel non amittendum, vel adipiscendum." Augustine, *De duab. an.* 10, 14.
22. Kant, *Critique of Practical Reason*, 5:33.
23. Kant, *Groundwork of the Metaphysics of Morals*, 4:430-31.
24. Søren Kierkegaard, *Fear and Trembling*, in *Fear and Trembling. Repetition.*, trans. and ed. Howard V. Hong and Edna Hong (Princeton, NJ: Princeton University Press, 1983), 53.
25. Martin Luther, *Die Letzte Predigt D. Mart. Lutheri zu Wittenburg*, 17 January 1546, in vol. 51 of *Werke: Kritische Gesamtausgabe* (Weimar: Herman Boehlaus Nachfolger, 1914), 126.
26. Fyodor Dostoevsky, preparatory notes for *The Brothers Karamazov*, in *Bratya Karamazovy: Knigi XI–XII/Epilog: Rukopisnye redaktsii*, vol. 15 of *Polnoe sobranie sochinenij v tridcati tomah* (St. Petersburg: Nauka, 1976), 232.
27. On Willkür, see Immanuel Kant, *Critique of Pure Reason*, trans. and ed. Paul Guyer and Allen Wood (Cambridge: Cambridge University Press, 1998); originally published as *Kritik der Reinen Vernunft* A533-34/B561-62; A552-53/B580-81; A800/B828, A802/B830.
28. See Kant, *The Metaphysics of Morals*, 6:213.
29. Kant, *Critique of Practical Reason*, 5:31.
30. Kant, *Critique of Practical Reason*, 5:47.
31. Descartes, *Disc.* IV, AT 6:32; *Med.* II, AT 7:25; *Princ.* I, AT 8:7. See also Augustine, *De civ. Dei* XI.26. For Leibniz, consciousness is achieved only with apperception, or the reflective knowledge of the internal perception that represents external things. See Gottfried Wilhelm Leibniz, *Principles of Nature and Grace, Based on Reason*, in *Philosophical Essays*, trans. Daniel Garber and Roger Ariew (Indianapolis: Hackett, 1989), §4.
32. William McDonald, "Kierkegaard's Demonic Boredom," in *Essays on Boredom and Modernity*, ed. Barbara Dalle Pezze and Carlo Salzani (Amsterdam: Rodopi, 2009), 65.
33. Aristotle, *Met.* Γ 3, 1005b19-20.

34. See Dan Zahavi, *Self and Other: Exploring Subjectivity, Empathy, and Shame* (Oxford: Oxford University Press, 2014), 86, 189-92.
35. Perhaps reflection even is a modern madness. See Jacques Derrida, "Cogito and the History of Madness," in *Writing and Difference*, trans. Alan Bass (Chicago: University of Chicago Press, 1978), 31-63.
36. See Plato. *Phaedr.* 273a-c; Sextus Empiricus, *Adv. Math.* II.96-99; Thomas Cole, "Who Was Corax?," *Illinois Classical Studies* 16 (1991): 65-84, repr. in *The Attic Orators*, ed. Edwin Carawan (Oxford: Oxford University Press, 2007), 37-59.
37. *Prolegomenon Sylloge*, ed. Hugo Rabe, vol. 14 of *Rhetores Graeci* (Leipzig: Teubner, 1931), 26.6-27.10.
38. See Socrates's account of his own life in an imaginary dialogue in Epictetus: "I have taken care of...that which is up to me [τὸ ἐπ' ἐμοί]....I have never done anything unjust either in private or public life [οὔτ' ἰδίᾳ οὔτε δημοσίᾳ]." Epictetus, *Disc.* II 2.9-10.
39. "ἴδιον δ' ἐστὶν ὃ μὴ δηλοῖ μὲν τὸ τί ἦν εἶναι, μόνῳ δ' ὑπάρχει καὶ ἀντικατηγορεῖται τοῦ πράγματος" (*Top.* 102a18-19). When Aristotle does not pay attention to essentiality but to substitutability only, he claims that essence *is* the proper of a thing, and hence the proper is predicated in essence, since the thing and its essence should be convertible: "τὸ δὲ τί ἐστιν ἴδιόν τε, καὶ ἐν τῷ τί ἐστι κατηγορεῖται. ταῦτα δ' ἀνάγκη ἀντιστρέφειν" (*An. post.* 91a15-16).
40. Before Porphyry, Alexander of Aphrodisias already uses laughter as the example of the *proprium* in humans: see *In an. prior.* 125.22-23; 274.1-3 (also learning grammar and music); 380.4-5; *In Top.* 2.10-12; 192.5-6.
41. Aristotle, *Top.* 102a20; see also142b31.
42. Aristotle, *An. priora* 43b28-29; *Top.* 137a17-18.
43. See Lucian, *Vit. auctio* 26: "A man is capable of laughter, but an ass is not capable of laughter, nor designing, nor sailing [ὡς ἄνθρωπος μὲν γελαστικόν, ὄνος δὲ οὐ γελαστικὸν οὐδὲ τεκταινόμενον οὐδὲ πλωϊζόμενον]."
44. See Aristotle, *Phys.* 191b36-192a1 passim.
45. In Hegel's concise formulation, in his habilitation thesis: "Contradictio est regula veri, non contradictio falsi." G. W. F. Hegel, *Habilitationsthesen*, in *Jenaer Schriften 1801–1807*, vol. 2 of *Werke* (Frankfurt: Suhrkamp, 1986), 533.
46. Aristotle, *An. post.* 72a12-14; *Cat.* 11b16-23, 13b36-14a25; see also *Phys.* 189a35ff; and Plato, *Phaedo* 103c-e. See also "ἀεὶ γάρ ἐστι μεταξύ, ὥσπερ τοῦ εἶναι καὶ μὴ εἶναι γένεσις" (Aristotle, *Met.* 994a27-28).
47. Aristotle, *Met.* 1046b22-24; 1051a10-12.
48. Nicolas of Cusa, *De docta ignorantia* I.13.
49. Μουσαγέτης, Homer. *Il.* 1.603-4; Aristophanes, *Aves* 584; Apollodorus. *Lib.* III.10.4.
50. Homer. *Il.* 1.47; *Hom. hymn.* 3.447; Apollodorus, *Lib.* I.4.2; Diodorus Siculus III.58.3; Pausanias 1.24.1; Aelian, *Var. hist.* 13.21; Ovid, *Fasti* 6.695-710. The competition between Apollo and Marsyas becomes a favorite subject of depiction both in ancient and Renaissance art. See the painting *Apollo and Marsyas* by Michelangelo Anselmi, ca. 1540, in the National Gallery in Washington, DC.
51. Homer. *Il.* 1.43-52; *Hom. Hymn.* 3.67, 215; Apollodorus, *Lib.* I.3.3; I.4.1; I.9.26; III.5.6; III.10.3; III.10.4.

3. Critique of Bored Reason

52. Apollodorus. *Lib.* I.8.1; III.5.1. See the reverse of the bronze coin of Pergamum from the time of Marcus Aurelius, SNG France 2123-2125.
53. See Cornelius Castoriadis, *The Imaginary Institution of Society*, trans. Kathleen Blamey (Cambridge: Polity, 1987), 132-64.
54. "φαντασία γὰρ ἕτερον καὶ αἰσθήσεως καὶ διανοίας." Aristotle, *De an.* 427b14-15.
55. Aristotle, *De an.* 428a11-12; see also *Met.* 1024b24-1025a6; and Plato, *Theaet.* 152c. Negativity in antiquity is associated with materiality, so no wonder that Proclus further connects imagination with the intelligible matter. *In Eucl.* 48.15-56.22, 93.18-19. See Plato, *Tim.* 51a, 52a-b; and Aristotle, *Met.* 1036a9-12.
56. Aristotle, *De an.* 428a3-4; 431a16-17.
57. Aristotle, *De mem.* 449b31-450a2.
58. See also Nicolas of Cusa, *De coniecturis*, II.14.
59. Proclus, *Procli Diadochi in primum Euclidis Elementorum librum commentarii*, ed. Gottfried Friedlein (Hildesheim: Georg Olms, 1992), 1.1-7; translated and edited by Glenn R. Morrow as *A Commentary on the First Book of Euclid's Elements* (Princeton, NJ: Princeton University Press, 1992), 3.
60. Proclus, *In Eucl.* 49.5-6; 51.9ff.
61. See Dmitri Nikulin, *Matter, Imagination and Geometry: Ontology, Natural Philosophy and Mathematics in Plotinus, Proclus and Descartes* (Aldershot, UK: Ashgate, 2002), 187-92. See Descartes to Gibieuf, 19 January 1642, AT 3:479; *The Correspondence*, vol. 3 of *The Philosophical Writings of Descartes*, trans. John Cottingham et al. (Cambridge: Cambridge University Press, 1991), 203.
62. Christian Wolff, *Vernünftige Gedanken von Gott, der Welt und der Seele des Menschen, auch allen Dingen überhaupt*, vol. 2.1 of *Deutsche Schriften*, ser. 1 of *Gesammelte Werke*, ed. Jean École et al. (Hildesheim: Georg Olms, 1983), §§273, 277ff; Alexander Gottlieb Baumgarten, *Metaphysica* (Hildesheim: Georg Olms, 1963); *Metaphysics: A Critical Translation with Kant's Elucidations, Selected Notes, and Related Material*, trans. Courtney D. Fugate and John Hymers (New York: Bloomsbury, 2014), §§520-21.
63. Kant, *Critique of Pure Reason*, A51/B75, A100-102, A115-16.
64. See Beatrice Longuenesse, *Kant and the Capacity to Judge* (Princeton, NJ: Princeton University Press, 1998), 35ff.
65. Kant, *Critique of Pure Reason*, A78-79/B104.
66. "Now there belongs to a representation by which an object is given, in order for there to be cognition of it in general, *imagination* for the composition of the manifold of intuition and *understanding* for the unity of the concept that unifies the representations." Kant, *Critique of the Power of Judgment*, §9, 5:217. See also Kant, *Critique of Pure Reason*, B151-52.
67. Aristotle, *De an.* 427b17-18.
68. See Gottfried Wilhelm Leibniz, *Monadology*, in *Discourse on Metaphysics and Other Essays*, §87.
69. "Concepts of objects often prompt a spontaneously produced image (through the productive power of imagination), which we attach to them involuntarily." Kant, *Anthropology* §30, 7:173; see also §28, 7:167-69.
70. Kant, *Anthropology*, §31, 7:175.

71. Kant, *Critique of Judgment* §9, 5:216-19; §16, 5:229-31; §23, 5:244-46; §35, 5:286-87; §58, 5:346-51 passim.
72. Kant, *Anthropology*, §5, 7:136.
73. Kant, *Anthropology*, §5, 7:136; §14, 7:151-53.
74. See Sigmund Freud, *The Interpretation of Dreams*, trans. and ed. James Strachey (New York: Basic, 2010); and Edmund Husserl, *Analysen zur Passiven Synthesis*, ed. Margot Fleischer, *Husserliana XI* (The Hague: Martinus Nijhoff, 1966), 308-9, 499-500.
75. See Immanuel Kant, *Lectures on Pedagogy*, trans. Robert B. Louden, in *Anthropology, History, and Education*, ed. Günther Zoller and Robert B. Louden (Cambridge: Cambridge University Press, 2007), 9:476.
76. Xavier De Maistre, *Voyage Around My Room*, trans. and ed. Stephen Sartarelli (New York: New Direction, 1994), 8.
77. De Maistre, *Voyage*, 11.
78. In the famous example of Descartes, one can think a chiliagon but one cannot imagine it. See *Med.* VI, AT 7:72. See Nicholas of Cusa, *De docta ignorantia* I.14; and Leibniz, *Discourse on Metaphysics*, §25.
79. For Proudhon, every human being "seeks society but avoids constraint and monotony." Pierre-Joseph Proudhon, *What Is Property?*, trans. and ed. Donald R. Kelley and Bonnie Smith (Cambridge: Cambridge University Press, 1994), 190.
80. "Three elements or, if you like, three fundamental principles constitute the essential conditions of all human development, collective or individual, in history: 1. human animality; 2. thought; and 3. rebellion." Mikhail Bakunin, "God and the State," in *Selected Writings*, ed. Michael Lehning (London: Johnathan Cape, 1973), 114.

4. BEING AND BOREDOM

1. See, e.g., Claude Lévi-Strauss, *La pensée sauvage* (Paris: Plon, 1962), 26ff.; Proclus, *Théologie platonicienne*, trans. and ed. H. D. Saffrey and L. G. Westerink (Paris: Les Belles Lettres, 1968-97); G. W. F. Hegel, *The Science of Logic*, trans. and ed. George di Giovanni (Cambridge: Cambridge University Press, 2010).
2. Pierre-Joseph Proudhon, *What Is Property?*, trans. and ed. Donald R. Kelley and Bonnie Smith (Cambridge: Cambridge University Press, 1994), 13.
3. Gilles Deleuze, *Difference and Repetition*, trans. Paul Patton (New York: Columbia University Press, 1994), 42-50 passim.
4. Viktor Shklovsky, "Искусство как прием," in *О теории прозы* (Moscow: Federatsia, 1929), 14. Shklovsky ascribes the device of estrangement to Tolstoy, who describes the familiar thing without naming it as seen for the first time.
5. See Plato, *Rep.* 524bff.
6. Aristotle, *Cat.* 6a36-8b24.
7. Martin Heidegger, "The Principle of Identity," in *Identity and Difference*, trans. Joan Stambaugh (New York: Harper & Row, 1969), 24.
8. Nicholas of Cusa, *On God as Not-Other: A Translation and Appraisal of De li Non-Aliud*, trans. and ed. Jasper Hopkins (Minneapolis: University of Minnesota Press, 1979), 27-151.

4. Being and Boredom

9. Emmanuel Levinas, *Totality and Infinity: An Essay on Exteriority*, trans. Alphonso Lingis (The Hague: Martinus Nijhof, 1979), 197-219.
10. In modern philosophy, "*repetition* is a crucial expression for what 'recollection' was to the Greeks. Just as they taught that all knowing is recollecting, modern philosophy will teach that all life is a repetition.... Repetition—that is the actuality and the earnestness of existence." Kierkegaard, *Repetition*, in *Fear and Trembling. Repetition* (Princeton, NJ: Princeton University Press, 1983), 131-33; originally published as *Gjentadelsen*, in vol. 5 of *Samlede vaerker*, ed. A. B. Drachmann, J. L. Heiberg, and H. O. Lange (Copenhagen: Gyldendal, 1963), 116. See Deleuze, *Difference and Repetition*, trans. Paul Patton (New York: Columbia University Press, 1994), 85-91 (repetition as temporality).
11. Aristotle, *Met.* 1005b19-20.
12. Gottfried Wilhelm Leibniz, *Principles of Nature and Grace*, in *Philosophical Essays*, trans. Daniel Garber and Roger Ariew (Indianapolis: Hackett, 1989), §7.
13. Aristotle, *An. post.* 92b4-11.
14. Both Plato and Aristotle use the infinitive, τὸ θαυμάζειν, in order to describe the beginning of philosophy: Plato, *Theaet.* 155d3; Aristotle, *Met.* 982b12.
15. Augustine (*si enim fallor, sum, De civ. Dei* 11.26; see also *Lib. arb.* 2.3.7; *Trin.* 15.12.21); Descartes to Colvius, 14 November 1640, AT 3:247: "I am thinking, therefore I exist [Ie pense, donc ie suis].... I use it to demonstrate that this *I* that thinks is *an immaterial substance*, and that it has nothing of the corporeal [je m'en sers pour faire connoistre que ce *moy*, qui pense, est *vne substance immaterielle*, et qui n'a rien d'incorporel]." Descartes speaks from the first-person singular. See *Disc.* IV, AT 6:32: "ie pense, donc ie suis."
16. "τὸ δὲ ὄν λέγεται μὲν πολλαχῶς" (Aristotle, *Met.* 1003a33); "τὸ ταὐτὸν καὶ τὸ ἕτερον πολλαχῶς λέγεται" (Aristotle, *Top.* 133b15).
17. Cory J. Gerritsen, Maggie E. Toplak, Jessica Sciaraffa, and John Eastwood, "I Can't Get No Satisfaction: Potential Causes of Boredom," *Consciousness and Cognition* 27 (2014): 27-41.
18. Yael Goldberg and James Danckert, "Traumatic Brain Injury, Boredom and Depression," *Behavioral Sciences* 3 (2013): 435.
19. McWelling Todman, "Boredom and Psychotic Disorders: Cognitive and Motivational Issues," *Psychiatry* 66 (2003): 146-67.
20. Thomas Goetz, Anne C. Frenzel, Nathan C. Hall, Ulrike E. Nett, Reinhard Pekrun, and Anastasiya A. Lipnevich, "Types of Boredom: An Experience Sampling Approach," *Motivation and Emotion* 38 (2014): 401-19.
21. Martin Doehlemann, *Langeweile? Deutung eines verbreiteten Phänomens* (Frankfurt: Suhrkamp, 1991), 22-23.
22. When we are bored, "Time seems endless, there is no distinction between past, present, and future. There seems to be only an endless present." Martin Wangh, "Boredom in Psychoanalytic Perspective," *Social Research* 42 (1975): 538-50, especially 541.
23. "When the days are so long and the hours so many, and then after a month one cries out in surprise: my God, how fleeting is the time! Where have these four weeks gone?" Ludwig Tieck, *William Lovell* (Berlin: Carl August Nicolai, 1795; repr., Stuttgart: Philipp Reclam, 1986), 215.

24. Reinhart Koselleck, "Is There an Acceleration of History?," in *High-Speed Society: Social Acceleration, Power, and Modernity*, ed. H. Rosa and W. E. Scheuermann (University Park: Pennsylvania State University Press, 2009), 113-34.
25. Yet slow motion in film might not be boring at all, once it communicates the unfolding careful and attentive vision, as in Eisenstein's *Alexander Nevsky*, Tarkovsky's *Stalker*, or Tsai Ming-Liang's *Stray Dogs*.
26. See Andrew C. Gallup, Lexington Swartwood, Janine Militello, and Serena Sackett, "Experimental Evidence of Contagious Yawning in Budgerigars (*Melopsittacus undulatus*)," *Animal Cognition* 18 (2015): 1051-58; Alessandra Zannella, Ivan Norscia, Roscoe Stanyon, and Elisabetta Palagi, "Testing Yawning Hypotheses in Wild Populations of Two Strepsirrhine Species: *Propithecus verreauxi* and *Lemur catta*," *American Journal of Primatology* 77 (2015): 1207-15.
27. "Die Langeweile gleicht auch in ihrer Entstehungsart der Stickluft, wie in den Wirkungen. Beide entwickeln sich gern, wo eine Menge Menschen im eingeschlossenen Raum beisammen ist." Friedrich Schlegel, *Kritische Friedrich-Schlegel-Ausgabe (KFSA)*, ed. Ernst Behler et al. (Munich: Ferdinand Schöningh, Zurich: Thomas, 1958-ongoing) 2:165.
28. Erich Fromm, *The Dogma of Christ: And Other Essays on Religion, Psychology, and Culture* (New York: Routledge, 2004, first published 1963), 150.
29. Bernard Williams, "The Makropulos Case: Reflections on the Tedium of Immortality," in *Problems of the Self: Philosophical Papers 1956–1972* (Cambridge: Cambridge University Press, 1973), 82-100. See Karel Čapek, *The Makropulos Case*, in *Four Plays*, trans. Peter Majer and Cathy Porter (London: Methuen, 1999).
30. See Lisa Bortolotti and Yujin Nagasawa, "Immortality Without Boredom," *Ratio* 22 (2009): 261-77; Donald W. Bruckner, "Against the Tedium of Immortality," *International Journal of Philosophical Studies* 20 (2012): 623-44; and Philip Kitcher, *Life After Faith: The Case for Secular Humanism* (New Haven, CT: Yale University Press, 2014), 99, 113.
31. Hans Jonas, "The Burden and Blessing of Mortality," *Hastings Center Report* 22 (1992): 34-40.
32. F. W. J. Schelling, "Ist eine Philosophie der Geschichte möglich? (1798)," in vol. 1 of *Ausgewählte Schriften*, ed. Manfred Frank (Frankfurt: Suhrkamp, 1985), 304.
33. "Gegen die Langeweile kämpfen die Götter selbst vergebens" (Friedrich Nietzsche, *Der Antichrist: Fluch auf das Christentum*, in vol. 6 of *Kritische Studienausgabe (KSA)*, ed. Giorgio Colli and Mazzino Montinari [Berlin: De Gruyter, 1988], 226; *The Anti-Christ*, in *The Anti-Christ, Ecce Homo, Twilight of the Idols, and Other Writings*, trans. Judith Norman [Cambridge: Cambridge University Press, 2005], §48).
34. *The Twilight Zone*, season 1, episode 6 (1959).
35. In modernism, "No longer does a clear line divide tedious from 'interesting' experience." Patricia Meyer Spacks, *Boredom: The Literary History of a State of Mind* (Chicago: University of Chicago Press, 1995), 219.
36. Immanuel Kant, *Lectures on Anthropology*, ed. Allen W. Wood and Robert B. Louden (Cambridge: Cambridge University Press, 2012), 441.
37. Jean-Baptiste Du Bos, *Critical Reflections on Poetry, Painting and Music*, trans. Thomas Nugent (New York: AMS, 1978; first published London: John Nourse, 1748), 1:5.

38. Friedhelm Decher, *Besuch vom Mittagsdämon: Philosophie der Langeweile* (Lüneburg: zu Klampen, 2000), 96-100; Paul North, *The Problem of Distraction* (Stanford: Stanford University Press, 2012), 143-74.
39. Brian Eno's *Ambient 1: Music for Airports* (1978) is an expression of endless repetition without meaning. As Eno notes on the insert to the record, such music "must be as ignorable as it is interesting."
40. The absurdity of such repetition is exemplified in the life-long project of Roman Opałka, who from 1965 until his death in 2011 only painted consecutive natural numbers beginning with one until infinity, eventually reaching 5607249.
41. Aristotle, *Met.* 1011b16-18.
42. Aristotle, *Cat.* 2a12-14; 5, 3a7-8, 3b24-25, 4a10-11; *Phys.* 189a32-33, 190a36-190b1, 191a12-14.
43. Aristotle, *Met.* 1004a14-16; see also 1056a15-16.
44. Aristotle, *Phys.* 192a5, 208a1, 229b26.
45. Aristotle, *De gen. et corr.* 318b16-17; *Met.* 1011b18-19.
46. Thus, the mole is blind because of the privation of sight in the genus, whereas a person is blind because of the privation of sight in this person. See Aristotle, *Met.* 1011b19-20; *Cat.* 12a26-27.
47. Aristotle, *Cat.* 11b16-23, 13b36, 14a1-2.
48. Dmitri Nikulin, *On Dialogue* (Lanham, MD: Lexington, 2006), 134-40.
49. See Timothy D. Wilson, David A. Reinhard, Erin C. Westgate, Daniel T. Gilbert, Nicole Ellerbeck, Cheryl Hahn, Casey L. Brown, and Adi Shaked, "Just Think: The Challenges of the Disengaged Mind," *Science* 345 (2014): 75-77. "In 11 studies, we found that participants typically did not enjoy spending 6 to 15 minutes in a room by themselves with nothing to do but think, that they enjoyed doing mundane external activities much more, and that many preferred to administer electric shocks to themselves instead of being left alone with their thoughts. Most people seem to prefer to be doing something rather than nothing, even if that something is negative" (75).
50. As Spacks argues, in modernity boredom becomes a mark of moral failure and is perceived as "diabolic," a temptation, a "mark of moral inadequacy" (Spacks, *Boredom*, 219). Boredom appears as the vacuity of mind that wants but cannot find proper occupation, and thus recognizes this idle lack of occupation as morally doubtful (46).
51. "The universal laws of the understanding, which are at the same time laws of nature, are equally as necessary to it (though they have originated from spontaneity) as the laws of motion are to matter." Immanuel Kant, *Critique of the Power of Judgment*, trans. Paul Guyer and Eric Matthews (Cambridge: Cambridge University Press, 2000), 5:186.
52. "By a 'method' I mean reliable rules which are easy to apply, and such that if one follows them exactly, one never will take what is false to be true or fruitlessly expend one's mental efforts, but will gradually and constantly increase one's knowledge till one arrives at a true understanding of everything within one's capacity." Descartes, *Reg.* IV, AT 10:372; and *Disc.* I, AT 6:3. See also Francis Bacon, *The New Organon*, ed. Lisa Jardine and Michael Silverthorne (Cambridge: Cambridge University Press, 2000), bk. II.
53. Descartes, *Reg.* IV, AT 6:372; XI, AT 6:407-8.
54. Plato, *Polit.* 305e-306a.

55. Descartes, *Reg.* IV, AT 10:378, 451.
56. Descartes, *Reg.* IV, AT 10:373-77; *Disc.* II, AT 6:21. Descartes himself stresses the importance of analysis, because of its simplicity, although both constituents are an integral part of the method. See Descartes, *Disc.* II, AT 6:17. The ideal of such a method is *mathematics*; see Descartes, *Med. Synopsis*, AT 7:13.
57. Aristotle, *NE* 1106b36-1107a1; See also William James, *Talks to Teachers on Psychology and to Students on Some of Life's Ideas* (New York: Henry Holt, 1899), 64-78.
58. Gottfried Wilhelm Leibniz, *Monadology*, in *Discourse on Metaphysics and Other Essays*, trans. Daniel Garber and Roger Ariew (Indianapolis: Hackett, 1991), §7.
59. Kant, *Anthropology*, 12:442, 444.
60. Byron, *Don Juan* 13:751-52, 759-60.
61. "It is false that the infinite is understood through the negation of a boundary or limit; on the contrary, all limitation implies a negation of the finite" (Descartes, *Fifth Set of Replies*, AT VII 365). See Descartes, *Conversation with Burman*, 16 April 1648, AT V 154; Nicolas of Cusa, *De li non aliud*; Pascal, *Pensées*, fr. 185; and Deleuze, *Difference and Repetition*, 46-47, 176-82.
62. The infinite "is not that outside or beyond [ἔξω] which there is nothing, but that which always has something outside or beyond" (Aristotle, *Phys.* 207a1-2). See Aristotle, *Met.* 987b25-26; *De bono*, fr. 2 Ross; Speusippus, fr. 62 Lang = fr. 29 Isnardi Parente = Simplicius, *In Phys.* 151.6-7; Xenocrates, fr. 27 Heinze = fr. 98 Isnardi Parente; Theophrastus, *Met.* 6a24-6b17; 11b2-7; Alexander of Aphrodisias, *In Met.* 85.15-86.23; and Philoponus, *In de gen. et corr.* 226.16-30. See also Dmitri Nikulin, *Matter, Imagination and Geometry* (Aldershot, UK: Ashgate, 2002), 34-58.
63. Descartes. *Princ.* I 27, AT VIII 15; G. W. F. Hegel, *Hegel's Logic*, trans. William Wallace (Oxford: Oxford University Press, 1975), §§93-94.
64. Aristotle, *Polit.* 1279b18-19, 1290b17-20.

5. THE NONBORING WELL-BEING

1. On the boredom of the sublime, see Patrick Hutchings, "Reflections on Boredom and the Sublime," *Literature and Aesthetics* 5 (1995): 104-22.
2. "ἡ δὲ πόλις κοινωνία τίς ἐστι τῶν ὁμοίων, ἕνεκεν δὲ ζωῆς τῆς ἐνδεχομένης ἀρίστης." Aristotle, *Polit.* 1328a35-37.
3. Dmitri Nikulin, *On Dialogue* (Lanham, MD: Lexington, 2006), 55-67, 141ff.; *Dialectic and Dialogue* (Stanford: Stanford University Press, 2010), 95-118.
4. Aurel Kolnai, "On the Concept of the Interesting," *British Journal of Aesthetics* 39 (1964): 25, 33.
5. "What lies at the end of the road we keep walking all our lives is death. Every present moment is governed by imminence. Human life is always 'not yet.' All 'having' is governed by fear, all 'not having' by desire." Hannah Arendt, *Love and Saint Augustine*, ed. Joanna Vecchiarelli Scott and Judith Chelius Stark (Chicago: University of Chicago Press, 1996), 13.
6. The modern attitude toward comedy is clearly expressed by Du Bos: "Thus the terror and pity, which the picture of tragical events excites in our souls, engages us much more than all the laughter and contempt excited by the several incidents of comedies."

Jean-Baptiste Du Bos, *Critical Reflections on Poetry, Painting and Music*, trans. Thomas Nugent (New York: AMS, 1978; first published London: John Nourse, 1748), 1:51.

7. As Schiller observes, "Furcht zielt auf Stillstand.... Freude auf Fortschreitung.... Furcht existiert in den Grenzen dessen, was da ist. Freude schafft, was nicht da ist [Fear aims at stillness.... Joy at progression.... Fear exists in the limits of that which is. Joy creates that which is not]." Friedrich Schiller, "Zwei philosophische Entwürfe," in vol. 5 of *Sämtliche Werke*, ed. Wolfgang Riedel (Munich: Deutscher Tauschenbuch, 2004), 1019.

8. See Richard L. Hunter, *New Comedy of Greece and Rome* (Cambridge: Cambridge University Press, 1985); Dmitri Nikulin, *Comedy, Seriously* (New York: Palgrave Macmillan, 2014).

9. See Carol Gould, *Interactive Democracy: The Social Roots of Global Justice* (Cambridge: Cambridge University Press, 2014).

10. In comedy, we find not only a structural analogy between plot and argument but also a comic parody of philosophical dialectical argument and argumentation, for instance, in Aristophanes's mocking of the Sophists in the *Clouds* or in Menander's debate between Daos and Syros portrayed as a dialectical legal argument (*Epitr.* 305ff.).

11. See Menander, *Samia* 140-43.

12. Plato, *Theaet.* 174a.

13. Dio Chrysostom, *Disc.* X.32.

14. Plato, *Legg.* 816e.

15. Hans Blumenberg, *Das Lachen der Thrakerin: Eine Urgeschichte der Theorie* (Frankfurt: Suhrkamp, 1987), 33-41 passim.

16. Such are the courtesan Habrotonon in Menander's *Epitrepontes* (538ff.), as well as the slaves Doris in Menander's *Perikeiromene* (982-83) and Syrus in Terence's *Adelphoe* (960). See Véronique Sternberg, *La poétique de la comédie* (Paris: Sedes, 1999), 182-85; T. G. A. Nelson, *Comedy: An Introduction to Comedy in Literature, Drama, and Cinema* (Oxford: Oxford University Press, 1990), 89-102; and Diego Lanza, *Lo stolto: Di Socrate, Eulenspiegel, Pinocchio e altri trasgressori del senso comune* (Turin: Einaudi, 1997).

17. An anecdote about the famous Parisian comic told by Benjamin runs: "Boredom began to be experienced in epidemic proportions during the 1840s. Lamartine is said to be the first to have given expression to the malady [*Leiden*]. It plays a role in a little story about the famous comic Deburau. A distinguished Paris neurologist was consulted one day by a patient whom he had not seen before. The patient complained of the typical illness of the times—weariness of life, depression, boredom [*die Krankheir der Zeit, Unlust zu Leben, tiefe Verstimmungen*]. 'There's nothing wrong with you,' said the doctor after a thorough examination. 'You need to relax—do something for entertainment [*Zerstreuung*]. Go see Deburau one evening, and life will look different to you.' 'Ah, dear sir,' answered the patient, 'I *am* Deburau'" (AP D3a,4). Yet Deburau became famous as representing Pierrot, who in modern interpretation became a decadent, melancholic, and tragic character out of a comic buffoon, and as such the embodiment of the modern subject who oxymoronically laughs through tears.

18. See Heinrich Niehues-Pröbsting, "The Modern Reception of Cynicism: Diogenes in the Enlightenment," in R. Bracht Branman and Marie-Odile Goulet-Cazé, eds., *The Cynics: The Cynic Movement in Antiquity and Its Legacy* (Berkeley: University of California Press, 1996), 329-65; David Mazella, *The Making of Modern Cynicism* (Charlottesville, VA:

University of Virginia Press, 2007), 110-42; and Louisa Shea, *The Cynic Enlightenment: Diogenes in the Salon* (Baltimore: Johns Hopkins University Press, 2010), 45-73.

19. See Plato, *Meno* 81b-86e. As Foucault observes, there is, however, an important difference between Socrates, who targets *ignorance* ("to show someone that he is ignorant of his own ignorance"), and Diogenes, who targets *pride*. See Michel Foucault, *Fearless Speech*, ed. Joseph Pearson (Los Angeles: Semiotext(e), 2001), 127.
20. As Kolnai observes, "interesting" is primarily present in the narrative and the comic. See "On the Concept of the Interesting," 27, 38.
21. As Benjamin observes, "Preformed in the figure of the flâneur is that of the detective.... It suited him very well to see his indolence presented as a plausible front, behind which, in reality, hides the riveted attention of an observer who will not let the unsuspecting malefactor out of his sight" (AP M13a,2; see also M11a,5; 11a,6: flâneur as a hunter). Yet the flâneur is not really a detective, to the extent that the flâneur remains solitary among the crowd of the city and does not solve a problem for others but keeps entertaining himself with solving riddles, not even capable of sharing his findings with others. See Nikulin, *Comedy, Seriously*, 67-68.
22. See the Stoic ideal of the good life as the life according to nature (τὸ ἀκολούθως τῇ φύσει ζῆν), "which is the same as a virtuous life, virtue being the goal toward which nature guides us." Zeno, ap. Diogenes Laertius, *Vitae phil.* VII.88.
23. Such is life for Aristotle: practical, and not productive. "ὁ δὲ βίος πρᾶξις, οὐ ποίησίς ἐστιν" (*Polit.* 1254a7).
24. See Sandi Mann and Rebekah Cadman, "Does Being Bored Make Us More Creative?," *Creativity Research Journal* 24 (2014): 165-73.
25. Ernst Ludwig Gerber, s.v. "Bach (Joh. Sebastian)," *Historisch-biographisches Lexikon der Tonkünstler* (Leipzig: Johann Gottlob Immanuel Breitkopf, 1790-92), vol. 1, col. 90.
26. ἕτερος ἐγώ, *heteros egō* (Aristotle, *MM* 1213a12); ἕτερος αὐτός, *heteros aytos* (*NE* 1169b6-7, 1161b28-29); ἄλλος αὐτός, *allos aytos* (*NE* 1166a31-32). See *Anon proleg.* III 13.
27. Aristotle is the first attested author to use the term φίλαυτος, *philaytos*, although he probably did not coin it. See *NE* 1168a30.
28. Aristotle, *NE* 1155b17-19.
29. Aristotle cites and often hints at κοινὰ τὰ φίλων: *NE* 1159b31. Another Pythagorean formula is "friendship (friendliness) is equality [φιλότης ἡ ἰσότης]," (*NE* 1157b36), which becomes a proverb. See Plato, *Legg.* 757a; Diog. Laert. VIII.10; and Terence, *Ad.* 804: "communia esse amicorum inter se omnia."
30. "For friendship is communication [κοινωνία γὰρ ἡ φιλία]" (Aristotle, *NE* 1171b32-33); see also *NE* 1161b14 and Plato, *Gorg.* 507e. See also *NE* 1155a4-5 (friendship as most necessary in life).
31. In Aristotle, friendship is mutual, ἀντιφίλησις: *NE* 1155b28; see also *EE* 1237a23-33; *MM* 1209a3-b20. In comedy, enemies leave the stage as friends, and unlike in tragedy, nobody dies as a result of other people's actions. See Aristotle, *Poet.* 1453a36-39.
32. Aristotle, *NE* 1166a12-13.
33. Immanuel Kant, *The Metaphysics of Morals*, in *Practical Philosophy*, trans. and ed. Mary J. Gregor (Cambridge: Cambridge University Press, 1996), 6:313-16.
34. Aristotle. *Polit.* 1253a7.
35. See Plato, *Prot.* 323d.

36. Mihaly Csikszentmihalyi, *Flow: The Psychology of Optimal Experience* (New York: Harper & Row, 1990), 67. Csikszentmihalyi describes the positive experience as follows: "First, the experience usually occurs when we confront tasks we have a chance of completing. Second, we must be able to concentrate on what we are doing. Third and fourth, the concentration is usually positive, because the task undertaken has clear goals and provides immediate feedback. Fifth, one acts with a deep but effortless involvement that removes from awareness the worries and frustrations of everyday life. Sixth, enjoyable experiences allow people to exercise a sense of control over their actions. Seventh, concern for the self disappears, yet paradoxically the sense of self emerges stronger after the flow experience is over. Finally, the sense of the duration of time is altered; hours pass by in minutes and can stretch out to seem like hours" (49).
37. Csikszentmihalyi, 107-26 passim.
38. Csikszentmihalyi, 39-40, 74-75, 168-73.
39. Diogenes Laertius., *Vitae phil.* VII.88.
40. Arendt, *The Human Condition*, 79-174.
41. Before the seventeenth century, "all activities of the *vita activa* had been judged and justified to the extent that they made the *vita contemplative* possible" (Arendt, *The Human Condition*, 291-92).
42. See Marcus Greil, *Lipstick Traces: A Secret History of the Twentieth Century* (Cambridge, MA: Harvard University Press, 1989), 51.
43. Sebastian de Grazia, *Of Time, Work, and Leisure* (New York: Twentieth Century Fund, 1962), 283; see also 202-3. See Patricia Meyer Spacks, *Boredom: The Literary History of a State of Mind* (Chicago: University of Chicago Press, 1995), 17ff.
44. See Martin Heidegger, *Sein und Zeit* (Tübingen, Germany: Max Niemeyer, 1993), 188 (§40): "In anxiety one is 'uncanny' [In der Angst ist einem '*unheimlich*']." An important analysis of anxiety also comes in Freud, who distinguishes different forms of anxiety throughout his writings, where it is variously connected to repression and trauma. See Sigmund Freud, *The Problem of Anxiety* (New York: Norton, 1936).
45. Søren Kierkegaard, *The Concept of Anxiety: A Simple Psychologically Orienting Deliberation on the Dogmatic Issue of the Hereditary Sin*, trans. and ed. Reidard Thomte and Albert B. Anderson (Princeton, NJ: Princeton University Press, 1980), 197; *Begrebet Angest*, in vol. 6 of *Samlede vaerker*, ed. A. B. Drachmann, J. L. Heiberg, and H. O. Lange (Copenhagen: Gyldendal, 1963), henceforth cited as BA followed by page number.
46. Dio Chrysostom, *Disc.* VI.41.
47. "οὐ γὰρ μήποτε τοῦτο δαμῆι εἶναι μὴ ἐόντα· ἀλλὰ σὺ τῆσδ᾽ ἀφ᾽ ὁδοῦ διζήσιος εἶργε νόημα" (Parmenides, 28B7 DK).
48. Aristotle, *Met.* 1049a27.
49. Plato, *Rep.* 509b.
50. The demonic boredom, which for Kierkegaard is a *mood* (*Stemning*) can be only countered by faith and love. See William McDonald, "Kierkegaard's Demonic Boredom," in *Essays on Boredom and Modernity*, ed. Barbara Dalle Pezze and Carlo Salzani (Amsterdam: Rodopi, 2009), 61-84.
51. Søren Kierkegaard, "Rotation of Crops: A Venture in a Theory of Social Prudence," in *Either/Or, Part I*, trans. and ed. Howard V. Hong and Edna Hong (Princeton, NJ: Princeton University Press, 1987), 288-91.

52. Kierkegaard, "Rotation of Crops," 292-93, 299.
53. "Kedsommeligheden, Uddøedheden er hemlig en Continuitet i Intet" (BA 215).

6. SCANDAL

1. "Why, to be sure, a tale of scandal is as fatal to the credit of a prudent lady of her stamp as a fever is generally to those of the strongest constitutions." Richard Brinsley Sheridan, *The School for Scandal*, ed. Ann Blake (New York: Norton, 1979), 55 (act 1, scene 1).
2. For Burke, loudness causes the passion of the sublime. See Edmund Burke, *A Philosophical Inquiry Into the Origin of Our Ideas of the Sublime and Beautiful*, ed. Adam Phillips (Oxford: Oxford University Press, 1990), 75-76. In a sense, the sublime is a scandal for the sensation, imagination, and reason, which, unable to embrace their objects, retreat in awe.
3. See Luc H. Arnal et al., "Human Screams Occupy a Privileged Niche in the Communication Soundscape," in *Current Biology* 25, no. 15 (2015): 2051-56.
4. Max Weber, *The Protestant Ethic and the Spirit of Capitalism*, trans. Talcott Parsons (London: Routledge, 1992; first published 1905), 45, 67, 100-101.
5. "A scandal, that is, a publicly given example of contempt for the strict laws of duty [ein öffentlich gegebene Beispiel der Verachtung strenger Pflichtgesetze]." Immanuel Kant, *The Metaphysics of Morals*, in *Practical Philosophy*, trans. and ed. Mary J. Gregor (Cambridge: Cambridge University Press, 1996), 6:474.
6. Kant, *The Metaphysics of Morals*, 6:464.
7. Plato, *Phaedr.* 275d-e; Alcidamas, "On Those Who Write Written Speeches, or On Sophists," in *The Works and Fragments*, ed. J. V. Muir (London: Bristol Classical, 2001), 2-21; *Peri sophiston*, in *Orationes et fragmenta, adiunctis Gorgiae Antisthenis Alcidamantis declamationibus*, ed. F. Blass (Leipzig: Teubner, 1908).
8. See Protagoras, 80B6b DK, ap. Aristotle, *Rhet.* 1402a23-24.
9. See Aquinas, *Summa theol.* II.2, Q 43, A 1: Greek *skandalon* (with reference to Jerome) can be considered "offense, downfall and a stumbling of the foot [*offensionem vel ruinam et impactionem pedis*]." In spiritual life, Aquinas takes the obstacle (*obex*) of scandal to be sin (*peccatum*).
10. σκανδαλιστής means an acrobat who performs on a trapeze (σκάνδαλον).
11. Søren Kierkegaard, *Fear and Trembling*, in *Fear and Trembling; Repetition*, trans. and ed. Howard V. Hong and Edna Hong (Princeton, NJ: Princeton University Press, 1983), 62; originally published as *Frygt og Baeven*, in *Frygt og Baeven. Gjentadelsen*, in *Samlede vaerker*, vol. 5, ed. A. B. Drachmann, J. L. Heiberg, and H. O. Lange (Copenhagen: Gyldendal, 1963), 58.
12. See Hannah Arendt, "Socrates," in *The Promise of Politics* (New York: Schocken, 2005), 5-39.
13. Emmanuel Levinas, "Kierkegaard: Existence and Ethics," in *Proper Names*, trans. Michael B. Smith (Stanford: Stanford University Press, 1996), 72.
14. Adut has argued that scandal is an episodic event that transgresses and challenges moral norms, provokes public reaction, expresses a conflict, and encompasses all areas of life. See Ari Adut, *On Scandal: Moral Disturbances in Society, Politics, and Art* (Cambridge: Cambridge University Press, 2008), 9-37. On this interpretation, publicity is

central to scandal, which "in its bare form involves a transgression, a publicizer, and a public" (17). Yet, in a broader sense, since it is always public, scandal can work its way into the public debate quietly yet steadily, without an immediate advertisement and publicity.

15. "Tempus absolutum, verum et mathematicum, in se et natura sua sine relatione ad externum quodvis, aequabiliter fluit, alioque nomine dicitur duratio." Isaac Newton, *Philosophiae Naturalis Principia Mathematica: The Third Edition (1726) with Variant Readings*, ed. Alexander Koyré and I. Bernard Cohen (Cambridge, MA: Harvard University Press, 1972), 1:46.
16. Piet Mondrian, *Plastic and Pure Plastic Art* (New York: Wittenborn, 1945), 14.
17. Mondrian, *Plastic and Pure Plastic Art*, 25; see also 53. "When dynamic movement is established through *contrasts* or oppositions of the expressive means, relationship becomes the chief preoccupation of the artist who is seeking to create equilibrium. I found that the right angle is the sole constant relationship, and that, through the proportions of dimension, its constant expression can be given movement, that is, made *living*" (10). See also Terrell M. Butler, "Mimesis, Scandal, and the End of History in Mondrian's Aesthetics," *Journal of Mind and Behavior* 3 (1982): 411-26.
18. Mondrian, *Plastic and Pure Plastic Art*, 38.
19. Hans Jonas, *Ontologische und wissenschaftliche Revolution*, ed. Jens Peter Brune, vol. II.2 of *Kritische Gesamtausgabe der Werke von Hans Jonas (KGA)* (Freiburg: Rombach, 2012), 3-197, henceforth cited as OSR followed by page number.
20. "We speak of revolution when the change in question—a collective change in human affairs—is radical in nature, comprehensive in scope, and concentrated in time." Hans Jonas, "Seventeenth Century and After: The Meaning of the Scientific and Technological Revolution," in *Philosophical Essays: From Ancient Creed to Technological Man* (Englewood Cliffs, NJ: Prentice-Hall, 1974), 45.
21. See OSR 129, 133-34. See also Hannah Arendt, *On Revolution* (New York: Penguin, 1979; first published 1963), 42; and Reinhart Koselleck et al., s.v. "Revolution," *Geschichtliche Grundbegriffe: Historisches Lexikon zur politisch-sozialen Sprache in Deutschland*, ed. Otto Bruner, Werner Conze, and Reinhart Koselleck (Stuttgart: Klett-Cotta, 1984), 5:653-788.
22. The term "revolutio" first appears only in late antiquity, in the nonpolitical context of Christian literature as turning the stone of Christ's tomb, the return of the seasons (*revolutio temporis, revolutio temporum*), rotation of the stars, the completion of a year (*revolutio anno*), and the transmigration of the souls, and is only rarely said about the world (*revolutio mundi*). See Thomas Aquinas, *In libros physicorum*, in *Commentaria in Aristotelem et alios*, vol. 4 of *Opera Omnia*, ed. Roberto Busa (Stuttgart: F. Frommann-Holzboog, 1980), 72 (2, 7, 6). See also Koselleck et al., "Revolution," 669-71.
23. Koselleck et al., "Revolution," 653ff.
24. "Revolutionary desire to realize the kingdom of God is . . . the beginning of modern history." Friedrich Schlegel, *Athenäums-Fragmente (1798)*, in *Charakteristiken und Kritiken I*, vol. 2 of *Kritische Neuausgabe*, pt. 1 of *Kritische Friedrich-Schlegel-Ausgabe (KFSA)*, ed. Ernst Behler et al. (Munich: Ferdinand Schöningh, 1967), 201.
25. See Denis Diderot, s.v. "Encyclopédie," in *Encyclopédie ou Dictionnaire raisonné des sciences, des arts et des métiers*, ed. Denis Diderot and Jean d'Alembert (Paris: Breton, David,

Durand, and Briasson, 1755), 5:639: "Les révolutions sont nécessaires, il y en a toujours eu, et il y a en aura toujours." Yet Hobbes saw the English Revolution and the ensuing restoration of the monarchy as a circular motion, that is, in the traditional sense of "revolution." See Koselleck et al., "Revolution," 718, 720.

26. "Scientific revolutions are... those non-cumulative developmental episodes in which an older paradigm is replaced in whole or in part by an incompatible new one." Thomas S. Kuhn, *The Structure of Scientific Revolutions* (Chicago: Chicago University Press, 1996); first published 1962, 92; see also 10–11, 176–77.
27. "Spatium absolutum, natura sua sine relatione ad externum quodvis, semper manet similare et immobile." Newton, *Philosophiae naturalis principia mathematica*, 1:46.
28. Descartes, *Med.* I, AT VII 20.
29. Plato, *Tim.* 35cff. See Pherecydes, 7B5 DK.
30. See an ironic fable by Theodore T. Lafferty, "A Scandal in Philosophy, or How to Make Philosophy Interesting," *International Journal of Ethics* 43, no. 4 (1933): 439-43; and the response by Paul L. DeLargy, "A Scandal Scanned, or How To Keep Philosophy Respectable," *International Journal of Ethics* 44, no. 1 (1933): 129-33.
31. As Jonas argues, "these mathematical proportions... were at the same time *also* the *rational explanation* of *why* the planets moved this way... the *ideal* mathematical *form* of movements is the *reason* for the movements to be that way" (OSR 34). See Alfredo Ferrarin, *Galilei e la matematica della natura* (Pisa: Edizioni ETS, 2014), 85ff.
32. "Natura nihil agit frustra... Natura enim simplex est." Newton, *Philosophiae naturalis principia mathematica*, 2:550 (Rule I of *Rules of Reasoning in Philosophy*). See Aristotle. *Polit.* 1253a9.
33. See J. E. McGuire and M. Tamny, *Certain Philosophical Questions: Newton's Trinity Notebook* (Cambridge: Cambridge University Press, 1983), 336-37.
34. Descartes, *Disc.* II, AT VI 18ff.
35. Alcinous, *Didask.* 3.2, 5.1ff.
36. Descartes. *Reg.* IV, AT X 372; see also *Disc.* I, AT VI 3. See Daniel Garber, *Descartes' Metaphysical Physics* (Chicago: University of Chicago Press, 1992), 31ff. See Francis Bacon, *The New Organon*, ed. Lisa Jardine and Michael Silverthorne (Cambridge: Cambridge University Press, 2000), 102-221.
37. Descartes, *Reg.* IV, AT VI 372; XI, AT VI 407-8.
38. Plato, *Polit.* 305e-306a; Descartes, *Reg.* IV, AT X 378, 451.
39. Descartes, *Reg.* IV, AT X 373-77; *Disc.* II, AT VI 21.
40. Descartes, *Reg.* XIII, AT X 430-31; *Disc.* II, AT VI 17, 20; *Med. Synopsis*, AT VII 13.
41. Karl R. Popper, *The Logic of Scientific Discovery* (London: Routledge, 1997; first published 1959), 40-42.
42. Paul Feyerabend, *Against Method*, 3rd ed. (London: Verso, 1993), 106-22 passim.
43. Galileo Galilei, "Excerpts from *The Assayer*," in *Discoveries and Opinions of Galileo Galilei*, trans. Stillman Drake (Garden City, NY: Doubleday, 1957), 237-38.
44. Aristotle, *Phys.* 224a21ff.
45. "By 'extension' we mean whatever has length, breadth and depth, leaving aside the question whether it is a real body or merely a space" (Descartes, *Reg.* XIV, AT X 442). See also Dmitri Nikulin, *Matter, Imagination and Geometry* (Aldershot, UK: Ashgate, 2002), 210-30.

46. Descartes, *Med.* III, AT VII 44-45.
47. See Descartes, *La Geometrie*, AT VI 367-485; and Ernst Cassirer, *Substance and Function*, trans. W. C. Swabey and M. Collins (New York: Dover, 1953).
48. Gottfried Wilhelm Leibniz, *Discourse on Metaphysics*, in *Discourse on Metaphysics and Other Essays*, trans. Daniel Garber and Roger Ariew (Indianapolis: Hackett, 1991), §6.
49. Jonas writes, "The simplicity of nature is equivalent to its mathematical form. The simplicity and mathematics have a certain relation to each other. Mathematics can be complex, but the mathematical solution to a problem is always the simplest" (OSR 63).
50. Aristotle, *Phys.* 207a1-2.
51. "It is not true that the infinite is understood through the negation of a boundary or limit; on the contrary, all limitation implies a negation of the infinite [Nec verum est intelligi infinitum per finis sive limitationis negationem, cùm e contrà omnis limitatio negationem infiniti contineat]." Descartes, *Med., Fifth Set of Replies*, AT VII 365.
52. Alexandre Koyré, *From the Closed World to the Infinite Universe* (Baltimore: Johns Hopkins University Press, 1957), 99-109 passim.
53. Nicolas of Cusa, *De docta ignorantia* I.12-14.
54. Descartes, *Princ.* I.26, AT VIIIA 15; see also *Disc.* IV, AT VI 36; to Chanut, 6 June 1647, AT V 51; and to More, 15 April 1649, AT V 344.
55. As Descartes explains, "For although we cannot include in Geometry any lines that are like cords—that is to say, sometimes straight and sometimes—because the ratios between straight and curved lines are unknown, and even, I believe, unknowable to men, so that we cannot thereby reach any exact and assured conclusions: nevertheless, because we use cords in these constructions only to determine straight lines whose length we know exactly, we must not entirely reject them." Descartes, *Geometry* II, AT VI 412.
56. Descartes, *Med., Fifth Set of Replies*, AT VII 385. See Nikulin. *Matter, Imagination and Geometry*, 117-20.
57. Aristotle, *Phys.* 207b1-27, 232a23-25.
58. Leibniz to Christian Goldbach, 17 April 1712, in vol. 3 of *Opera Omnia*, ed. Louis Dutens (Geneva: Fratres de Tournes, 1768), 437, ap. Arthur Schopenhauer, *Die Welt als Wille und Vorstellung* (Leipzig: Reclam, 1891), 1:338.
59. Pierre Cabanne, *Dialogues with Marcel Duchamp, with an Appreciation by Jasper Johns*, trans. Ron Padgett (Boston: Da Capo, 1979), 45, 55.
60. Adut presents the "shock" of contemporary art as coming in two forms: the ugly and the immoral, which often are associated with and imply each other. See Adut, *On Scandal*, 224-86, esp. 228. Cabanne further speaks about two forms of art scandal: internal, which concerns the change of technique, style, and antagonisms among artists (which mostly remain concealed from the general public)—and external, which shocks the spectators, the state, and the church. See Pierre Cabanne, *Le Scandale dans l'art* (Paris: Éditions de la Différence, 2007), 33. See Maria Karlsson and Måns Wrange, "Scandal Success! The Political Economy of the Art Scandal," in *Scandalous: A Reader on Art and Ethics*, ed. Nina Möntmann (Berlin: Sternberg, 2013), 88-105, who argue that because contemporary art lives off the norm of transgression, scandals in modern art are easily manipulated through contemporary media and become usurped by populist politicians for creating political scandals. Seijun Suzuki said in an interview that he does not want his spectators to get bored, which is the motivation, at least in part, behind his

deliberately scandalous B-movies, including The Taisho Trilogy—*Zigeunerweisen*, *Kageroza*, and *Yumeji*.
61. See The Clash's "I'm So Bored with the USA."
62. *New York Times*, 15 June 2014.
63. See Clement Greenberg, *Art and Culture: Critical Essays* (Boston: Beacon, 1989; first published 1961), 133-38, 158-77.
64. As Cassirer argues, "Whereas formerly imagination had to fight for recognition and equal rights, it is now treated as the fundamental power of the soul, as the leader and ruler to whom all other faculties of the mind must submit." Ernst Cassirer, *The Philosophy of the Enlightenment*, trans. Fritz Koelln and James P. Pettegrove (Princeton, NJ: Princeton University Press, 1951), 305.
65. See Dmitri Nikulin, *On Dialogue* (Lanham, MD: Lexington, 2006), 165-66; see also 99-140.
66. Following the aesthetics of the Enlightenment, Batteux considers the genius differently, as the one who follows and is bound by nature: "If genius capriciously assembles ideas in a manner that violates natural laws ... [it] is reduced to a type of insanity." Genius, for Batteux, should follow not the capricious imagination but strict reason, thus becoming the inventor of the imitative means that display and discover being itself as the very being of nature. Genius, then, is the natural philosopher, since the task of genius is "not to imagine what cannot be but to discover what is. Invention in the arts does not consist in creating things. Rather, it is discovering how things are and what they are like. The profoundest geniuses discover only what was already there." Charles Batteux, *The Fine Arts Reduced to a Single Principle*, trans. James O. Young (Oxford: Oxford University Press, 2015), 5.
67. Immanuel Kant, *Lectures on Anthropology*, trans. Robert R. Clewis et al., ed. Allen W. Wood and Robert B. Louden (Cambridge: Cambridge University Press, 2012), 7:318n.
68. Immanuel Kant, *Critique of the Power of Judgment*, trans. Paul Guyer and Eric Matthews (Cambridge: Cambridge University Press, 2000), §§49-50, 5:313-20. On the freedom of imagination, see Jane Kneller, *Kant and the Power of Imagination* (Cambridge: Cambridge University Press, 2007), 38-59.
69. Kant, *Critique of the Power of Judgment* §49, 5:317-18.
70. Kant, *Anthropology*, §30, 7:172. See Henry E. Allison, *Kant's Theory of Taste: A Reading of the Critique of Aesthetic Judgment* (Cambridge: Cambridge University Press, 2001), 271-301.
71. Hans-Georg Gadamer, *Truth and Method*, 2nd. ed., trans. W. Glen-Doepel, Joel Weinsheimer, and Donald G. Marshall (New York: Continuum, 2004), 47-52. Genius is the "enlivening spirit. Against the pedant's rigid adherence to rules, genius demonstrates a free sweep of invention and thus the originality that creates new models" (46).
72. Gadamer, 50, 61-70.
73. See W. K. C. Guthrie, *The Sophists* (Cambridge: Cambridge University Press, 1971), 55-134. Sometimes, nature or *physis* is identified with the "unwritten laws," which were opposed to the conventional law or *nomos* (118-30).
74. See Nikulin, *Matter, Imagination and Geometry*, 210ff.
75. "ἡ τέχνη μιμεῖται τὴν φύσιν." Aristotle, *Phys.* 194a21-22.

76. Ágnes Heller, *The Concept of the Beautiful*, ed. Marcia Morgan (Lanham, MD: Lexington, 2012), henceforth cited as CB followed by page number.
77. Pliny, *Nat. hist.* XXXV.36, §§66–67.
78. R. G. Collingwood, *The Principles of Art* (Oxford: Oxford University Press, 1958; first published 1938), 36–41. It is a grilled steak that should be called beautiful, according to Collingwood (40).
79. Heller writes, "Works of art do not need observers, but observers need works of art. There is no reciprocity between the work and the observer, but every piece of art needs a creator" (CB 107).
80. Plotinus, *Enn.* I.6 [1].1–6; I.6.9.13. Against the Stoics, Plotinus argues that if beauty is proportion (συμμετρία), then no single thing can be considered beautiful but only a composite one, since proportion is between parts, *Enn.* I.6.1.25–30. See also CB xlii, 19–24.
81. See Walter Benjamin, "Goethe's Elective Affinities," in vol. 1 of *Selected Writings*, 350–51.
82. Plotinus, *Enn.* I.6.2.12; I.6.5.19–20; I.6.6.26–32; I.6.8.2; I.6.9.43.
83. "ζωῆς... αἴτιος καὶ νοῦ καὶ τοῦ εἶναι" (Plotinus, *Enn.* I.6.7.11). As Heller puts it, "if there is no sole source of all beauties, there is no beauty" (CB 19).
84. Plotinus, *Enn.* I.6.7.28–29; I.6.9.39–42.
85. Plotinus, *Enn.* I.6.7.1.
86. Horace, *Ars poët.* 189–90.
87. Heller even speaks of "a terror of taste." See Ágnes Heller, "Autonomy of Art or the Dignity of the Artwork," in *Aesthetics and Modernity: Essays by Agnes Heller*, ed. John Rundell (Lanham, MD: Lexington, 2011), 49.
88. Unlike in Kant, for Descartes the beautiful still signifies a relation between our judgment and an object: "generalement ny le beau, ny l'agreable, ne signifie rien qu'vn rapport de nostre iugement à l'objet" (Letter to Mersenne, 18 March 1630, AT I 133).
89. Kant, *Critique of the Power of Judgment* §§42, 49, 5:298–303, 313–19. See Gadamer, *Truth and Method*, 43–46.
90. F. W. J. Schelling, *The Philosophy of Art*, trans. and ed. Douglas W. Scott (Minneapolis: University of Minnesota Press, 1989), 31. See also Theodor W. Adorno, *Aesthetic Theory*, trans. and ed. Robert Hullot-Kentor (Minneapolis: University of Minnesota Press, 1997), 61–100.
91. Cicero, *De nat. deor.* I.47–49.
92. Plato, *Lys.* 216d; *Gorg.* 474d.
93. G. W. F. Hegel, *Grundlinien der Philosophie des Rechts*, vol. 7 of *Werke* (Frankfurt: Suhrkamp, 1986), §31, 84. See also CB xl–xli.
94. Heller draws on Adorno's famous suggestion, which itself is a reference to Stendhal's claim that art is the *promesse du bonheur*. See Adorno, *Aesthetic Theory*, 311. See also Alexander Nehamas, *Only a Promise of Happiness: The Place of Beauty in a World of Art* (Princeton, NJ: Princeton University Press, 2007), 1–3, 70ff.
95. Plato, *Charm.* 167e. It is worth noting that Plotinus, who closely follows Plato in the discussion of beauty and love, dedicates his first treatise to beauty (*Enn.* I.6 [1]), but only one of the last, written before death, to love (*Enn.* III.5 [50]). His whole life of thinking and writing thus takes the comic path.
96. Plato, *Phaedr.* 248b–c; see also *Symp.* 199c–212c.

97. Plato, *Rep.* 517b-534e.
98. Friedrich Nietzsche, *Die Geburt der Tragödie aus dem Geiste der Musik*, in vol. 1 of *Kritische Studienausgabe (KSA)*, ed. Giorgio Colli and Mazzino Montinari (Berlin: De Gruyter, 1988), 26-28, 40-41, 51, 67, 70-72, 103, 115 passim.
99. Nietzsche, 28, 30, 33-35, 41, 56, 103.
100. This is also Adorno's and Freud's position. See Adorno, *Aesthetic Theory*, 45-61. It is worth noting that today we expect mass-produced things to be kitsch and unappealing. However, in an anonymously published essay of 1935, "Art and Craftsmanship in Industry," Aldous Huxley has argued that mass production will not proliferate ugly things but only beautiful ones, because the design will be made by the best artists and no one will want to reproduce ugly things (*Aldous Huxley Annual* 6 [2006], 35-37).
101. See *Sylloge Nummorum Graecorum, France 5, Mysie* (Paris: Bibliothéque nationale de France, 2001), No. 1342ff. (Parium).
102. Hesiod, *Theog.* 585.
103. See Cornelius Castoriadis, *The Imaginary Institution of Society*, trans. Kathleen Blamey (Cambridge: Polity, 1987), 127ff; Martha Nussbaum, *Poetic Justice: The Literary Imagination and Public Life* (Boston: Beacon, 1995), 3-12; and Charles Taylor, *Modern Social Imaginaries* (Durham: Duke University Press, 2004), 23-30: social imaginary is "what enables, through making sense of, the practices of society" (2).
104. Kant remarks, "Russians and Poles are not capable of any autonomy. The former, because they want to be *without absolute masters*; the latter, because *they all want to be masters*" (Kant, *Anthropology, Marginal note in H*, 411, italics added).
105. Aristotle, *Polit.* 1279b18-19, 1290b17-20.
106. Martin Breaugh, *The Plebeian Experience: A Discontinuous History of Political Freedom*, trans. Lazer Lederhendler (New York: Columbia University Press, 2007), xvi.
107. Walter Benjamin, "Experience and Poverty [1933]," in vol. 2.2 of *Selected Writings*, 731-36.
108. Jacques Rancière, "Ten Theses on Politics," *Theory and Event* 5:3 (2001), https://muse.jhu.edu/article/32639 (accessed April 15, 2019), thesis 1.
109. Aristotle, *Rhet.* 1360b15; see also *Polit.* 1256b31-32; and *De gener. anim.* 776b8.
110. Aristotle, *Polit.* 1253a2. When asked who is really rich, Diogenes replied, "the self-sufficient" (ὁ αὐτάρκης) (*Gnomologium Vaticanum* 743, n.180 = G 241).
111. Cornelius Castoriadis, "On the Content of Socialism, II," in *1955–1966*, vol. 2 of *Political and Social Writings*, trans. and ed. David Ames Curtis (Minneapolis: University of Minnesota Press, 1988), 92, 101; see also 102-14.
112. Aristotle, *Polit.* 1317b2-3, 15-16.
113. "τὸ δίκαιον τὸ δημοτικὸν τὸ ἴσον ἔχειν ἐστὶ κατ' ἀριθμὸν ἀλλὰ μὴ κατ' ἀξίαν" (Aristotle, *Polit.* 1317b3-4).
114. Aristotle, *Polit.* 1317b17.
115. Aristotle, *Polit.* 1317b11-12.
116. Carl Schmitt, *Political Theology: Four Chapters on the Concept of Sovereignty*, trans. George Schwab (Chicago: University of Chicago Press, 2005), 5.
117. Livy, *Ab urbe cond.* II.18, III.26-29. See Cicero, *De leg.* III.9.
118. Giorgio Agamben, *Homo Sacer: Sovereign Power and Bare Life*, trans. Daniel Heller-Roazen (Stanford: Stanford University Press, 1998), 17-19; *State of Exception*, trans. Kevin Attell (Chicago: University of Chicago Press, 2005), 1-31.

119. Schmitt, *Political Theology*, 13.
120. Schmitt, *Political Theology*, 6.
121. Diog. Laert. VI.20; Dio Chrysostom, *Disc.* VI 1, VIII 1. See Léonce Paquet, *Les Cyniques grecs: Fragments et témoignages* (Ottawa: Les presses de l'Université d'Ottawa, 1988; first published 1975), 10: "Le déracinement volontaire."
122. Diog. Laert. VI.63. See [Lucian], *Cynicus* 15, in vol. 4 of *Luciani Opera*, ed. M. D. Macleod (Oxford: Clarendon, 1987), 134-46.
123. "μόνην τε ὀρθὴν πολιτείαν εἶναι τὴν ἐν κόσμῳ." Diog. Laert. VI.72.
124. See Koselleck et al., "Revolution," 766-74.
125. The Florentine chronist Giovanni Villani in 1348 (*Chroniche* XII.19) describes the events as "che in così piccolo tempo la città nostra ebbe tante novità e varie revoluzioni." Giovanni Villani, *Croniche di Giovanni, Matteo e Filippo Villani* (Trieste: Sezione letterario-artistica del Lloyd Austriaco, 1857), 457).
126. Isidore, *Etym.* 5.26.11. Following Isidore, Aquinas makes a distinction between war (*bellum*) as the fight against the multitude of external enemies, strife (*rixa*) between two or several people, and *seditio*, the discord between parts of the same (political) unity. See Aquinas, *Summa theol.* II.2, Q 42, A 1: "Bellum proprie est contra extraneos et hostes, quasi multitudinis ad multitudinem; rixa autem est unius ad unum, vel paucorum ad paucos; seditio autem proprie est inter partes unius multitudinis inter se dissentientes, puta cum pars civitatis excitatur in tumultum contra alium." *Seditio* is opposite to both justice and the common good: *Summa theol.* II.2, Q 43, A 2.
127. On civil war, see Koselleck et al., "Revolution," 678-79, 699-700, 712-18, 725ff, 769-79.
128. In a dictionary published in 1690, Furetière defines civil war as "Guerre civile ou intestine, est celle qui se fait entre les sujets d'un même Royaume, entre les parties d'un meme Estat," in which "l'un des parties ne voulant pas tolérer l'autre" (Koselleck et al., "Revolution," 713).
129. Democritus, 68B249 DK.
130. See J. C. A. Gaskin, introduction to Thomas Hobbes, *Leviathan*, ed. J. C. A. Gaskin (Oxford: Oxford University Press, 1996), 7.
131. Hobbes, *Leviathan*, 385 (III.XLII.125).
132. In a widely popular treatise that saw 77 editions in its time, Justus Lipsius's *Politicorum sive civilis doctrinae libri sex* mentions two main causes of civil war: divine *fatum*, and luxury, the *nimia felicitas*, "excessive happiness," which inevitably leads to corruption. See Justus Lipsius, *Politicorum sive civilis doctrinae libri sex* (Leiden: Franciscum Raphelengien, 1599), 344ff (VI.2).
133. As Condorcet has argued, revolution is made for the sake of *liberté*, and for Robespierre, revolution "n'est que le passage du règne du crime à celui de la justice" (Koselleck et al., "Revolution," 733, 736).
134. Arendt, *On Revolution*, 29: "It might be a truism to say that liberation and freedom are not the same; that liberation may be the condition of freedom but by no means leads automatically to it; that the notion of liberty implied in liberation can only be negative and hence, that even the intention of liberating is not identical with the desire for freedom. Yet if these truisms are frequently forgotten, it is because liberation has always loomed large and the foundation of freedom has always been uncertain, if not

altogether futile." Also Arendt: "There is nothing more futile than rebellion and liberation unless they are followed by the constitution of the newly won freedom" (142). As Richard Bernstein comments, "Liberty is always liberation *from* something, whether it is liberation *from* poverty, or *from* oppressive rulers, tyrants, and dictators. Liberty is a *necessary* condition for freedom, but not a *sufficient* condition. Freedom is a positive political *achievement* of individuals acting together." Richard J. Bernstein, *The Abuse of Evil: The Corruption of Politics and Religion since 9/11* (Cambridge: Polity, 2005), 74.

135. Arendt, *On Revolution*, 11, 29.
136. Freedom of speech is calling a thing plainly by its proper name. See Cicero, *Fam.* 9.22.
137. τὸ κάλλιστον, Diog. Laert. VI.69; ἥδιστον, Dio Chrysostom, *Disc.* IV.15.
138. In this respect, truth-telling is akin to prophesizing (see CB 124).
139. For Aristotle, magnanimous is the one who speaks freely (παρρησιαστής), because to care for opinion more than for truth and hide one's thought is cowardly. See Aristotle, *NE* 1124b26-31.
140. "But in the final analysis, only the revolution creates an open space for the city [*das Freie der Stadt*]. Fresh air doctrines [*Pleinairismus*] of revolutions. Revolution disenchants [*entzaubert*] the city." Benjamin, AP M3,3.
141. Karl Kautsky, *Die soziale Revolution* (Berlin: Vorwärts, 1903), 48; V. I. Lenin, *State and Revolution*, in vol. 25 of *Collected Works* (Moscow: Foreign Languages Publishing House, 1964), 381-492; *Gosudartsvo i revoljucija*, in vol. 21 of *Sochinenija* (Moscow: Partizdat, 1935), 365-455.
142. Schlegel speaks about revolution, exemplified in the French Revolution, as the "prototype of revolutions, as the revolution as such [Urbild der Revolution, als die Revolution schlechthin]." Schlegel, *Athenäums-Fragmente*, 247-48.
143. See C. L. R. James, *Black Jacobins: Toussaint L'Ouverture and the San Domingo Revolutions*, 2nd rev. ed. (New York: Vintage, 1989); and Michel-Rolph Trouillot, "An Unthinkable History: The Haitian Revolution as a Non-Event," in *Silencing the Past: Power and the Production of History* (Boston: Beacon, 2015; first published 1995), 70-107, 167-76.
144. Friedrich Engels, "Interview mit der Zeitung 'Le Figaro' am 8. Mai 1893" in vol. 22 of Karl Marx and Friedrich Engels, *Marx-Engels-Werke (MEW)* (Berlin: Dietz, 1963), 542.
145. Koselleck connects the revolutionary acceleration of modern life with the nineteenth-century industrial revolution that changes the speed of locomotion. See Koselleck, "Is There an Acceleration of History?," 114-15.
146. G. W. F. Hegel, *Phenomenology of Spirit*, trans. A. V. Miller (Oxford: Oxford University Press, 1977), 111-19 (§§178-96); Karl Marx and Friedrich Engels, *The Communist Manifesto*, ed. Phil Gasper (Chicago: Haymarket, 2005); Manfred Riedel, s.v. "Bürger, Staatsbürger, Bürgertum," in *Geschichtliche Grundbegriffe Historisches Lexikon*, 672-725.
147. "In so far as the English bourgeoisie regards pauperism as the *fault of politics* the Whigs put the blame on the Tories and the Tories put it on the Whigs.... Neither party discovers the explanation in politics itself but only in the politics of the other party. Neither party would even dream of a reform of society as a whole." Karl Marx, "Critical Notes on the 'King of Prussia and Social Reform. By a Prussian,'" 406. See William E. Connolly, *Political Theory and Modernity* (Ithaca, NY: Cornell University Press, 1993), 125-28.

276   6. Scandal

148. See Dmitri Nikulin, *Comedy, Seriously* (New York: Palgrave Macmillan, 2014), 120–24 passim.
149. When asked what he could do if sold as a slave, Diogenes replied: "rule over people [ἀνδρῶν ἄρχειν]" (Diog. Laert. VI.29). See Dio Chrysostom, *Disc.* IV 48 (the king is often a slave in a children's game).
150. Aristotle, *Polit.* 1295b1–3.
151. J. Mark Rowland and Douglas J. Emlen, "Two Thresholds, Three Male Forms Result in Facultative Trimorphism in Beetles," *Science* 323 (6 February 2009): 773–76.
152. "La contrerévolution ne sera point une révolution contraire, mais le contraire de la révolution" (Joseph de Maistre, *Considérations sur la France* [London: Bâle, 1797], 210); cited in Arendt, *On Revolution*, 18. See Herbert Marcuse, *Counterrevolution and Revolt* (Boston: Beacon, 1972), 1–57.
153. The concept of conservative revolution is already used by Marx ("Der 'Débat social' vom 6. Februar über die Association démocratique," in vol. 4 of Karl Marx and Friedrich Engels, *Marx-Engels-Werke (MEW)* [Berlin: Dietz, 1972], 513), but only becomes widespread in the twentieth century. See Koselleck et al., "Revolution," 784.

IN PLACE OF A CONCLUSION

1. See Dmitri Nikulin, *Dialectic and Dialogue* (Stanford: Stanford University Press, 2010), 32.
2. According to Kuleshov, "apart from montage, nothing exists in cinema ... the work of the actor is absolutely irrelevant" (L. V. Kuleshov, "The Principles of Montage," in *Kuleshov on Film: Writings by Lev Kuleshov*, trans. and ed. Ronald Levaco [Berkeley: University of California Press, 1974], 194). Later, however, he revoked this thesis, recognizing the importance of *what* is shown and that for *the sake of which* it is shown. See L. V. Kuleshov, *Osnovy kinorezhissury*, in *Uroki kinorezhissury* (Moscow: VGIK, 1999), 174–75.
3. See Kuleshov, *Osnovy kinorezhissury*, 40. See also L. V. Kuleshov, *Azbuka kinorezhissury* (Moscow: Iskusstvo, 1961), 15–16.
4. Kuleshov, *Uroki kinorezhissury*, 189.
5. S. M. Eisenstein, *Montage* (Moscow: Muzey kino, 2000); Kuleshov, *Azbuka kinorezhissury*, 23–24ff.
6. Kuleshov, *Azbuka kinorezhissury*, 52.
7. Kuleshov, 20.
8. Kuleshov, 180.
9. Kuleshov, 183–88.
10. Kuleshov, 179.
11. In a famous letter to Strakhov, Tolstoy writes: "In everything, almost everything that I wrote, I was led by the need of bringing together the thoughts concatenated with each other, in order that they might express themselves; but every thought, being individually expressed by words, loses its meaning and is terribly demeaned once it is taken on its own and without that concatenation [сцепление] in which it resides. Concatenation itself is not composed by thought (I think) but by something else, and one cannot express the ground of this concatenation immediately by words, but only as mediated by words, describing images, actions, situations." Leo Tolstoy to Nikolai Strakhov, 23

and 26 April 1876, in Leo Tolstoy, *Pis'ma 1873–1879*, vol. 62 of *Polnoe sobranie sochineniy* (Moscow: Khudozhestvennaia Literatura, 1953), 269.
12. Kuleshov, "The Principles of Montage," 194.
13. Kuleshov, *Osnovy kinorezhissury*, 175, 178.
14. See Kuleshov, *Azbuka kinorezhissury*, 21.

Bibliography

Adorno, Theodor W. *Aesthetic Theory*. Translated and edited by Robert Hullot-Kentor. Minneapolis: University of Minnesota Press, 1997.
Adut, Ari. *On Scandal: Moral Disturbances in Society, Politics, and Art*. Cambridge: Cambridge University Press, 2008.
Aelian. *Varia Historia*. Edited by Rudolf Hercher. 2 vols. Leipzig: Teubner, 1864–66.
Agamben, Giorgio. *Homo Sacer: Sovereign Power and Bare Life*. Translated by Daniel Heller-Roazen. Stanford: Stanford University Press, 1998.
———. *State of Exception*. Translated by Kevin Attell. Chicago: University of Chicago Press, 2005.
Alcidamas. "On Those Who Write Written Speeches, or On Sophists." In *The Works and Fragments*, edited by J. V. Muir, 2–21. London: Bristol Classical, 2001.
———. *Peri sophiston*. In *Orationes et fragmenta, adiunctis Gorgiae Antisthenis Alcidamantis declamationibus*, edited by F. Blass. Leipzig: Teubner, 1908.
Alcinous. *The Handbook of Platonism*. Translated and edited by John Dillon. Oxford: Oxford University Press, 1996.
Alexander of Aphrodisias. *In Aristotelis analyticorum priorum librum 1 commentarium*. Edited by Max Wallies. In *Commentaria in Aristotelem Graeca*, vol. 2.1. Berlin: Reimer, 1883.
———. *In Aristotelis metaphysica commentaria*. Edited by Michael Hayduck. In *Commentaria in Aristotelem Graeca*, vol. 1. Berlin: Reimer, 1891.
———. *In Aristotelis topicorum libros octo commentaria*. Edited by Max Wallies. In *Commentaria in Aristotelem Graeca*, vol. 2.2. Berlin: Reimer, 1891.
Allison, Henry E. *Kant's Theory of Taste: A Reading of the Critique of Aesthetic Judgment*. Cambridge: Cambridge University Press, 2001.
Ameriks, Karl. *Kant and the Problem of Autonomy: Problems of the Appropriation of the Critical Philosophy*. Cambridge: Cambridge University Press, 2000.
Apollodorus. *The Library*. Translated by J. G. Frazer. 2 vols. Cambridge, MA: Harvard University Press, 1921.
Aquinas, Thomas. *Opera Omnia*. Edited by Roberto Busa. 7 vols. Stuttgart: F. Frommann-Holzboog, 1980.
———. *Summa Theologiae*. Edited by Thomas Gilby et al. 61 vols. New York: McGraw-Hill, 1964–1981.

Arendt, Hannah. *The Human Condition*. Chicago: University of Chicago Press, 1998. First published 1958.
—. *The Life of the Mind*. San Diego: Harcourt, 1978.
—. *Love and Saint Augustine*. Edited by Joanna Vecchiarelli Scott and Judith Chelius Stark. Chicago: University of Chicago Press, 1996.
—. "Socrates." In *The Promise of Politics*, 5-39. New York: Schocken, 2005.
—. "What Is Freedom?" In *Between Past and Future*, 142-69. New York: Penguin, 1968.
Aristophanes, *Fabulae*. Edited by N. G. Wilson. 2 vols. Oxford: Oxford University Press, 2008.
Aristotle, *Opera*. Edited by Immanuel Bekker. 5 vols. Berlin: G. Reimer, 1831.
Arnal, Luc H., et al. "Human Screams Occupy a Privileged Niche in the Communication Soundscape." *Current Biology* 25, no. 15 (2015): 2051-56.
Arnim, Hans von, ed. *Stoicorum Veterum Fragmenta* (SVF). 4 vols. Stuttgart: Teubner, 1964.
Augustine. *Confessions*. Translated by John Ryan. Garden City, NY: Doubleday, 1960.
—. *De civitate dei*. Edited by B. Dombart and A. Kalb. 2 vols. Turnhout, Belgium: Brepols, 1955.
—. *De duabus animabus*, in vol. 8 of *Opera Omnia*, edited by J.-P. Migne, 93-110. Paris: Vrayet, 1841.
—. *De libero arbitrio*, in vol. 1 of *Opera Omnia*, edited by J.-P. Migne, 1221-310. Paris: Vrayet, 1845.
—. *De Trinitate*. In vol. 8 of *Opera Omnia*, edited by J.-P. Migne, 819-1098. Paris: Vrayet, 1841.
Auty, Robert, et al., eds. *Lexikon des Mittelalters*. 9 vols. Stuttgart: Deutscher Taschenbuch, 2003.
Bacin, Stefano, and Oliver Sensen, eds. *The Emergence of Autonomy in Kant's Moral Philosophy*. Cambridge: Cambridge University Press, 2019.
Bacon, Francis. *The New Atlantis*. In *The Major Works*, edited by Brian Vickers, 457-89. Oxford: Oxford University Press, 2002.
——. *The New Organon*. Edited by Lisa Jardine and Michael Silverthorne. Cambridge: Cambridge University Press, 2000.
Bakunin, Mikhail. "God and the State." In *Selected Writings*, edited by Michael Lehning, 111-35. London: Johnathan Cape, 1973.
Balibar, Etienne. *Spinoza: From Individuality to Transindividuality*. Delft, Netherlands: Eburon, 1997.
Barthes, Roland. *Le plaisir du texte*. Paris: Éditions du Seuil: 1973.
—. *Michelet*. Paris: Seuil, 1995. First published 1954.
Batteux, Charles. *The Fine Arts Reduced to a Single Principle*. Translated by James O. Young. Oxford: Oxford University Press, 2015.
Baudelaire, Charles. "The Painter of Modern Life." In *The Painter of Modern Life and Other Essays*, translated by Jonathan Mayne, 1-41. New York: Da Capo, 1986.
Baumgarten, Alexander Gottlieb. *Metaphysica*. Hildesheim: Georg Olms, 1963. Translated by Courtney D. Fugate and John Hymers as *Metaphysics: A Critical Translation with Kant's Elucidations, Selected Notes, and Related Material*. New York: Bloomsbury, 2014.
Benjamin, Andrew. "Boredom and Distraction: The Moods of Modernity." In *Walter Benjamin and History*, edited by Andrew Benjamin, 156-70. London: Continuum, 2005.
Benjamin, Walter. *The Arcades Project*. Translated by Howard Eiland and Kevin McLaughlin. Edited by Rolf Tiedemann. New York: Belknap, 2002. Originally published as *Das Passagen-Werk*. In *Gesammelte Schriften*, vol. 5., edited by Rolf Tiedemann. Frankfurt: Suhrkamp, 1982.

———. *Charles Baudelaire: A Lyric Poet in the Era of High Capitalism.* Translated by Harry Zohn. London: Verso, 1997.
———. "Ein Aussenseiter macht sich bemerkbar. Zu S. Kracauer, 'Die Angestellten.'" In *Gesammelte Schriften*, vol. 3, edited by Hella Tiedemann-Bartels, 219-25. Frankfurt: Suhrkamp, 1972.
———. *Selected Writings.* Vols. 1-4. Edited by Marcus Bullock, Michael W. Jennings, and Howard Eiland et al. Cambridge, MA: Belknap, 1996-2003.
———. "Theses on the Philosophy of History." In *Illuminations*, translated by Harry Zohn, edited by Hannah Arendt, 253-64. New York: Schocken, 1968.
———. *The Writer of Modern Life: Essays on Charles Baudelaire.* Edited by Michael W. Jennings. Translated by Howard Eiland. Cambridge, MA: Belknap, 2006.
Bergson, Henri. *Laughter: An Essay on the Meaning of the Comic.* Translated by Cloudesley Brereton and Fred Rothwell. Minneola, FL: Dover, 2005.
Bernstein, Richard J. *The Abuse of Evil: The Corruption of Politics and Religion since 9/11.* Cambridge: Polity, 2005.
Blanqui, Auguste. *L'Éternité par les Astres: Hypothèse Astronomique.* Paris: Librarie Germer Baillière, 1872.
Blumenberg, Hans. *Das Lachen der Thrakerin: Eine Urgeschichte der Theorie.* Frankfurt: Suhrkamp, 1987.
Boethius. *The Consolation of Philosophy.* In *Theological Tractates and The Consolation of Philosophy*, translated by H. F. Stewart, E. K. Rand, and S. J. Tester, 130-435. Cambridge, MA: Harvard University Press, 1973.
Bortolotti, Lisa, and Yujin Nagasawa. "Immortality Without Boredom." *Ratio* 22 (2009): 261-77.
Bouchez, Madeleine. *L'ennui de Sénèque à Moravia.* Paris: Bordas, 1973.
Braudel, Fernand. *The Mediterranean and the Mediterranean World in the Age of Philip II.* Translated by Siân Reynolds. 2 vols. New York: Harper & Row, 1972-73. First published 1949.
Breaugh, Martin. *The Plebeian Experience: A Discontinuous History of Political Freedom.* Translated by Lazer Lederhendler. New York: Columbia University Press, 2007.
Brodsky, Joseph. "In Praise of Boredom." In *On Grief and Reason: Essays*, 104-13. New York: Farrar, Strauss and Giroux, 1995.
Bruckner, Donald W. "Against the Tedium of Immortality." *International Journal of Philosophical Studies* 20 (2012): 623-44.
Bruner, Otto. Werner Conze, and Reinhart Koselleck, eds. *Geschichtliche Grundbegriffe: Historisches Lexikon zur politisch-sozialen Sprache in Deutschland.* 8 vols. Stuttgart: Klett-Cotta, 1972-97.
Bruss, Kristine. "Searching for Boredom in Ancient Greek Rhetoric: Clues in Isocrates." *Philosophy and Rhetoric* 45 (2012): 312-34.
Burke, Edmund. *A Philosophical Inquiry Into the Origin of Our Ideas of the Sublime and Beautiful.* Edited by Adam Phillips. Oxford: Oxford University Press, 1990.
Butler, Terrell M. "Mimesis, Scandal, and the End of History in Mondrian's Aesthetics." *Journal of Mind and Behavior* 3 (1982): 411-26.
Byron, George Gordon. *Don Juan.* New York: Penguin, 1973.
Cabanne, Pierre. *Dialogues with Marcel Duchamp, with an Appreciation by Jasper Johns.* Translated by Ron Padgett. Boston: Da Capo, 1979.

———. *Le Scandale dans l'art*. Paris: Éditions de la Différence, 2007.
Camus, Albert. *Le mythe de Sisyphe*. Paris: Gallimard, 1965. First published 1942.
Čapek, Karel. *The Makropulos Case*. In *Four Plays*, translated by Peter Majer and Cathy Porter. London: Methuen, 1999.
Cassian. *De Institutis Coenobiorum*. Edited by Michael Petschenig. In vol. 17 of *Corpus Scriptorum Ecclesiasticorum Latinorum*. Vienna: Tempsky, 1888.
Cassirer, Ernst. *The Philosophy of the Enlightenment*. Translated by Fritz Koelln and James P. Pettegrove. Princeton, NJ: Princeton University Press, 1951.
———. *Substance and Function*. Translated by W. C. Swabey and M. Collins. New York: Dover, 1953.
Castoriadis, Cornelius. *The Imaginary Institution of Society*. Translated by Kathleen Blamey. Cambridge: Polity, 1987.
———. "On the Content of Socialism, II." In *Political and Social Writings*, vol. 2, *1955–1966*, translated and edited by David Ames Curtis, 90-154. Minneapolis: University of Minnesota Press, 1988.
Catullus, *Carmina*. Edited by Roger Mynors. Oxford: Clarendon, 1958.
Cicero. *Letters to Atticus* [*Epistulae ad Atticum*]. Translated by D. R. Shackleton Bailey. 4 vols. Cambridge, MA: Harvard University Press, 1999.
———. *Letters to Friends* [*Epistulae ad Familiares*]. Translated by D. R. Shackleton Bailey. 3 vols. Cambridge, MA: Harvard University Press, 2001.
———. *On Ends* [*De finibus*]. Translated by H. Rackham. Cambridge, MA: Harvard University Press, 1914.
———. *On the Laws* [*De legibus*]. In *On the Republic/ On the Laws*, translated by Clinton W. Keyes. Cambridge, MA: Harvard University Press, 1928.
———. *On the Nature of the Gods* [*De natura deorum*]. Translated by H. Rackham. Cambridge, MA: Harvard University Press, 1933.
———. *On the Orator* [*De oratore*]. Translated by E. W. Sutton and H. Rackham. 2 vols. Cambridge, MA: Harvard University Press, 1942.
Cole, Thomas. "Who Was Corax?" *Illinois Classical Studies* 16 (1991): 65-84. Reprinted in *The Attic Orators*, edited by Edwin Carawan, 37-59. Oxford: Oxford University Press, 2007.
Collingwood, R. G. *The Principles of Art*. Oxford: Oxford University Press, 1958. First published 1938.
Connolly, William E. *Political Theory and Modernity*. Ithaca, NY: Cornell University Press, 1993.
Crangle, Sara. *Prosaic Desires: Modernist Knowledge, Boredom, Laughter, and Anticipation*. Edinburgh: Edinburgh University Press, 2010.
Csikszentmihalyi, Mihaly. *Creativity: Flow and the Psychology of Discovery and Invention*. New York: Harper & Row, 1996.
———. *Flow: The Psychology of Optimal Experience*. New York: Harper & Row, 1990.
De Beauvoir, Simone. *The Ethics of Ambiguity*. Translated by Bernard Frechtman. New York: Philosophical Library, 2015. Originally published as *Pour une morale de l'ambiguïté* (Paris: Gallimard, 2003).
De Beistegui, Miguel. "'Boredom: Between Existence and History': On Heidegger's Pivotal *The Fundamental Concepts of Metaphysics*." *Journal of the British Society for Phenomenology* 31 (2000): 145-58.
De Grazia, Sebastian. *Of Time, Work, and Leisure*. New York: Twentieth Century Fund, 1962.

De Leon, Charles A. "The Special Significance of Boredom in Medical Students." *Journal of the National Medical Association* 50 (1958): 43-45.
De Maistre, Joseph. *Considérations sur la France*. London: Bâle, 1797.
De Maistre, Xavier. *Voyage Around My Room: Selected Works of Xavier de Maistre*. Translated and edited by Stephen Sartarelli. New York: New Direction, 1994.
De Mandeville, Bernard. *The Fable of Bees, or Private Vices, Publick Benefits*. London: Penguin Classics, 1989. First published 1714.
D'Ennery, Adolphe, and Eugène Grangé. *Les bohémiens de Paris: drame en cinq actes et huit tableaux*. Paris: Dondey-Dupré, 1843.
De Vaan, Michel. Edited by *Etymological Dictionary of Latin and the Other Italic Languages*. Leiden: Brill, 2008.
Decher, Friedhelm. *Besuch vom Mittagsdämon: Philosophie der Langeweile*. Lüneburg: zu Klampen, 2000.
DeLargy, Paul L. "A Scandal Scanned, or How To Keep Philosophy Respectable." *International Journal of Ethics* 44, no. 1 (1933): 129-33.
Deleuze, Gilles. *Difference and Repetition*. Translated by Paul Patton. New York: Columbia University Press, 1994.
Derrida, Jacques. "Cogito and the history of madness." In *Writing and Difference*, translated by Alan Bass, 31-63. Chicago: University of Chicago Press, 1978.
Descartes, René. *The Correspondence*. Translated by John Cottingham et al. Vol. 3 of *The Philosophical Writings of Descartes*. Cambridge: Cambridge University Press, 1991.
———. *Meditations on First Philosophy*. Translated by John Cottingham. In *The Philosophical Writings of Descartes*, vol. 2. Cambridge: Cambridge University Press, 1984.
———. *Oeuvres de Descartes*. Edited by Charles Adam and Paul Tannery, 12 vols. Paris: J. Vrin, 1964-76.
———. *The Passions of the Soul*. In *The Philosophical Writings of Descartes*, vol. 1. Translated by John Cottingham, Robert Stoothoff, and Dugald Murdoch, 328-403. Cambridge: Cambridge University Press, 1985.
———. *Rules for the Direction of the Mind*. Translated by Dugald Murdoch. In *The Philosophical Writings of Descartes*, vol. 1, 7-78. Cambridge: Cambridge University Press, 1985.
Desmond, William. *Cynics*. Berkeley: University of California Press, 2008.
Diderot, Denis, and Jean d'Alembert, eds. *Encyclopédie ou Dictionnaire raisonné des sciences, des arts et des métiers*. 28 vols. Paris: Breton, David, Durand, and Briasson, 1751-72.
Diels, Hermann and Walter Kranz, eds. *Die Fragmente der Vorsokratiker*. 3 vols. Zurich: Weidmann, 1951-52. First published 1903.
Dio Chrysostom. *Discourses [Orationes]*. Translated by J. W. Cohoon, J. W. Crosby, and H. Lamar. 5 vols. Cambridge, MA: Harvard University Press, 1932-51.
Diodorus Siculus. *Library of History*. Translated by C. H. Oldfather, et al. 12 vols. Cambridge, MA: Harvard University Press, 1933-57.
Diogenes Laertius. *Lives of Eminent Philosophers*. Translated by R. D. Hicks. 2 vols. Cambridge, MA: Harvard University Press, 1925.
Diogenes the Cynic. *Sayings and Anecdotes, with Other Popular Moralists*. Translated by Robin Hard. Oxford: Oxford University Press, 2012.
Doehlemann, Martin. *Langeweile? Deutung eines verbreiteten Phänomens*. Frankfurt: Suhrkamp, 1991.

Dostoevsky, Fyodor. *Bratya Karamazovy: Knigi XI–XII/Epilog: Rukopisnye redaktsii*. Vol. 15 of *Polnoe sobranie sochinenij v tridcati tomah*. St. Petersburg: Nauka, 1976.
Du Bos, Jean-Baptiste. *Critical Reflections on Poetry, Painting, and Music*. Translated by Thomas Nugent. 3 vols. New York: AMS, 1978. First published London: John Nourse, 1748.
Durkheim, Émile. "Representations individuelles et representations collectives." *Revue de métaphysique et de morale* 6 (1898): 273–302.
Eisenstein, S. M. *Montage*. Moscow: Muzey kino, 2000.
Engels, Friedrich. *The Condition of the Working Class in England*. Translated by Florence Wischnewetzky. Revised by V. G. Kierran. London: Penguin, 1987. Originally published as *Die Lage der arbeitenden Klasse in England*. Leipzig: O. Wigand, 1848.
——. "Interview mit der Zeitung 'Le Figaro' am 8. Mai 1893." In Karl Marx and Friedrich Engels, *Marx-Engels-Werke (MEW)*, vol. 22, 538–43. Berlin: Dietz, 1963.
Epictetus. *Discourses*. Translated by W. A. Oldfather. 2 vols. Cambridge, MA: Harvard University Press, 1925–28.
Erasmus. *Praise of Folly*. In *Praise of Folly and Letter to Maarten van Dorp, 1515*. Translated by Betty Radice, edited by A. H. T. Levi. London: Penguin, 1993.
Ernout, Alfred, and Antoine Meillet, eds. *Dictionnaire étymologique de la langue latine*. Paris: Klincksieck, 2001.
Euripides. *Euripidis fabulae*. Vol. 1, *Cyclops; Alcestis; Medea; Heraclidae; Hippolytus; Andromacha; Hecuba*. Edited by J. Diggle. Oxford: Oxford University Press, 1984.
Ferrarin, Alfredo. *Galilei e la matematica della natura*. Pisa: Edizioni ETS, 2014.
Feyerabend, Paul. *Against Method*. 3rd ed. London: Verso, 1993.
Foucault, Michel. *Fearless Speech*. Edited by Joseph Pearson. Los Angeles: Semiotext(e), 2001.
Fraser, Nancy. *Scales of Justice*. New York: Columbia University Press, 2009.
Freud, Sigmund. *The Interpretation of Dreams*. Translated and edited by James Strachey. New York: Basic, 2010.
——. *The Problem of Anxiety*. New York: Norton, 1936.
Friedlander, Eli. *Walter Benjamin: A Philosophical Portrait*. Cambridge, MA: Harvard University Press, 2012.
Fromm, Erich. *The Dogma of Christ: And Other Essays on Religion, Psychology, and Culture*. New York: Routledge, 2004. First published 1963.
Gabbey, Alan. "Force and Inertia in the Seventeenth Century: Descartes and Newton." In *Descartes: Philosophy, Mathematics and Physics*, edited by S. Gaukroger, 230–320. Sussex: Harvester, 1980.
Gadamer, Hans-Georg. *Truth and Method*. 2nd ed. Translated by W. Glen-Doepel, and revised by Joel Weinsheimer and Donald G. Marshall. New York: Continuum, 2004. Originally published as *Wahrheit und Methode: Grundzüge einer philosophischen Hermeneutik*. Vol. 1 of *Gesammelte Werke*. Tübingen, Germany: J. C. B Mohr [Paul Siebeck], 1990.
Galilei, Galileo. *Discoveries and Opinions of Galileo Galilei*. Translated by Stillman Drake. Garden City, NY: Doubleday, 1957.
Gallup, Andrew C., Lexington Swartwood, Janine Militello, and Serena Sackett. "Experimental Evidence of Contagious Yawning in Budgerigars (*Melopsittacus undulatus*)." *Animal Cognition* 18 (2015): 1051–58.
Garber, Daniel. *Descartes' Metaphysical Physics*. Chicago: University of Chicago Press, 1992.

Gelley, Alexander. *Benjamin's Passages: Dreaming, Awakening*. Fordham: Fordham University Press, 2015.
Gerber, Ernst Ludwig. *Historisch-biographisches Lexikon der Tonkünstler*. 2 vols. Leipzig: Johann Gottlob Immanuel Breitkopf, 1790-92.
Gerritsen, Cory J., Maggie E. Toplak, Jessica Sciaraffa, and John Eastwood. "I Can't Get No Satisfaction: Potential Causes of Boredom." *Consciousness and Cognition* 27 (2014): 27-41.
Giannantoni, Gabriele, ed. *Socratis et Socraticorum Reliquiae*. 4 vols. Naples: Bibliopolis, 1990.
Gilloch, Graeme. *Myth and Metropolis: Walter Benjamin and the City*. Cambridge: Polity, 1996.
Goetz, Thomas, Anne C. Frenzel, Nathan C. Hall, Ulrike E. Nett, Reinhard Pekrun, and Anastasiya A. Lipnevich. "Types of Boredom: An Experience Sampling Approach." *Motivation and Emotion* 38 (2014): 401-19.
Goldberg, Yael, and James Danckert. "Traumatic Brain Injury, Boredom and Depression." *Behavioral Sciences* 3 (2013): 434-44.
Goodstein, Elizabeth S. *Experience Without Qualities: Boredom and Modernity*. Stanford: Stanford University Press, 2005.
Gould, Carol. *Interactive Democracy: The Social Roots of Global Justice*. Cambridge: Cambridge University Press, 2014.
Greenberg, Clement. *Art and Culture: Critical Essays*. Boston: Beacon, 1989. First published 1961.
Greil, Marcus. *Lipstick Traces: A Secret History of the Twentieth Century*. Cambridge, MA: Harvard University Press, 1989.
Guthrie, W. K. C. *The Sophists*. Cambridge: Cambridge University Press, 1971.
Halbwachs, Maurice. *On Collective Memory*. Translated and edited by Lewis A. Coser. Chicago: University of Chicago Press, 1992.
Hammer, Espen. "Heidegger's Theory of Boredom." *Graduate Faculty Philosophy Journal* 29, no. 1 (2008): 199-225.
Hansen, Miriam. *Cinema and Experience: Siegfried Kracauer, Walter Benjamin, and Theodor W. Adorno*. Berkeley: University of California Press, 2012.
Harries, Karsten. "The Infinite Sphere: Comments on the History of a Metaphor." *Journal of the History of Philosophy* 13 (1975): 5-15.
Healy, Seán Desmond. *Boredom, Self, and Culture*. Rutherford, NJ: Fairleigh Dickinson University Press, 1984.
Hegel, G. W. F. *Grundlinien der Philosophie des Rechts*. Vol. 7 of *Werke*. Frankfurt: Suhrkamp, 1986.
———. *Habilitationsthesen*. In *Jenaer Schriften 1801–1807*, vol. 2 of *Werke*. Frankfurt: Suhrkamp, 1986.
———. *Hegel's Logic*. Translated by William Wallace. Oxford: Oxford University Press, 1975.
———. *Phenomenology of Spirit*. Translated by A. V. Miller. Oxford: Oxford University Press, 1977.
———. *The Science of Logic*. Translated and edited by George di Giovanni. Cambridge: Cambridge University Press, 2010.
Heidegger, Martin. *Being and Time*. Translated by John Macquarrie and Edward Robinson. Oxford: Basil Blackwell, 1962. Originally published as *Sein und Zeit* (Tübingen, Germany: Max Niemeyer, 1993).
———. "Brief über den 'Humanismus' (1946)." In *Gesamtausgabe*, vol. 9. Frankfurt: Vittorio Klostermann, 1976.
———. *Einführung in die Metaphysik*. Tübingen, Germany: Max Niemeyer, 1976. First published 1935.

———. *The End of Philosophy*. Translated by Joan Stambaugh. Chicago: University of Chicago Press, 2003.
———. *The Fundamental Concepts of Metaphysics: World, Finitude, Solitude*. Translated by William McNeill and Nicholas Walker. Bloomington: Indiana University Press, 1995. Originally published as *Die Grundbegriffe der Metaphysik: Welt—Endlichkeit—Einsamkeit*, vols. 29-30 of *Gesamtausgabe* (Frankfurt: Vittorio Klostermann, 1983).
———. *Holzwege*. In *Gesamtausgabe*, vol. 5. Frankfurt: Vittorio Klostermann, 1977. First published 1935-46.
———. *Nietzsche*. 2 vols. Stuttgart: Klett-Cotta, 2008.
———. *Parmenides*. Vol. 54 of *Gesamtausgabe*. Frankfurt: Vittorio Klostermann, 1982.
———. "The Principle of Identity." In *Identity and Difference*, translated by Joan Stambaugha, 23-41. New York: Harper & Row, 1969.
———. *Zur Sache des Denkens*. Vol. 14 of *Gesamtausgabe*. Frankfurt: Vittorio Klostermann, 2007.
Heller, Ágnes. "Autonomy of Art or the Dignity of the Artwork." In *Aesthetics and Modernity: Essays by Agnes Heller*, edited by John Rundell. Lanham, MD: Lexington, 2011.
———. *The Concept of the Beautiful*. Edited by Marcia Morgan. Lanham, MD: Lexington, 2012.
Hesiod. *Theogonia, Opera et dies, Scutum*. Edited by Friedrich Solmsen. Oxford: Oxford University Press, 1990.
Hobbes, Thomas. *Leviathan*. Edited by J. C. A. Gaskin. Oxford: Oxford University Press, 1996.
Homer. *Opera*. Edited by D. B. Monro and T. W. Allen. 5 vols. Oxford: Oxford University Press, 1920-22.
Horace. *Ars Poetica*. In *Satires, Epistles, and The Art of Poetry*, translated by H. Rushton Fairclough. Cambridge, MA: Harvard University Press, 1926.
Hudry, Françoise, ed. *Liber Viginti Quattuor Philosophorum*. Turnhout, Belgium: Brepols, 1997.
Hunter, Richard L. *New Comedy of Greece and Rome*. Cambridge: Cambridge University Press, 1985.
Husserl, Edmund. *Analysen zur Passiven Synthesis*. Edited by Margot Fleischer. In *Husserliana XI*, edited by Julia Jansen. The Hague: Martinus Nijhoff, 1966.
Hutchings, Patrick. "Reflections on Boredom and the Sublime." *Literature and Aesthetics* 5 (1995): 104-22.
Huxley, Aldous. "Art and Craftsmanship in Industry." *Aldous Huxley Annual* 6 (2006): 35-37.
[Iamblichus]. *The Theology of Arithmetic*. Translated by Robin Waterfield. Grand Rapids, MI: Phanes, 1988.
Isidore de Séville. *Étymologies*. 20 vols. Paris: Les Belles Lettres, 1981-2010.
Jackson, Stanley W. *Melancholia and Depression: From Hippocratic Times to Modern Times*. New Haven, CT: Yale University Press, 1986.
James, C. L. R. *The Black Jacobins: Toussaint L'Ouverture and the San Domingo Revolutions*. 2nd rev. ed. New York: Vintage, 1989.
James, William. *Talks to Teachers on Psychology and to Students on Some of Life's Ideas*. New York: Henry Holt, 1899.
———. "The Will to Believe." In *The Will to Believe and Other Essays in Popular Philosophy*, 1-31. New York: Longmans Green.
Jankélévitch, Vladimir. *L'aventure, l'ennui, le sérieux*. Paris: Aubier-Montaigne, 1963.
Jaran, Francois, and Christophe Perrin. *The Heidegger Concordance*. 3 vols. London: Bloomsbury, 2013.

Jonard, Norbert. *L'ennui dans la litérature européenne: Des origins à l'aube du XXe siècle*. Paris: Honoré Champion Éditeur, 1997.
Jonas, Hans. "The Burden and Blessing of Mortality." *Hastings Center Report* 22 (1992): 34-40.
—. *Ontologische und wissenschaftliche Revolution*. Edited by Jens Peter Brune. Vol. II.2 of *Kritische Gesamtausgabe der Werke von Hans Jonas. KGA*. Freiburg: Rombach, 2012.
—. "Seventeenth Century and After: The Meaning of the Scientific and Technological Revolution." In *Philosophical Essays: From Ancient Creed to Technological Man*, 45-80. Englewood Cliffs, NJ: Prentice-Hall, 1974. First published in *Philosophy Today* 15 (1971): 76-101.
Kant, Immanuel. *Anthropology from a Pragmatic Point of View*. Translated by Robert B. Louden. In *Anthropology, History, and Education*, edited by Günther Zoller and Robert B. Louden. Cambridge: Cambridge University Press, 2007.
—. *Critique of Practical Reason*. In *Practical Philosophy*, translated and edited by Mary J. Gregor. Cambridge: Cambridge University Press, 1996.
—. *Critique of Pure Reason*. Translated and edited by Paul Guyer and Allen Wood. Cambridge: Cambridge University Press, 1998.
—. *Critique of the Power of Judgment*. Translated by Paul Guyer and Eric Matthews. Cambridge: Cambridge University Press, 2000.
—. *Gesammelte Schriften*. Edited by Preussischen Akademie der Wissenschaften (vols. 1-22), Deutschen Akademie der Wissenschaften zu Berlin (vol. 23), and Akademie der Wissenschaften zu Göttingen (vols. 24-29), 29 vols. Berlin: De Gruyter, 1902-2009.
—. *Groundwork of the Metaphysics of Morals*. In *Practical Philosophy*, translated and edited by Mary J. Gregor. Cambridge: Cambridge University Press, 1996.
—. "Idea for Universal History with a Cosmopolitan Purpose." Translated by H. B. Nisbet. In *Political Writings*, edited by Hans Reiss. Cambridge: Cambridge University Press, 1991.
—. *Lectures on Anthropology*. Translated by Robert R. Clewis, Robert B. Louden, G. Felicitas Munzel, and Allen W. Wood. Edited by Allen W. Wood and Robert B. Louden. Cambridge: Cambridge University Press, 2012.
—. *Lectures on Pedagogy*. Translated by Robert B. Louden. In *Anthropology, History, and Education*, edited by Günther Zoller and Robert B. Louden. Cambridge: Cambridge University Press, 2007.
—. *The Metaphysics of Morals*. In *Practical Philosophy*. Translated and edited by Mary J. Gregor. Cambridge: Cambridge University Press, 1996.
—. *Religion Within the Bounds of Mere Reason*. Translated by George di Giovanni, in *Religion and Rational Theology*, edited by Allen W. Wood and George di Giovanni. Cambridge: Cambridge University Press, 1996.
—. "Toward Perpetual Peace." In *Practical Philosophy*, translated and edited by Mary J. Gregor. Cambridge: Cambridge University Press, 1996.
—. "What Real Progress Has Philosophy Made in Germany Since the Time of Leibniz and Wolff?" Translated by Peter Heath. In *Theoretical Philosophy After 1781*, edited by Henry Allison and Peter Heath. Cambridge: Cambridge University Press, 2002.
Karlsson, Maria, and Måns Wrange. "Scandal Success! The Political Economy of the Art Scandal." In *Scandalous: A Reader on Art and Ethics*, edited by Nina Möntmann. Berlin: Sternberg, 2013.
Kautsky, Karl. *Die soziale Revolution*. Berlin: Vorwärts, 1903.
Kessel, Martina. *Langeweile. Zum Umgang mit Zeit und Gefühlen in Deutschland vom späten 18. bis zum frühen 20. Jahrhundert*. Göttingen: Wallstein, 2001.

Kierkegaard, Søren. *The Concept of Anxiety*. Translated and edited by Reidard Thomte and Albert B. Anderson. Princeton, NJ: Princeton University Press, 1980. Originally published as *Begrebet Angest. Samlede vaerker*, vol. 6, edited by A. B. Drachmann, J. L. Heiberg, and H. O. Lange (Copenhagen: Gyldendal, 1963).

—. *Der Augenblick*. Jena: Eugen Diederichs, 1923.

—. *Fear and Trembling. Repetition*. Translated and edited by Howard V. Hong and Edna Hong. Princeton, NJ: Princeton University Press, 1983. Originally published as *Frygt og Baeven. Gjentadelsen*. In *Samlede vaerker*, vol. 5, edited by A. B. Drachmann, J. L. Heiberg, and H. O. Lange. Copenhagen: Gyldendal, 1963.

—. "Rotation of Crops: A Venture in a Theory of Social Prudence." In *Either/Or, Part I*, translated and edited by Howard V. Hong and Edna Hong, 281–300. Princeton, NJ: Princeton University Press, 1987.

Kitcher, Philip. *Life After Faith: The Case for Secular Humanism*. New Haven, CT: Yale University Press, 2014.

Klein, Lawrence E. *Shaftesbury and the Culture of Politeness: Moral Discourse and Cultural Politics in Early Eighteenth-Century Europe*. Cambridge: Cambridge University Press, 1994.

Klibansky, Raymond, Erwin Panofsky, and Fritz Saxl. *Saturn and Melancholy: Studies in the History of Natural Philosophy, Religion, and Art*. London: Thomas Nelson, 1964.

Kneller, Jane. *Kant and the Power of Imagination*. Cambridge: Cambridge University Press, 2007.

Kolnai, Aurel. "On the Concept of the Interesting." *British Journal of Aesthetics* 39 (1964): 22–39.

Korsgaard, Christine M. "The Normative Question." In *The Sources of Normativity*. Cambridge: Cambridge University Press, 1996.

Koselleck, Reinhart. "Is There an Acceleration of History?" In *High-Speed Society: Social Acceleration, Power, and Modernity*, edited by H. Rosa and W. E. Scheuermann, 113–34. University Park: Pennsylvania State University Press, 2009.

Koyré, Alexandre. *From the Closed World to the Infinite Universe*. Baltimore: Johns Hopkins University Press, 1957.

Kracauer, Siegfried. "Boredom." In *The Mass Ornament: Weimar Essays*, translated and edited by Thomas Y. Levin, 331–34. Cambridge, MA: Harvard University Press, 1995.

—. "Langeweile." In *Essays, Feuilletons, Rezensionen, 1924–1927*, part 2, edited by Inka Mülder-Bach, vol. 5 of *Werke*. Berlin: Suhrkamp, 2011.

Kuhn, Reinhard. *The Demon of Noontide: Ennui in Western Literature*. Princeton, NJ: Princeton University Press, 1976.

Kuhn, Thomas S. *The Structure of Scientific Revolutions*. Chicago: Chicago University Press, 1996. First published 1962.

Kuleshov, L. V. *Azbuka kinorezhissury*. Moscow: Iskusstvo, 1961.

—. *Osnovy kinorezhissury*. In *Uroki kinorezhissury*, 26–188. Moscow: VGIK, 1999.

—. "The Principles of Montage (1935)." In *Kuleshov on Film: Writings by Lev Kuleshov*, translated and edited by Ronald Levaco, 183–95. Berkeley: University of California Press, 1974.

Lafferty, Theodore T. "A Scandal in Philosophy, or How to Make Philosophy Interesting." *International Journal of Ethics* 43, no. 4 (1933): 439–43.

Lanza, Diego. *Lo stolto: Di Socrate, Eulenspiegel, Pinocchio e altri trasgressori del senso comune*. Turin: Einaudi, 1997.

La Rochefoucauld, François de. *Maximes*. In *Oeuvres complètes de La Rochefoucauld*, edited by Louis Martin-Chauffier. Paris: Gallimard, 1964.

Lefebvre, Henri. *Critique of Everyday Life*. Vol. 1. Translated by John Moore. London: Verso, 1991.

Leibniz, Gottfried Wilhelm. *Discourse on Metaphysics*. In *Discourse on Metaphysics and Other Essays*, translated by Daniel Garber and Roger Ariew. Indianapolis: Hackett, 1991.

—. *Monadology*. In *Discourse on Metaphysics and Other Essays*. Translated by Daniel Garber and Roger Ariew. Indianapolis: Hackett, 1991.

—. *Opera Omnia*. Edited by Ludovic Dutens, 6 vols. Geneva: Fratres de Tournes, 1768.

—. *Principles of Nature and Grace, Based on Reason*. In *Philosophical Essays*. Translated by Daniel Garber and Roger Ariew. Indianapolis: Hackett, 1989.

Lenin, V. I. *State and Revolution*. In *Collected Works*, vol. 25, 381-492. Moscow: Foreign Languages Publishing House, 1964. Originally published as *Gosudartsvo i revoljucija*. In *Sochinenija*, vol. 21, 365-455. Moscow: Partizdat, 1935.

Lepenies, Wolf. *Melancholy and Society*. Translated by Jeremy Gaines and Doris Jones. Cambridge, MA: Harvard University Press, 1992.

Leslie, Esther. "Ruins and Rubble in the Arcades." In *Walter Benjamin and the Arcades Project*, edited by Beatrice Hanssen, 87-112. London: Continuum, 2006.

Levinas, Emmanuel. "Kierkegaard: Existence and Ethics." In *Proper Names*, translated by Michael B. Smith, 66-74. Stanford: Stanford University Press, 1996.

—. *Totality and Infinity: An Essay on Exteriority*. Translated by Alphonso Lingis. The Hague: Martinus Nijhof, 1979.

Lévi-Strauss, Claude. *La pensée sauvage*. Paris: Plon, 1962.

Liddell, Henry George, and Robert Scott, eds. *Greek-English Lexicon: With a Revised Supplement*. 9th ed. Oxford: Clarendon, 1996.

Lipsius, Justus. *Politicorum sive civilis doctrinae libri sex*. Leiden: Franciscum Raphelengien, 1599.

Livy. *History of Rome* [*Ab urbe condita*]. Translated by B. O. Foster. 14 vols. Cambridge, MA: Harvard University Press, 1919-51.

Longuenesse, Beatrice. *Kant and the Capacity to Judge*. Princeton, NJ: Princeton University Press, 1998.

Lucian. *Luciani Opera*. Edited by M. D. Macleod. 4 vols. Oxford: Clarendon, 1972-87.

—. *Philosophies for Sale* (*Vitarum auctio*). In *Lucian*, vol. 2, translated by A. M. Harmon, 449-512. Cambridge, MA: Harvard University Press, 1915.

Lucretius. *De Rerum Natura*. Edited by Cyril Bailey. Oxford: Oxford University Press, 1922.

Luther, Martin. *Die Letzte Predigt D. Mart. Lutheri zu Wittenburg*, 17 January 1546. In *Werke: Kritische Gesamtausgabe*, 51:123-34. Weimar: Herman Boehlaus Nachfolger, 1914.

Malevich, Kazimir. *Len' kak deystvitelnaya istina chelovechestva*. Moscow: Gilea, 1994.

Mann, Sandi, and Rebekah Cadman. "Does Being Bored Make Us More Creative?" *Creativity Research Journal* 24 (2014): 165-73.

Marcuse, Herbert. *Counterrevolution and Revolt*. Boston: Beacon, 1972.

Marx, Karl. *Capital: A Critique of Political Economy*. Vol. 1. Translated by Samuel Moore and Edward Aveling. New York: International, 1967.

—. "Critical Notes on the 'King of Prussia and Social Reform. By a Prussian.'" In *Early Writings*, translated by Rodney Livingstone and Gregor Benton. London: Penguin, 1992.

—. "Der 'Débat social' vom 6. Februar über die Association démocratique." In Karl Marx and Friedrich Engels, *Marx-Engels-Werke (MEW)*, vol. 4, 511-13. Berlin: Dietz, 1972.

———. *The Economic and Philosophic Manuscripts of 1844*. Translated by Martin Milligan. New York: International, 1964. Originally published as *Der historische Materialismus: die Frühschriften*. Edited by S. Landshut and J. P. Mayer. 2 vols. Leipzig: A Kröner, 1932.

Marx, Karl, and Friedrich Engels. *The Communist Manifesto*. Edited by Phil Gasper. Chicago: Haymarket, 2005.

Mazella, David. *The Making of Modern Cynicism*. Charlottesville: University of Virginia Press, 2007.

McDonald, William. "Kierkegaard's Demonic Boredom." In *Essays on Boredom and Modernity*, edited by Barbara Dalle Pezze and Carlo Salzani, 61–84. Amsterdam: Rodopi, 2009.

McGuire, J. E., and M. Tamny. *Certain Philosophical Questions: Newton's Trinity Notebook*. Cambridge: Cambridge University Press, 1983.

McNeill, William. *The Glance of the Eye: Heidegger, Aristotle, and the Ends of Theory*. Albany: SUNY Press, 1999.

———. *The Time of Life: Heidegger and Ethos*. Albany: SUNY Press, 2006.

Menander. *Reliquiae Selectae*. Edited by F. H. Sandbach. Oxford: Clarendon, 1990.

Méry, Joseph. "Le Climat de Paris." In *Le Diable à Paris*, vol. 1, *Paris et les Parisiens*. Paris: Hetzel, 1845.

Momigliano, Arnaldo. "Ancient History and the Antiquarian (1950)." In *Studies in Historiography*. New York: Harper & Row, 1966.

Mondrian, Piet. *Plastic and Pure Plastic Art*. New York: Wittenborn, 1945.

Nelson, T. G. A. *Comedy: An Introduction to Comedy in Literature, Drama, and Cinema*. Oxford: Oxford University Press, 1990.

Newton, Isaac. *Philosophiae Naturalis Principia Mathematica: The Third Edition (1726) with Variant Readings*. Edited by Alexander Koyré and I. Bernard Cohen. 2 vols. Cambridge, MA: Harvard University Press, 1972.

Nicolas of Cusa. *De coniecturis*. In *Philosophisch-Theologische Schriften*, vol. 2, edited by Leo Gabriel. Vienna: Herder, 1967.

———. *De docta ignorantia*. 3 vols. Hamburg: Felix Meiner, 1964–1977.

———. *On God as Not-Other: A Translation and Appraisal of De li Non-Aliud*. Translated and edited by Jasper Hopkins. Minneapolis: University of Minnesota Press, 1979.

Niehues-Pröbsting, Heinrich. "The Modern Reception of Cynicism: Diogenes in the Enlightenment." In R. Bracht Branman and Marie-Odile Goulet-Cazé, eds., *The Cynics: The Cynic Movement in Antiquity and Its Legacy*, 329–65. Berkeley: University of California Press, 1996.

Nietzsche, Friedrich. *The Anti-Christ*. In *The Anti-Christ, Ecce Homo, Twilight of the Idols, and Other Writings*, translated by Judith Norman. Cambridge: Cambridge University Press, 2005. Originally published as *Der Antichrist: Fluch auf das Christentum*. In *Kritische Studienausgabe (KSA)*, vol. 6, edited by Giorgio Colli and Mazzino Montinari (Berlin: De Gruyter, 1988).

———. *Beyond Good and Evil: Prelude to a Philosophy of the Future*. Translated by Judith Norman. Edited by Rolf-Peter Horstmann. Cambridge: Cambridge University Press, 2002. Originally published as *Jenseits von Gut und Böse*. In *Kritische Studienausgabe (KSA)*, edited by Giorgio Colli and Mazzino Montinari (Berlin: De Gruyter, 1999).

———. *The Birth of Tragedy*. In *The Birth of Tragedy and the Case of Wagner*. Translated by Walter Kaufmann. New York: Vintage, 1967. Originally published as *Die Geburt der Tragödie aus dem Geiste der Musik*. In *Kritische Studienausgabe (KSA)*, vol. 1, edited by Giorgio Colli and Mazzino Montinari (Berlin: De Gruyter, 1988).

―. *The Gay Science*. Translated by Walter Kaufman. New York: Vintage, 1974. Originally published as *Die fröhliche Wissenschaft*. In *Kritische Studienausgabe (KSA)*, vol. 3, edited by Giorgio Colli and Mazzino Montinari (Berlin: De Gruyter, 1988).

―. *The Will to Power*. Translated by Walter Kaufmann and R. J. Hollingdale. New York: Vintage, 1968. Originally published as *Der Wille zur Macht*. Vols. 18-19 of *Gesammelte Werke*. Edited by Richard Oehler, Max Oehler, and Friedrich Würzbach. Munich: Musarion, 1926.

Nikulin, Dmitri. *Comedy, Seriously*. New York: Palgrave Macmillan, 2014.

―. *The Concept of History*. London: Bloomsbury, 2017.

―. *Dialectic and Dialogue*. Stanford: Stanford University Press, 2010.

―. *Matter, Imagination and Geometry: Ontology, Natural Philosophy and Mathematics in Plotinus, Proclus and Descartes*. Aldershot, UK: Ashgate, 2002.

―. *On Dialogue*. Lanham, MD: Lexington, 2006.

Nora, Pierre. *Realms of Memory*. Translated by Arthur Goldhammer. Edited by Lawrence D. Kritzman. 3 vols. New York: Columbia University Press, 1996-98.

North, Paul. *The Problem of Distraction*. Stanford: Stanford University Press, 2012.

Novalis. *Das Philosophische Werke I*. Vol. 2 of *Schriften*. Edited by J. Minor. Jena: Eugen Diederichs, 1923.

Nussbaum, Martha. *Poetic Justice: The Literary Imagination and Public Life*. Boston: Beacon, 1995.

O'Connor, Brian. *Idleness: A Philosophical Essay*. Princeton, NJ: Princeton University Press, 2018.

Ovid. *Fasti*. Translated by James G. Frazer. Cambridge, MA: Harvard University Press, 1931.

Paquet, Léonce. *Les Cyniques grecs: Fragments et témoignages*. Ottawa: Les presses de l'Université d'Ottawa, 1988. First published 1975.

Pascal, Blaise. *Pensées and Other Writings*. Translated by Honor Levi. Edited by Anthony Levi. Oxford: Oxford University Press, 1995. Originally published as *Pensées*, edited by Michel Le Guern (Paris: Gallimard, 1977).

Pausanius. *Description of Greece* [*Periēgēsis*]. Translated by W. H. S. Jones and H. A. Ormerod. 5 vols. Cambridge, MA: Harvard University Press, 1918-35.

Philoponus. *In Aristotelis libros de generatione et corruption*. Vol. 14.3 of *Commentaria in Aristotelem Graeca*. Berlin: Reimer, 1897.

Plato. *Platonis opera*. Edited by John Burnet. 5 vols. Oxford: Clarendon, 1900-1907.

Pliny. *Natural History* [*Naturalis Historia*]. Translated by H. Rackham, W. H. S. Jones, and D. E. Eichholz. 10 vols. Cambridge, MA: Harvard University Press, 1938-62.

Plotinus. *Enneads*. Translated by A. H. Armstrong. 7 vols. Cambridge, MA: Harvard University Press, 1966-88.

Plutarch. *Lives*. Translated by Bernadotte Perrin. 11 vols. Cambridge, MA: Harvard University Press, 1914-26.

Pöggeler, Otto. "Destruction and Moment." In *Reading Heidegger from the Start: Essays in His Earliest Thought*, edited by Theodore Kisiel and John van Buren. Albany: SUNY Press, 1994.

Popper, Karl R. *The Logic of Scientific Discovery*. London: Routledge, 1997. First published 1959.

Porphyry. *Porphyrii Isagoge et in Aristotelis Categorias Commentarium*. Vol. 4.1 of *Commentaria in Aristotelem Graeca*. Edited by Adolfus Busse. Berlin: Reimer, 1887.

Postman, Neil. *Amusing Ourselves to Death: Public Discourse in the Age of Show Business*. New York: Penguin, 1985.

Prins, Arend Weert. *Uit verveling. Being bored*. Kampen: Klement, 2007.

Proclus. *Procli Diadochi in primum Euclidis Elementorum librum commentarii*. Edited by Gottfried Friedlein. Hildesheim: Georg Olms, 1992. Translated and edited by Glenn R. Morrow as *A Commentary on the First Book of Euclid's Elements*. Princeton, NJ: Princeton University Press, 1992.

——. *Théologie platonicienne*. Translated and edited by H. D. Saffrey and L. G. Westerink. 6 vols. Paris: Les Belles Lettres, 1968-97.

Proudhon, Pierre-Joseph. *What Is Property?* Translated and edited by Donald R. Kelley and Bonnie Smith. Cambridge: Cambridge University Press, 1994.

Quintilian. *The Orator's Education* [*De institutione oratoria*]. Translated by Donald A. Russell. 5 vols. Cambridge, MA: Harvard University Press, 2002.

Rabe, Hugo. Edited by *Prolegomenon Sylloge*. Vol. 14 of *Rhetores Graeci*. Leipzig: Teubner, 1931.

Rahlfs, Alfred and Robert Hanhart, eds. *Septuaginta*. 2nd ed. Stuttgart: Deutsche Bibelgesellschaft, 2006.

Ross, Alison. *Walter Benjamin's Concept of the Image*. London: Routledge, 2015.

Rousseau, Jean-Jacques. *Reveries of the Solitary Walker*. Translated by Russell Goulbourne. Oxford: Oxford University Press, 2011.

Rowland, J. Mark, and Douglas J. Emlen. "Two Thresholds, Three Male Forms Result in Facultative Trimorphism in Beetles." *Science* 323 (6 February, 2009): 773-76.

Saito, Yuriko. "The Japanese Aesthetics of Imperfection and Insufficiency." *Journal of Aesthetics and Art Criticism* 55, no. 4 (1997): 377-85.

Salzani, Carlo. "The Atrophy of Experience: Walter Benjamin and Boredom." In *Essays on Boredom and Modernity*, edited by Barbara Dalle Pezze and Carlo Salzani, 127-54. Amsterdam: Rodopi, 2009.

Sartre, Jean-Paul. *La Nausée*. Paris: Gallimard, 1972. First published 1938.

Schelling, F. W. J. "Ist eine Philosophie der Geschichte möglich? (1798)." In *Ausgewählte Schriften*, vol. 1, edited by Manfred Frank, 295-304. Frankfurt: Suhrkamp, 1985.

——. *The Philosophy of Art*. Translated and edited by Douglas W. Scott. Minneapolis: University of Minnesota Press, 1989.

Schiller, Friedrich. "Zwei philosophische Entwürfe." In *Sämtliche Werke*, vol. 5, edited by Wolfgang Riedel. 5 vols. Munich: Deutscher Tauschenbuch, 2004.

Schlegel, Friedrich. *Kritische Friedrich-Schlegel-Ausgabe (KFSA)*. Edited by Ernst Behler et al. 35 vols. Munich: Ferdinand Schöningh, 1958-ongoing.

Schlovsky, Viktor. "Iskusstvo kak priem." In *O teorii prozy*, 7-23. Moscow: Federatsiya, 1929.

Schmitt, Carl. *Political Theology: Four Chapters on the Concept of Sovereignty*. Translated by George Schwab. Chicago: University of Chicago Press, 2005.

Schopenhauer, Arthur. *Die Welt als Wille und Vorstellung*. 2 vols. Leipzig: Reclam, 1891.

Schwarz, Christopher. *Langeweile und Identität. Eine Studie zur Entstehung und Krise des romantischen Selbstgefühls*. Heidelberg: Universitätsverlaf C. Winter, 1993.

Seneca. *Epistles* [*Epistulae*]. Translated by Richard M. Gummere. 3 vols. Cambridge, MA: Harvard University Press, 1917-25.

Sextus Empiricus. *Sextus Empiricus*. Edited by Immanuel Bekker. Berlin: Reimer, 1842.

Shea, Louisa. *The Cynic Enlightenment: Diogenes in the Salon*. Baltimore: Johns Hopkins University Press, 2010.

Sheridan, Richard Brinsley. *The School for Scandal*. Edited by Ann Blake. New York: Norton, 1979.

Simmel, Georg. "The Metropolis and Mental Life." In *The Sociology of Georg Simmel*, translated and edited by Kurt H. Wolff, 409-24. New York: Free Press, 1950.
Simplicius. *In Aristotelis Physicorum libros commentaria*. Edited by Hermann Diels. Vols. 9-10 of *Commentaria in Aristotelem Graeca*. Berlin: Reimer, 1882-95.
Sloterdijk, Peter. *Critique of Cynical Reason*. Translated by Michael Eldred. Minneapolis: University of Minnesota Press, 1987; Originally published as *Kritik der Zynischen Vernunft*, 2 vols. Frankfurt: Suhrkamp, 1983.
Spacks, Patricia Meyer. *Boredom: The Literary History of a State of Mind*. Chicago: University of Chicago Press, 1995.
Starobinski, Jean. *History of the Treatment of Melancholy from the Earliest Times to 1900*. Basel: J. P. Geigy, 1962.
Sternbach, Leo. Edited by *Gnomologium Vaticanum*. Berlin: De Gruyter, 1963.
Sternberg, Véronique. *La poétique de la comédie*. Paris: Sedes, 1999.
Strässle, Thomas. *Gelassenheit: Über eine andere Haltung zur Welt*. Munich: Carl Hanser, 2001.
Strauss, Leo. *On Tyranny*. Edited by Victor Gourevitsch and Michael S. Roth. Chicago: University of Chicago Press, 2000.
Sulzer, Johann Georg. *Vermischte philosophische Schriften*. 2 vols. Leipzig: Weidmann, 1781-82.
Svendsen, Lars. *A Philosophy of Boredom*. Translated by John Irons. London: Reaktion, 2005.
Sylloge Nummorum Graecorum, France 5, Mysie. Paris: Bibliothéque nationale de France, 2001.
Taylor, Charles. *Modern Social Imaginaries*. Durham: Duke University Press, 2004.
—. *Sources of the Self: The Making of the Modern Identity*. Cambridge, MA: Harvard University Press, 1989.
Terence. *Comoediae*. Edited by Robert Kauer and Wallace M. Lindsay. Oxford: Clarendon, 1926.
Themistius. *Themistii in libros de anima paraphrasis*. Vol. 5.3 of *Commentaria in Aristotelem Graeca*. Edited by R. Heinze. Berlin: Georg Reimer, 1899.
Theophrastus. *Metaphysics*. Edited by W. D. Ross and F. H. Fobes. Oxford: Clarendon, 1929.
Tieck, Ludwig. *William Lovell*. Berlin: Carl August Nicolai, 1795. Reprint, Stuttgart: Philipp Reclam Jun., 1986.
Todman, McWelling. "Boredom and Psychotic Disorders: Cognitive and Motivational Issues." *Psychiatry* 66 (2003): 146-67.
Tolstoy, Leo. *Anna Karenina*. Vols. 18-19 of *Polnoe sobranie sochinenii*. Edited by V.D. Chertkov. Moscow: Khudozhestvennaia Literatura, 1949.
—. *Pis'ma 1873–1879*. Vol. 62 of *Polnoe sobranie sochineniy*. Moscow: Khudozhestvennaia Literatura, 1953.
—. "Why Do Men Stupefy Themselves (1889)." In *Recollections and Essays*, translated by Aylmer Maude, 67-89. London: Oxford University Press, 1937.
Toohey, Peter. *Boredom: A Lively Story*. New Haven, CT: Yale University Press, 2011.
—. *Melancholy, Love and Time: Boundaries of the Self in Ancient Literature*. Ann Arbor: University of Michigan Press, 2004.
Trouillot, Michel-Rolph. "An Unthinkable History: The Haitian Revolution as a Non-Event." In *Silencing the Past: Power and the Production of History*, 70-107, 167-176. Boston: Beacon, 2015. First published 1995.
Tyutchev, F. I. *Lirika*. Edited by K. V. Pigarev. 2 vols. Moscow: Nauka, 1965.
Veuillot, Louis. *Les odeurs de Paris*. Paris: G. Crés, 1914.

Villani, Giovanni. *Croniche di Giovanni, Matteo e Filippo Villani*. Trieste: Sezione letterario-artistica del Lloyd Austriaco, 1857.

Ward, Koral. *Augenblick: The Concept of the "Decisive Moment" in 19th- and 20th-Century Western Philosophy*. Burlington, VT: Ashgate, 2008.

Waugh, Evelyn. *The Diaries of Evelyn Waugh*. Edited by Michael Davie. Boston: Little, Brown, 1976.

Weber, Max. *The Protestant Ethic and the Spirit of Capitalism*. Translated by Talcott Parsons. London: Routledge, 1992. First published 1905.

Weisel, Ori, and Shaul Shalvi. "The Cooperative Roots of Corruption." *Proceedings of the National Academy of Sciences* 112, no. 34 (2015), http://www.pnas.org/content/112/34/10651.full.

Westerink, L. G. *Anonymous Prolegomena to Platonic Philosophy*. Rev. ed. Westbury: Prometheus Trust, 2010.

Whitehead, Alfred North. *Process and Reality*. Edited by David Ray Griffin and Donald W. Sherburne. New York: Free Press, 1974.

Williams, Bernard. "The Makropulos Case: Reflections on the Tedium of Immortality." In *Problems of the Self: Philosophical Papers 1956–1972*, 82-100. Cambridge: Cambridge University Press, 1973.

Wilson, Timothy D., David A. Reinhard, Erin C. Westgate, Daniel T. Gilbert, Nicole Ellerbeck, Cheryl Hahn, Casey L. Brown, and Adi Shaked. "Just Think: The Challenges of the Disengaged Mind." *Science* 345 (2014): 75-77.

Wolff, Christian. *Vernünftige Gedanken von Gott, der Welt und der Seele des Menschen, auch allen Dingen überhaupt*. Vol. 2.1 of *Deutsche Schriften*, ser. 1 of *Gesammelte Werke*. Edited by Jean École et al. Hildesheim: Georg Olms, 1983.

Zahavi, Dan. *Self and Other: Exploring Subjectivity, Empathy, and Shame*. Oxford: Oxford University Press, 2014.

Zannella, Alessandra, Ivan Norscia, Roscoe Stanyon, and Elisabetta Palagi. "Testing Yawning Hypotheses in Wild Populations of Two Strepsirrhine Species: *Propithecus verreauxi* and *Lemur catta*." *American Journal of Primatology* 77 (2015): 1207-15.

Index

aesthetics, 204, 208; and imperfection, 63-64; and scientific revolution, 190-92. *See also* scandal
allonomy, 100, 126. *See also* dialogue
ancient philosophy, 95, 111
Angst. See anxiety
antithesis, 76. *See also* boredom; rain; repetition; waiting
anxiety, 5, 12, 31, 166, 168-69, 217; and freedom, 172-73; and nothing, 169-71; and pure reason, 99; as fundamental mood of Dasein, 39. *See also* dread; fear; Heidegger, Martin; Kierkegaard, Søren; modern subject
Apollonian and Dionysian, the, 51, 110, 179, 211-12
Arendt, Hannah, 167; on freedom, 221, 255, 274
Aristotle, viii, 31, 38, 95, 120, 126, 145, 189, 260; on democracy, 214, 216; on friendship, 164-65, 265; on imagination, 111; on movement, 82; on opposites, 109; on privation, 134-35, 262; on the proper, 106-7, 257
Augenblick, 48-50, 248-49
autarchy, 215
autonomy, 87-88, 92, 99, 101, 213; as freedom of the will, 95; and loneliness, 93, 150; moral, 89-91. *See also* autarchy; comedy; Kant, Immanuel: on moral autonomy; modern subject

Bakunin, Mikhail, 231, 259
Baudelaire, Charles, ix, 56, 72; on dandyism, 252-53
beauty, 206; loss of, 208-10; and the ugly, 212; warm and cold, 211. *See also* Heller, Ágnes, on the beautiful; taste
Benjamin, Walter, ix, 3, 38; *Arcades Project*, 53; boredom in, three types of, 54-63; on eternal return, 62; on the flâneur, 72, 75, 252-53, 265; on Kracauer, 16; and Proust, 63; on rain, 54-56, 60, 151; types of the bored, 67, 251. *See also* flâneur, the; gambler, the
Blanqui, Louis Auguste, 55, 60, 231
Boethius, 5, 39
boredom, viii, xi; in antiquity, 2, 242; antithesis to, 75-78, 179; and death, 12-13; ideological, 64-66; and immortality, 130-32; legitimate, 17-18; and leisure, 15-17; as long while (*Langeweile*), 50, 128; and mediation, lack of, 117-18; as modern malaise, 13-14; as painful gift of nature, 6, 248; productivity of, 162-63; as proprium of modern subject, viii, 85, 106, 108, 127; and psychology, x-xi, 14, 81; radical, 17-19; of repetition, 60-63; as short while/repetition, 132-33; three forms of, 127-47; and time, 33-34, 37; and waiting, 27-31, 33, 56-59, 250; of weather, 54-56; and work, 7-9, 12. *See also* anxiety; dread; ennui; fear; profound boredom

bourgeois, 14; modern, 13–14, 58, 65; petit, 15, 51; revolution, 187, 223, 231

capitalism, 59, 64–65, 215
Cassirer, Ernst, 22, 271
categorical imperative, 92, 95
Cicero, 5, 209
city, 13–14, 16, 54–56, 201, 265, 275; and the flâneur, 69–71, 73, 75. *See also* city life; polis
city life, 15–16, 21–22, 55; as locus of boredom, 15
comedy, 12, 108, 157, 161; aim of, 174; and argumentation, 264; and autonomy, 94; and comic character, 158–60; and freedom, 156, 229, 230; modern attitude to, 263; power distribution in, 226–32; social justice in, xiii; vs. tragedy, 153–55, 158, 265. *See also* dialogue; comic reason; comic subject; New Comedy. philosophy; politics; well-being
comic reason, 93, 100–1, 153, 156–57
comic subject, xiii, 94, 108, 153–56, 216
crisis, 184–85. *See also* scandal
critique, 21
culture, 12
cunning of nature, 3, 6, 11, 163

dandy, the, 71–74. *See also* Baudelaire, Charles
Dasein, x, 22–24; essence of our, 40, 48; fate of, 52; fundamental mood of, 36, 39; and profound boredom, 46–49; and time, 45–47, 50–51;
death, 174; of the author, 13, 87. *See also* boredom
deception, art of, 10–12
delay, 34–37, 41
de Maistre, Joseph, 230, 276
de Maistre, Xavier, 116, 246, 252
democracy, 214, 228; radical, 215–16; as regulative ideal, 99. *See also* autarchy; politics
demontage, x, 237–40
deontology, 94–95

Descartes, René, 6, 29, 31, 144, 190; on beauty, 272; on boredom, 79; on geometry, 199, 270; on imagination, 113, 259; on infinity, 198, 263; on method, 192–93, 262–63; on nature, 205; on passions, 241
dialogical being, 149, 155, 162, 185
dialogue; and allonomy, 149; and comedy, xii–xiii; and interruption, 130, 150, 177, 180, 250; as nonboring, 150–52. *See also* dialogical being; philosophy; politics; scandal; well-being
Diogenes the Cynic, 16, 182, 218, 265, 273, 276; on free speech, 222
Dostoevsky, Fyodor, ix, 96
dread, 5, 168, 211. *See also* anxiety; fear
dreams, 5, 59, 170, 211–12
Durkheim, Émile, 14, 59

Eisenstein, Sergei, 75, 234, 261
elision, 19, 37, 43
ellipsis, 19
emptiness, 34, 37–38, 46, 174; and time, 35. *See also* profound boredom
Engels, Friedrich, 66, 225
ennui, xi, 78, 80–81, 137, 253. *See also* Pascal, Blaise
entertainment, 32, 35. *See also* repetition
enthymeme, 28, 181, 237
estrangement, ix, 120, 133, 206. *See also* Shklovsky, Viktor
eternal recurrence. *See* eternal return; repetition: eternal
eternal return, 62, 99, 130. *See also* Benjamin, Walter; Nietzsche, Friedrich
eternity, 38–39, 61, 247
ethics, deontological, 94–95
exclusion, 146–47

fear, 6, 35, 79, 86, 140, 154, 222, 254, 263–64
film. *See* montage
flâneur, the, 68–72; as observer and consumer, 72–75. *See also* Benjamin, Walter; city; dandy, the; memory
forgetfulness, 19, 46

forgetting, 38, 81, 84, 104, 174. *See also* forgetfulness; memory; recollection
Foucault, Michel, 183, 265
freedom, 92, 151, 161, 223; and democracy, 216; jump toward, the, 173; and liberation, 19, 51–52, 221–22, 224, 274. *See also* Arendt, Hannah; autonomy; comedy; free speech; revolution
freedom of will. *See* free will
free speech, 221–24
free will, 89–90, 97–98; and autonomy, 92; and pure reason, 203; and reason, 96
French Revolution, 187, 223, 275
friendship, 174. *See also under* Aristotle; well-being
Fromm, Erich, 14, 130
fundamental mood, 24, 26–28, 30–33, 51, 138, 168. *See also under* Dasein

Galilei, Galileo, 191, 195, 197, 205
gambler, the, 67, 251
genius, 202–3, 206, 209, 271. *See also* language; novelty; scandal
Goethe, Johann Wolfgang von, 28
Gogol, Nikolai, 17
good life, the, 9–10

Haitian Revolution, 223
Halbwachs, Maurice, 14, 59, 244
Hausmann, Georges-Eugène, 13
Hegel, G. W. F., 63, 155, 165, 194, 206, 208, 210, 236, 239
Heidegger, Martin, ix–x, 21, 27, 29, 120, 133; analysis of boredom in, 31–45; on anxiety, 30, 39, 266; *Being and Time*, 15, 20, 22–23, 249; on freedom and liberation, 52; *The Fundamental Concepts of Metaphysics*, 20, 30; and language, 26–28, 30, 41, 43, 45, 47–48; on mood (*Stimmung*), 22–51, 247; poetics of boredom, 20–24; on unconcealment, 26–28, 246. *See also* Dasein; profound boredom
Heller, Ágnes, on the beautiful, 205–13
Heraclitus, 25–26
home, 146

homesickness, 26, 30–31
Horkheimer, Max, 55, 71
hypocrisy, 11, 141–44, 177

imagination, 111–17; as fundamental power of soul, 271; productive, 29, 114, 124, 203–4, 236
infinity, 60, 82, 110, 144, 198
intersubjectivity, 13, 87, 90, 103

Jonas, Hans, 131, 183, 187, 268–70
journalism, 22, 74
judgment, 89, 91, 184, 238

kairos, 42–43
Kant, Immanuel, ix, 84, 165, 243; on beauty, 209; on boredom, 3–13; *Critique of Pure Reason*, 89, 190, 197, 205; on emptiness, 4–5; on imagination, 113–15, 258; on laziness and work, 6–9; on long and short while, 4, 12, 133; on lying, 10–12; on moral autonomy, 90–92; on nature, 205; and Stoicism, 5–6, 9. *See also* categorical imperative
Kierkegaard, Søren, 30, 102, 168, 182–83; on anxiety, 168–74; on boredom, 174, 266; on faith, 96; on repetition, 260
kingdom of ends, 90, 114, 138, 146, 189, 217
Koselleck, Reinhart, 128, 188, 225
Kracauer, Siegfried, ix–x, 3, 32; boredom, paradoxes of, 14–20; on city life, 15–16
Kuhn, Thomas, 189, 269
Kuleshov, Lev, 234, 236, 276
Kuleshov effect, 237

language, 29, 126; genius of, 32, 40; logos of, 30–31. *See also* Heidegger, Martin
laziness, 6, 7, 9, 17, 174. *See also* Kant, Immanuel
Leibniz, Gottfried Wilhelm, 143, 191, 197, 200
leisure, 15–17
Levinas, Emmanuel, 183–84
life, 5; preserving, 7, 9. *See also* good life, the
logos, 26, 28, 126–27, 173. *See also* language

loneliness, 47, 84, 130, 166. *See also* autonomy; modern subject
long while (*Langeweile*), 30, 32, 39, 48, 53, 80, 128, 147. *See also* boredom; Kant, Immanuel; short while
Luther, Martin, 96, 168

Marx, Karl, 66, 214; on pauperism, 227, 275; on production, 64; on value, 74
mathematics, 195-99, 209. *See also* Plato; world, mathematization of
mediation, 61, 68, 76, 130; and imagination, 113, 117; impossibility of, 108-11; and the infinite, 198; of same and other, 121-22, 124, 126; and scandal, 179. *See also* opposites, unmediated; reflection; revolution
melancholy, 31, 60
memory, 38; and flâneur, the, 69-71; theater, 237. *See also* forgetting; recollection
method, 233; new scientific, 192-95. *See also* Descartes, René
modernity, vii, 7, 21, 58, 145, 167, 194; critics of, 53, 72; diagnosis of, 19; and modern subject, 185; and the novel, ix; and the primacy of will, 95. *See also* revolution
modern science, 60, 186, 191, 196, 199, 200
modern subject, the, vii, 42, 88, 104; and anxiety, 31; atomization of, 140, 142-43; autonomy of, 79, 88, 207, 217; constitutive features of, 85; and entertainment, xii; and imagination, 117; loneliness of, 87, 90, 101; and pure reason, 95-96, 101, 114; reflexivity of, 101-3; sovereignty and exception of, 217-18; as tragic, 87, 94, 122, 153-55, 165, 227; and will, 96. *See also* comic subject
monotony, 61, 69
montage, 234-37. *See also* demontage; Kuleshov, Lev; Kuleshov effect
mood. *See* fundamental mood; Heidegger, Martin; *Stimmung*
morality, 7, 91, 144, 254

nature, 6, 26, 89, 104, 122, 139, 162, 166, 189-90, 194, 203, 209, 212, 265, 271; loss of, 186, 219; and simplicity, 191. *See also* Heller, Ágnes, on the beautiful; world, mathematization of
negativity, 5, 8, 123, 169, 224; power of, 203; as productive, 125-26; unmediated, 183
New Comedy, 155-56, 158-59, 229, 264, 286
Newton, Isaac, 144, 190-191, 197; on nature, 205
Nietzsche, Friedrich, 23, 29, 110, 155, 212; on boredom of gods, 131; on eternal return, 62; on work and pleasure, 8. *See also* Apollonian and Dionysian, the
noncontradiction, law of, 102, 109
nothing, 169-71; as possibility, 172. *See also* anxiety; privation
Novalis, 30-31
novelty, 13, 58, 77, 152, 187-88; genius as creator of, 202-3

one who waits, 67-68
ontology, 120, 145, 149, 161, 191, 199, 202. *See also* deontology
opposites, unmediated, 76, 117, 186, 225, 227; antidote to, 228. *See also* boredom: and mediation, lack of; mediation; negativity; reflection
oracle, 26-27, 29, 40, 67
original sin, 168
otherness, 5, 9, 121-22, 126. *See also* allonomy; same and other; sameness

Paris, 53-54, 56
Pascal, Blaise, ix, 3. on ennui, 78-84
pauperism, 117, 227, 275
philosophy: beginning of, 9; and comedy, 160; and dialogue, 182; modern, 22, 111, 127, 130, 139, 210; and philosophizing, 24-31, 51; and poetry, 23, 26, 30-31, 36, 41; as rooted in boredom, 31; and scandal, 182-83
physics, 186, 193
Plato, 2, 29, 63, 109, 116, 158, 193, 207, 260; on beauty, 211; on mathematics, 190
Plotinus, 247; on beauty, 207, 272
poetry, 28-29, 31, 65, 145, 178, 201. *See also* philosophy

polis, 5, 14, 54, 142, 158, 215, 218, 223, 226
politeness, 142-43
politics, 145, 187, 275; approaches, types of, 230; as comic, 157; democratic, 99, 101; dialogical, 165; of radical inclusion, 218. *See also* autarchy; democracy; polis; scandal: political
poverty, 145-46, 214
power, 228, 251; cosmic, 54; establishing, 250; and modern nation-state, 145; tragic, 227. *See also* comedy; politics; revolution
privation, xi, 132, 168, 173, 198; and nothing, 5, 172. *See also* Aristotle
Proclus, 112-13, 258
profound boredom, 39-41, 47, 52, 67, 200, 210, 217; and delay, 43-44; and emptiness as indifference, 41-42; metaphorical description of, 50-51; and repetition, 133; structural moments of, 41-44. *See also* Dasein
Proust, Marcel, 55, 70, 201. *See also* Benjamin, Walter
psychology, 60, 127, 185. *See also* boredom
pure reason, 88, 92, 98, 194; and impure reason, 99-100; as a myth, 101; as tragic reason, 93-94; and *Willkür*, 97
Pythia, the, 27, 29, 30

rain, 56, 63, 69; antithesis to, 76; the power of, 53-54; and waiting, 61. *See also* Benjamin, Walter; repetition; weather
reason, vii; impure, 99-100; modern, 96, 114, 169, 180; and will, 95-96. *See also* comic reason; pure reason; tragic reason
recollection, 71, 81, 104, 260
reflection, 171; act of, 102, 109; mediated, 123; and revolution, 224; unmediated, 122-23
reflexivity, 97, 171; as malaise, 103-4. *See also* modern subject
repetition, xi, 63, 69, 142, 174, 250; boredom as, antithesis to, 77; and dialogue, 148-49; as entertainment, 133-34; eternal, 61, 64-66; and infinity, 134, 262; and modern subject, 125; and rain, 60-61;

of the same, ix, 39, 60, 64-66, 77, 81, 117, 131-32, 144. *See also* Kierkegaard, Søren; monotony
revolt, 217, 219, 220. *See also* revolution
revolution, xii; characteristics of, 187-89; and freedom, 223-24; and mediation, 224-26; and modernity, 219-20; political meanings of, 218-21; and power, 231; vs. revolt, 223; scientific, 189-90. *See also* bourgeois; French Revolution; Haitian Revolution; reflection; scandal
Romanticism, 31, 36, 78, 208, 251; and landscape, 70
Romantics, the, 1, 87, 131, 203
rupture, 5, 49, 136-37, 151, 161, 225

same and other, 121-27. *See also* allonomy; mediation; otherness
sameness, 2, 5-6, 9-10, 122, 141. *See also* allonomy; otherness
scandal, xii, 267, 181-82; aesthetic, 200-2; in art, 270; and beauty, 186, 213; characteristics of, 175-78; as crisis and critique, 183-85; as dialogue (dialogical), 176-79, 184; and genius, 204-5; and the infinite, 198-200; modern, 89, 178-80; and plagiarism, 180-81; political, 213-15; and revolution, 185-89. *See also* mediation; philosophy; world, mathematization of
Schelling, F. W. J., 131, 209
Shklovsky, Viktor, 120, 236, 259. *See also* estrangement
short while, 48, 80, 132, 137; of Dasein, 50. *See also* boredom; long while (*Langeweile*)
Simmel, Georg, ix, 13
simplicity, 270
Sisyphus, 66, 72
skepticism, 14, 244
Socrates, 16, 25, 57, 160, 182, 212, 257, 265
sound, 20, 145, 177
Stimmung, 22, 24, 59, 246, 252
Stoics, the, 2, 5, 272
Subject. *See* modern subject

subjectivity, 2; modern, 3, 11, 82, 85, 168, 174; *See also* intersubjectivity

suicide, 13, 79, 87, 118, 125, 154, 179, 185, 227, 231, 238

taste, 204, 208, 210, 272

temporality, 44-45

theater, 11, 12, 16

time, 35, 260; lingering, 33-34; spell of, 45-47; standing, 38-39. *See also* boredom; Dasein; delay; emptiness; kairos; temporality

Tolstoy, Leo, 83, 236, 241, 254, 276

tragedy, 12, 47, 51, 157, 202; and the beautiful, 211. *See also* comedy; modern subject: as tragic; will: tragic

tragic reason, 100, 209

vision: moment of, 48-52, 249; simplicity of, 47-48. *See also* Augenblick

waiting, 18, 48, 54, 128, 150; antithesis to, 76-77. *See also* boredom; one who waits; rain

weather, 54, 56. *See also* boredom; rain

Weber, Max, 13, 179

well-being, 162; as being in dialogue, 148-52; as comedy, 152-56; comic, 174; as flow, 166-67; as friendship, 163-65; nonboring, xii, 126, 155, 175

will: act of, 24, 93, 140, 168-73, 203; tragic, 96-97. *See also* free will; reason

Willkür, 52, 96-97, 114. *See also* pure reason

world, mathematization of, 195-98

GPSR Authorized Representative: Easy Access System Europe, Mustamäe tee
50, 10621 Tallinn, Estonia, gpsr.requests@easproject.com

www.ingramcontent.com/pod-product-compliance
Lightning Source LLC
Chambersburg PA
CBHW021935290426
44108CB00012B/841